Irene

Your Grandma Rocks, Mine Rolls

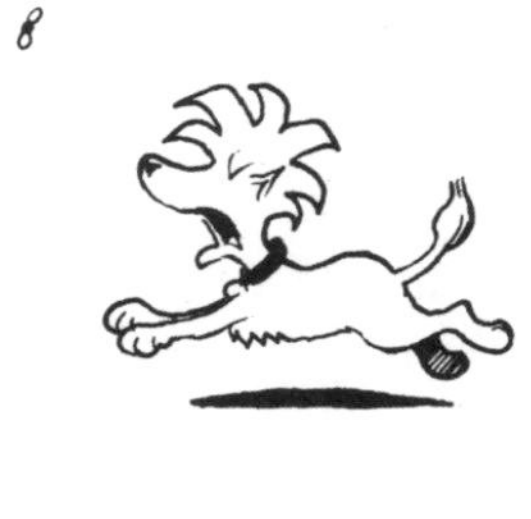

8

Your Grandma Rocks, Mine Rolls

A Grand Avenue Collection
By Steve Breen

**Andrews McMeel
Publishing**

Kansas City

Grand Avenue is distributed internationally by United Feature Syndicate, Inc.

Your Grandma Rocks, Mine Rolls copyright © 2001 by United Feature Syndicate, Inc. All rights reserved. Printed in the United States of America. No part of this book may be used or reproduced in any manner whatsoever without written permission except in the case of reprints in the context of reviews. For information write Andrews McMeel Publishing, an Andrews McMeel Universal company, 4520 Main Street, Kansas City, Missouri 64111.

01 02 03 04 05 BAH 10 9 8 7 6 5 4 3 2 1

ISBN: 0-7407-1849-5

Library of Congress Control Number: 2001087671

Grand Avenue can be viewed on the Internet at:
www.comics.com/comics/grandave

To Mom and Dad

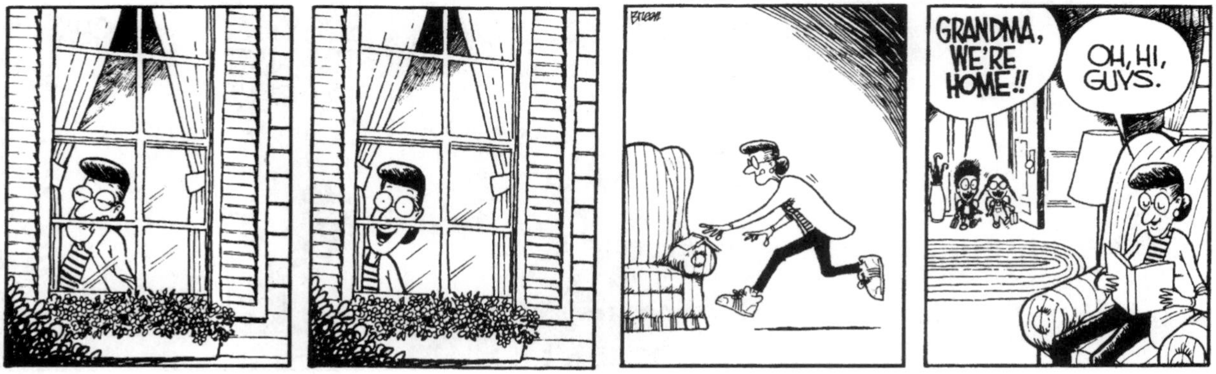
GRANDMA, WE'RE HOME!!
OH, HI, GUYS.

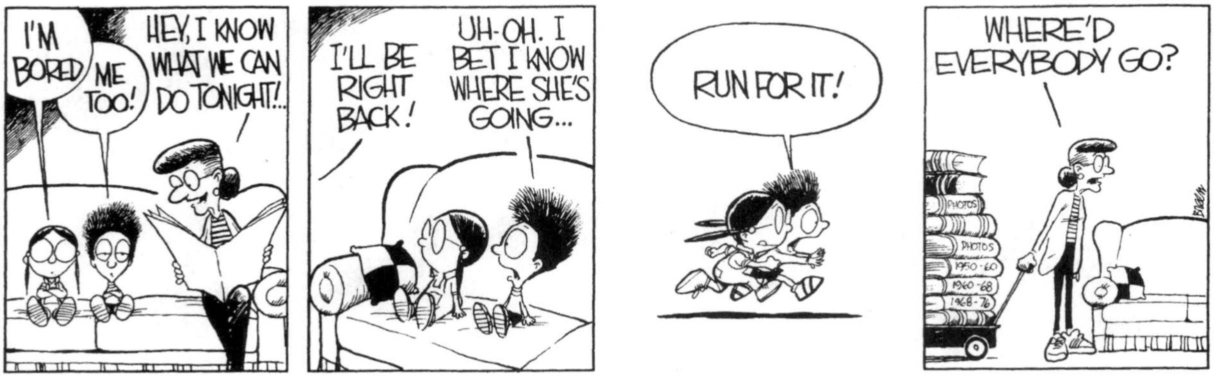
I'M BORED
ME TOO!
HEY, I KNOW WHAT WE CAN DO TONIGHT!...
I'LL BE RIGHT BACK!
UH-OH. I BET I KNOW WHERE SHE'S GOING...
RUN FOR IT!
PHOTOS
PHOTOS
1950-60
1960-68
1968-76
WHERE'D EVERYBODY GO?

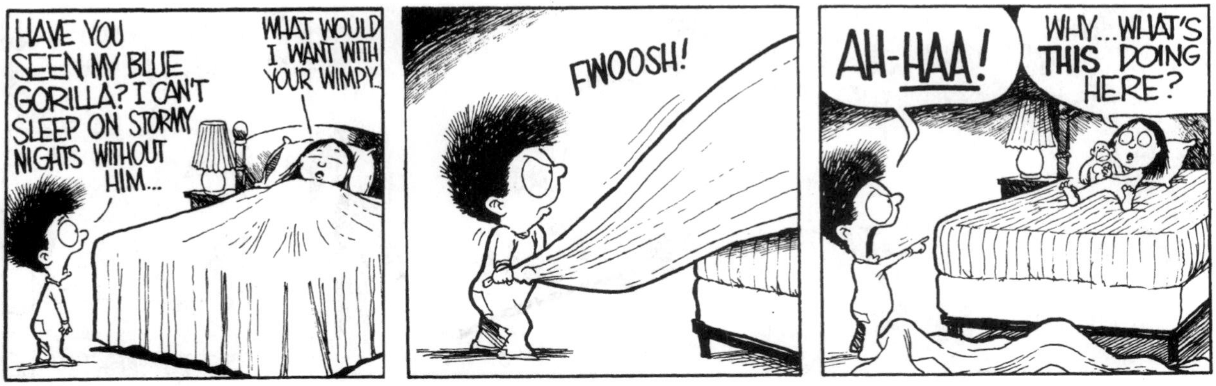
HAVE YOU SEEN MY BLUE GORILLA? I CAN'T SLEEP ON STORMY NIGHTS WITHOUT HIM...
WHAT WOULD I WANT WITH YOUR WIMPY...
FWOOSH!
AH-HAA!
WHY...WHAT'S THIS DOING HERE?

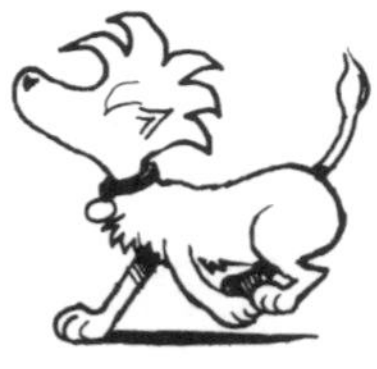

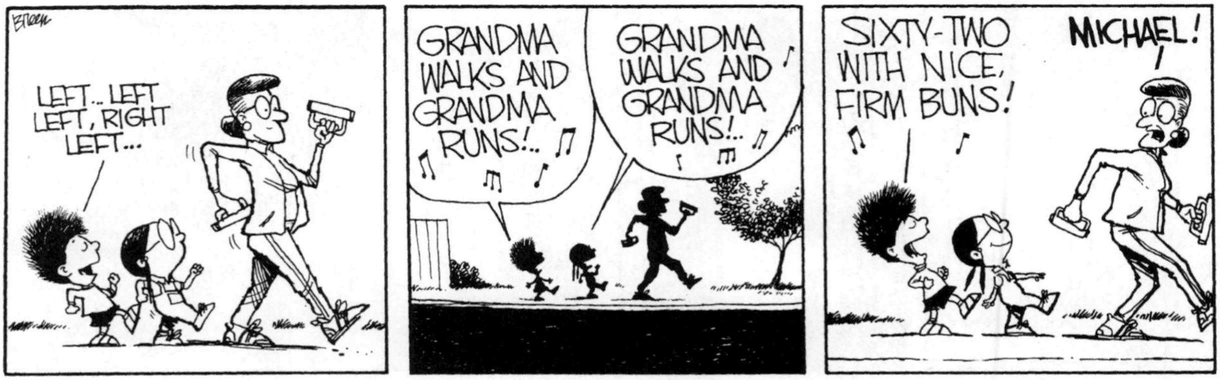
LEFT... LEFT
LEFT, RIGHT
LEFT...
GRANDMA WALKS AND GRANDMA RUNS!..
GRANDMA WALKS AND GRANDMA RUNS!..
SIXTY-TWO WITH NICE, FIRM BUNS!
MICHAEL!

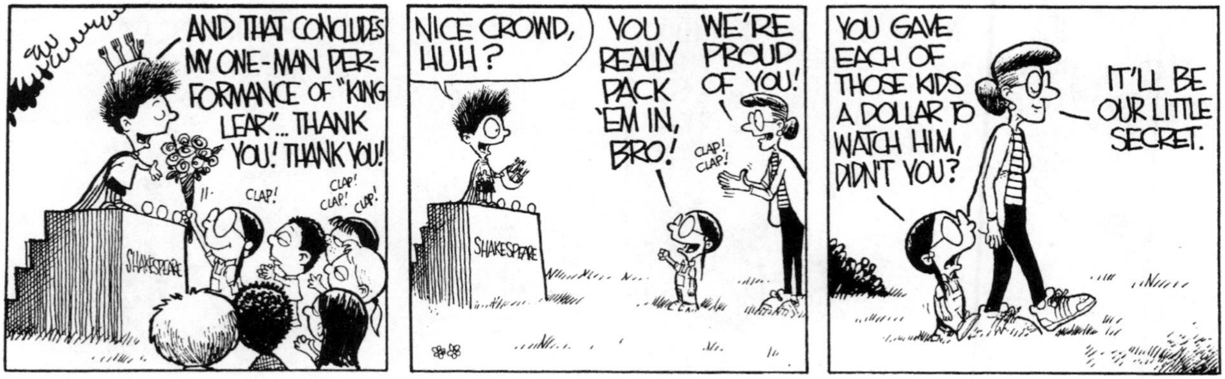
AND THAT CONCLUDES MY ONE-MAN PERFORMANCE OF "KING LEAR"... THANK YOU! THANK YOU!
SHAKESPEARE
CLAP!
CLAP! CLAP!
CLAP!
NICE CROWD, HUH?
YOU REALLY PACK 'EM IN, BRO!
WE'RE PROUD OF YOU!
CLAP! CLAP!
SHAKESPEARE
YOU GAVE EACH OF THOSE KIDS A DOLLAR TO WATCH HIM, DIDN'T YOU?
IT'LL BE OUR LITTLE SECRET.

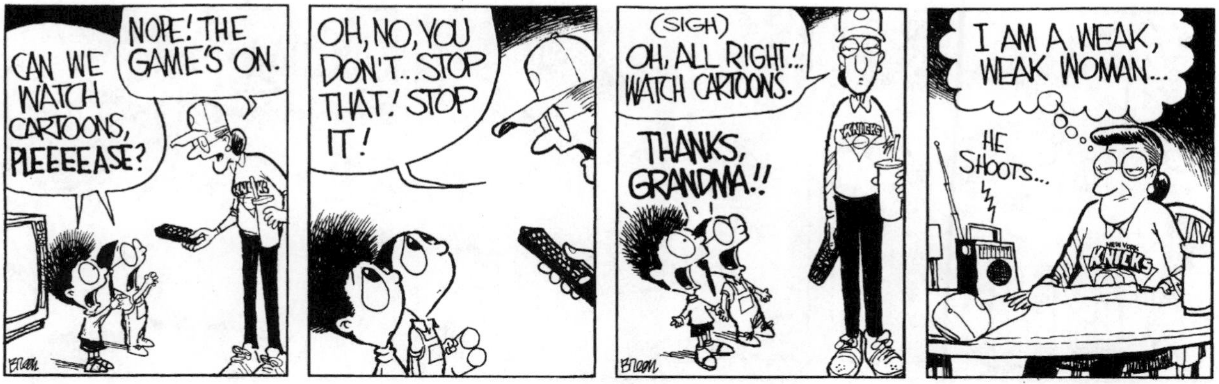
CAN WE WATCH CARTOONS, PLEEEEASE?
NOPE! THE GAME'S ON.
OH, NO, YOU DON'T... STOP THAT! STOP IT!
(SIGH)
OH, ALL RIGHT!.. WATCH CARTOONS.
THANKS, GRANDMA!!
KNICKS
I AM A WEAK, WEAK WOMAN...
HE SHOOTS...
NEW YORK KNICKS

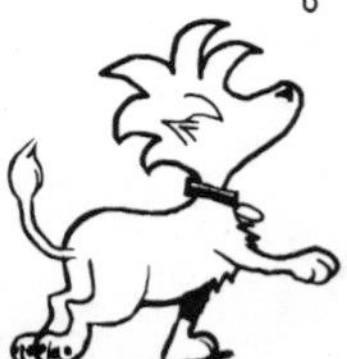

THAT'S A GREAT TIRE SWING!
THE SECRET IS TO FIND A NICE HIGH BRANCH...
...THAT ISN'T DEAD.

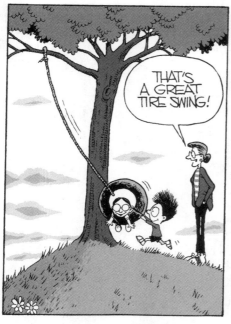

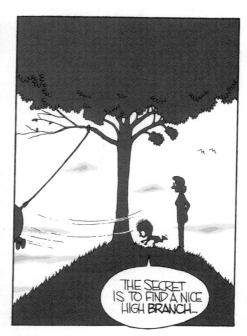

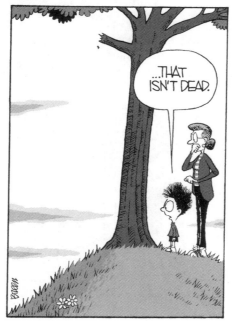

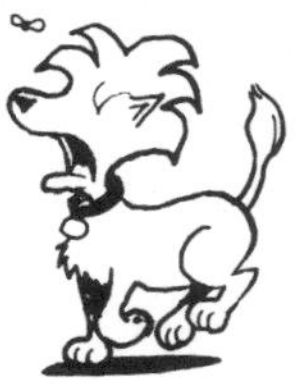

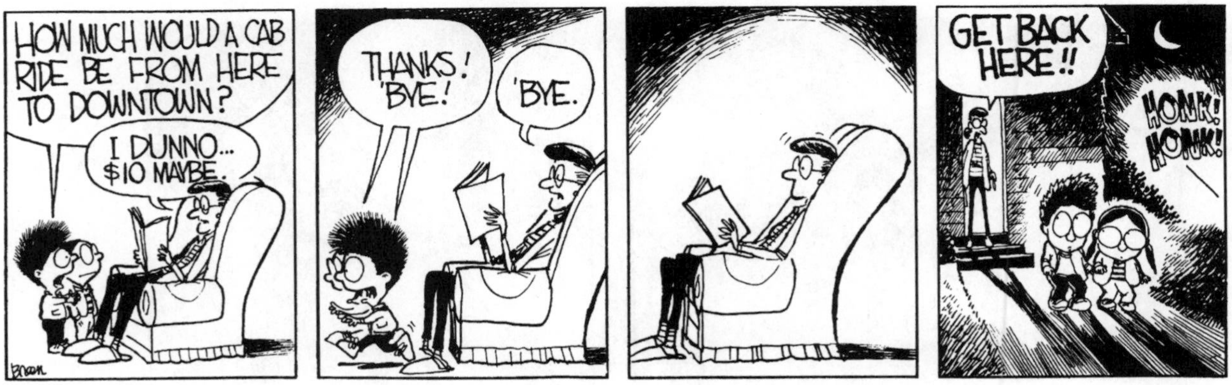
HOW MUCH WOULD A CAB RIDE BE FROM HERE TO DOWNTOWN?
I DUNNO... $10 MAYBE.
THANKS! 'BYE!
'BYE.
GET BACK HERE!!
HONK! HONK!

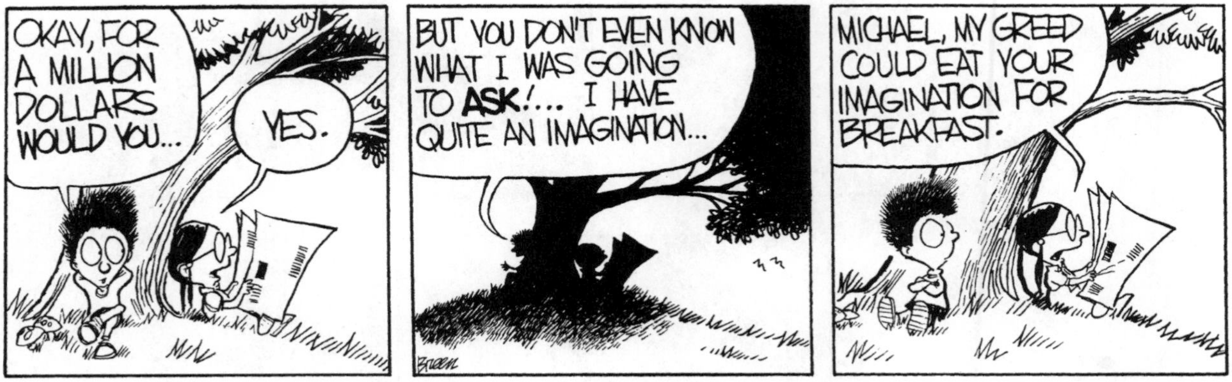
OKAY, FOR A MILLION DOLLARS WOULD YOU...
YES.
BUT YOU DON'T EVEN KNOW WHAT I WAS GOING TO ASK!... I HAVE QUITE AN IMAGINATION...
MICHAEL, MY GREED COULD EAT YOUR IMAGINATION FOR BREAKFAST.

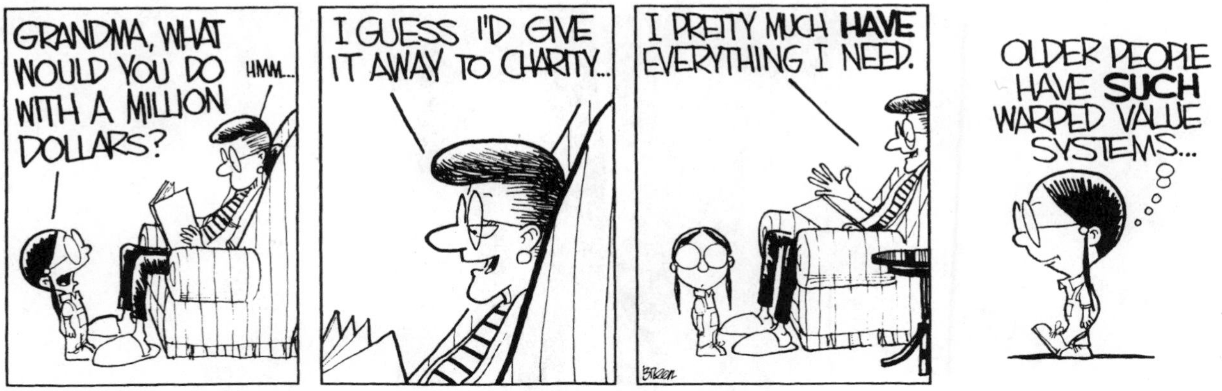
GRANDMA, WHAT WOULD YOU DO WITH A MILLION DOLLARS?
HMM...
I GUESS I'D GIVE IT AWAY TO CHARITY...
I PRETTY MUCH HAVE EVERYTHING I NEED.
OLDER PEOPLE HAVE SUCH WARPED VALUE SYSTEMS...

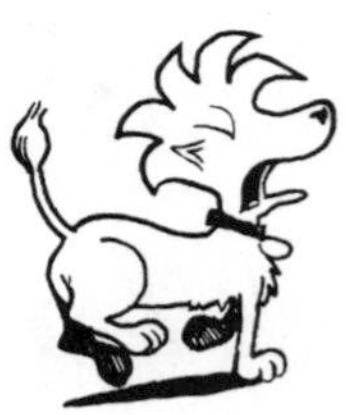

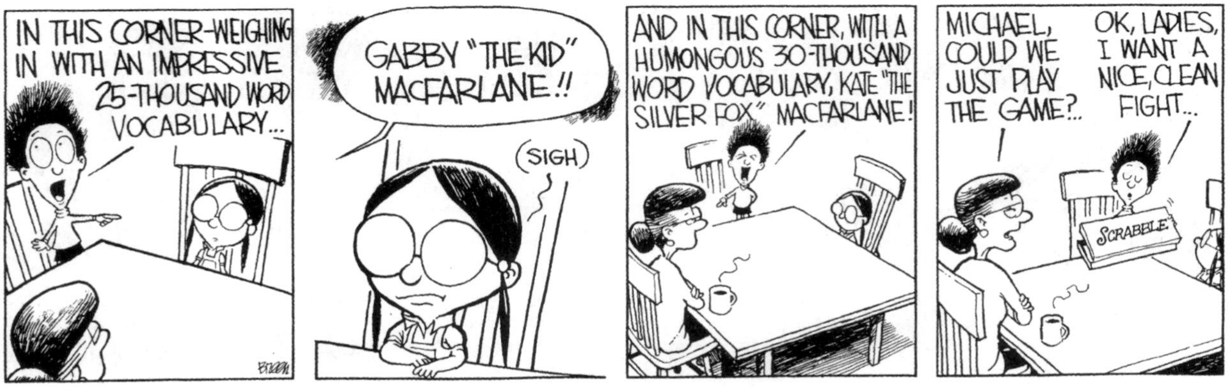
IN THIS CORNER-WEIGHING IN WITH AN IMPRESSIVE 25-THOUSAND WORD VOCABULARY...
GABBY "THE KID" MACFARLANE!!
(SIGH)
AND IN THIS CORNER, WITH A HUMONGOUS 30-THOUSAND WORD VOCABULARY, KATE "THE SILVER FOX" MACFARLANE!
MICHAEL, COULD WE JUST PLAY THE GAME?..
OK, LADIES, I WANT A NICE, CLEAN FIGHT...
SCRABBLE

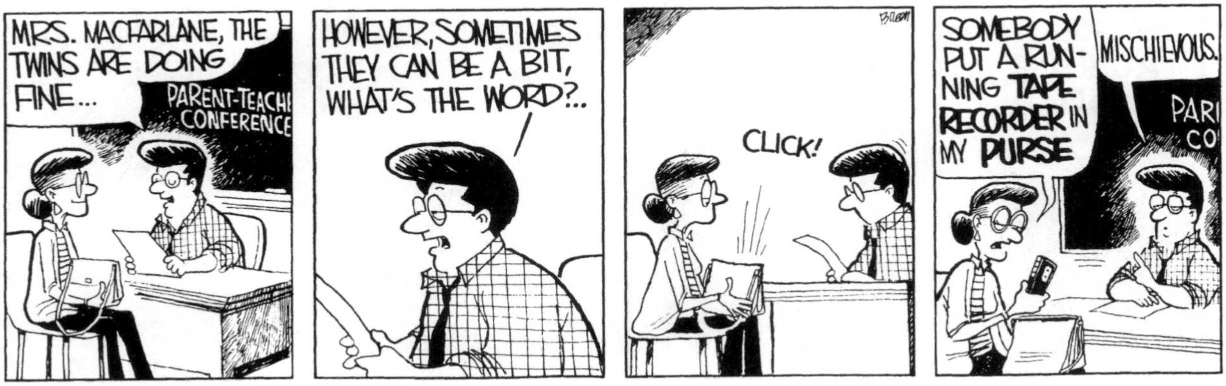
MRS. MACFARLANE, THE TWINS ARE DOING FINE...
PARENT-TEACH
CONFERENCE
HOWEVER, SOMETIMES THEY CAN BE A BIT, WHAT'S THE WORD?..
CLICK!
SOMEBODY PUT A RUN-NING TAPE RECORDER IN MY PURSE
MISCHIEVOUS.

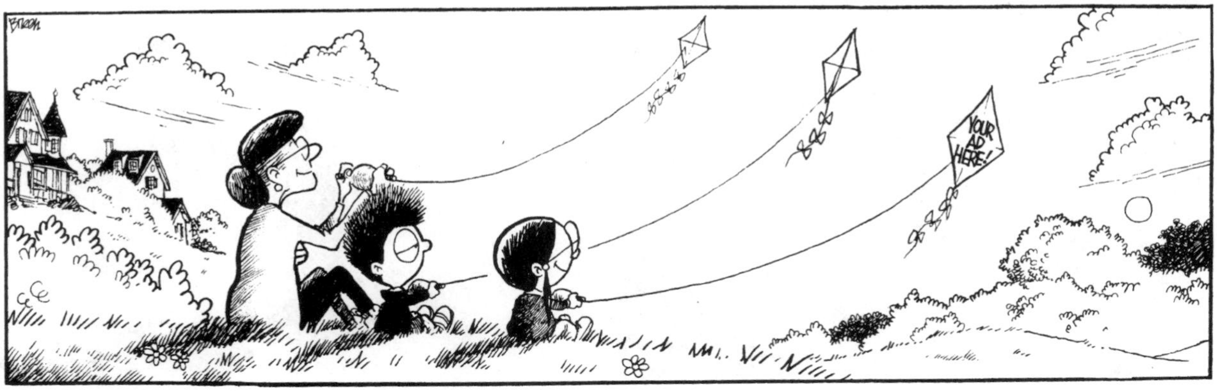
YOUR AD HERE!

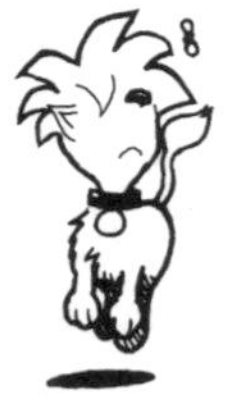

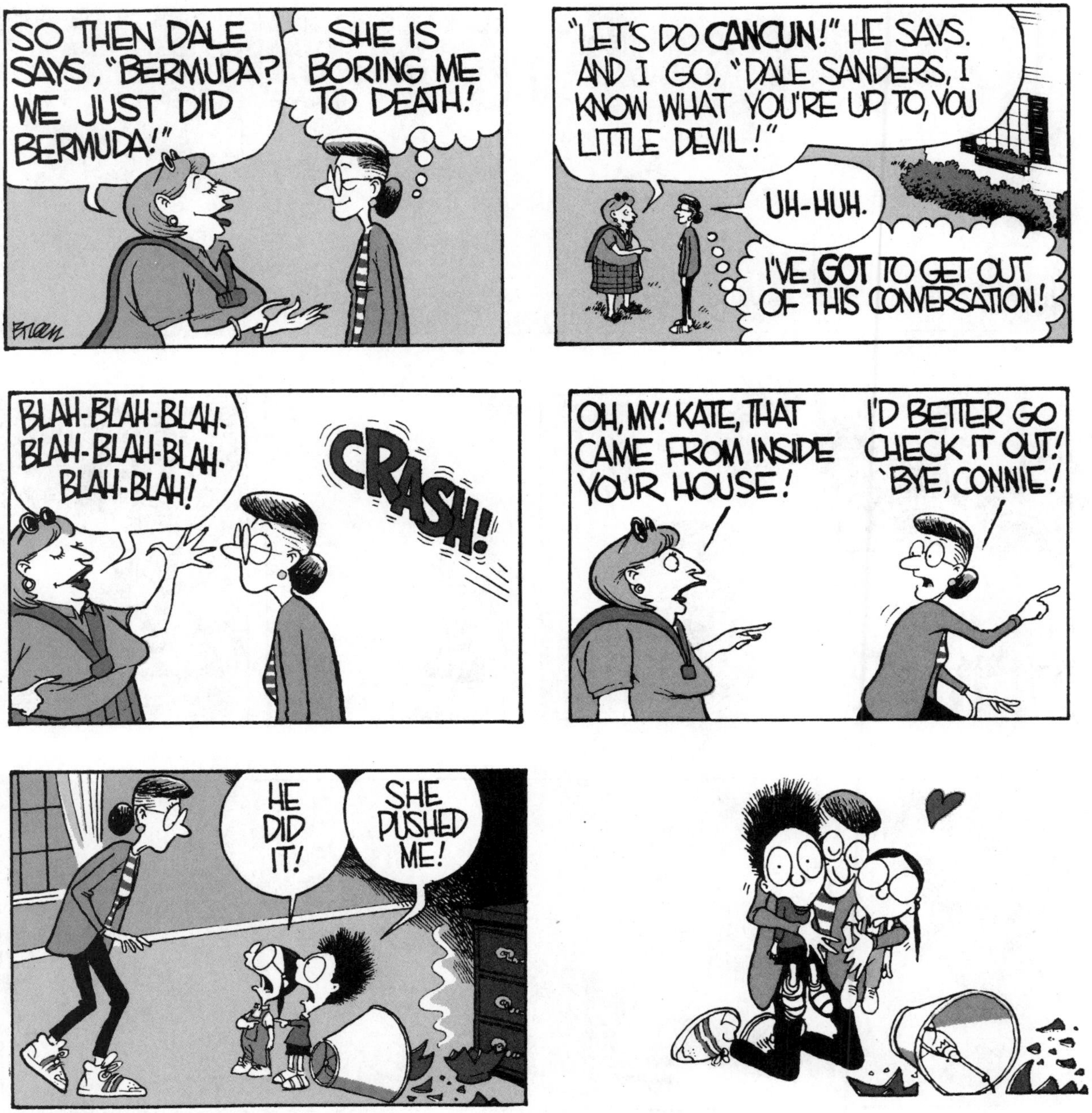
SO THEN DALE SAYS, "BERMUDA? WE JUST DID BERMUDA!"
SHE IS BORING ME TO DEATH!
"LET'S DO **CANCUN**!" HE SAYS. AND I GO, "DALE SANDERS, I KNOW WHAT YOU'RE UP TO, YOU LITTLE DEVIL!"
UH-HUH.
I'VE **GOT** TO GET OUT OF THIS CONVERSATION!
BLAH-BLAH-BLAH-BLAH-BLAH-BLAH-BLAH-BLAH!
CRASH!
OH, MY! KATE, THAT CAME FROM INSIDE YOUR HOUSE!
I'D BETTER GO CHECK IT OUT! 'BYE, CONNIE!
HE DID IT!
SHE PUSHED ME!

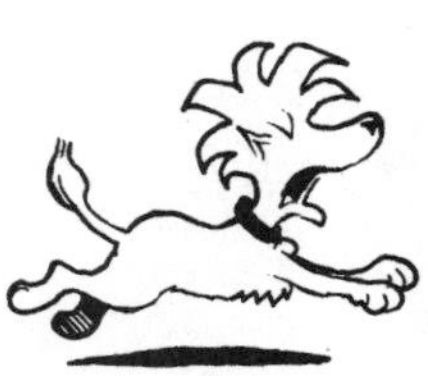

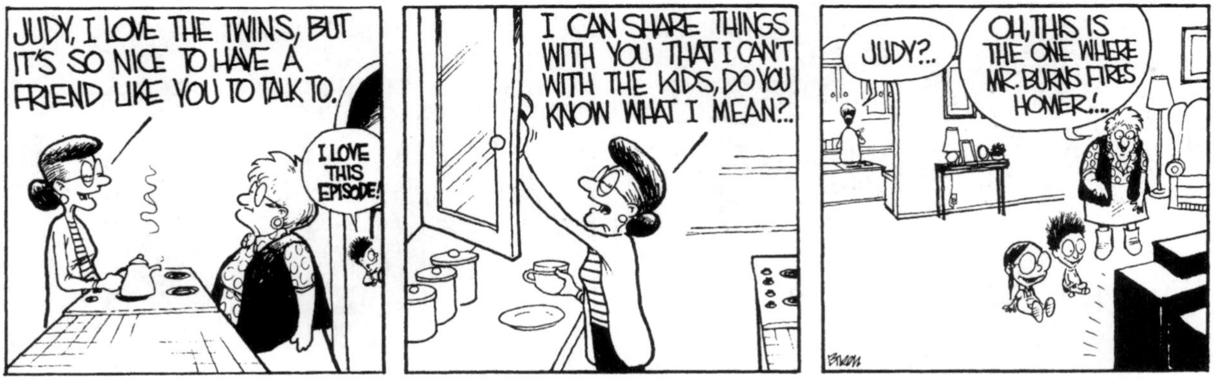
JUDY, I LOVE THE TWINS, BUT IT'S SO NICE TO HAVE A FRIEND LIKE YOU TO TALK TO.
I LOVE THIS EPISODE!
I CAN SHARE THINGS WITH YOU THAT I CAN'T WITH THE KIDS, DO YOU KNOW WHAT I MEAN?..
JUDY?..
OH, THIS IS THE ONE WHERE MR. BURNS FIRES HOMER!...

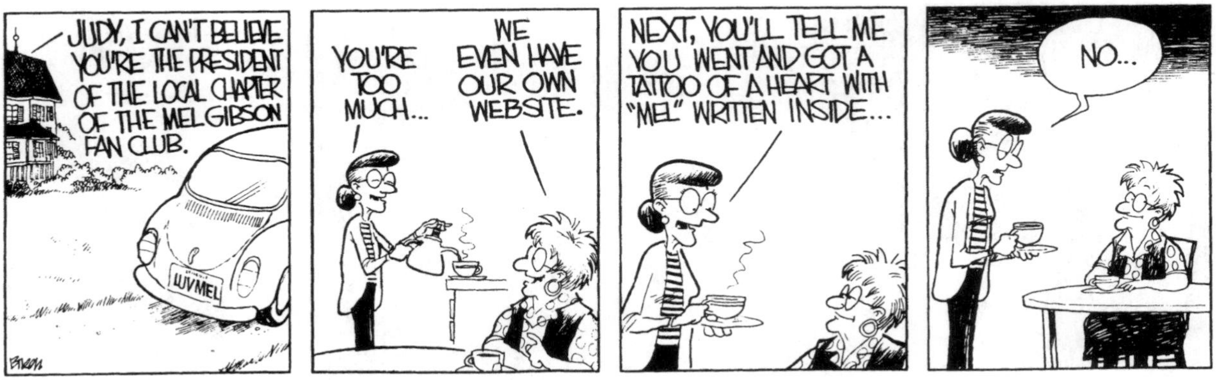
JUDY, I CAN'T BELIEVE YOU'RE THE PRESIDENT OF THE LOCAL CHAPTER OF THE MEL GIBSON FAN CLUB.
LUVMEL
YOU'RE TOO MUCH...
WE EVEN HAVE OUR OWN WEBSITE.
NEXT, YOU'LL TELL ME YOU WENT AND GOT A TATTOO OF A HEART WITH "MEL" WRITTEN INSIDE...
NO...

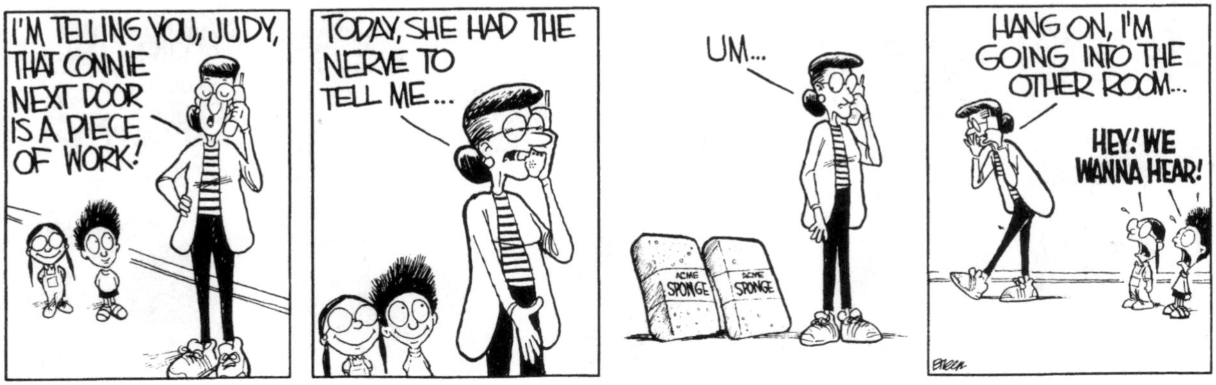
I'M TELLING YOU, JUDY, THAT CONNIE NEXT DOOR IS A PIECE OF WORK!
TODAY, SHE HAD THE NERVE TO TELL ME...
UM...
ACME SPONGE
ACME SPONGE
HANG ON, I'M GOING INTO THE OTHER ROOM...
HEY! WE WANNA HEAR!

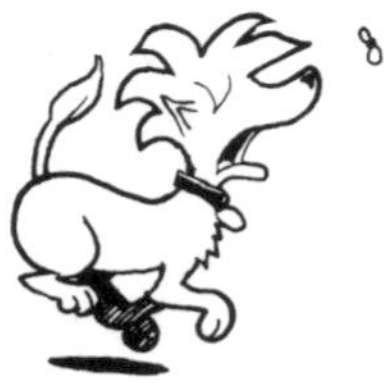

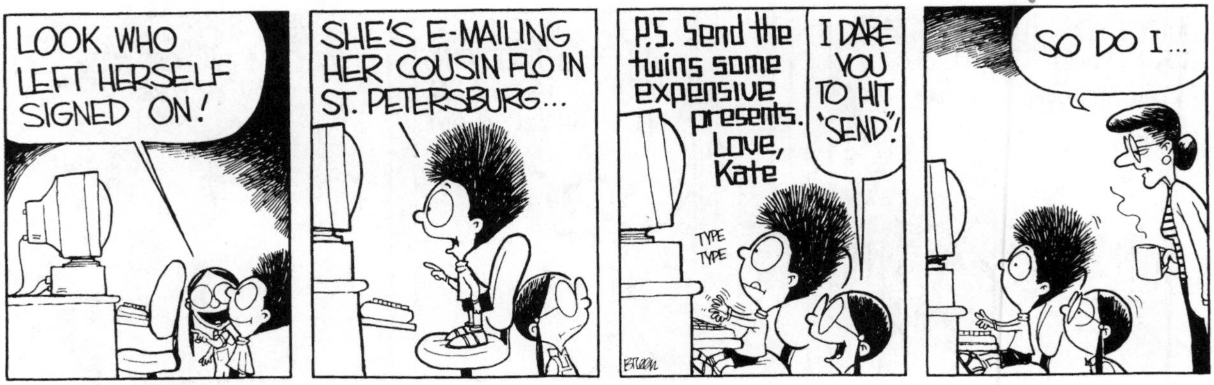
LOOK WHO LEFT HERSELF SIGNED ON!
SHE'S E-MAILING HER COUSIN FLO IN ST. PETERSBURG...
P.S. Send the twins some expensive presents. Love, Kate
TYPE TYPE
I DARE YOU TO HIT "SEND"!
SO DO I...

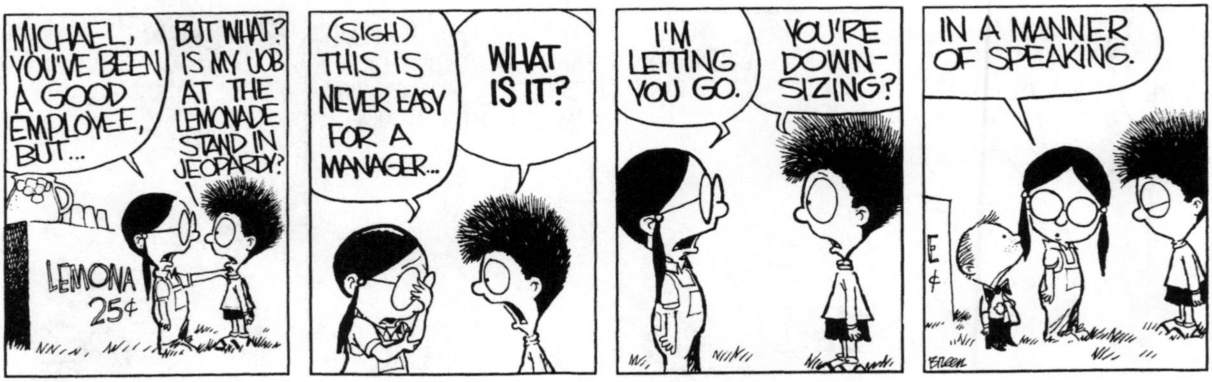
MICHAEL, YOU'VE BEEN A GOOD EMPLOYEE, BUT...
BUT WHAT? IS MY JOB AT THE LEMONADE STAND IN JEOPARDY?
LEMONA
25¢
(SIGH) THIS IS NEVER EASY FOR A MANAGER...
WHAT IS IT?
I'M LETTING YOU GO.
YOU'RE DOWN-SIZING?
IN A MANNER OF SPEAKING.

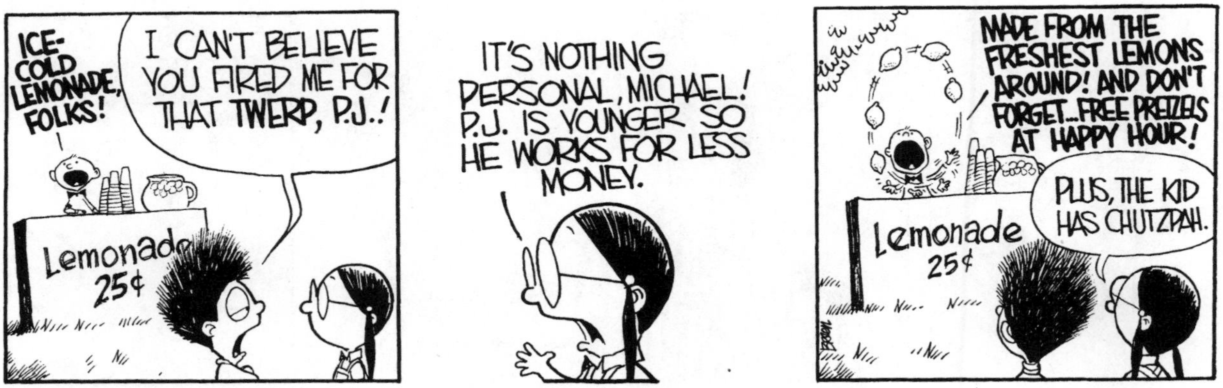
ICE-COLD LEMONADE, FOLKS!
I CAN'T BELIEVE YOU FIRED ME FOR THAT TWERP, P.J.!
Lemonade
25¢
IT'S NOTHING PERSONAL, MICHAEL! P.J. IS YOUNGER SO HE WORKS FOR LESS MONEY.
MADE FROM THE FRESHEST LEMONS AROUND! AND DON'T FORGET...FREE PRETZELS AT HAPPY HOUR!
Lemonade
25¢
PLUS, THE KID HAS CHUTZPAH.

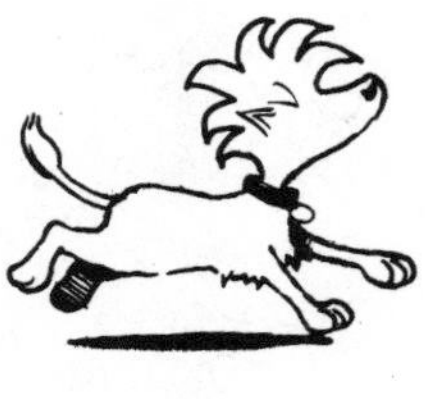

GRANDMA, WE'RE BORED. WHY CAN'T WE GET **CABLE TV**?
WE'D NEVER GET BORED WITH 80 CHANNELS!
FOLLOW ME INTO THE DEN, YOU TWO...
BOOKS ARE THE ANSWER TO BOREDOM!
SHE WAS RIGHT!
AND THE NEIGHBORS EVEN HAVE **HBO**!

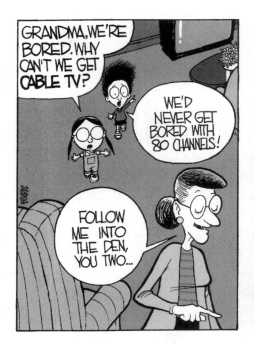

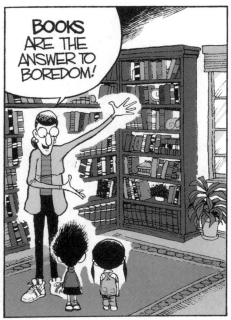

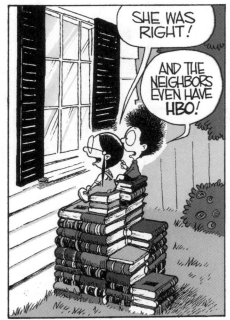

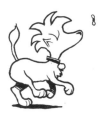

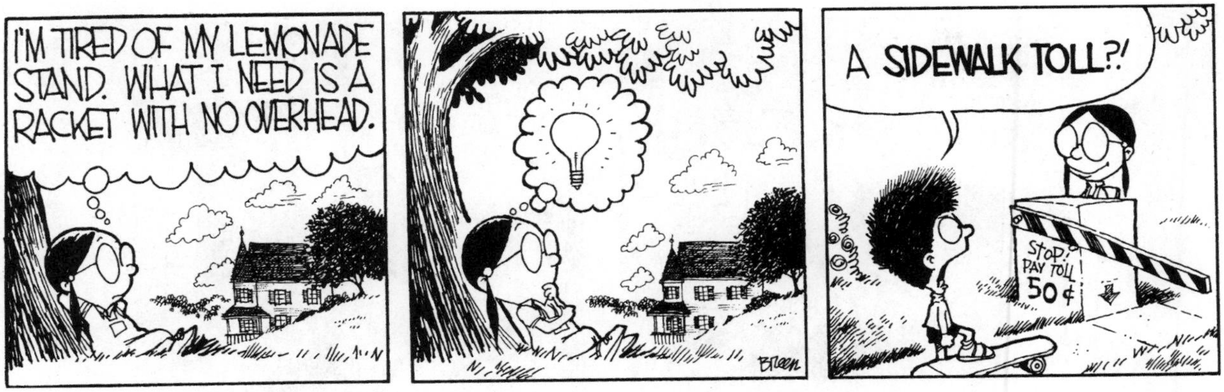
I'M TIRED OF MY LEMONADE STAND. WHAT I NEED IS A RACKET WITH NO OVERHEAD.
A **SIDEWALK TOLL**?!
STOP! PAY TOLL 50¢

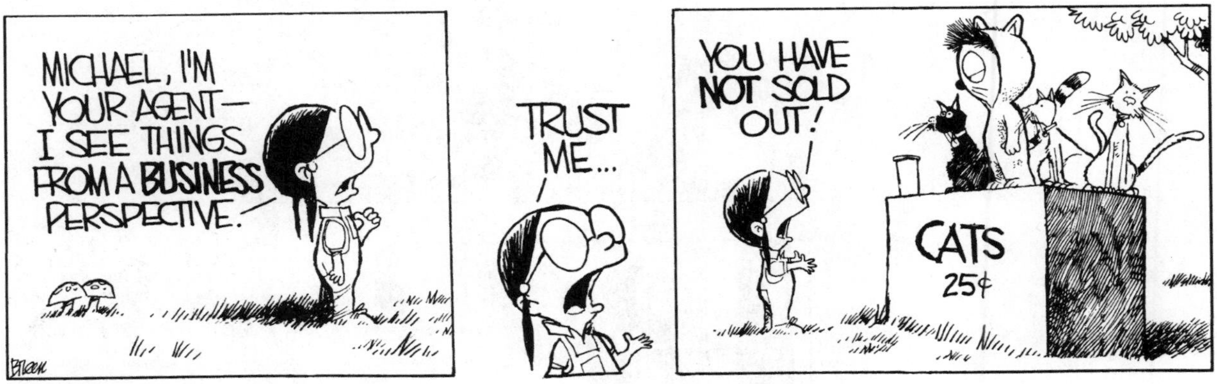
MICHAEL, I'M YOUR AGENT— I SEE THINGS FROM A **BUSINESS** PERSPECTIVE.
TRUST ME...
YOU HAVE **NOT** SOLD OUT!
CATS 25¢

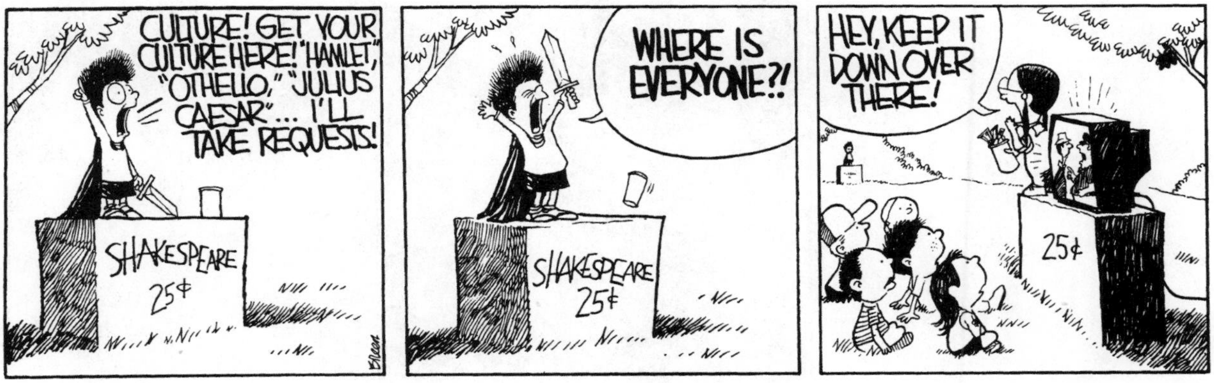
CULTURE! GET YOUR CULTURE HERE! "HAMLET," "OTHELLO," "JULIUS CAESAR"... I'LL TAKE REQUESTS!
SHAKESPEARE 25¢
WHERE IS EVERYONE?!
SHAKESPEARE 25¢
HEY, KEEP IT DOWN OVER THERE!
25¢

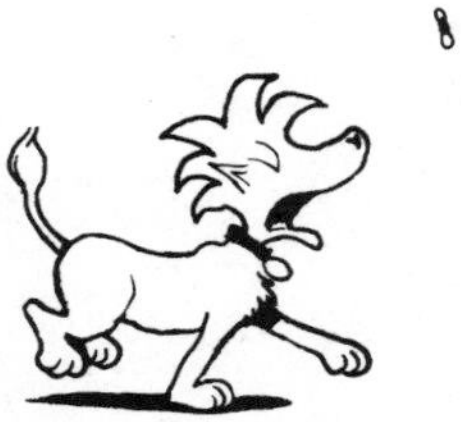

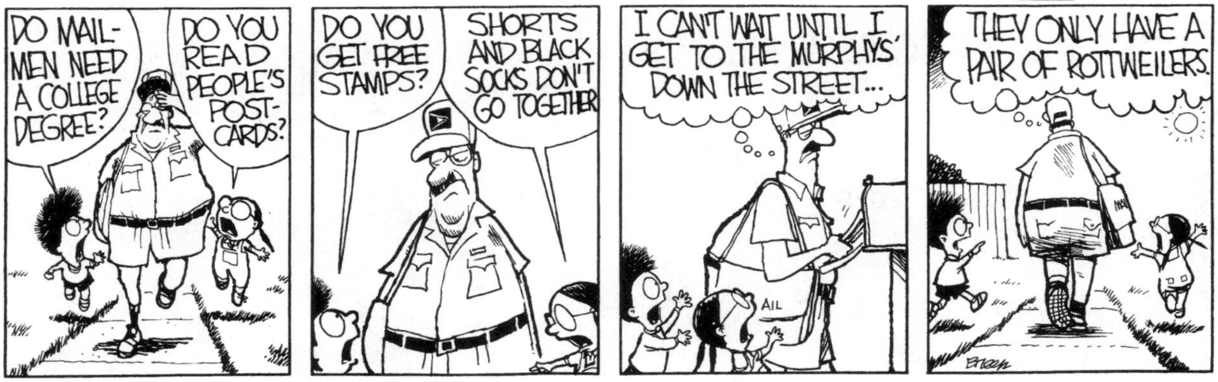
DO MAIL-MEN NEED A COLLEGE DEGREE?
DO YOU READ PEOPLE'S POST-CARDS?
DO YOU GET FREE STAMPS?
SHORTS AND BLACK SOCKS DON'T GO TOGETHER
I CAN'T WAIT UNTIL I GET TO THE MURPHYS' DOWN THE STREET...
THEY ONLY HAVE A PAIR OF ROTTWEILERS.

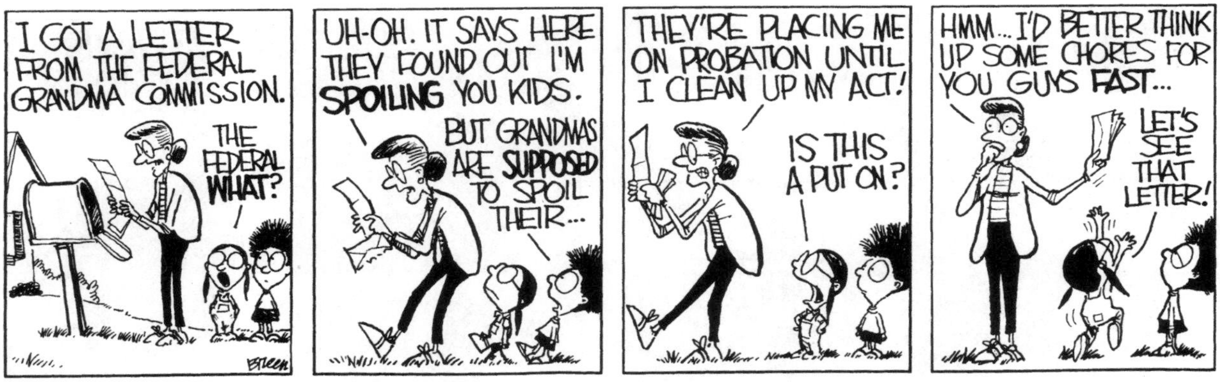
I GOT A LETTER FROM THE FEDERAL GRANDMA COMMISSION.
THE FEDERAL WHAT?
UH-OH. IT SAYS HERE THEY FOUND OUT I'M SPOILING YOU KIDS.
BUT GRANDMAS ARE SUPPOSED TO SPOIL THEIR...
THEY'RE PLACING ME ON PROBATION UNTIL I CLEAN UP MY ACT!
IS THIS A PUT ON?
HMM... I'D BETTER THINK UP SOME CHORES FOR YOU GUYS FAST...
LET'S SEE THAT LETTER!

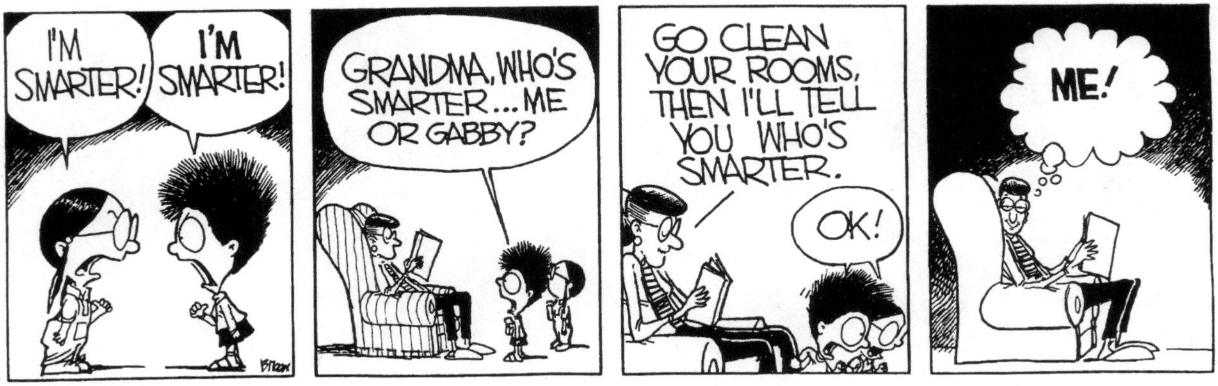
I'M SMARTER!
I'M SMARTER!
GRANDMA, WHO'S SMARTER... ME OR GABBY?
GO CLEAN YOUR ROOMS, THEN I'LL TELL YOU WHO'S SMARTER.
OK!
ME!

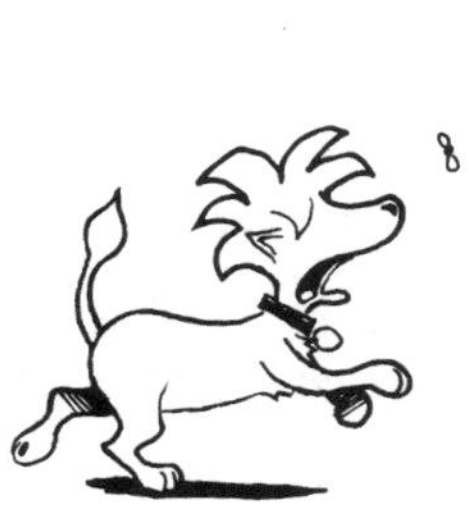

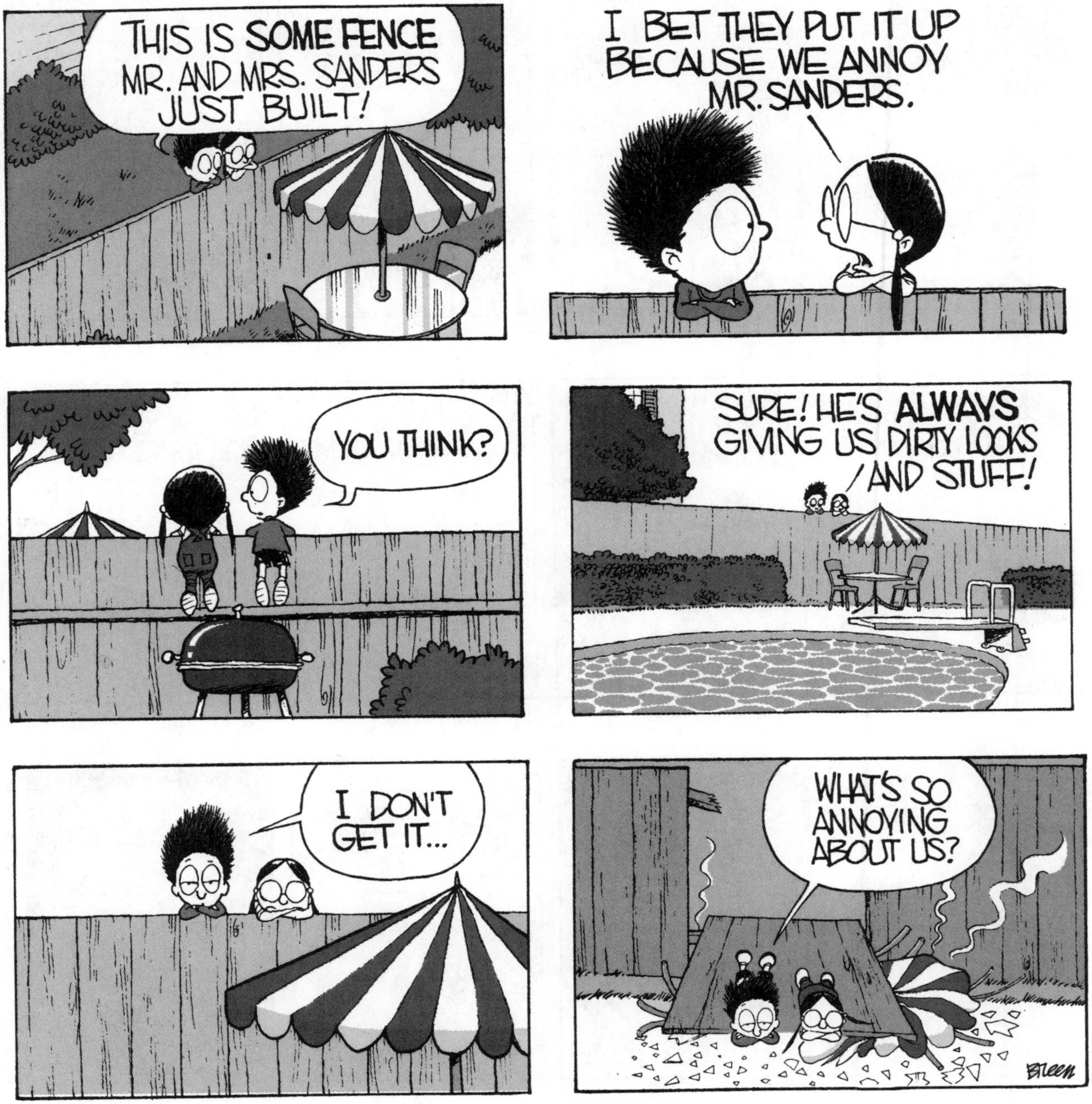
THIS IS SOME FENCE MR. AND MRS. SANDERS JUST BUILT!
I BET THEY PUT IT UP BECAUSE WE ANNOY MR. SANDERS.
YOU THINK?
SURE! HE'S ALWAYS GIVING US DIRTY LOOKS AND STUFF!
I DON'T GET IT...
WHAT'S SO ANNOYING ABOUT US?

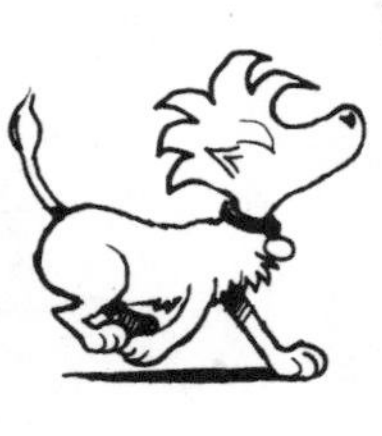

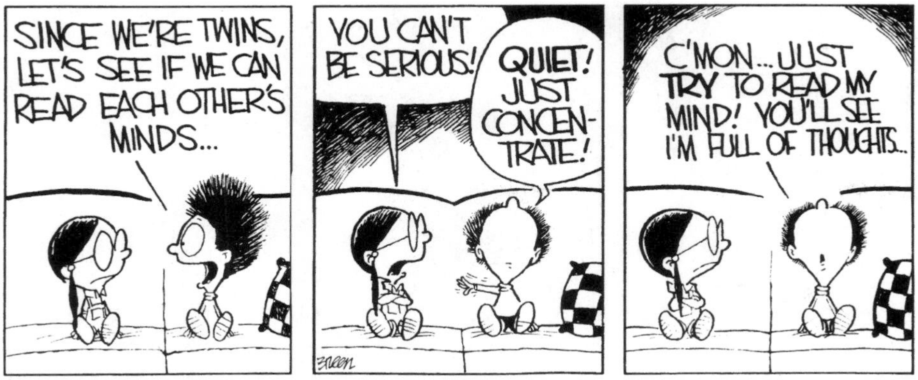
SINCE WE'RE TWINS, LET'S SEE IF WE CAN READ EACH OTHER'S MINDS...
YOU CAN'T BE SERIOUS!
QUIET! JUST CONCENTRATE!
C'MON... JUST **TRY** TO READ MY MIND! YOU'LL SEE I'M FULL OF THOUGHTS...
"THOUGHTS" ISN'T THE WORD I'D USE...

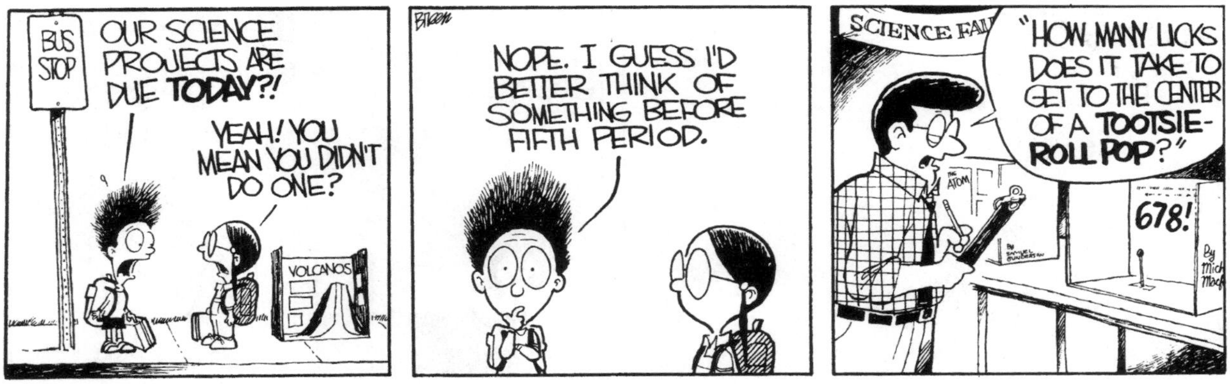
BUS STOP
OUR SCIENCE PROJECTS ARE DUE **TODAY**?!
YEAH! YOU MEAN YOU DIDN'T DO ONE?
VOLCANOS
NOPE. I GUESS I'D BETTER THINK OF SOMETHING BEFORE FIFTH PERIOD.
"HOW MANY LICKS DOES IT TAKE TO GET TO THE CENTER OF A **TOOTSIE-ROLL POP**?"
THE ATOM
678!

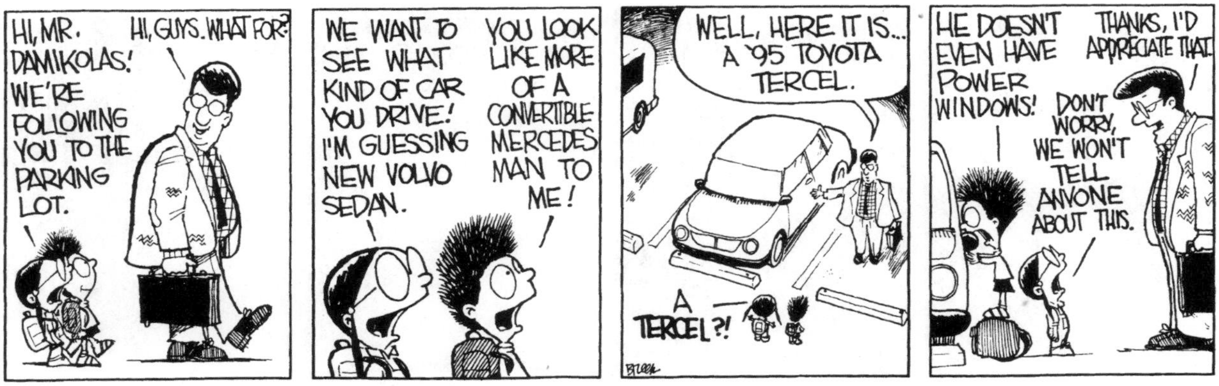
HI, MR. DAMIKOLAS! WE'RE FOLLOWING YOU TO THE PARKING LOT.
HI, GUYS. WHAT FOR?
WE WANT TO SEE WHAT KIND OF CAR YOU DRIVE! I'M GUESSING NEW VOLVO SEDAN.
YOU LOOK LIKE MORE OF A CONVERTIBLE MERCEDES MAN TO ME!
WELL, HERE IT IS... A '95 TOYOTA TERCEL.
A **TERCEL**?!
HE DOESN'T EVEN HAVE POWER WINDOWS!
THANKS, I'D APPRECIATE THAT.
DON'T WORRY, WE WON'T TELL ANYONE ABOUT THIS.

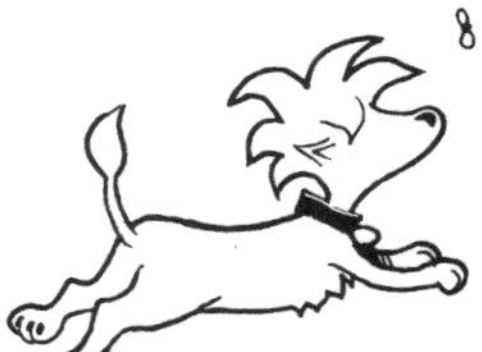

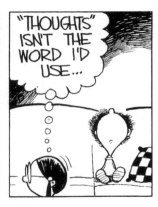

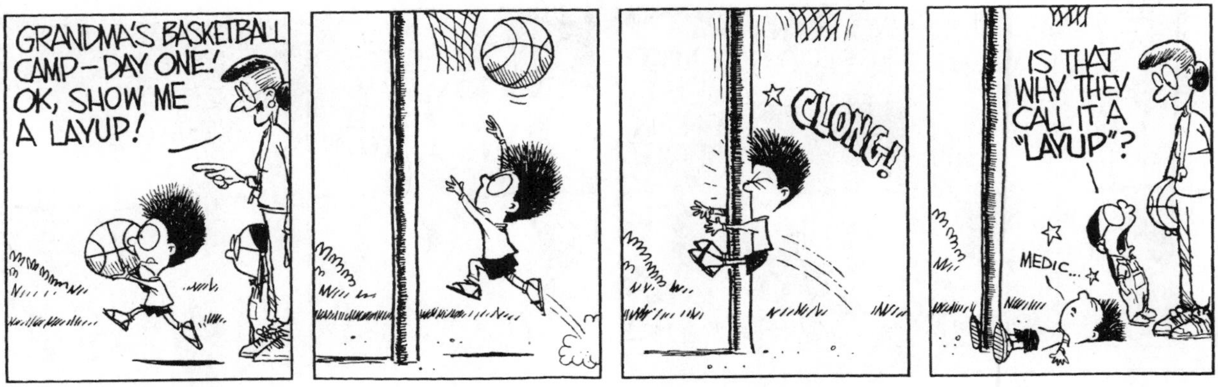
GRANDMA'S BASKETBALL CAMP–DAY ONE! OK, SHOW ME A LAYUP!
CLONG!
IS THAT WHY THEY CALL IT A "LAYUP"?
MEDIC...

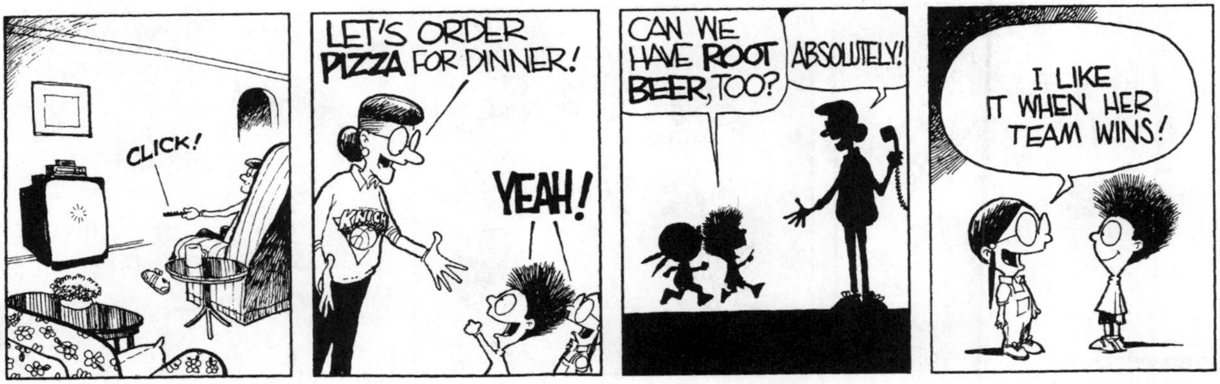
CLICK!
LET'S ORDER PIZZA FOR DINNER!
KNICKS
YEAH!
CAN WE HAVE ROOT BEER, TOO?
ABSOLUTELY!
I LIKE IT WHEN HER TEAM WINS!

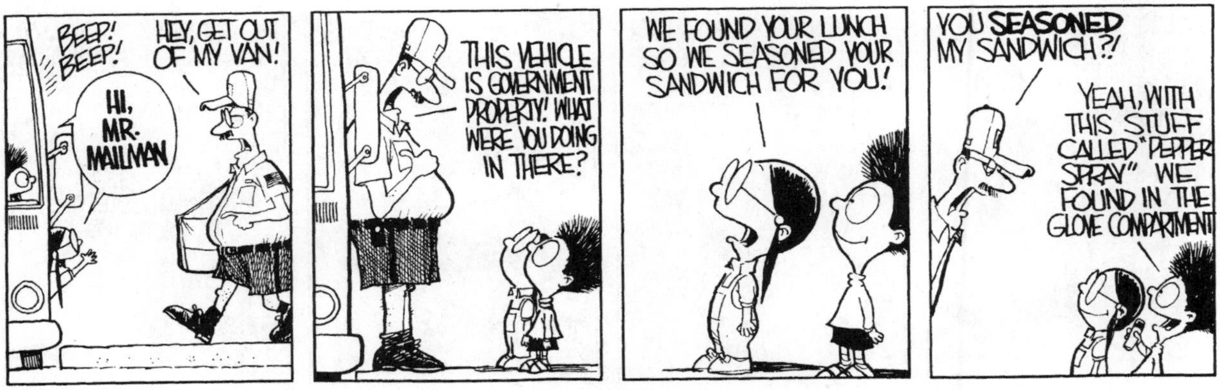
BEEP! BEEP!
HI, MR. MAILMAN
HEY, GET OUT OF MY VAN!
THIS VEHICLE IS GOVERNMENT PROPERTY! WHAT WERE YOU DOING IN THERE?
WE FOUND YOUR LUNCH SO WE SEASONED YOUR SANDWICH FOR YOU!
YOU SEASONED MY SANDWICH?!
YEAH, WITH THIS STUFF CALLED "PEPPER SPRAY" WE FOUND IN THE GLOVE COMPARTMENT

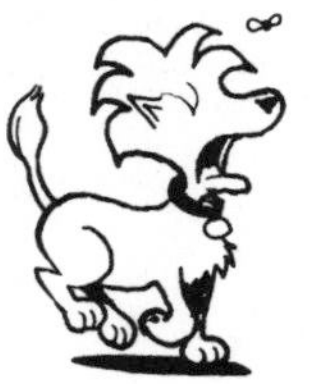

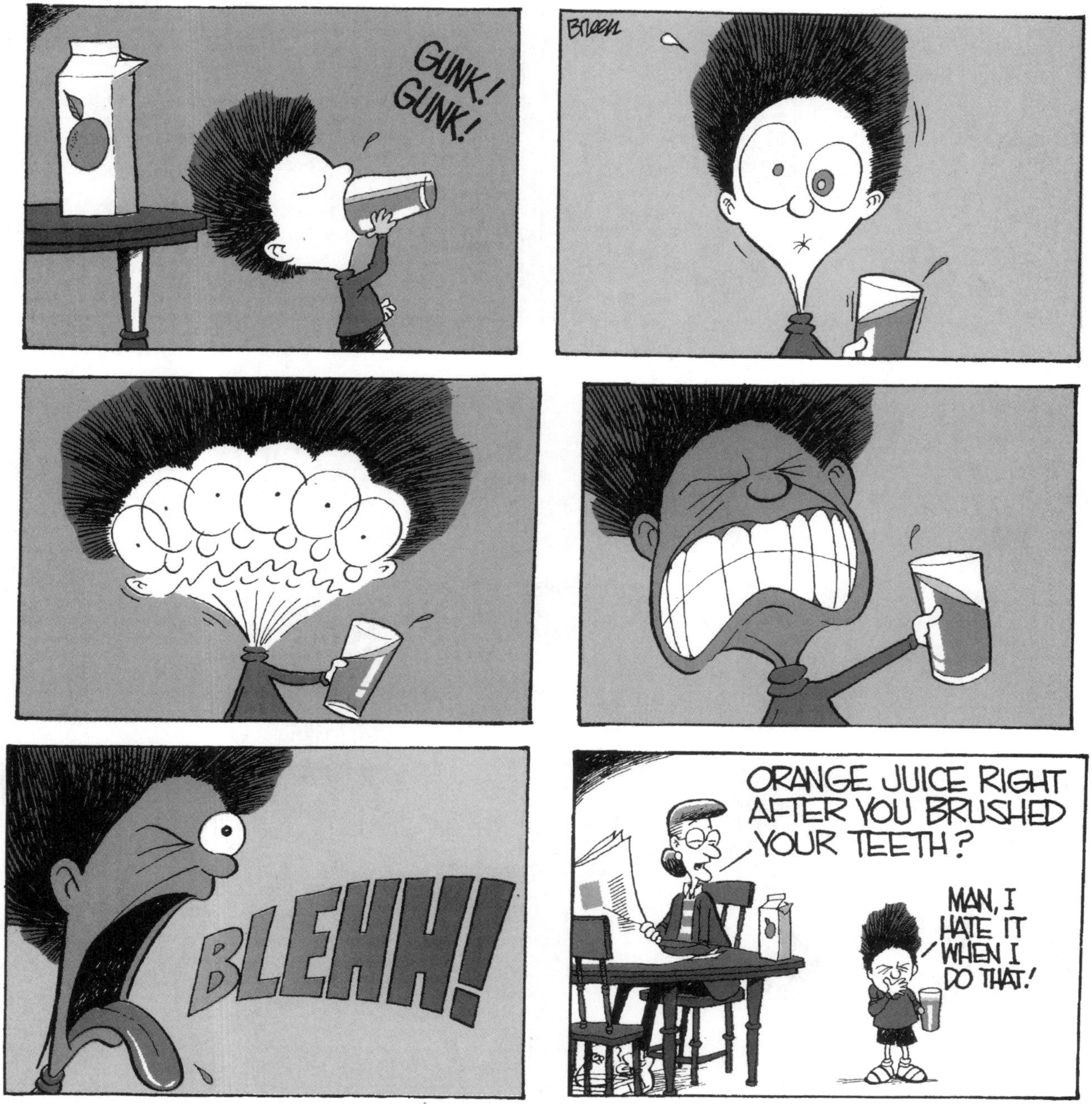
GUNK! GUNK!
BLEHH!
ORANGE JUICE RIGHT AFTER YOU BRUSHED YOUR TEETH?
MAN, I HATE IT WHEN I DO THAT!

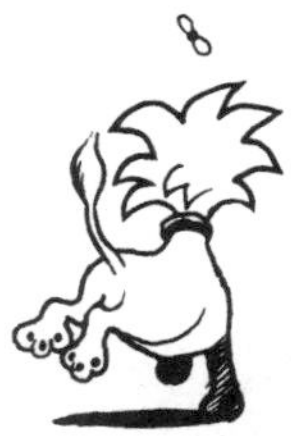

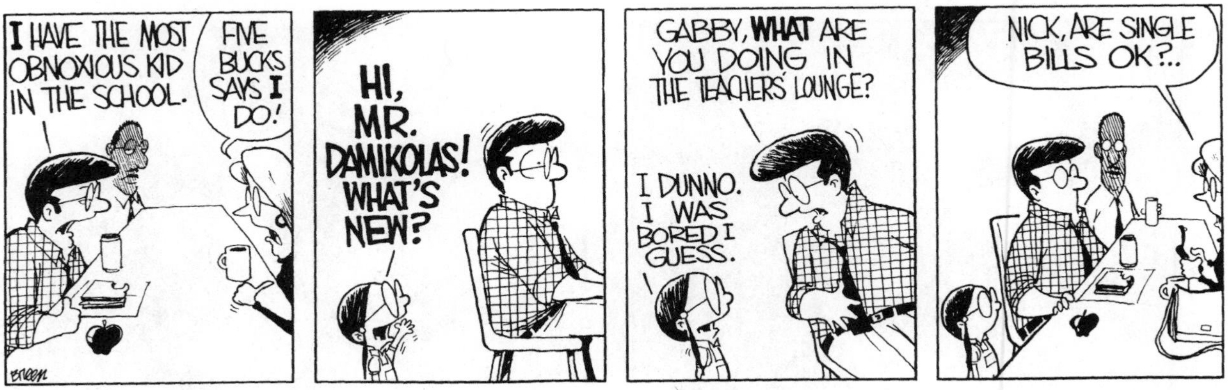
I HAVE THE MOST OBNOXIOUS KID IN THE SCHOOL.
FIVE BUCKS SAYS I DO!
HI, MR. DAMIKOLAS! WHAT'S NEW?
GABBY, WHAT ARE YOU DOING IN THE TEACHERS' LOUNGE?
I DUNNO. I WAS BORED I GUESS.
NICK, ARE SINGLE BILLS OK?..

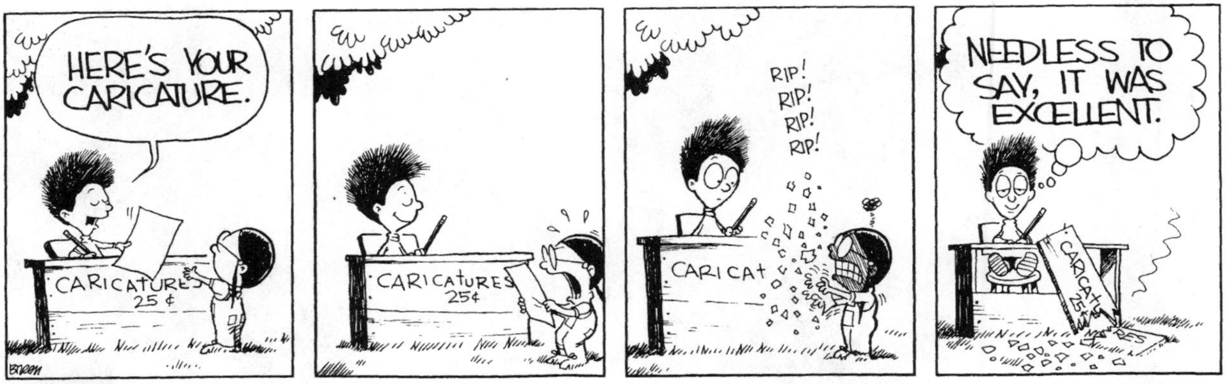
HERE'S YOUR CARICATURE.
CARICATURES 25¢
CARICATURES 25¢
RIP! RIP! RIP! RIP!
CARICAT
NEEDLESS TO SAY, IT WAS EXCELLENT.

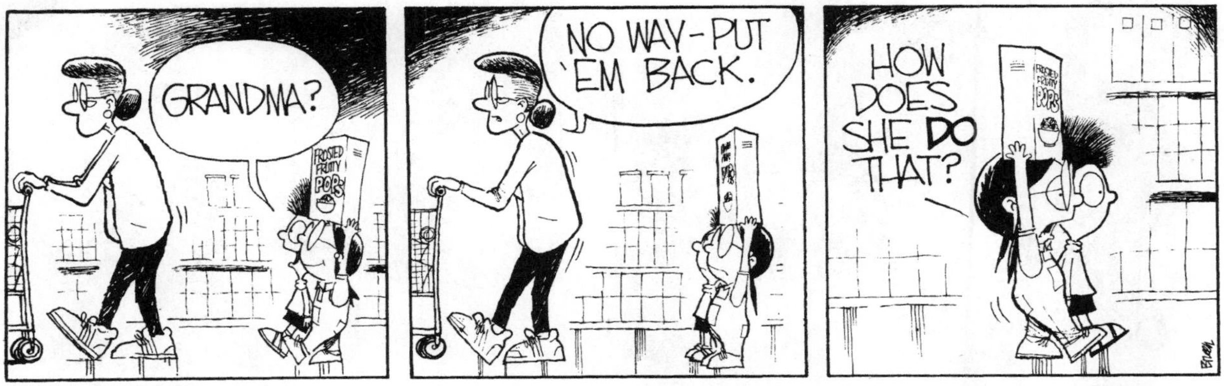
GRANDMA?
FROSTED FRUITY POPS
NO WAY-PUT 'EM BACK.
HOW DOES SHE DO THAT?

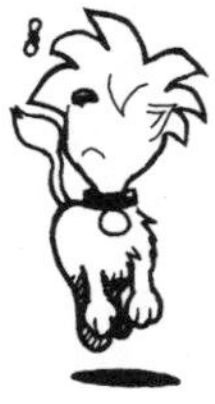

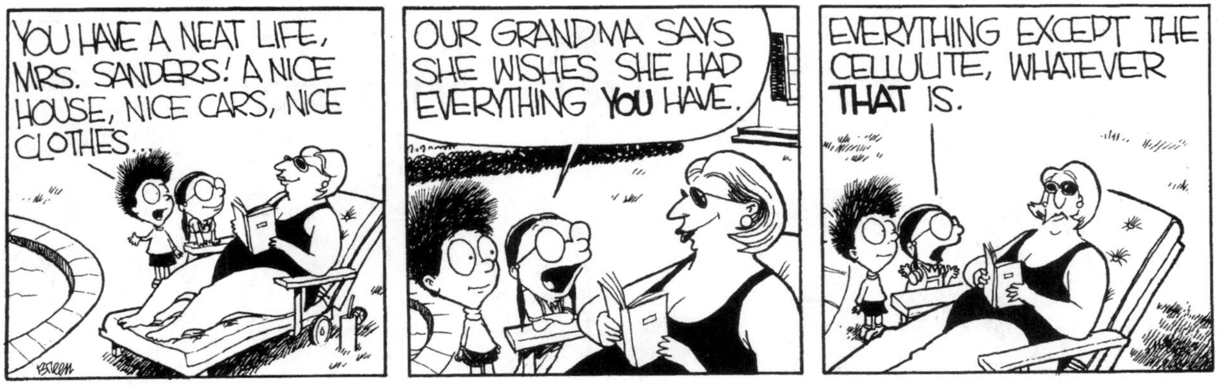
YOU HAVE A NEAT LIFE, MRS. SANDERS! A NICE HOUSE, NICE CARS, NICE CLOTHES...
OUR GRANDMA SAYS SHE WISHES SHE HAD EVERYTHING **YOU** HAVE.
EVERYTHING EXCEPT THE CELLULITE, WHATEVER **THAT** IS.

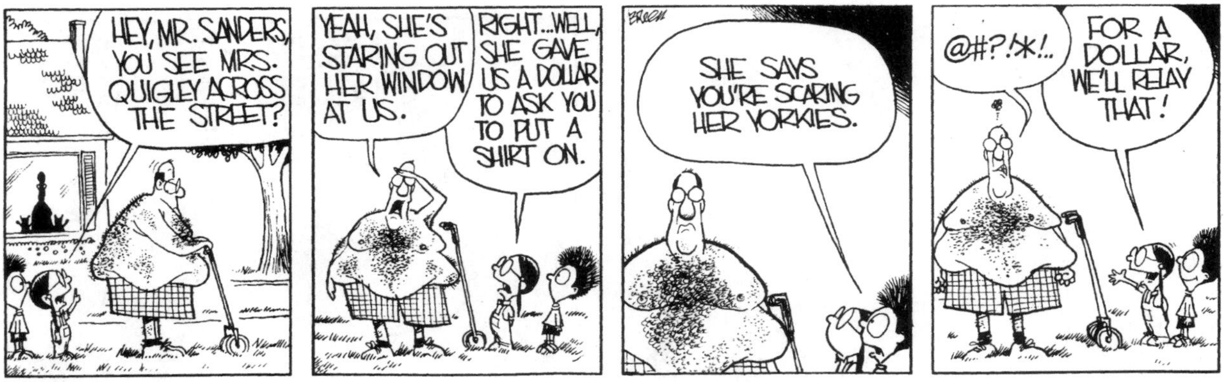
HEY, MR. SANDERS, YOU SEE MRS. QUIGLEY ACROSS THE STREET?
YEAH, SHE'S STARING OUT HER WINDOW AT US.
RIGHT...WELL, SHE GAVE US A DOLLAR TO ASK YOU TO PUT A SHIRT ON.
SHE SAYS YOU'RE SCARING HER YORKIES.
@#?!$*!..
FOR A DOLLAR, WE'LL RELAY THAT!

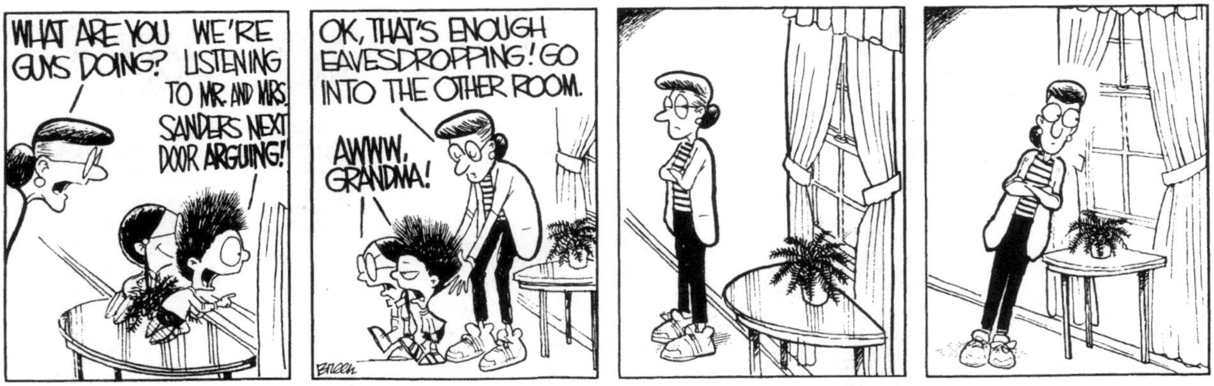
WHAT ARE YOU GUYS DOING?
WE'RE LISTENING TO MR. AND MRS. SANDERS NEXT DOOR **ARGUING**!
OK, THAT'S ENOUGH EAVESDROPPING! GO INTO THE OTHER ROOM.
AWWW, GRANDMA!

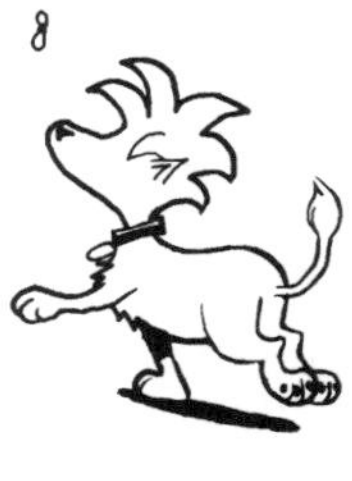

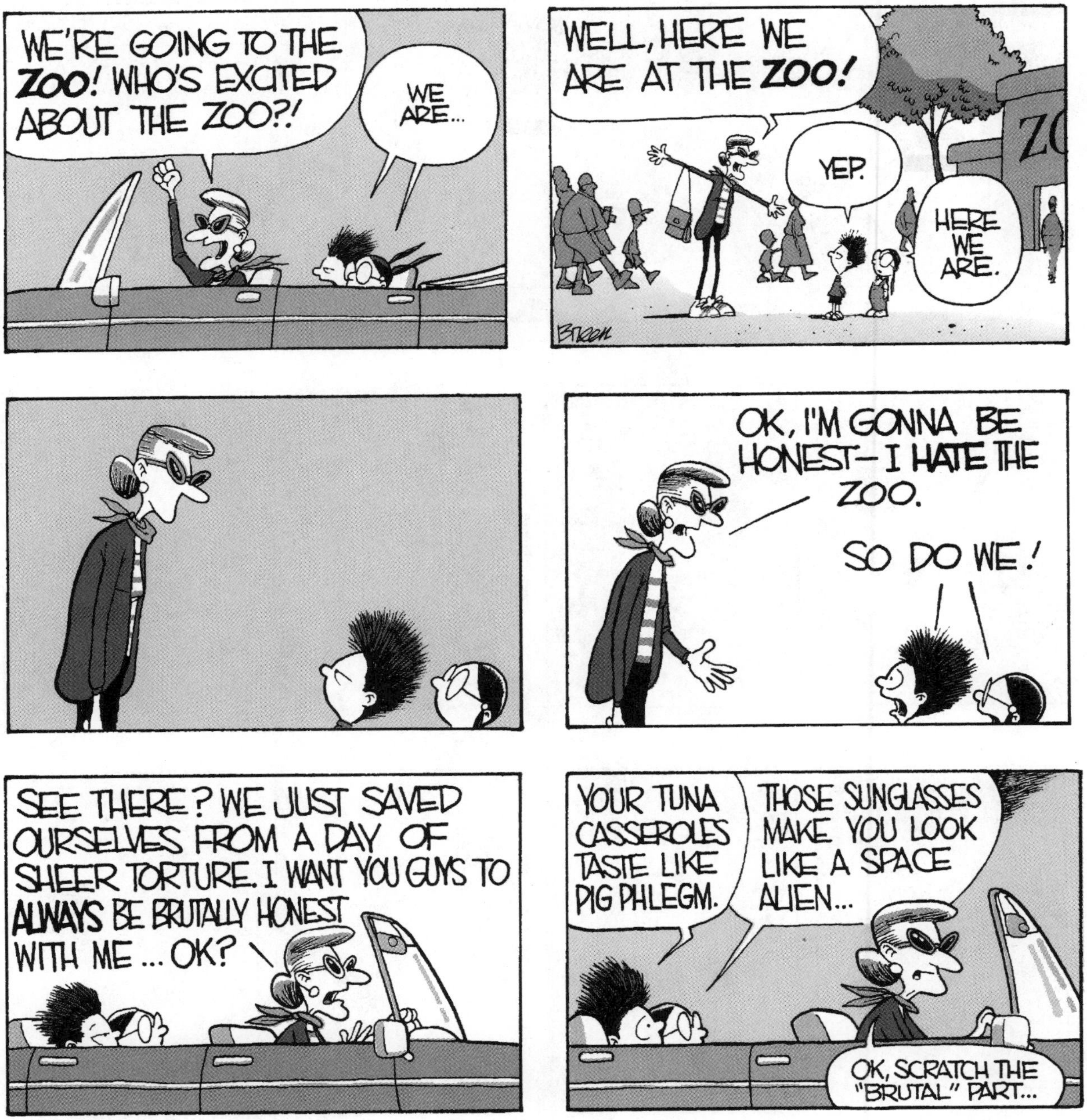
WE'RE GOING TO THE ZOO! WHO'S EXCITED ABOUT THE ZOO?!
WE ARE...
WELL, HERE WE ARE AT THE ZOO!
YEP.
HERE WE ARE.
OK, I'M GONNA BE HONEST– I HATE THE ZOO.
SO DO WE!
SEE THERE? WE JUST SAVED OURSELVES FROM A DAY OF SHEER TORTURE. I WANT YOU GUYS TO ALWAYS BE BRUTALLY HONEST WITH ME ... OK?
YOUR TUNA CASSEROLES TASTE LIKE PIG PHLEGM.
THOSE SUNGLASSES MAKE YOU LOOK LIKE A SPACE ALIEN...
OK, SCRATCH THE "BRUTAL" PART...

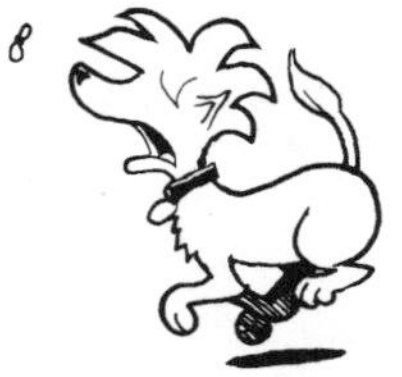

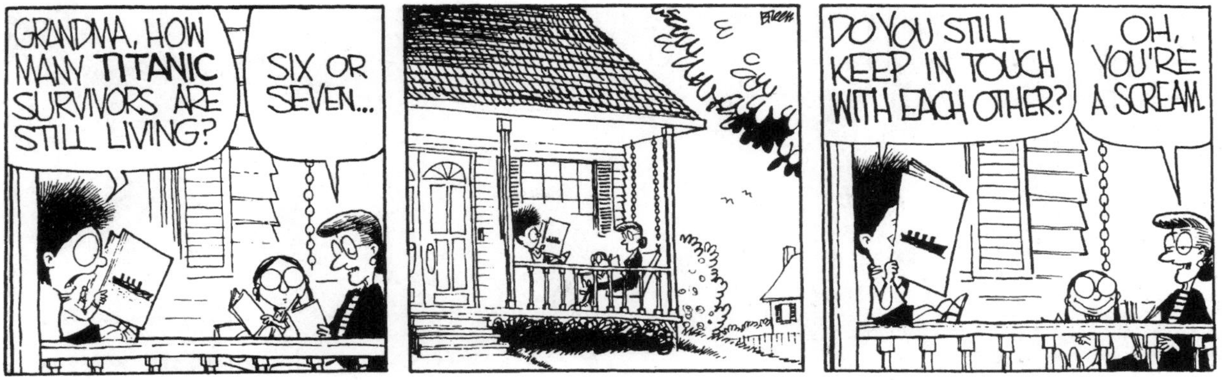
GRANDMA, HOW MANY **TITANIC** SURVIVORS ARE STILL LIVING?
SIX OR SEVEN...
DO YOU STILL KEEP IN TOUCH WITH EACH OTHER?
OH, YOU'RE A SCREAM.

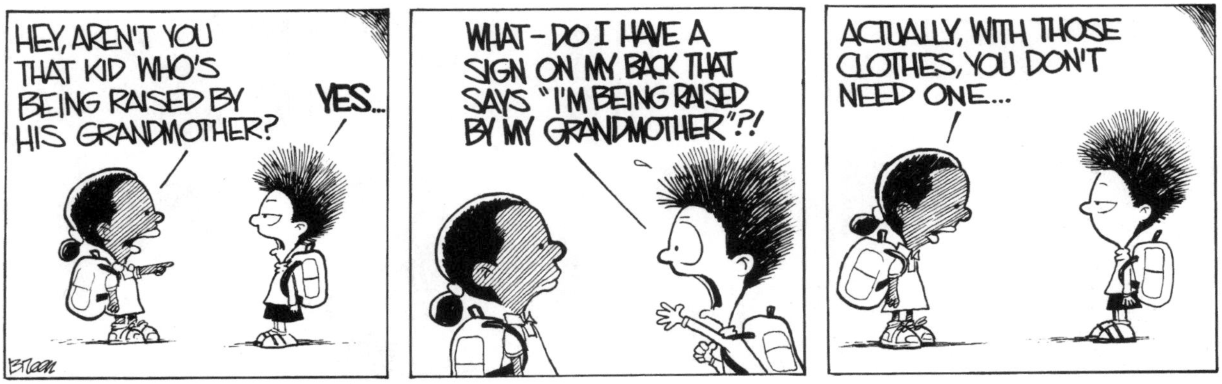
HEY, AREN'T YOU THAT KID WHO'S BEING RAISED BY HIS GRANDMOTHER?
YES...
WHAT- DO I HAVE A SIGN ON MY BACK THAT SAYS "I'M BEING RAISED BY MY GRANDMOTHER"?!
ACTUALLY, WITH THOSE CLOTHES, YOU DON'T NEED ONE...

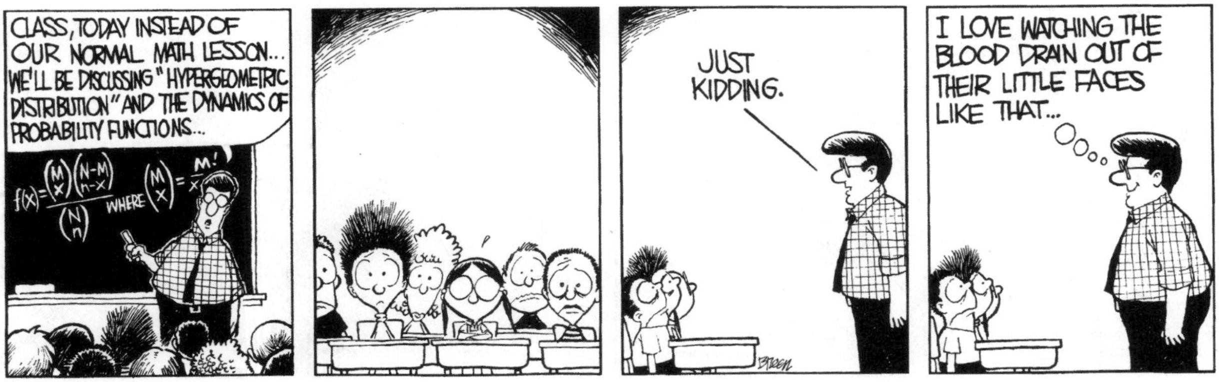
CLASS, TODAY INSTEAD OF OUR NORMAL MATH LESSON... WE'LL BE DISCUSSING "HYPERGEOMETRIC DISTRIBUTION" AND THE DYNAMICS OF PROBABILITY FUNCTIONS...
JUST KIDDING.
I LOVE WATCHING THE BLOOD DRAIN OUT OF THEIR LITTLE FACES LIKE THAT...

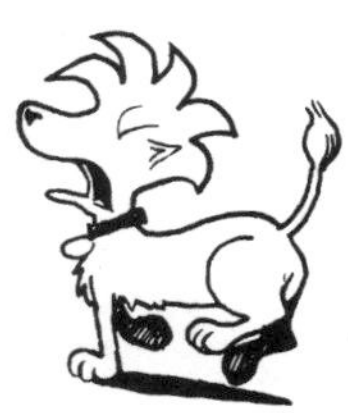

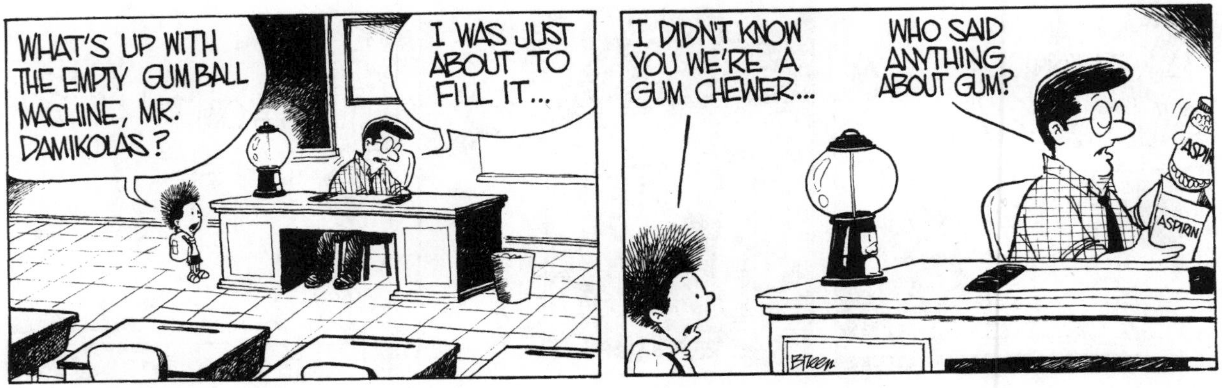
WHAT'S UP WITH THE EMPTY GUM BALL MACHINE, MR. DAMIKOLAS?
I WAS JUST ABOUT TO FILL IT...
I DIDN'T KNOW YOU WE'RE A GUM CHEWER...
WHO SAID ANYTHING ABOUT GUM?
ASPIRIN

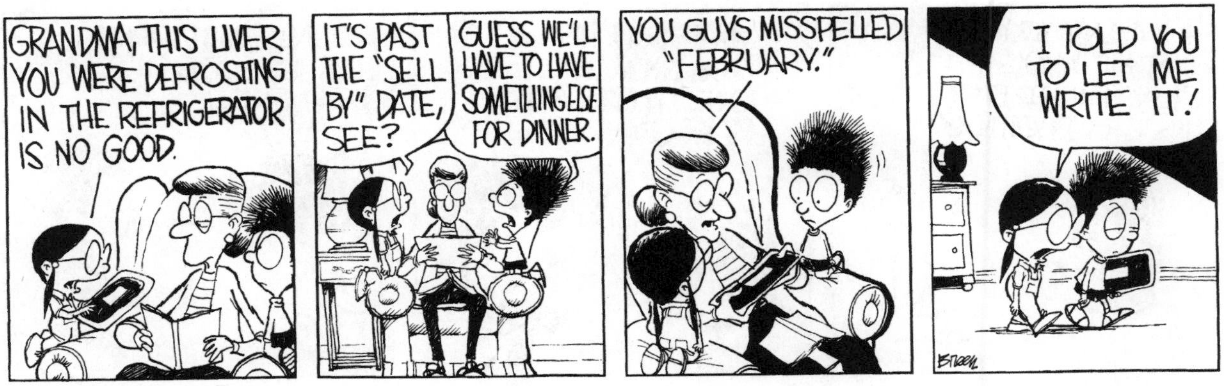
GRANDMA, THIS LIVER YOU WERE DEFROSTING IN THE REFRIGERATOR IS NO GOOD.
IT'S PAST THE "SELL BY" DATE, SEE?
GUESS WE'LL HAVE TO HAVE SOMETHING ELSE FOR DINNER.
YOU GUYS MISSPELLED "FEBRUARY."
I TOLD YOU TO LET ME WRITE IT!

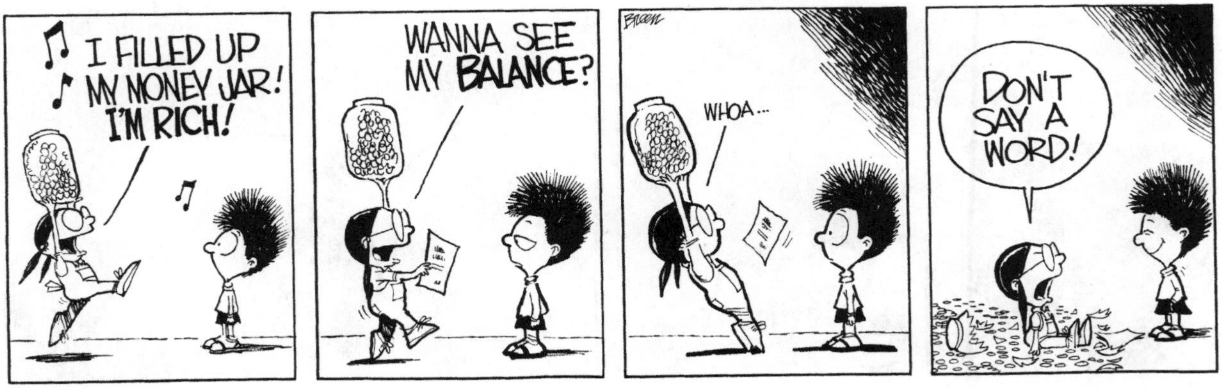
I FILLED UP MY MONEY JAR! I'M RICH!
WANNA SEE MY BALANCE?
WHOA...
DON'T SAY A WORD!

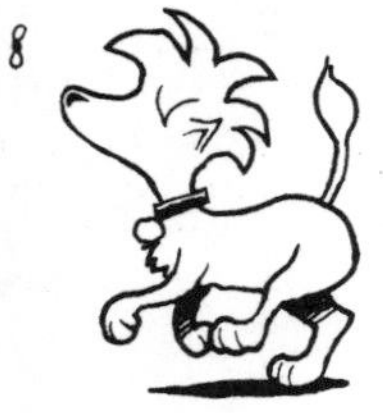

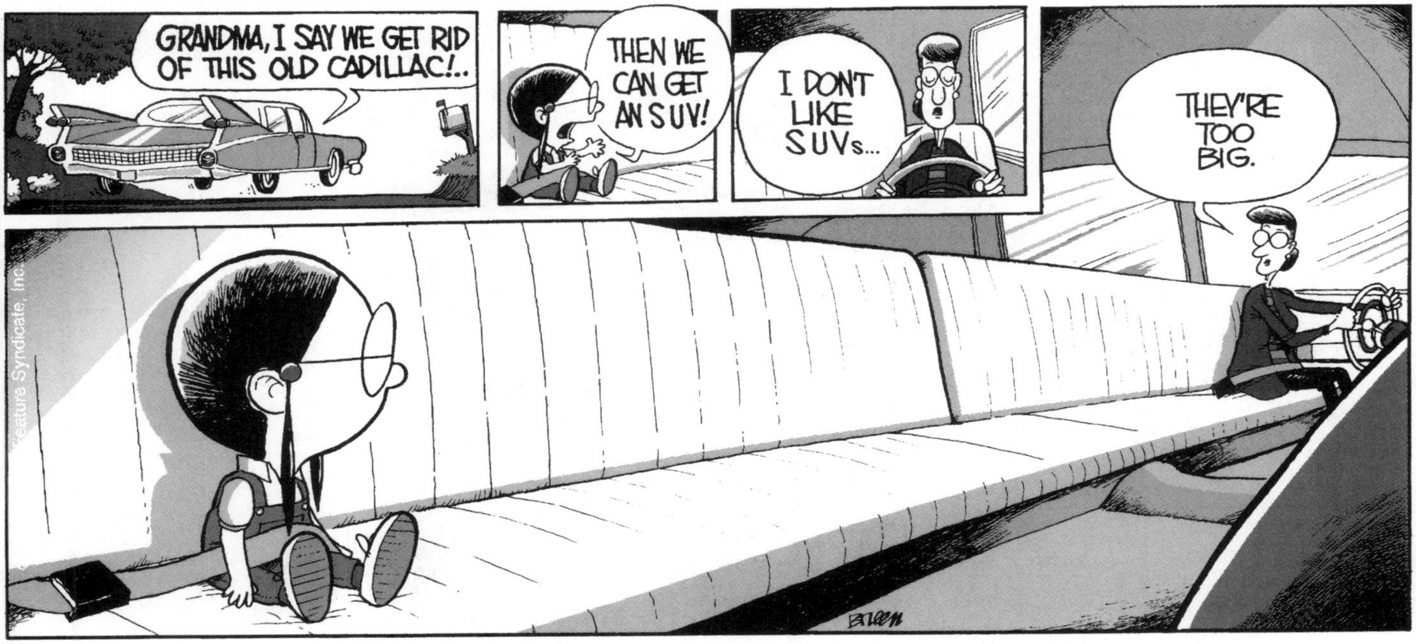
GRANDMA, I SAY WE GET RID OF THIS OLD CADILLAC!..
THEN WE CAN GET AN SUV!
I DON'T LIKE SUVs...
THEY'RE TOO BIG.

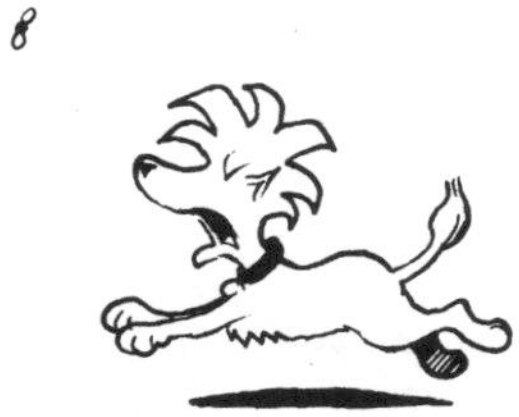

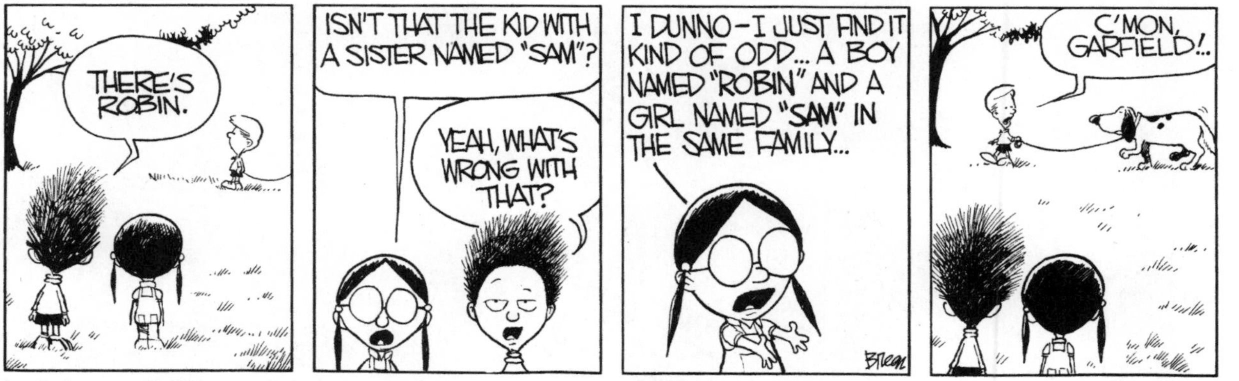
THERE'S ROBIN.
ISN'T THAT THE KID WITH A SISTER NAMED "SAM"?
YEAH, WHAT'S WRONG WITH THAT?
I DUNNO—I JUST FIND IT KIND OF ODD... A BOY NAMED "ROBIN" AND A GIRL NAMED "SAM" IN THE SAME FAMILY...
C'MON, GARFIELD!..

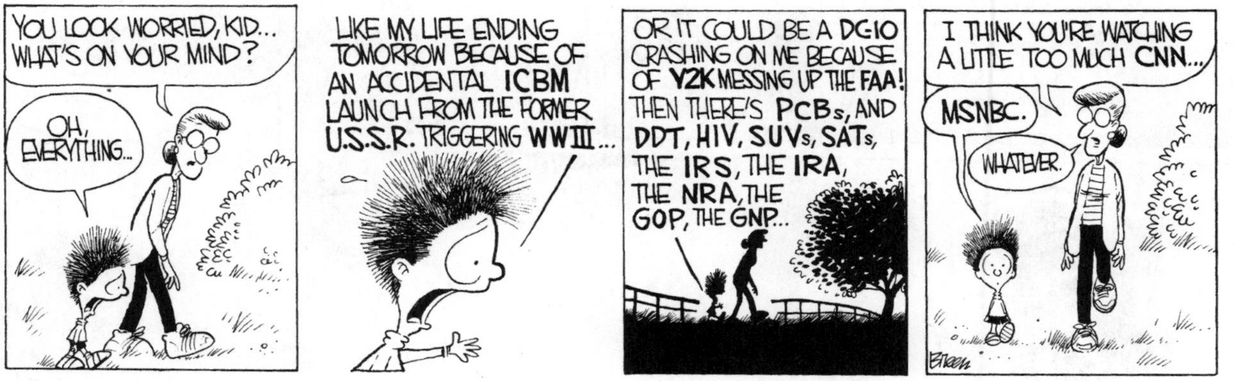
YOU LOOK WORRIED, KID... WHAT'S ON YOUR MIND?
OH, EVERYTHING...
LIKE MY LIFE ENDING TOMORROW BECAUSE OF AN ACCIDENTAL ICBM LAUNCH FROM THE FORMER U.S.S.R. TRIGGERING WWIII...
OR IT COULD BE A DC-10 CRASHING ON ME BECAUSE OF Y2K MESSING UP THE FAA! THEN THERE'S PCBs, AND DDT, HIV, SUVs, SATs, THE IRS, THE IRA, THE NRA, THE GOP, THE GNP...
I THINK YOU'RE WATCHING A LITTLE TOO MUCH CNN...
MSNBC.
WHATEVER.

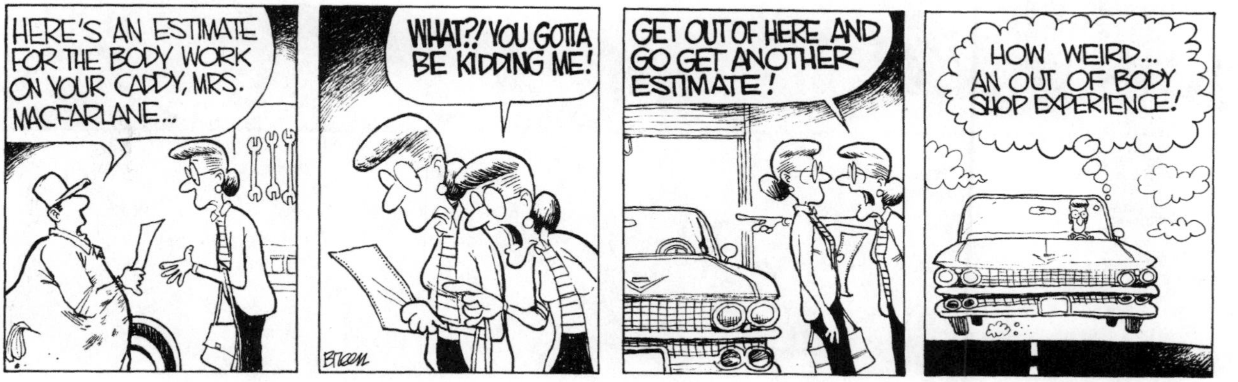
HERE'S AN ESTIMATE FOR THE BODY WORK ON YOUR CADDY, MRS. MACFARLANE...
WHAT?! YOU GOTTA BE KIDDING ME!
GET OUT OF HERE AND GO GET ANOTHER ESTIMATE!
HOW WEIRD... AN OUT OF BODY SHOP EXPERIENCE!

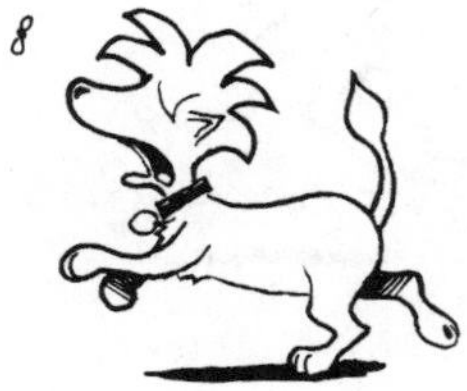

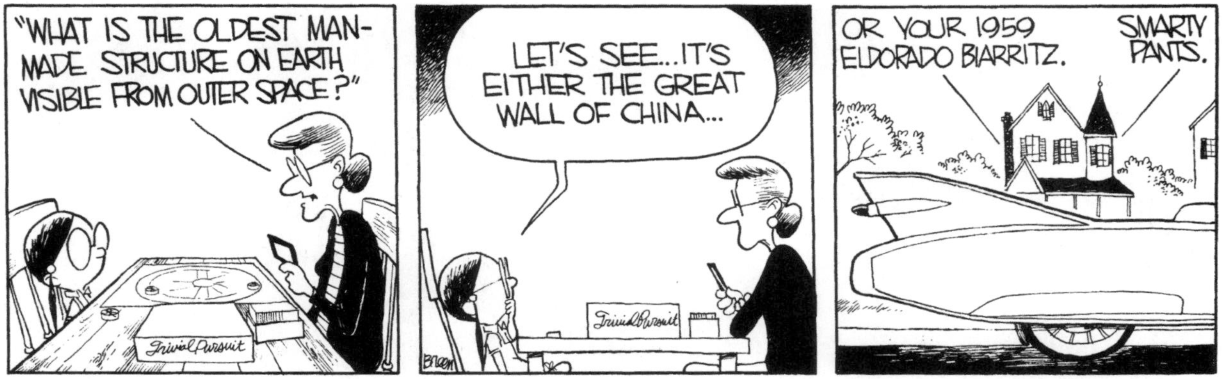
"WHAT IS THE OLDEST MAN-MADE STRUCTURE ON EARTH VISIBLE FROM OUTER SPACE?"
Trivial Pursuit
LET'S SEE...IT'S EITHER THE GREAT WALL OF CHINA...
Trivial Pursuit
OR YOUR 1959 ELDORADO BIARRITZ.
SMARTY PANTS.

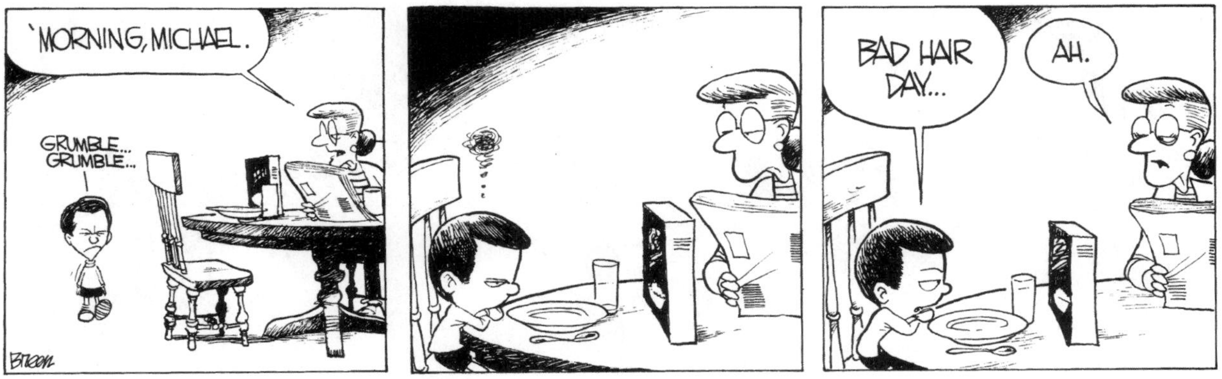
`MORNING, MICHAEL.
GRUMBLE... GRUMBLE...
BAD HAIR DAY...
AH.

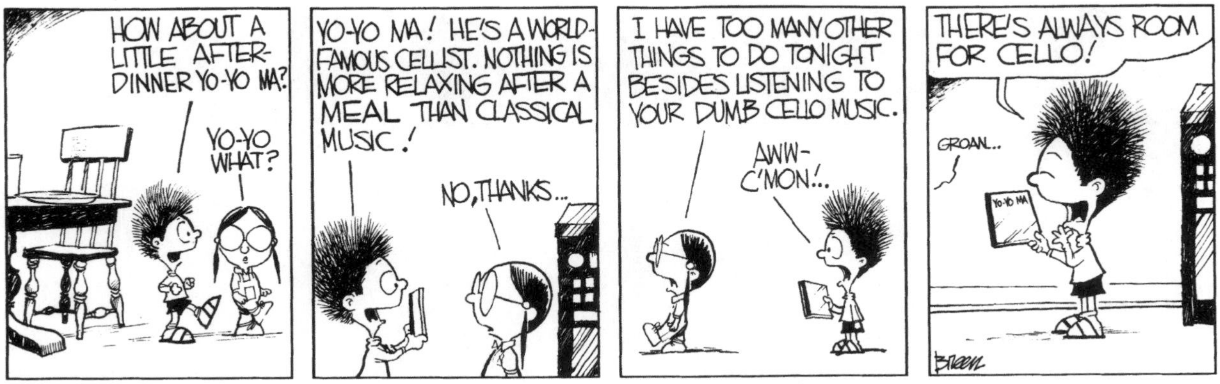
HOW ABOUT A LITTLE AFTER-DINNER YO-YO MA?
YO-YO WHAT?
YO-YO MA! HE'S A WORLD-FAMOUS CELLIST. NOTHING IS MORE RELAXING AFTER A MEAL THAN CLASSICAL MUSIC!
NO, THANKS...
I HAVE TOO MANY OTHER THINGS TO DO TONIGHT BESIDES LISTENING TO YOUR DUMB CELLO MUSIC.
AWW-C'MON!
THERE'S ALWAYS ROOM FOR CELLO!
GROAN...
YO-YO MA

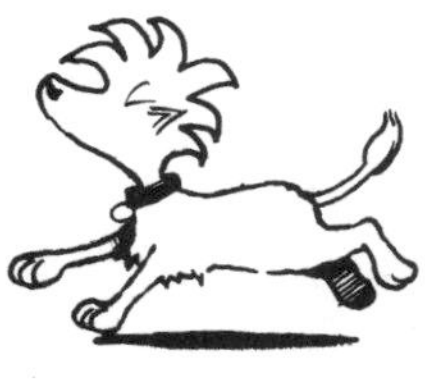

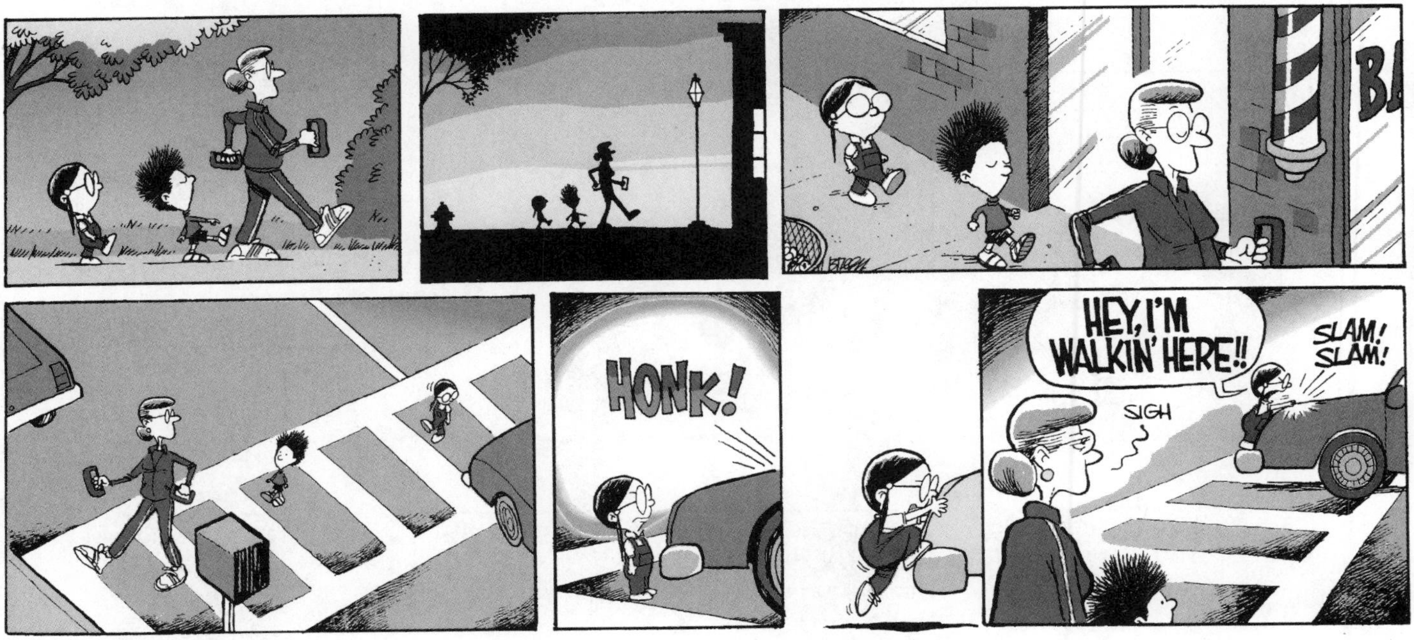
HONK!
HEY, I'M WALKIN' HERE!!
SIGH
SLAM! SLAM!

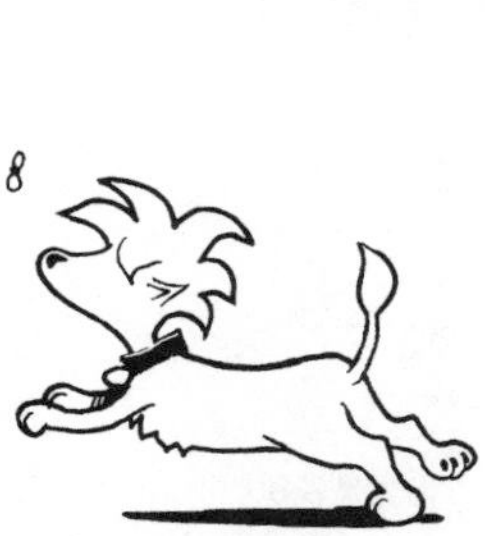

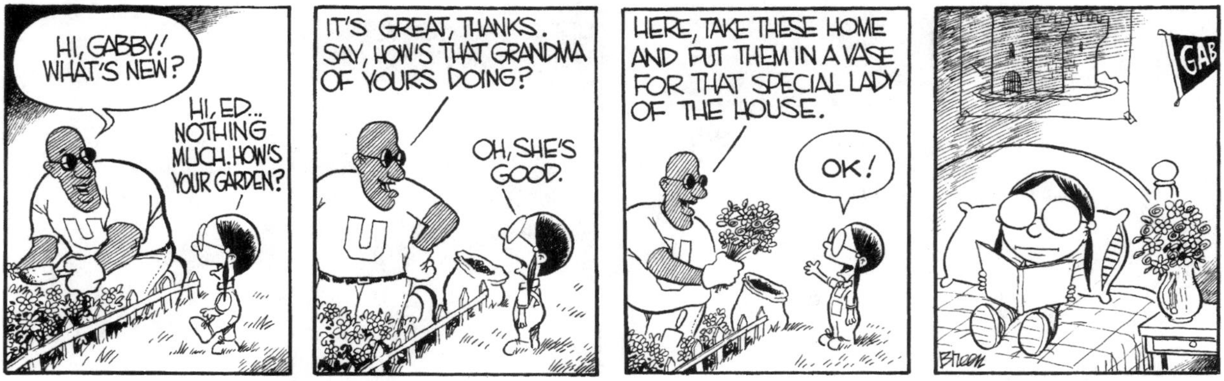
HI, GABBY! WHAT'S NEW?
HI, ED... NOTHING MUCH. HOW'S YOUR GARDEN?
IT'S GREAT, THANKS. SAY, HOW'S THAT GRANDMA OF YOURS DOING?
OH, SHE'S GOOD.
HERE, TAKE THESE HOME AND PUT THEM IN A VASE FOR THAT SPECIAL LADY OF THE HOUSE.
OK!
GAB

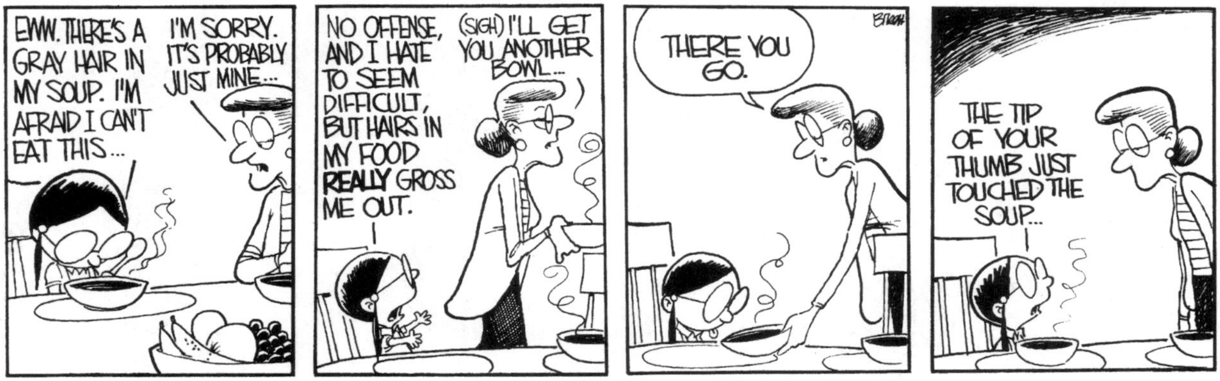
EWW. THERE'S A GRAY HAIR IN MY SOUP. I'M AFRAID I CAN'T EAT THIS...
I'M SORRY. IT'S PROBABLY JUST MINE...
NO OFFENSE, AND I HATE TO SEEM DIFFICULT, BUT HAIRS IN MY FOOD REALLY GROSS ME OUT.
(SIGH) I'LL GET YOU ANOTHER BOWL...
THERE YOU GO.
THE TIP OF YOUR THUMB JUST TOUCHED THE SOUP...

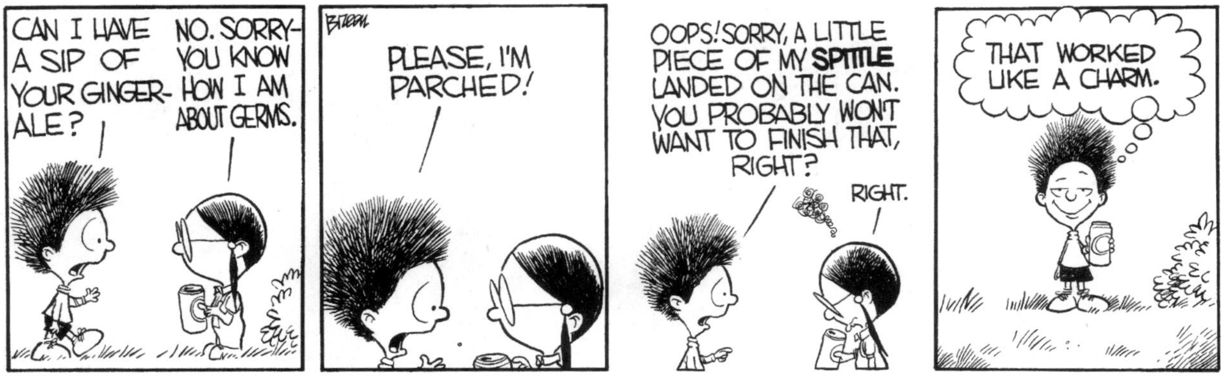
CAN I HAVE A SIP OF YOUR GINGER-ALE?
NO. SORRY- YOU KNOW HOW I AM ABOUT GERMS.
PLEASE, I'M PARCHED!
OOPS! SORRY, A LITTLE PIECE OF MY SPITTLE LANDED ON THE CAN. YOU PROBABLY WON'T WANT TO FINISH THAT, RIGHT?
RIGHT.
THAT WORKED LIKE A CHARM.

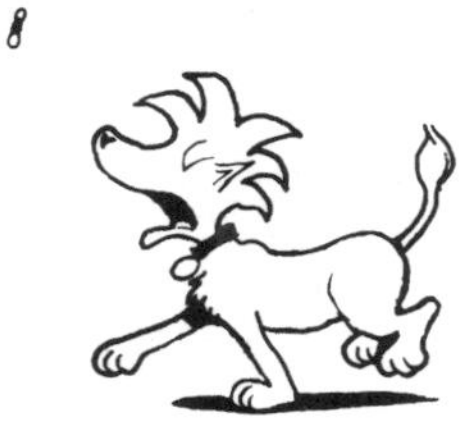

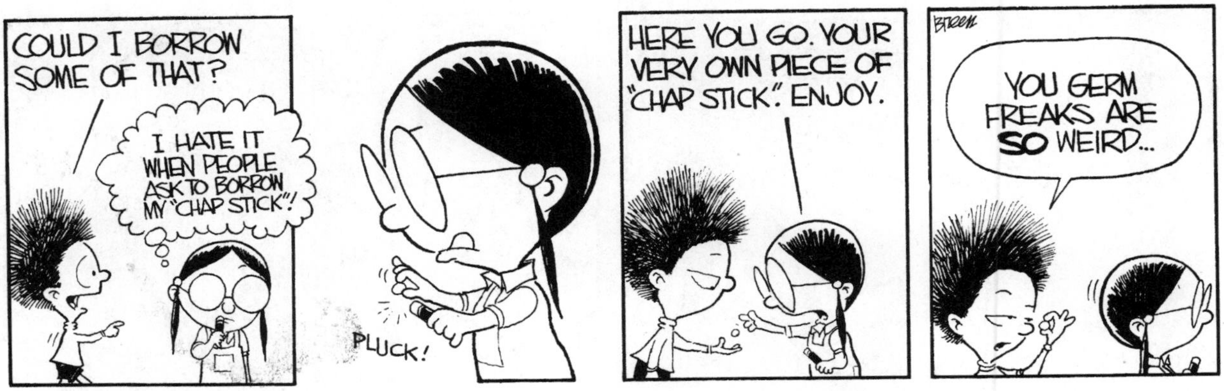
COULD I BORROW SOME OF THAT?
I HATE IT WHEN PEOPLE ASK TO BORROW MY "CHAP STICK"!
PLUCK!
HERE YOU GO. YOUR VERY OWN PIECE OF "CHAP STICK". ENJOY.
YOU GERM FREAKS ARE **SO** WEIRD...

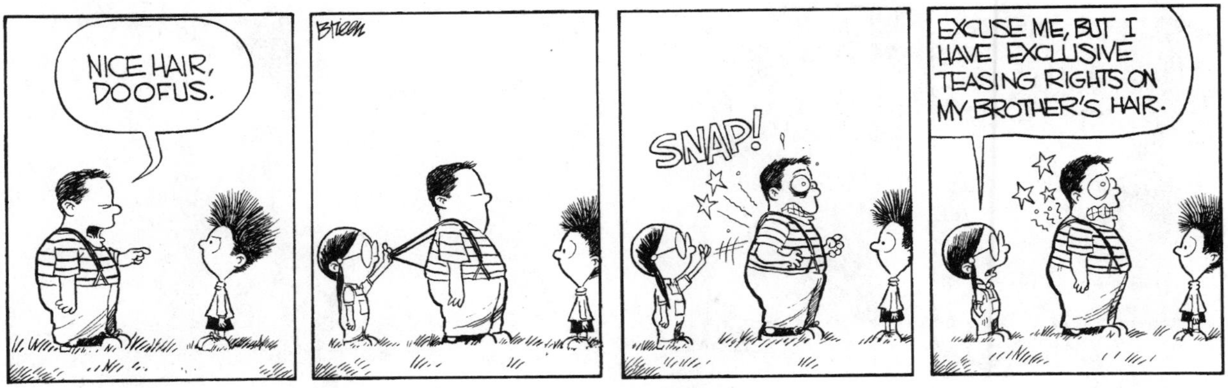
NICE HAIR, DOOFUS.
SNAP!
EXCUSE ME, BUT I HAVE EXCLUSIVE TEASING RIGHTS ON MY BROTHER'S HAIR.

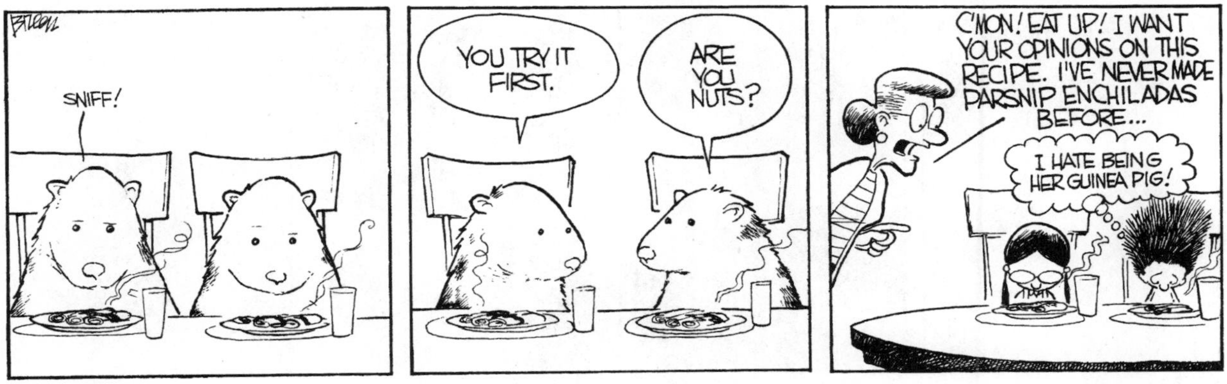
SNIFF!
YOU TRY IT FIRST.
ARE YOU NUTS?
C'MON! EAT UP! I WANT YOUR OPINIONS ON THIS RECIPE. I'VE NEVER MADE PARSNIP ENCHILADAS BEFORE...
I HATE BEING HER GUINEA PIG!

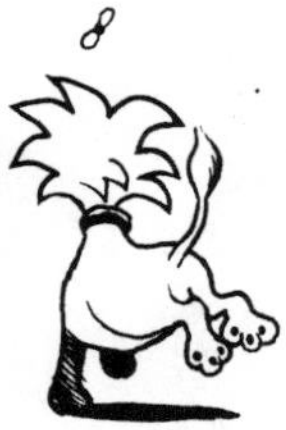

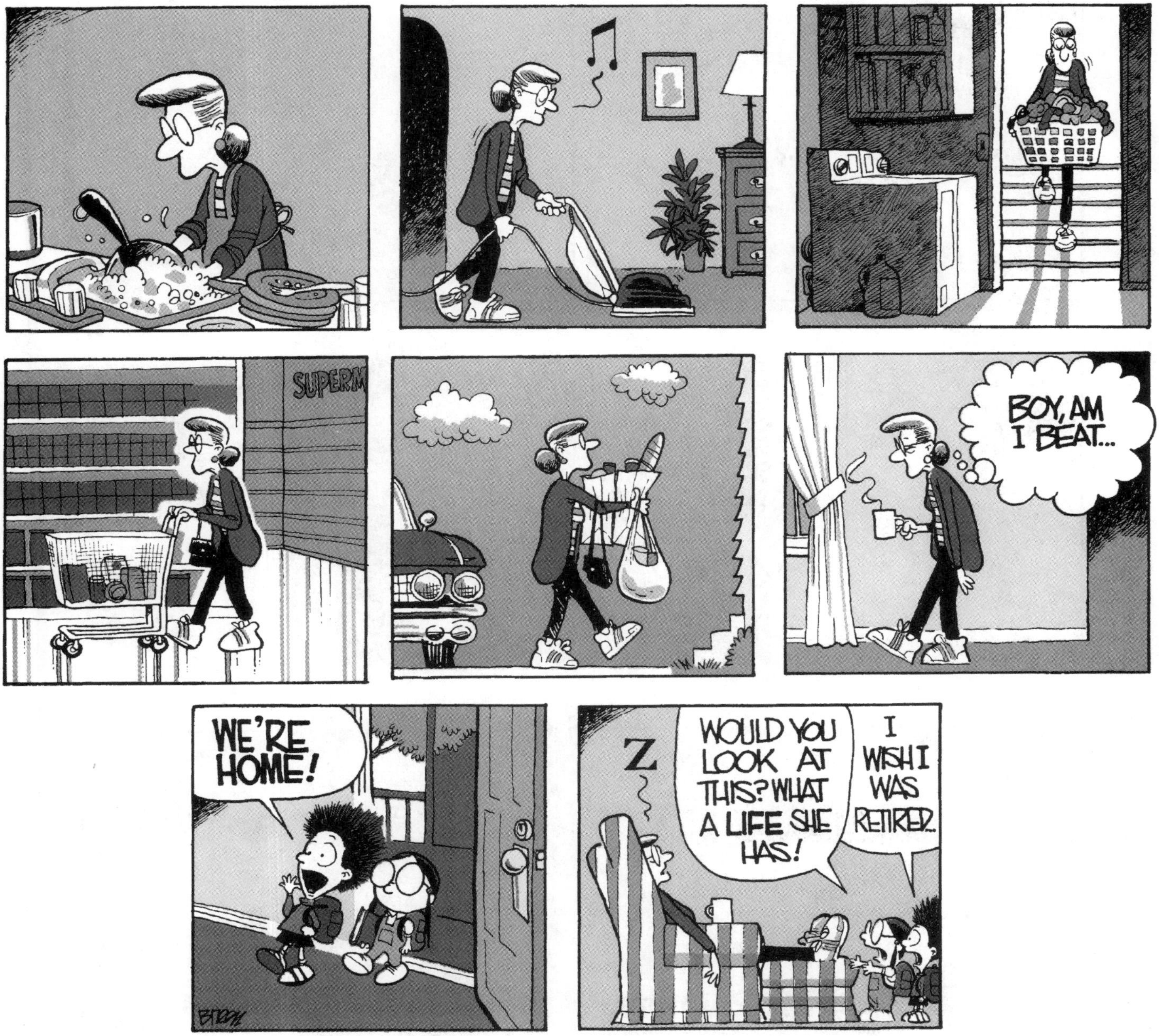
SUPERM
BOY, AM I BEAT...
WE'RE HOME!
Z
WOULD YOU LOOK AT THIS? WHAT A LIFE SHE HAS!
I WISH I WAS RETIRED..

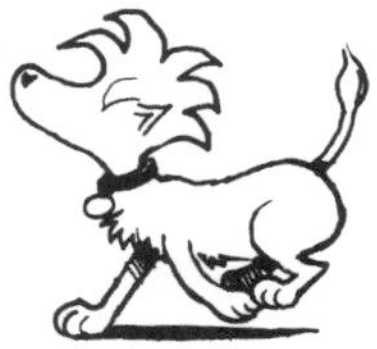

HIYA, TOOTS! NIFTY DAY, HUH? I MEAN, GOLLY! THIS WEATHER IS THE CAT'S PAJAMAS, ISN'T IT?
WHAT'S WITH YOU?
I'M GOING TO USE OLD-FASHIONED WORDS ALL WEEK LONG! IT'LL BE FUN!
IT'LL BE ANNOYING.
HORSEFEATHERS!
JEEPERS.

I JUST THOUGHT OF SOMETHING TOTALLY DEPRESSING...
I CAN'T WAIT TO HEAR IT...
I HAVE THE **TIME** TO GO SOMEWHERE EXCITING FOR SUMMER VACATION, BUT I DON'T HAVE THE **MONEY**. NEXT THING YOU KNOW, I'LL BE MIDDLE-AGED AND I'LL LIKELY HAVE THE MONEY BUT NO **TIME**.
THEN WHEN I'M OLD, I'LL PROBABLY HAVE THE TIME **AND** MONEY, BUT I'LL BE TOO SICK TO GO ANYWHERE.
...OR YOU'LL BE STUCK SOMEWHERE RAISING YOUR GRANDCHILDREN.
EXACTLY... **HEY!**

TOO HARD?
!

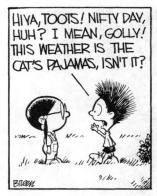

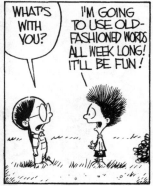

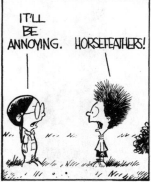

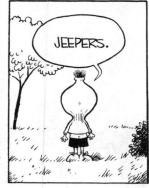

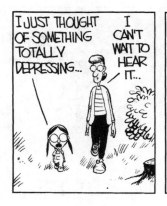

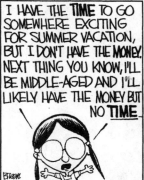

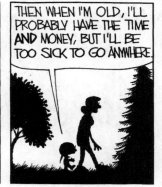

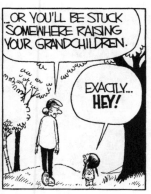

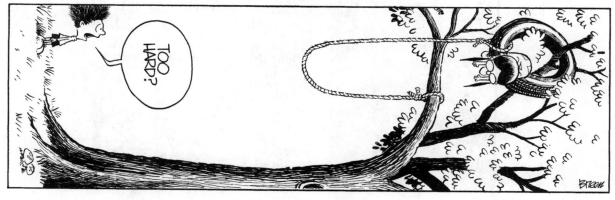

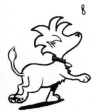

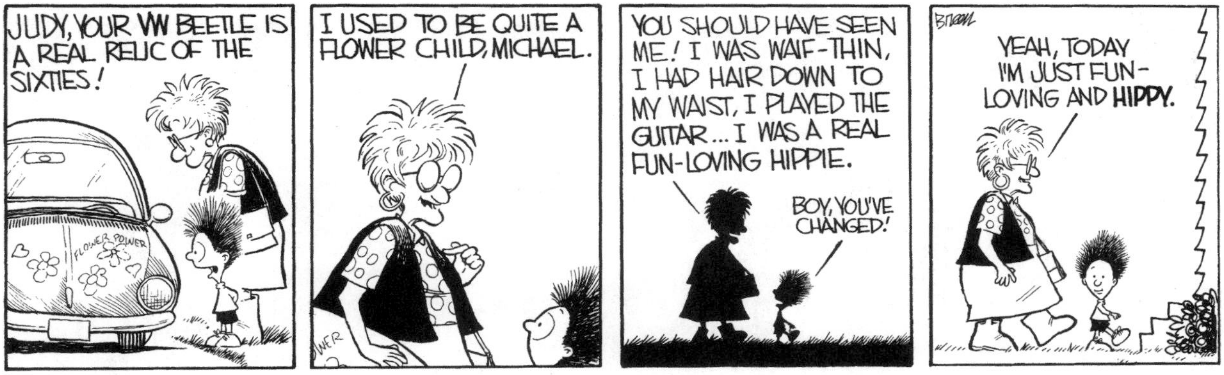
JUDY, YOUR VW BEETLE IS A REAL RELIC OF THE SIXTIES!
FLOWER POWER
I USED TO BE QUITE A FLOWER CHILD, MICHAEL.
YOU SHOULD HAVE SEEN ME! I WAS WAIF-THIN, I HAD HAIR DOWN TO MY WAIST, I PLAYED THE GUITAR... I WAS A REAL FUN-LOVING HIPPIE.
BOY, YOU'VE CHANGED!
YEAH, TODAY I'M JUST FUN-LOVING AND **HIPPY.**

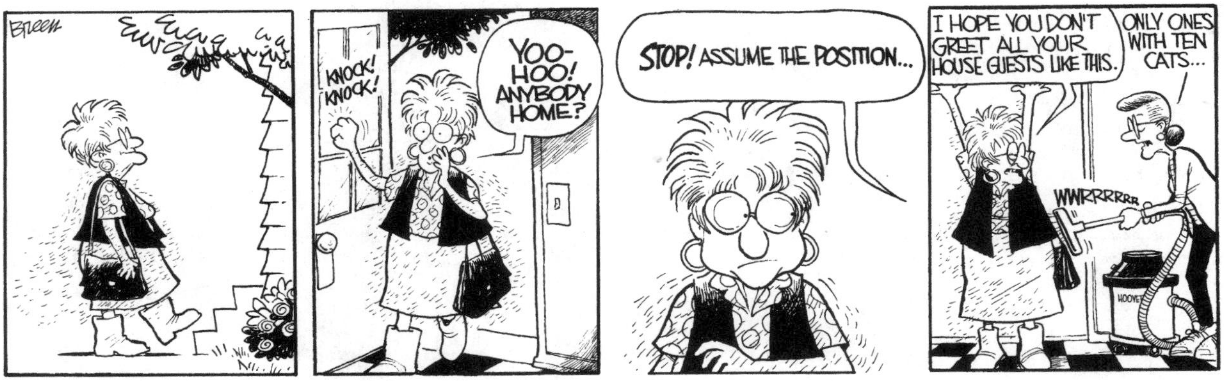
KNOCK! KNOCK!
YOO-HOO! ANYBODY HOME?
STOP! ASSUME THE POSITION...
I HOPE YOU DON'T GREET ALL YOUR HOUSE GUESTS LIKE THIS.
ONLY ONES WITH TEN CATS...
WWRRRRRR
HOOVER

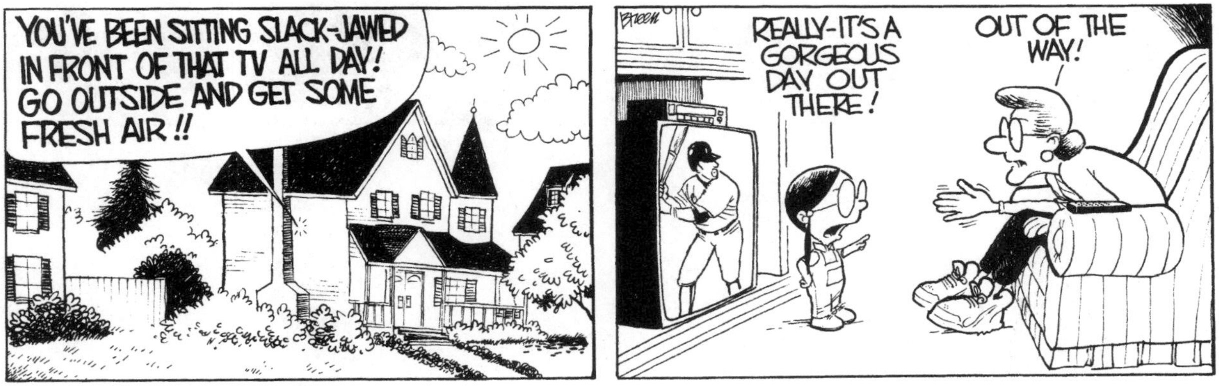
YOU'VE BEEN SITTING SLACK-JAWED IN FRONT OF THAT TV ALL DAY! GO OUTSIDE AND GET SOME FRESH AIR!!
REALLY-IT'S A GORGEOUS DAY OUT THERE!
OUT OF THE WAY!

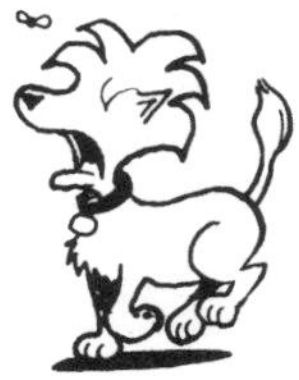

WHAT ARE YOU GUYS **LISTENING** TO?!
MY NEW HIP-HOP CD!
I CAN'T BELIEVE THAT'S WHAT PASSES FOR MUSIC THESE DAYS!
IT JUST SOUNDS LIKE A BUNCH OF NOISE TO ME!
AND I GENERALLY HAVE A **VERY** OPEN MIND WHEN IT COMES TO MUSIC
I LIKE ROCK AND ROLL, R AND B, JAZZ... REALLY!
UH-HUH
(SIGH) IT'S NO USE
YOU KIDS THINK OF ME AS SOME OLD-FASHIONED **FUDDY-DUDDY**, DON'T YOU?
NO-O-O...
NOT AT ALL...

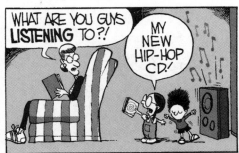

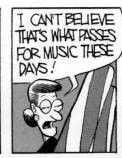

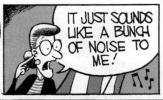

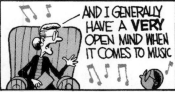

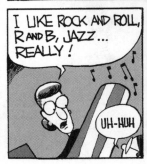

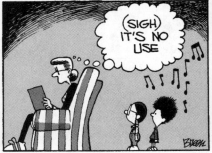

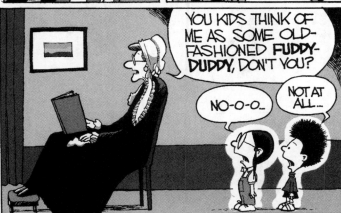

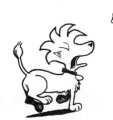

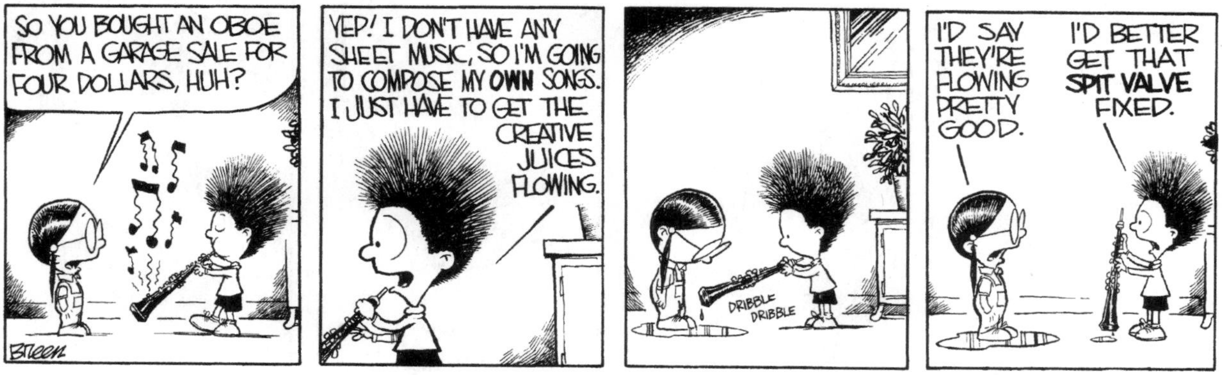
SO YOU BOUGHT AN OBOE FROM A GARAGE SALE FOR FOUR DOLLARS, HUH?
YEP! I DON'T HAVE ANY SHEET MUSIC, SO I'M GOING TO COMPOSE MY **OWN** SONGS. I JUST HAVE TO GET THE CREATIVE JUICES FLOWING.
DRIBBLE DRIBBLE
I'D SAY THEY'RE FLOWING PRETTY GOOD.
I'D BETTER GET THAT **SPIT VALVE** FIXED.
BREEN

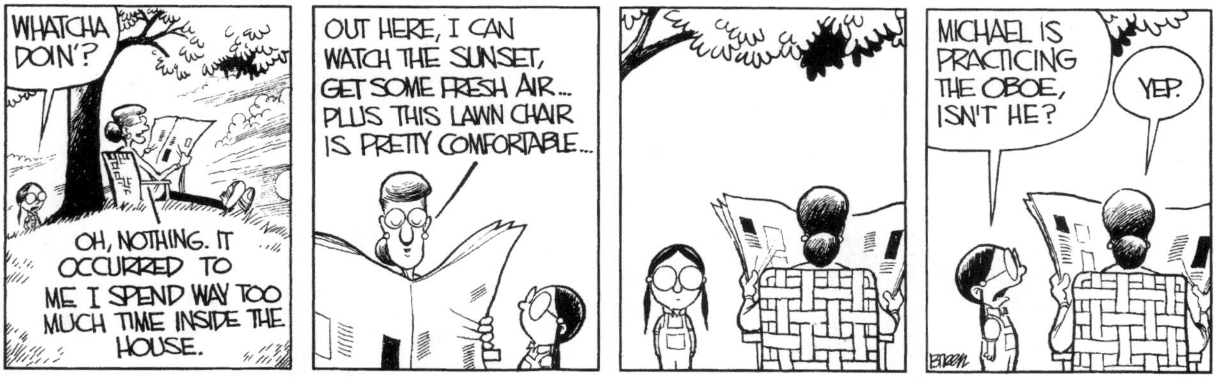
WHATCHA DOIN'?
OH, NOTHING. IT OCCURRED TO ME I SPEND WAY TOO MUCH TIME INSIDE THE HOUSE.
OUT HERE, I CAN WATCH THE SUNSET, GET SOME FRESH AIR... PLUS THIS LAWN CHAIR IS PRETTY COMFORTABLE...
MICHAEL IS PRACTICING THE OBOE, ISN'T HE?
YEP.
BREEN

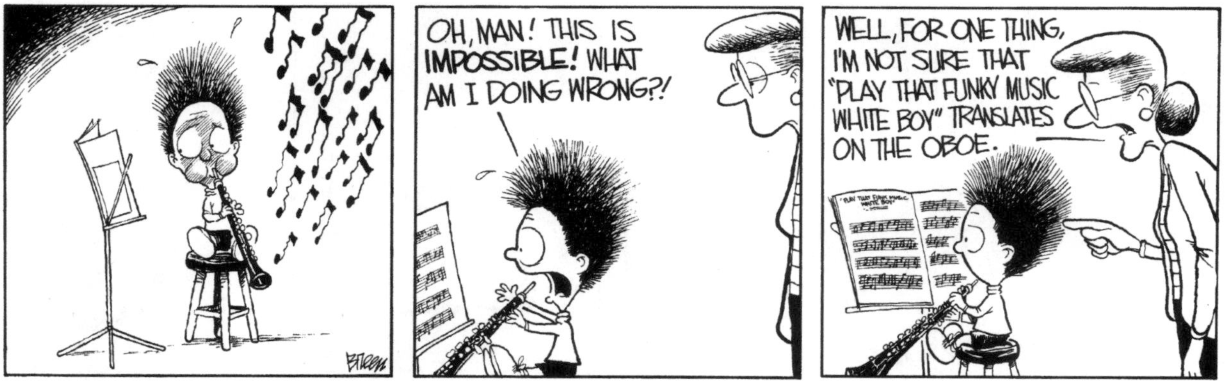
BREEN
OH, MAN! THIS IS **IMPOSSIBLE!** WHAT AM I DOING WRONG?!
WELL, FOR ONE THING, I'M NOT SURE THAT "PLAY THAT FUNKY MUSIC WHITE BOY" TRANSLATES ON THE OBOE.

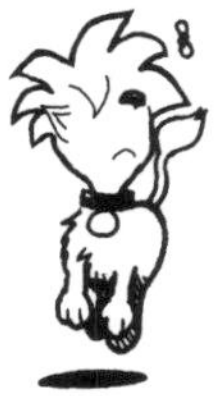

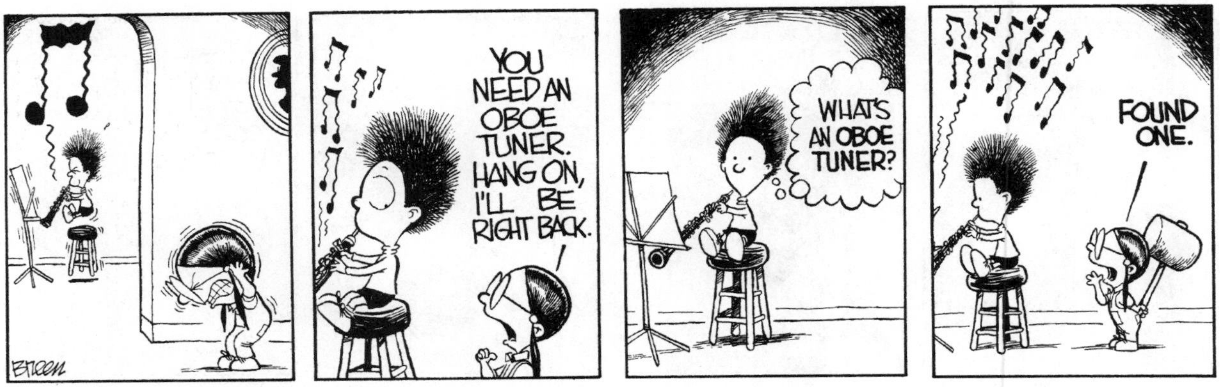
YOU NEED AN OBOE TUNER. HANG ON, I'LL BE RIGHT BACK.
WHAT'S AN OBOE TUNER?
FOUND ONE.

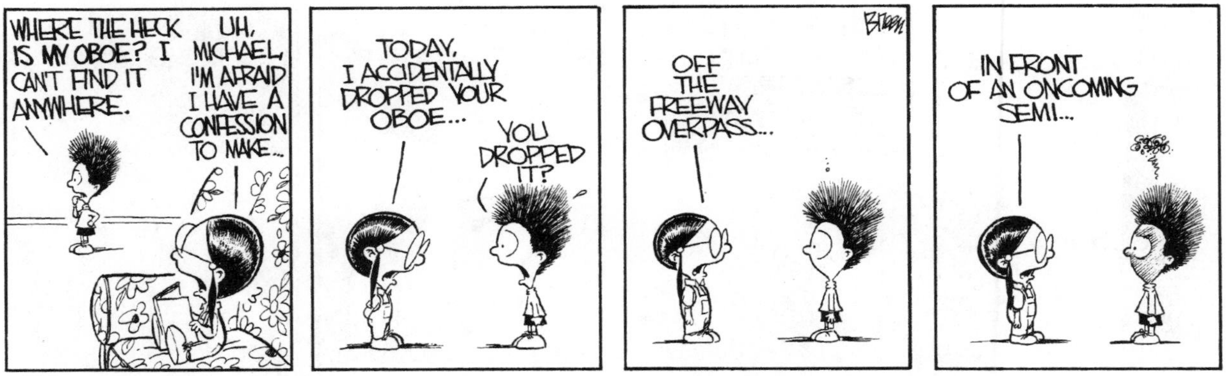
WHERE THE HECK IS MY OBOE? I CAN'T FIND IT ANYWHERE.
UH, MICHAEL, I'M AFRAID I HAVE A CONFESSION TO MAKE...
TODAY, I ACCIDENTALLY DROPPED YOUR OBOE...
YOU DROPPED IT?
OFF THE FREEWAY OVERPASS...
IN FRONT OF AN ONCOMING SEMI...

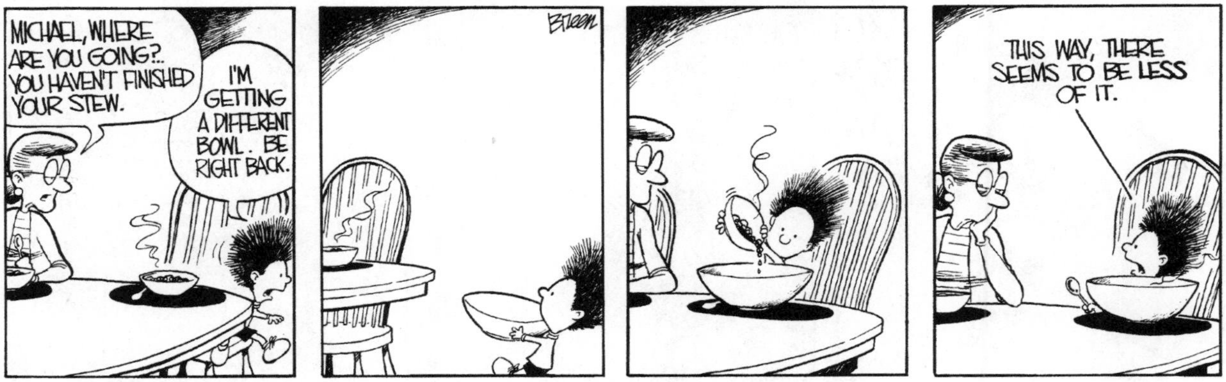
MICHAEL, WHERE ARE YOU GOING?.. YOU HAVEN'T FINISHED YOUR STEW.
I'M GETTING A DIFFERENT BOWL. BE RIGHT BACK.
THIS WAY, THERE SEEMS TO BE LESS OF IT.

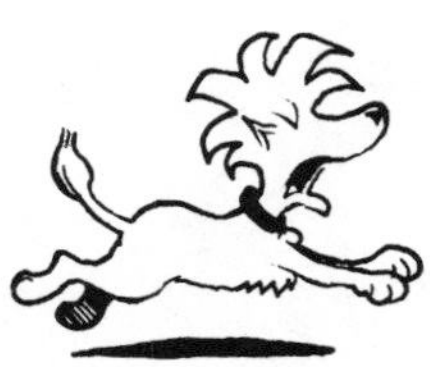

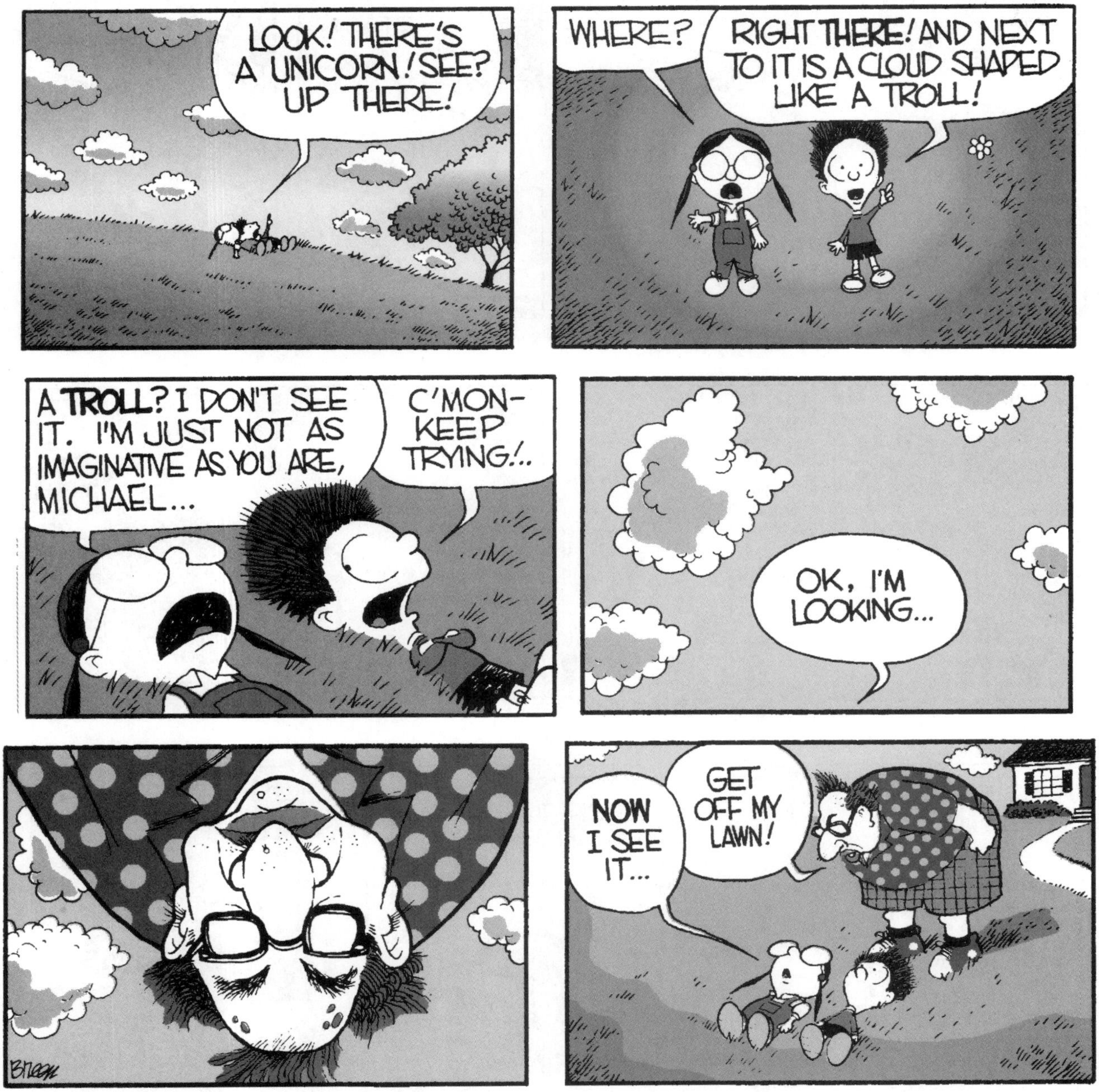
LOOK! THERE'S A UNICORN! SEE? UP THERE!
WHERE?
RIGHT THERE! AND NEXT TO IT IS A CLOUD SHAPED LIKE A TROLL!
A TROLL? I DON'T SEE IT. I'M JUST NOT AS IMAGINATIVE AS YOU ARE, MICHAEL...
C'MON- KEEP TRYING!..
OK, I'M LOOKING...
NOW I SEE IT...
GET OFF MY LAWN!

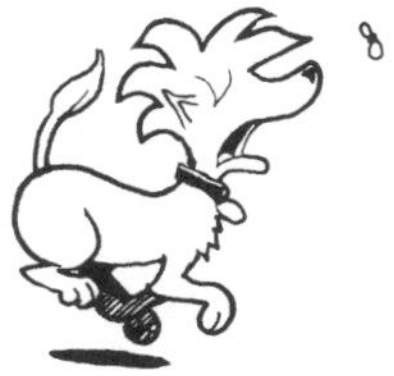

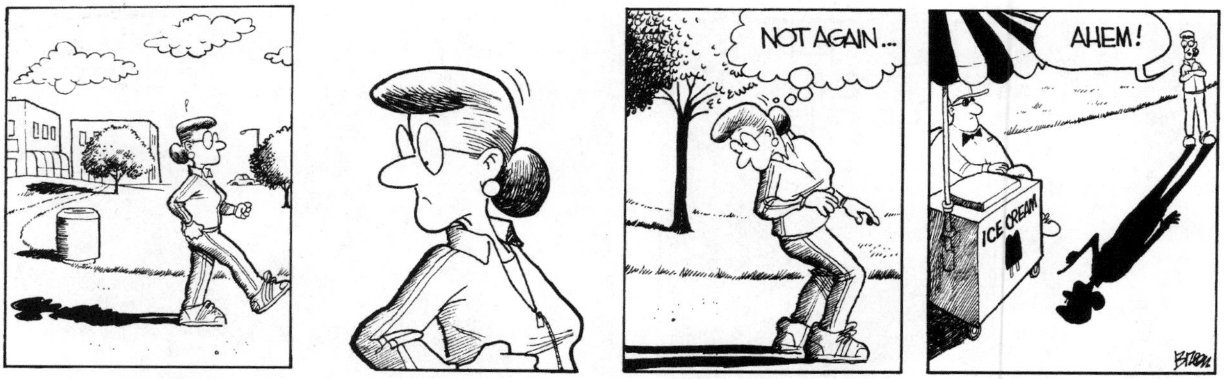
NOT AGAIN...
AHEM!
ICE CREAM

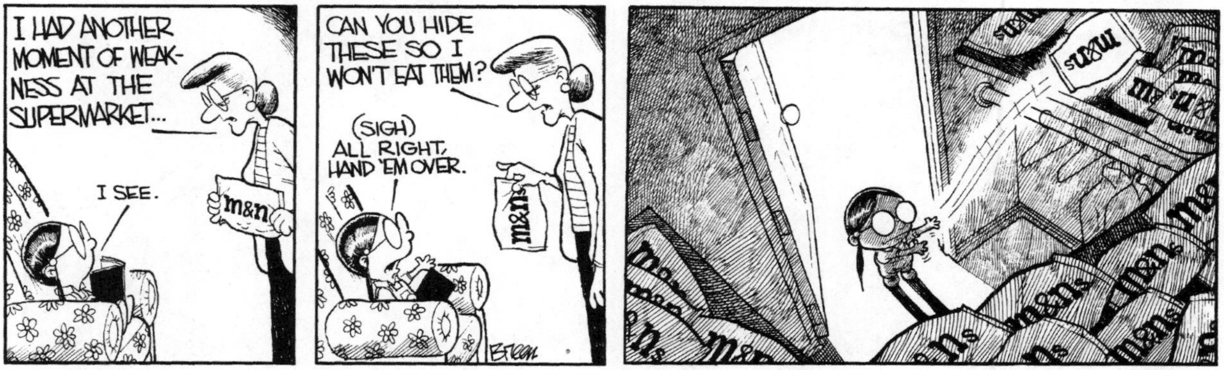
I HAD ANOTHER MOMENT OF WEAK-NESS AT THE SUPERMARKET...
I SEE.
m&n
CAN YOU HIDE THESE SO I WON'T EAT THEM?
(SIGH) ALL RIGHT, HAND 'EM OVER.

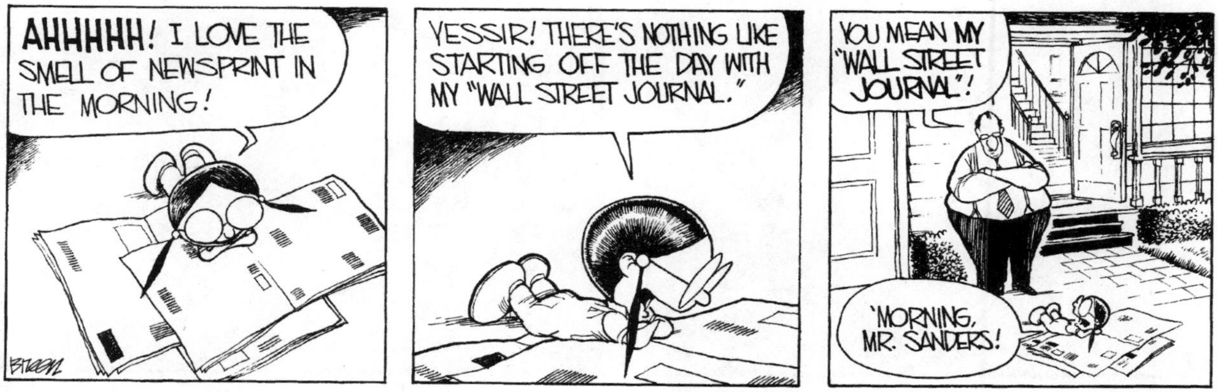
AHHHHH! I LOVE THE SMELL OF NEWSPRINT IN THE MORNING!
YESSIR! THERE'S NOTHING LIKE STARTING OFF THE DAY WITH MY "WALL STREET JOURNAL."
YOU MEAN MY "WALL STREET JOURNAL"!
'MORNING, MR. SANDERS!

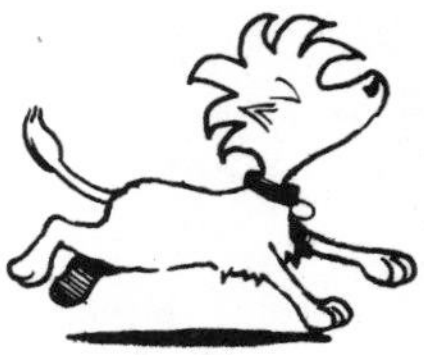

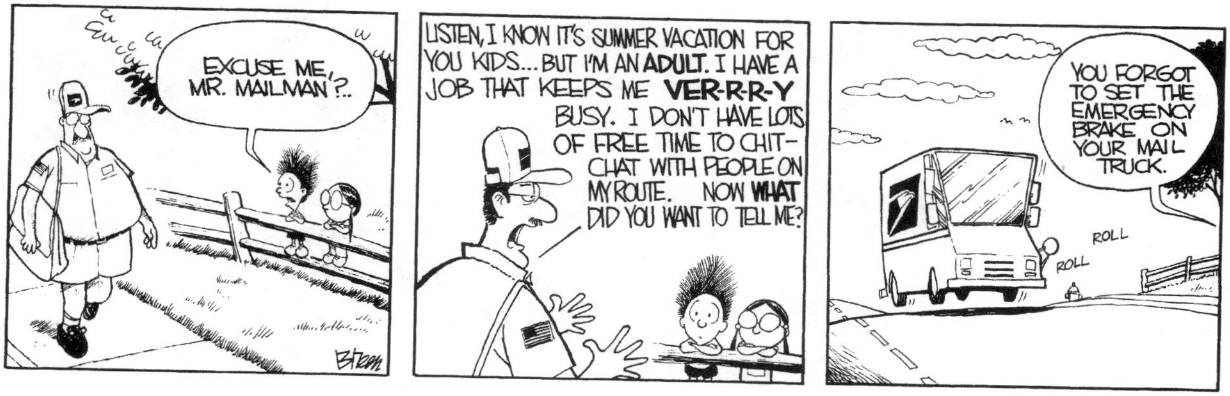
EXCUSE ME, MR. MAILMAN?..
LISTEN, I KNOW IT'S SUMMER VACATION FOR YOU KIDS... BUT I'M AN ADULT. I HAVE A JOB THAT KEEPS ME VER-R-R-Y BUSY. I DON'T HAVE LOTS OF FREE TIME TO CHIT-CHAT WITH PEOPLE ON MY ROUTE. NOW WHAT DID YOU WANT TO TELL ME?
YOU FORGOT TO SET THE EMERGENCY BRAKE ON YOUR MAIL TRUCK.
ROLL
ROLL

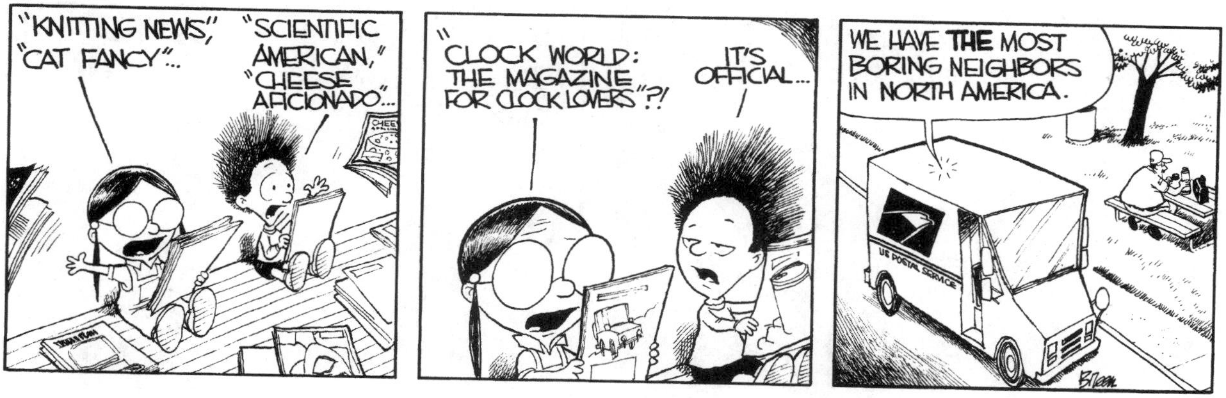
"KNITTING NEWS," "CAT FANCY"...
"SCIENTIFIC AMERICAN," "CHEESE AFICIONADO"...
"CLOCK WORLD: THE MAGAZINE FOR CLOCK LOVERS"?!
IT'S OFFICIAL...
WE HAVE THE MOST BORING NEIGHBORS IN NORTH AMERICA.

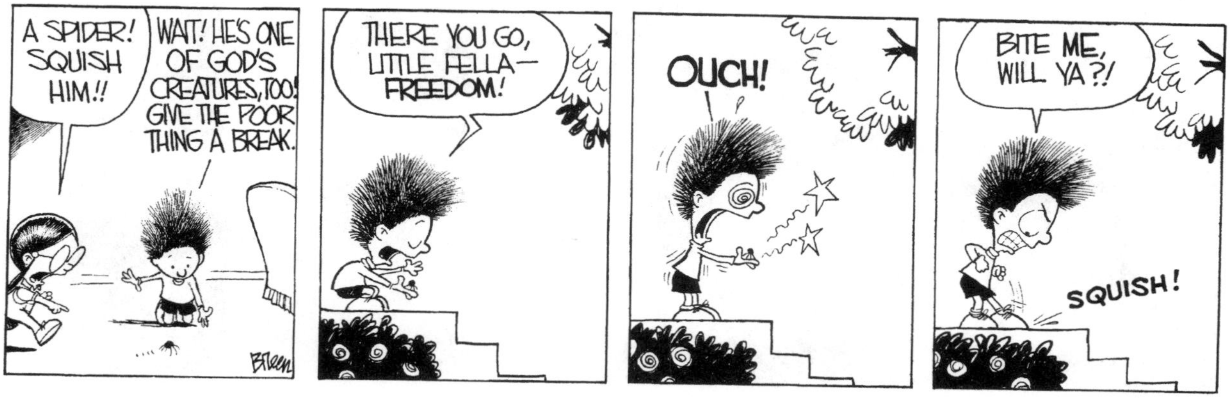
A SPIDER! SQUISH HIM!!
WAIT! HE'S ONE OF GOD'S CREATURES, TOO! GIVE THE POOR THING A BREAK.
THERE YOU GO, LITTLE FELLA— FREEDOM!
OUCH!
BITE ME, WILL YA?!
SQUISH!

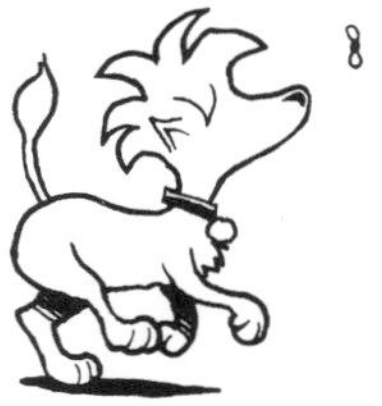

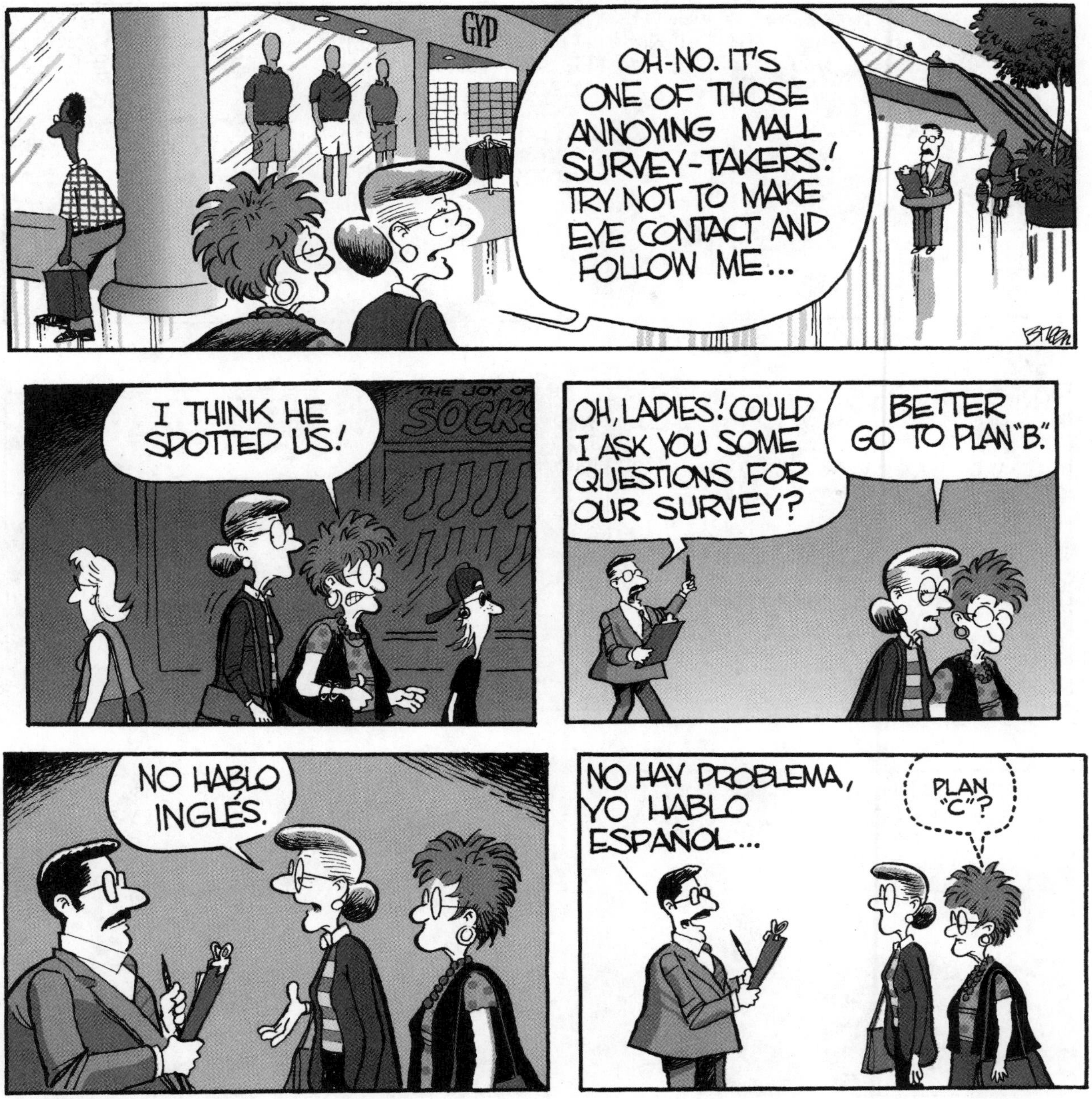
GYP
OH-NO. IT'S ONE OF THOSE ANNOYING MALL SURVEY-TAKERS! TRY NOT TO MAKE EYE CONTACT AND FOLLOW ME...
THE JOY OF SOCKS
I THINK HE SPOTTED US!
OH, LADIES! COULD I ASK YOU SOME QUESTIONS FOR OUR SURVEY?
BETTER GO TO PLAN "B."
NO HABLO INGLÉS.
NO HAY PROBLEMA, YO HABLO ESPAÑOL...
PLAN "C"?

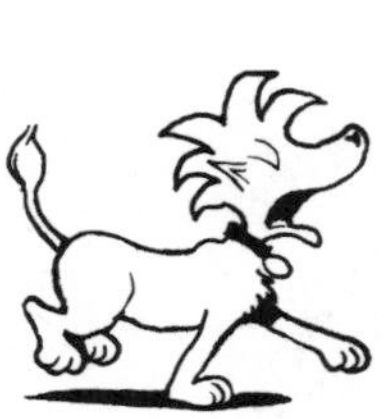

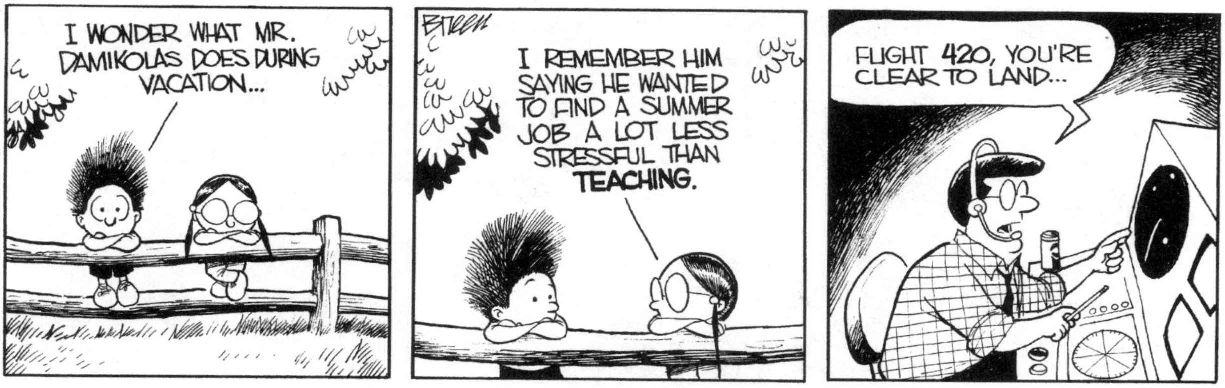
I WONDER WHAT MR. DAMIKOLAS DOES DURING VACATION...
I REMEMBER HIM SAYING HE WANTED TO FIND A SUMMER JOB A LOT LESS STRESSFUL THAN TEACHING.
FLIGHT 420, YOU'RE CLEAR TO LAND...

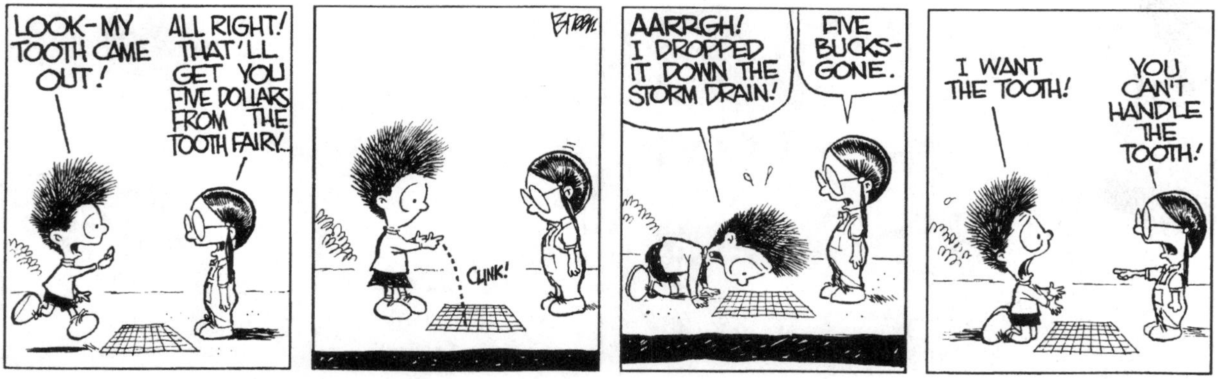
LOOK-MY TOOTH CAME OUT!
ALL RIGHT! THAT'LL GET YOU FIVE DOLLARS FROM THE TOOTH FAIRY...
CLINK!
AARRGH! I DROPPED IT DOWN THE STORM DRAIN!
FIVE BUCKS-GONE.
I WANT THE TOOTH!
YOU CAN'T HANDLE THE TOOTH!

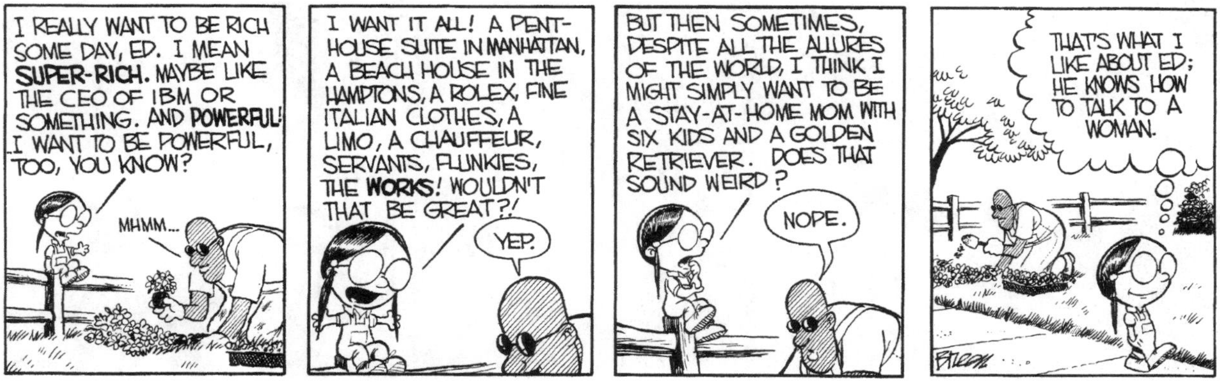
I REALLY WANT TO BE RICH SOME DAY, ED. I MEAN SUPER-RICH. MAYBE LIKE THE CEO OF IBM OR SOMETHING. AND POWERFUL! I WANT TO BE POWERFUL, TOO, YOU KNOW?
MHMM...
I WANT IT ALL! A PENTHOUSE SUITE IN MANHATTAN, A BEACH HOUSE IN THE HAMPTONS, A ROLEX, FINE ITALIAN CLOTHES, A LIMO, A CHAUFFEUR, SERVANTS, FLUNKIES, THE WORKS! WOULDN'T THAT BE GREAT?!
YEP.
BUT THEN SOMETIMES, DESPITE ALL THE ALLURES OF THE WORLD, I THINK I MIGHT SIMPLY WANT TO BE A STAY-AT-HOME MOM WITH SIX KIDS AND A GOLDEN RETRIEVER. DOES THAT SOUND WEIRD?
NOPE.
THAT'S WHAT I LIKE ABOUT ED; HE KNOWS HOW TO TALK TO A WOMAN.

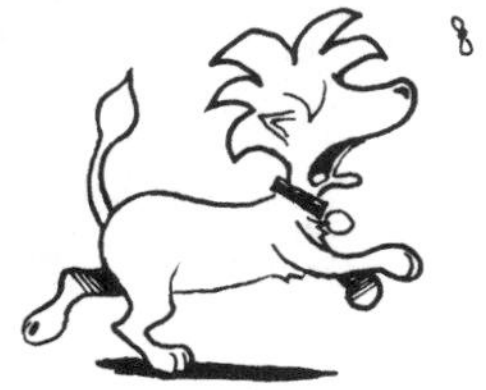

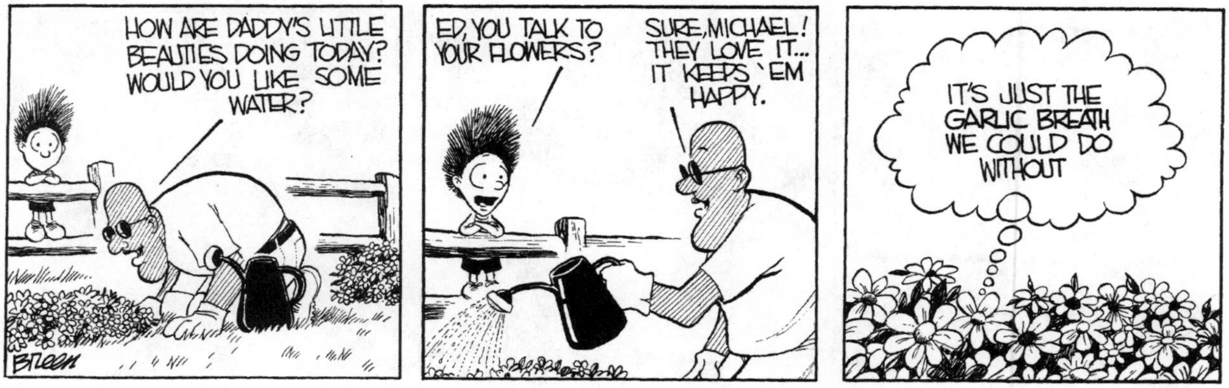
HOW ARE DADDY'S LITTLE BEAUTIES DOING TODAY? WOULD YOU LIKE SOME WATER?
ED, YOU TALK TO YOUR FLOWERS?
SURE, MICHAEL! THEY LOVE IT... IT KEEPS 'EM HAPPY.
IT'S JUST THE GARLIC BREATH WE COULD DO WITHOUT

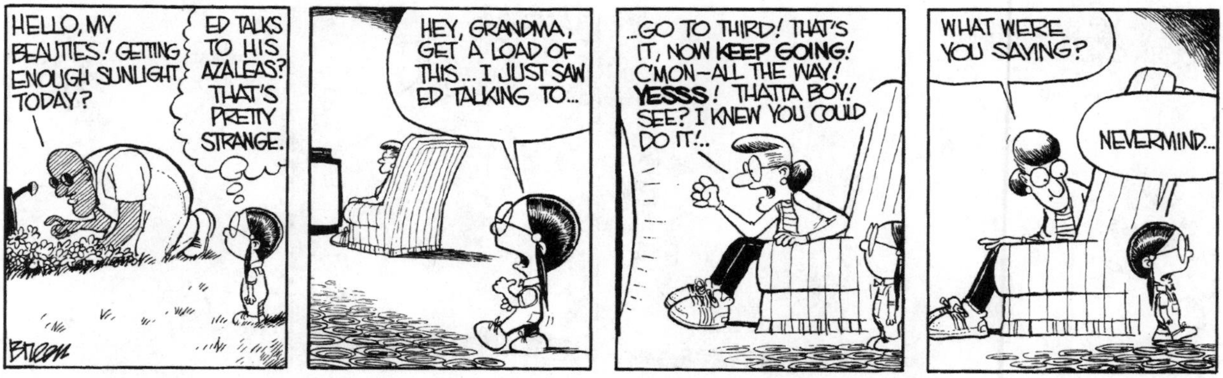
HELLO, MY BEAUTIES! GETTING ENOUGH SUNLIGHT TODAY?
ED TALKS TO HIS AZALEAS? THAT'S PRETTY STRANGE.
HEY, GRANDMA, GET A LOAD OF THIS... I JUST SAW ED TALKING TO...
...GO TO THIRD! THAT'S IT, NOW KEEP GOING! C'MON—ALL THE WAY! YESSS! THATTA BOY! SEE? I KNEW YOU COULD DO IT!..
WHAT WERE YOU SAYING?
NEVERMIND...

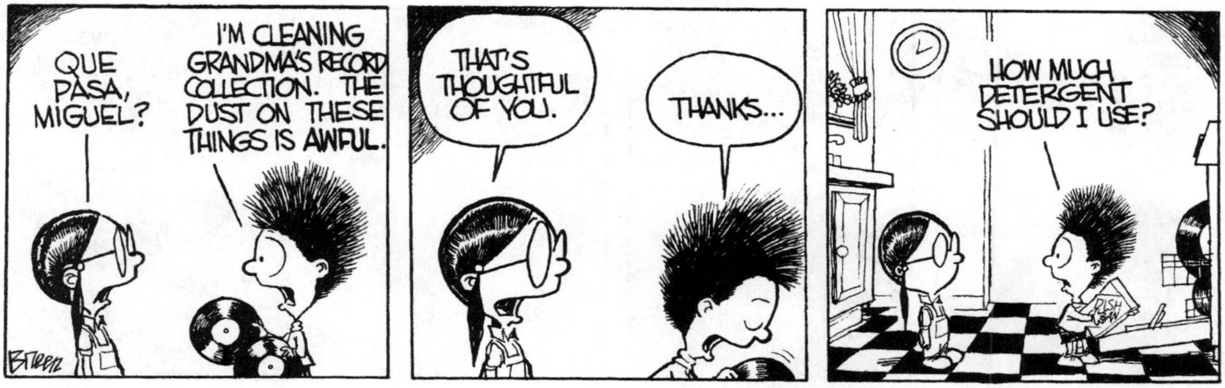
QUE PASA, MIGUEL?
I'M CLEANING GRANDMA'S RECORD COLLECTION. THE DUST ON THESE THINGS IS AWFUL.
THAT'S THOUGHTFUL OF YOU.
THANKS...
HOW MUCH DETERGENT SHOULD I USE?
DISH WASH

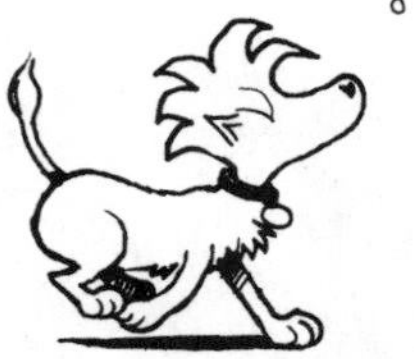

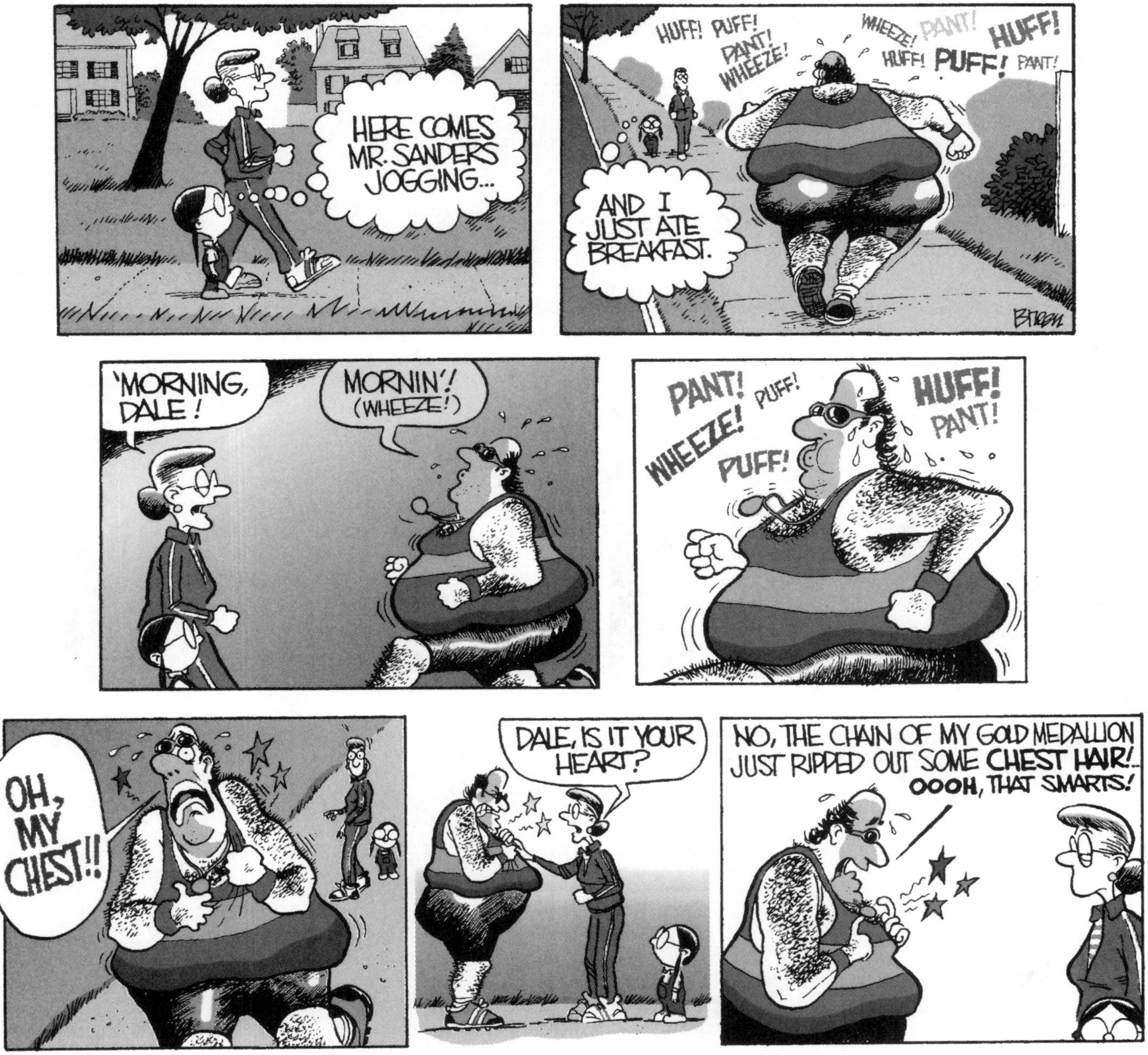
HERE COMES MR. SANDERS JOGGING...
HUFF! PUFF! PANT! WHEEZE!
WHEEZE! PANT! HUFF! PUFF! HUFF! PANT!
AND I JUST ATE BREAKFAST.
'MORNING, DALE!
MORNIN'! (WHEEZE!)
PANT! PUFF! WHEEZE! PUFF! HUFF! PANT!
OH, MY CHEST!!
DALE, IS IT YOUR HEART?
NO, THE CHAIN OF MY GOLD MEDALLION JUST RIPPED OUT SOME CHEST HAIR!..
OOOH, THAT SMARTS!

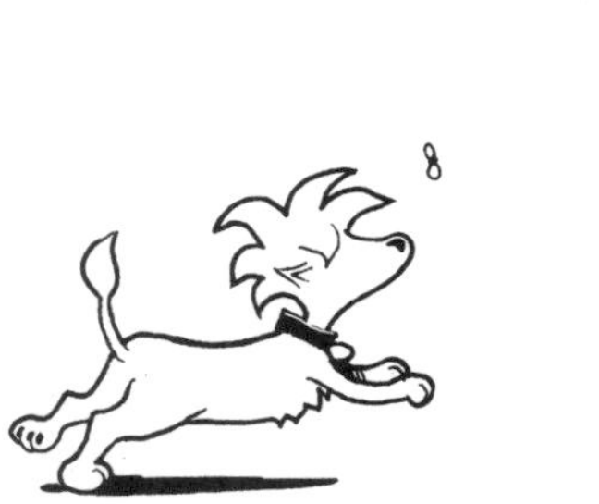

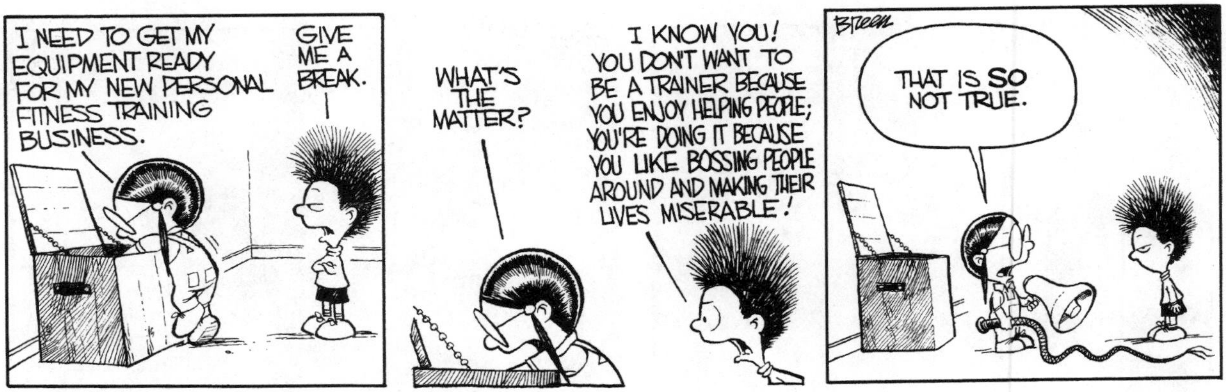
I NEED TO GET MY EQUIPMENT READY FOR MY NEW PERSONAL FITNESS TRAINING BUSINESS.
GIVE ME A BREAK.
WHAT'S THE MATTER?
I KNOW YOU! YOU DON'T WANT TO BE A TRAINER BECAUSE YOU ENJOY HELPING PEOPLE; YOU'RE DOING IT BECAUSE YOU LIKE BOSSING PEOPLE AROUND AND MAKING THEIR LIVES MISERABLE!
THAT IS SO NOT TRUE.

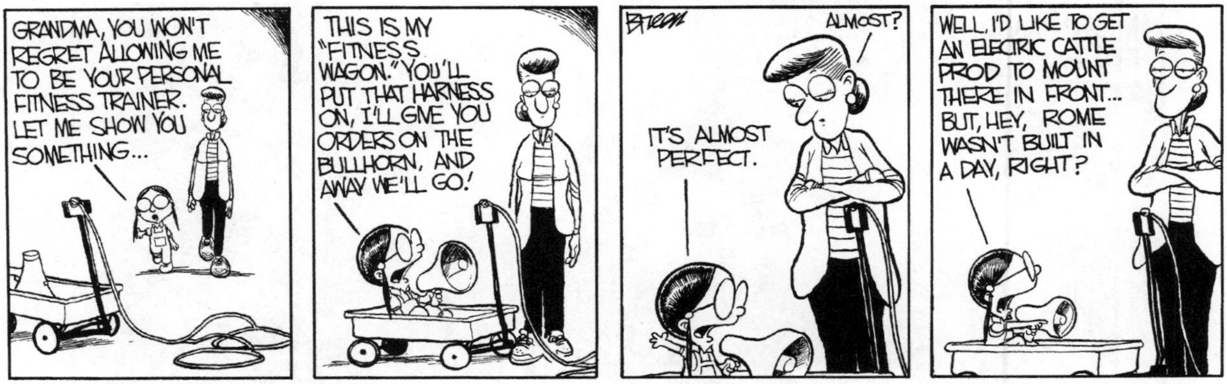
GRANDMA, YOU WON'T REGRET ALLOWING ME TO BE YOUR PERSONAL FITNESS TRAINER. LET ME SHOW YOU SOMETHING...
THIS IS MY "FITNESS WAGON." YOU'LL PUT THAT HARNESS ON, I'LL GIVE YOU ORDERS ON THE BULLHORN, AND AWAY WE'LL GO!
IT'S ALMOST PERFECT.
ALMOST?
WELL, I'D LIKE TO GET AN ELECTRIC CATTLE PROD TO MOUNT THERE IN FRONT... BUT, HEY, ROME WASN'T BUILT IN A DAY, RIGHT?

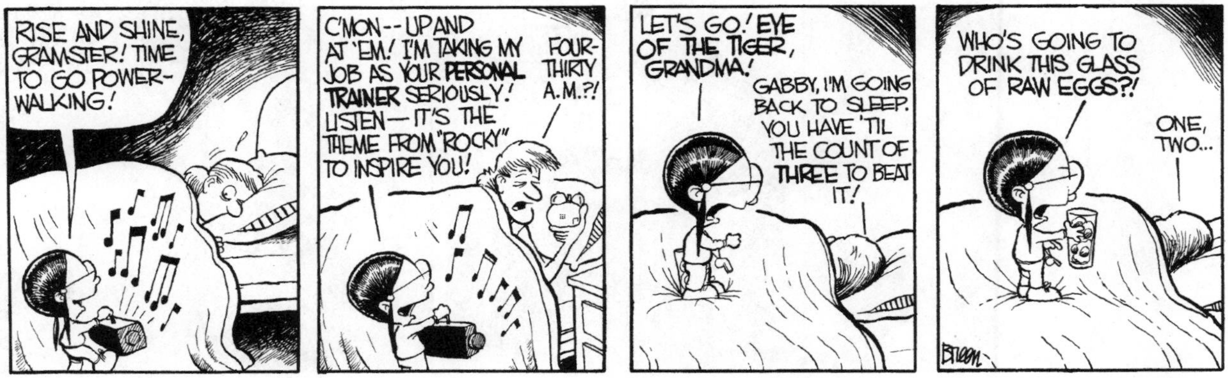
RISE AND SHINE, GRAMSTER! TIME TO GO POWER-WALKING!
C'MON--UP AND AT 'EM! I'M TAKING MY JOB AS YOUR PERSONAL TRAINER SERIOUSLY! LISTEN—IT'S THE THEME FROM "ROCKY" TO INSPIRE YOU!
FOUR-THIRTY A.M.?!
LET'S GO! EYE OF THE TIGER, GRANDMA!
GABBY, I'M GOING BACK TO SLEEP. YOU HAVE 'TIL THE COUNT OF THREE TO BEAT IT!
WHO'S GOING TO DRINK THIS GLASS OF RAW EGGS?!
ONE, TWO...

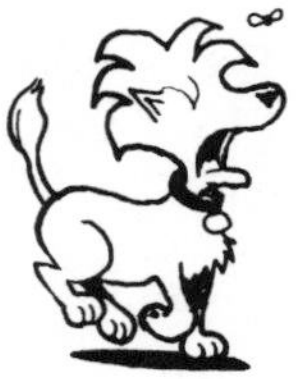

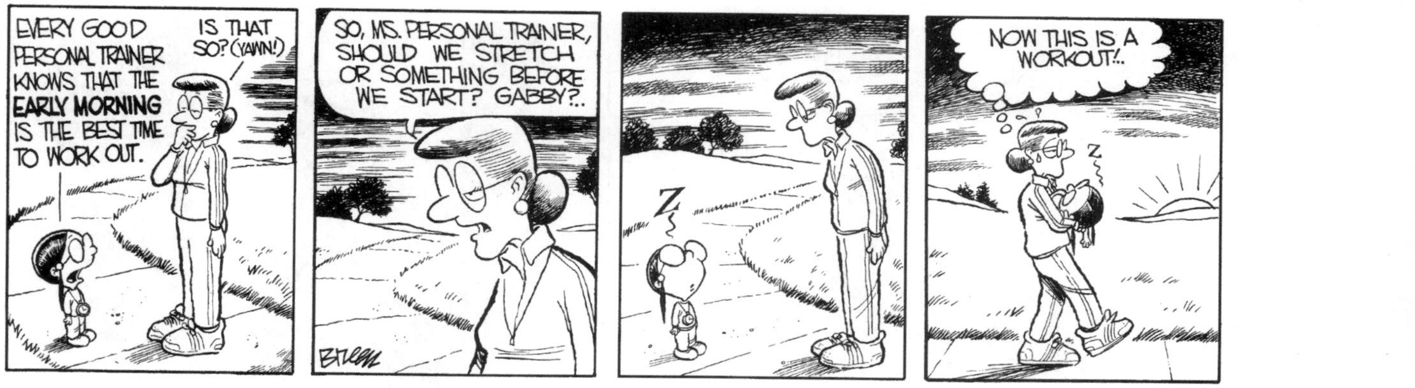
EVERY GOOD PERSONAL TRAINER KNOWS THAT THE **EARLY MORNING** IS THE BEST TIME TO WORK OUT.
IS THAT SO? (YAWN!)
SO, MS. PERSONAL TRAINER, SHOULD WE STRETCH OR SOMETHING BEFORE WE START? GABBY?..
Z
NOW THIS IS A WORKOUT!..
Z

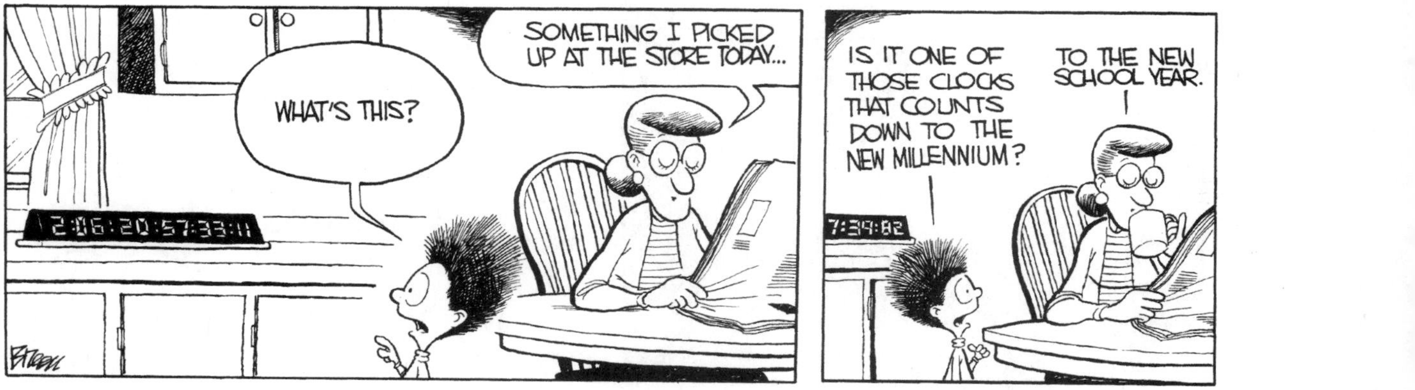
2:06:20:57:33:11
WHAT'S THIS?
SOMETHING I PICKED UP AT THE STORE TODAY...
7:39:82
IS IT ONE OF THOSE CLOCKS THAT COUNTS DOWN TO THE NEW MILLENNIUM?
TO THE NEW SCHOOL YEAR.

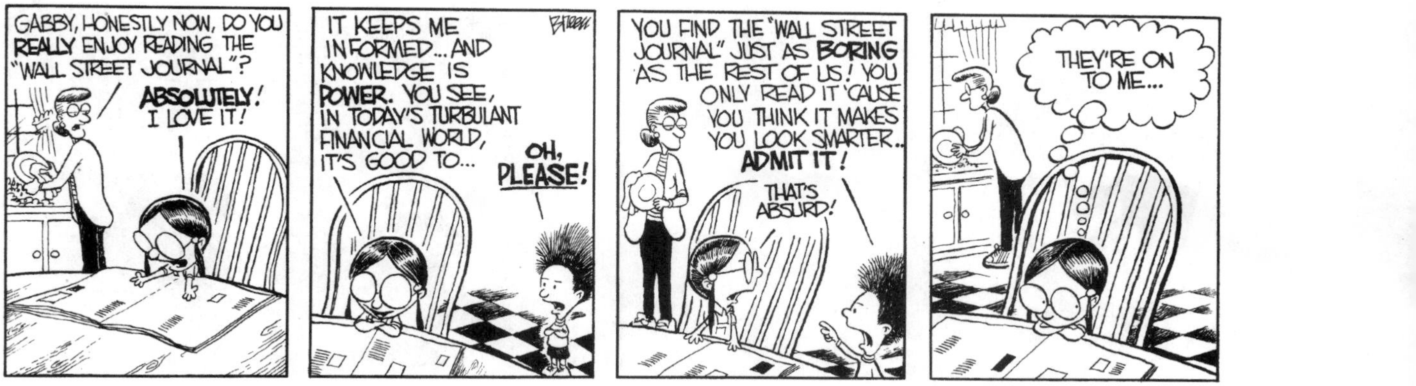
GABBY, HONESTLY NOW, DO YOU **REALLY** ENJOY READING THE "WALL STREET JOURNAL"?
ABSOLUTELY! I LOVE IT!
IT KEEPS ME INFORMED... AND KNOWLEDGE IS **POWER**. YOU SEE, IN TODAY'S TURBULANT FINANCIAL WORLD, IT'S GOOD TO...
OH, PLEASE!
YOU FIND THE "WALL STREET JOURNAL" JUST AS **BORING** AS THE REST OF US! YOU ONLY READ IT 'CAUSE YOU THINK IT MAKES YOU LOOK SMARTER.. **ADMIT IT**!
THAT'S ABSURD!
THEY'RE ON TO ME...

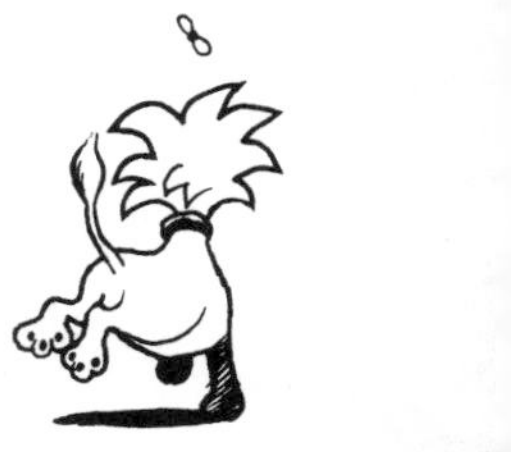

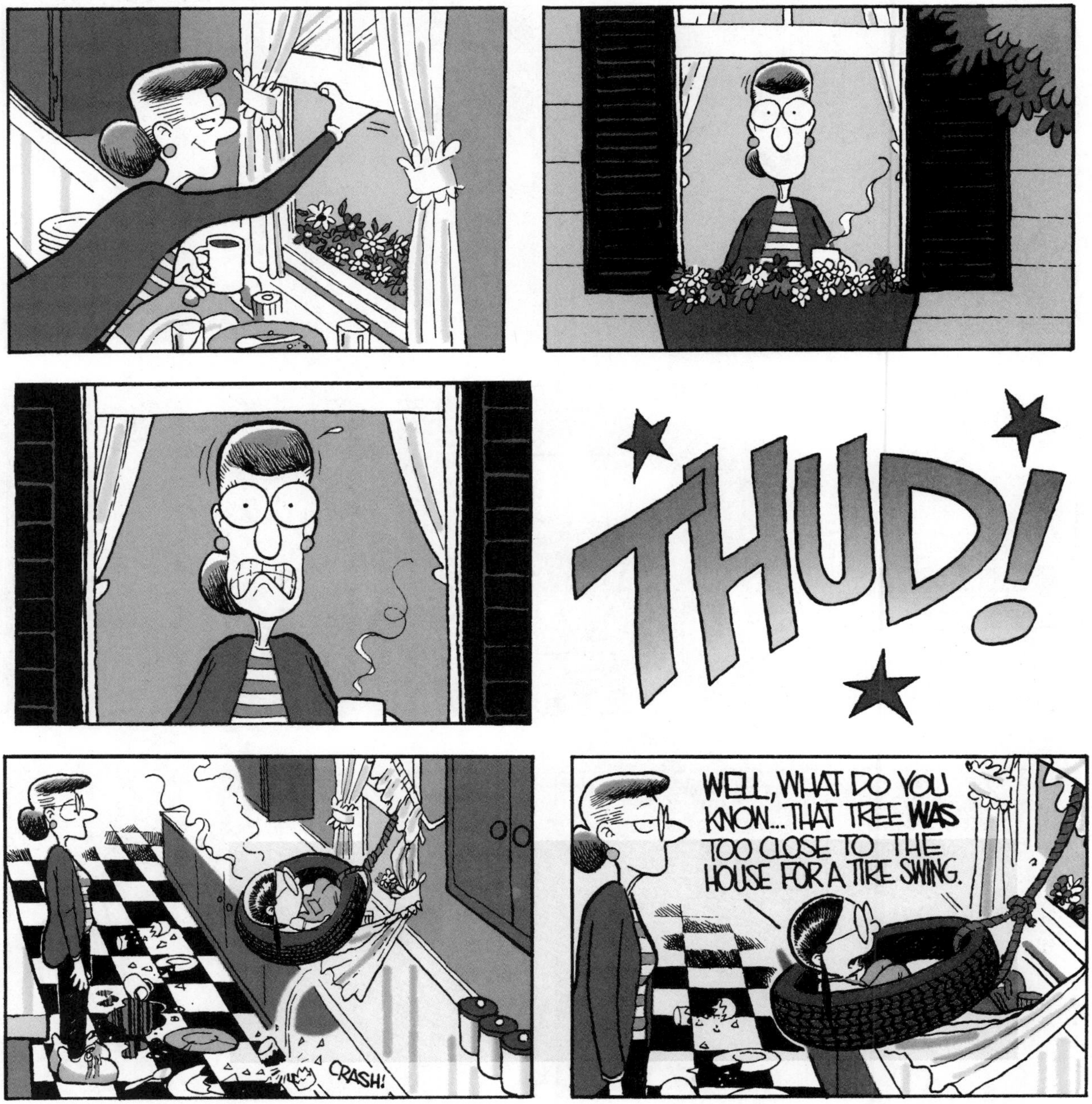
THUD!
CRASH!
WELL, WHAT DO YOU KNOW... THAT TREE **WAS** TOO CLOSE TO THE HOUSE FOR A TIRE SWING.

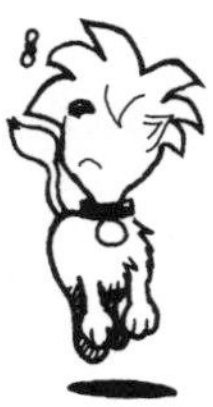

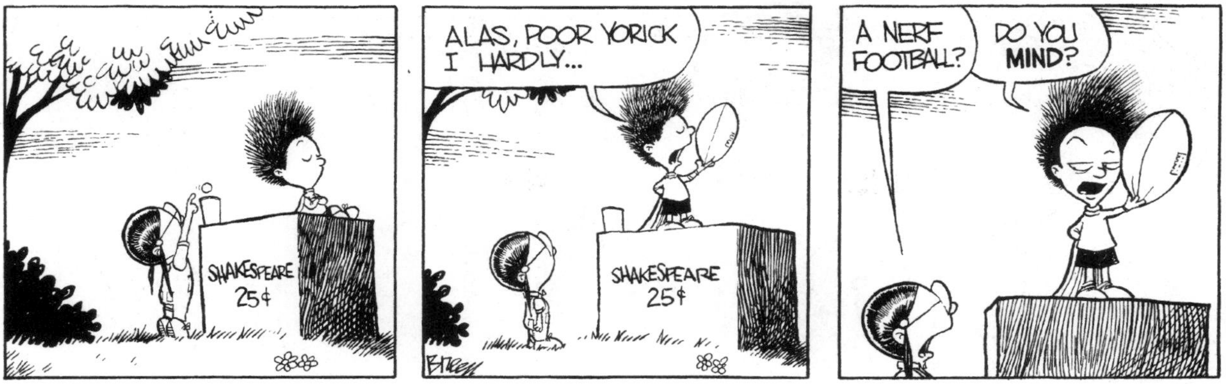
SHAKESPEARE 25¢
ALAS, POOR YORICK I HARDLY...
SHAKESPEARE 25¢
A NERF FOOTBALL?
DO YOU **MIND**?

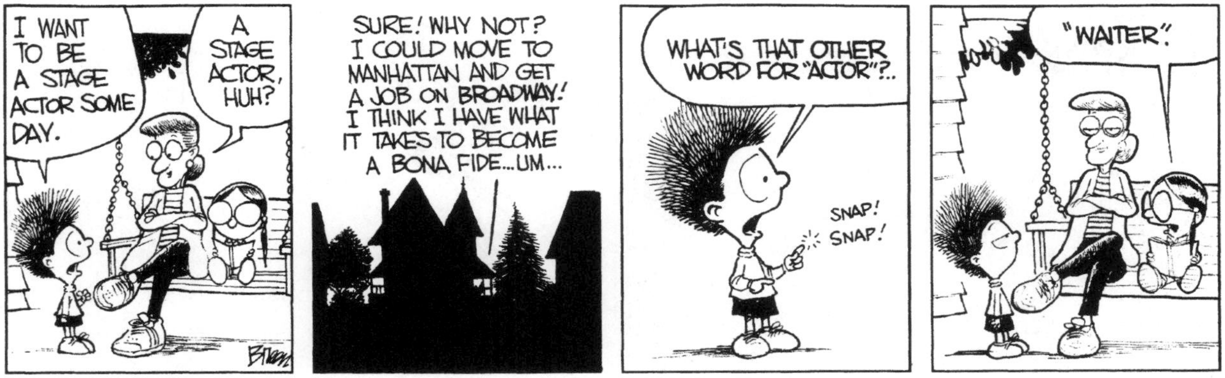
I WANT TO BE A STAGE ACTOR SOME DAY.
A STAGE ACTOR, HUH?
SURE! WHY NOT? I COULD MOVE TO MANHATTAN AND GET A JOB ON **BROADWAY**! I THINK I HAVE WHAT IT TAKES TO BECOME A BONA FIDE...UM...
WHAT'S THAT OTHER WORD FOR "ACTOR"?..
SNAP! SNAP!
"WAITER".

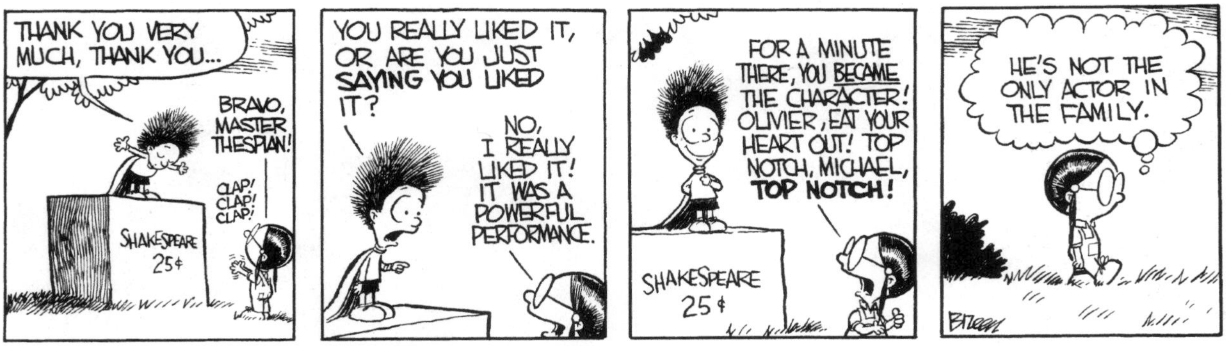
THANK YOU VERY MUCH, THANK YOU...
BRAVO, MASTER THESPIAN!
CLAP! CLAP! CLAP!
SHAKESPEARE 25¢
YOU REALLY LIKED IT, OR ARE YOU JUST **SAYING YOU LIKED** IT?
NO, I REALLY LIKED IT! IT WAS A POWERFUL PERFORMANCE.
FOR A MINUTE THERE, YOU BECAME THE CHARACTER! OLIVIER, EAT YOUR HEART OUT! TOP NOTCH, MICHAEL, **TOP NOTCH**!
SHAKESPEARE 25¢
HE'S NOT THE ONLY ACTOR IN THE FAMILY.

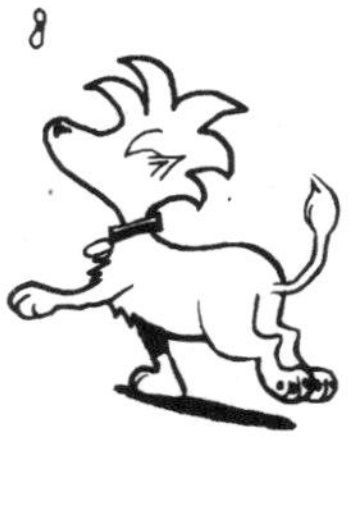

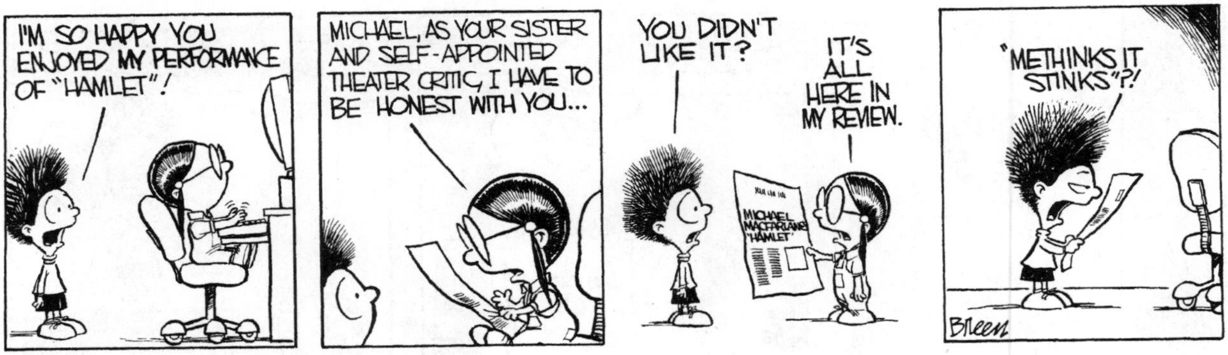
I'M SO HAPPY YOU ENJOYED MY PERFORMANCE OF "HAMLET"!
MICHAEL, AS YOUR SISTER AND SELF-APPOINTED THEATER CRITIC, I HAVE TO BE HONEST WITH YOU...
YOU DIDN'T LIKE IT?
IT'S ALL HERE IN MY REVIEW.
MICHAEL MACFARLANE'S "HAMLET"
"METHINKS IT STINKS"?!
BREEN

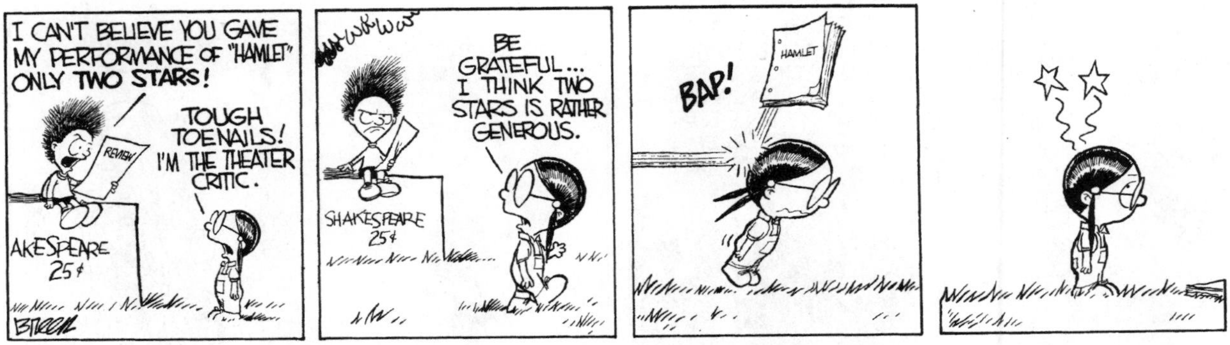
I CAN'T BELIEVE YOU GAVE MY PERFORMANCE OF "HAMLET" ONLY TWO STARS!
REVIEW
TOUGH TOENAILS! I'M THE THEATER CRITIC.
AKESPEARE 25¢
BREEN
BE GRATEFUL... I THINK TWO STARS IS RATHER GENEROUS.
SHAKESPEARE 25¢
BAP!
HAMLET

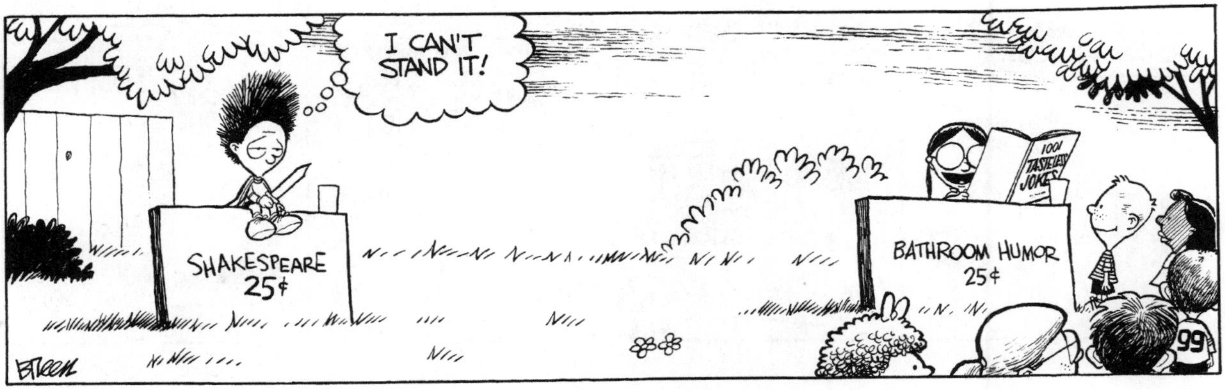
I CAN'T STAND IT!
SHAKESPEARE 25¢
1001 TASTELESS JOKES
BATHROOM HUMOR 25¢
99
BREEN

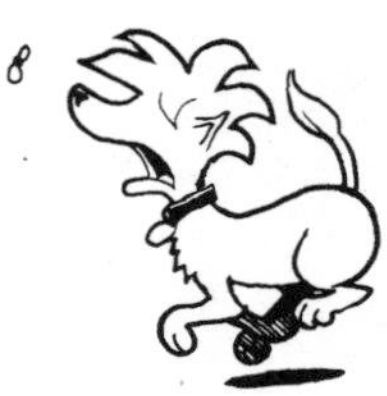

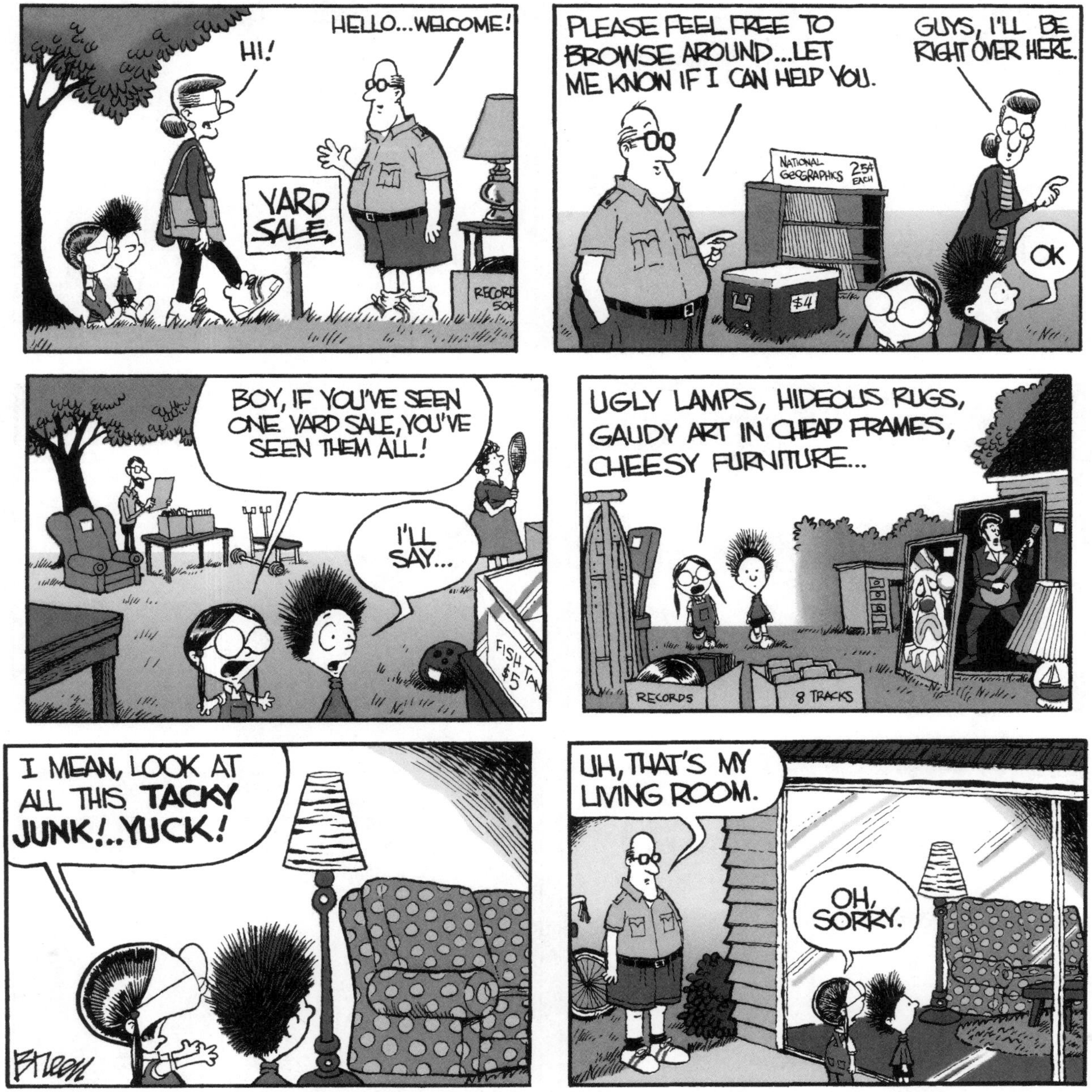
HI!
HELLO...WELCOME!
YARD SALE
PLEASE FEEL FREE TO BROWSE AROUND...LET ME KNOW IF I CAN HELP YOU.
GUYS, I'LL BE RIGHT OVER HERE.
NATIONAL GEOGRAPHICS 25¢ EACH
$4
OK
BOY, IF YOU'VE SEEN ONE YARD SALE, YOU'VE SEEN THEM ALL!
I'LL SAY...
FISH TANK $5
UGLY LAMPS, HIDEOUS RUGS, GAUDY ART IN CHEAP FRAMES, CHEESY FURNITURE...
RECORDS
8 TRACKS
I MEAN, LOOK AT ALL THIS **TACKY JUNK!**..**YUCK!**
UH, THAT'S MY LIVING ROOM.
OH, SORRY.

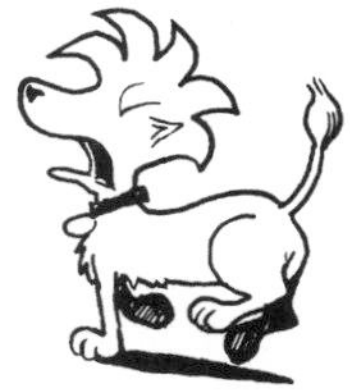

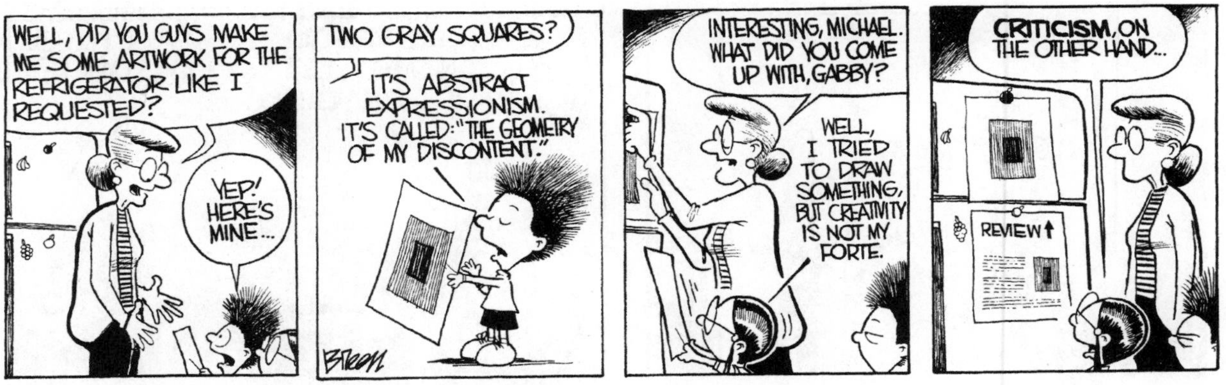
WELL, DID YOU GUYS MAKE ME SOME ARTWORK FOR THE REFRIGERATOR LIKE I REQUESTED?
YEP! HERE'S MINE...
TWO GRAY SQUARES?
IT'S ABSTRACT EXPRESSIONISM. IT'S CALLED: "THE GEOMETRY OF MY DISCONTENT."
BREEN
INTERESTING, MICHAEL. WHAT DID YOU COME UP WITH, GABBY?
WELL, I TRIED TO DRAW SOMETHING, BUT CREATIVITY IS NOT MY FORTE.
CRITICISM, ON THE OTHER HAND...
REVIEW ↑

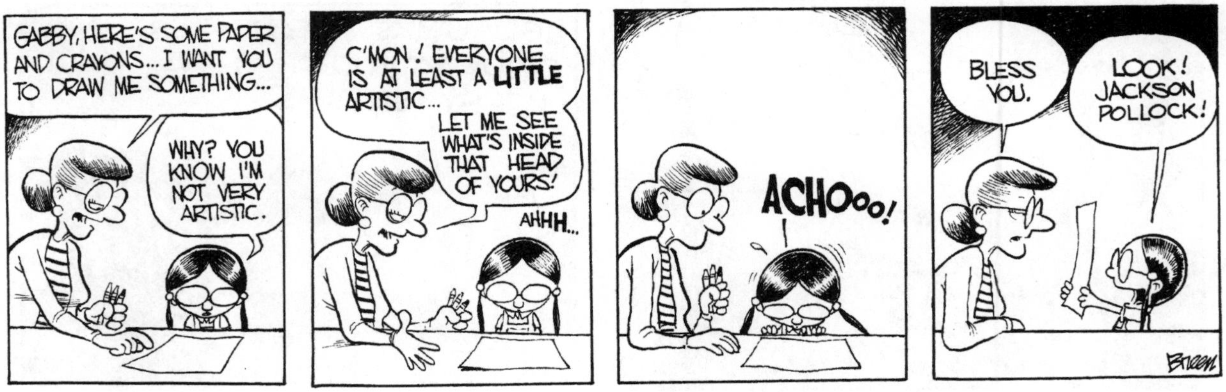
GABBY, HERE'S SOME PAPER AND CRAYONS... I WANT YOU TO DRAW ME SOMETHING...
WHY? YOU KNOW I'M NOT VERY ARTISTIC.
C'MON! EVERYONE IS AT LEAST A **LITTLE** ARTISTIC...
LET ME SEE WHAT'S INSIDE THAT HEAD OF YOURS!
AHHH...
ACHOoo!
BLESS YOU.
LOOK! JACKSON POLLOCK!
BREEN

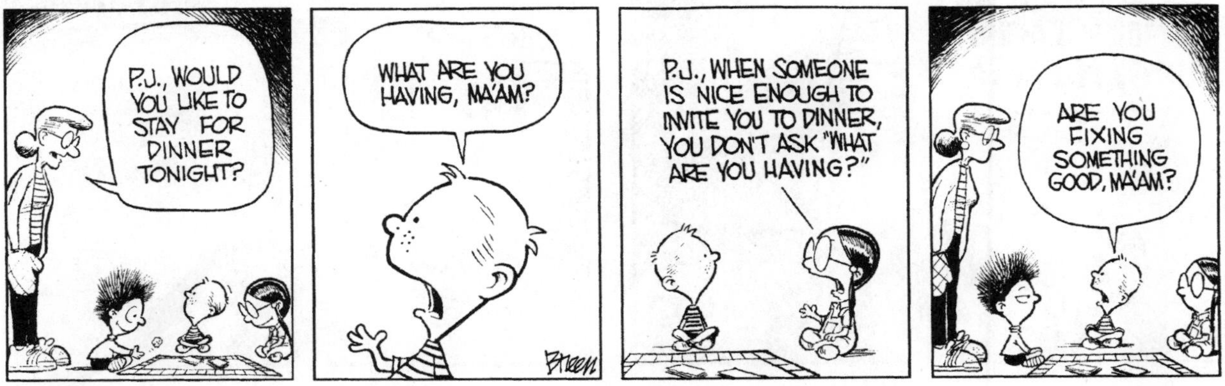
P.J., WOULD YOU LIKE TO STAY FOR DINNER TONIGHT?
WHAT ARE YOU HAVING, MA'AM?
BREEN
P.J., WHEN SOMEONE IS NICE ENOUGH TO INVITE YOU TO DINNER, YOU DON'T ASK "WHAT ARE YOU HAVING?"
ARE YOU FIXING SOMETHING GOOD, MA'AM?

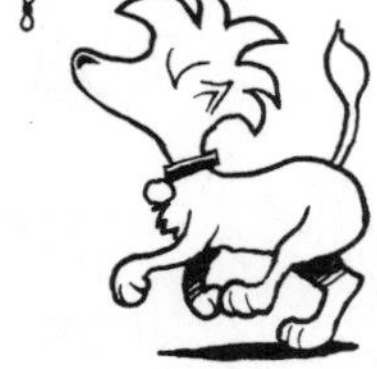

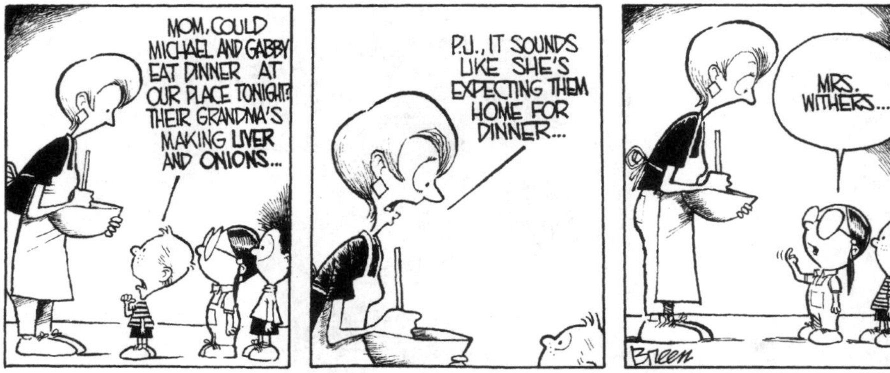
MOM, COULD MICHAEL AND GABBY EAT DINNER AT OUR PLACE TONIGHT? THEIR GRANDMA'S MAKING LIVER AND ONIONS...
P.J., IT SOUNDS LIKE SHE'S EXPECTING THEM HOME FOR DINNER...
MRS. WITHERS...
WOULD THIS GET US A TABLE ANY FASTER?

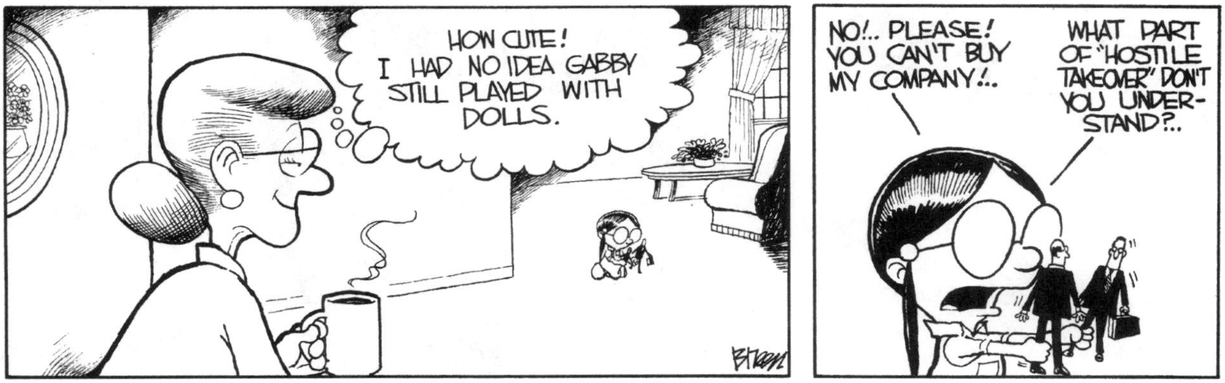
HOW CUTE! I HAD NO IDEA GABBY STILL PLAYED WITH DOLLS.
NO!.. PLEASE! YOU CAN'T BUY MY COMPANY!..
WHAT PART OF "HOSTILE TAKEOVER" DON'T YOU UNDERSTAND?..

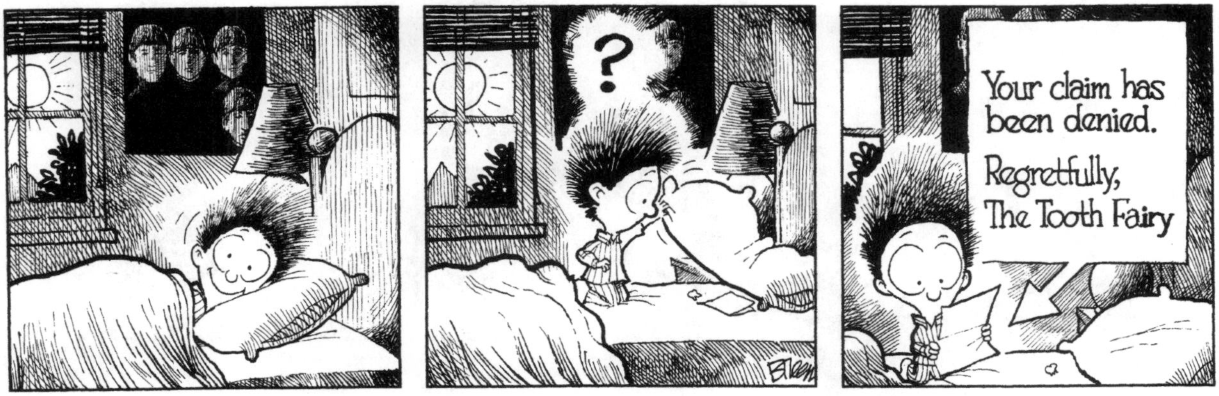
?
Your claim has been denied.
Regretfully,
The Tooth Fairy

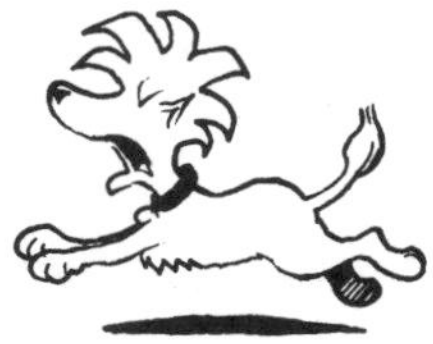

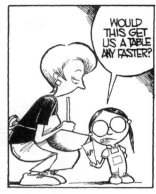

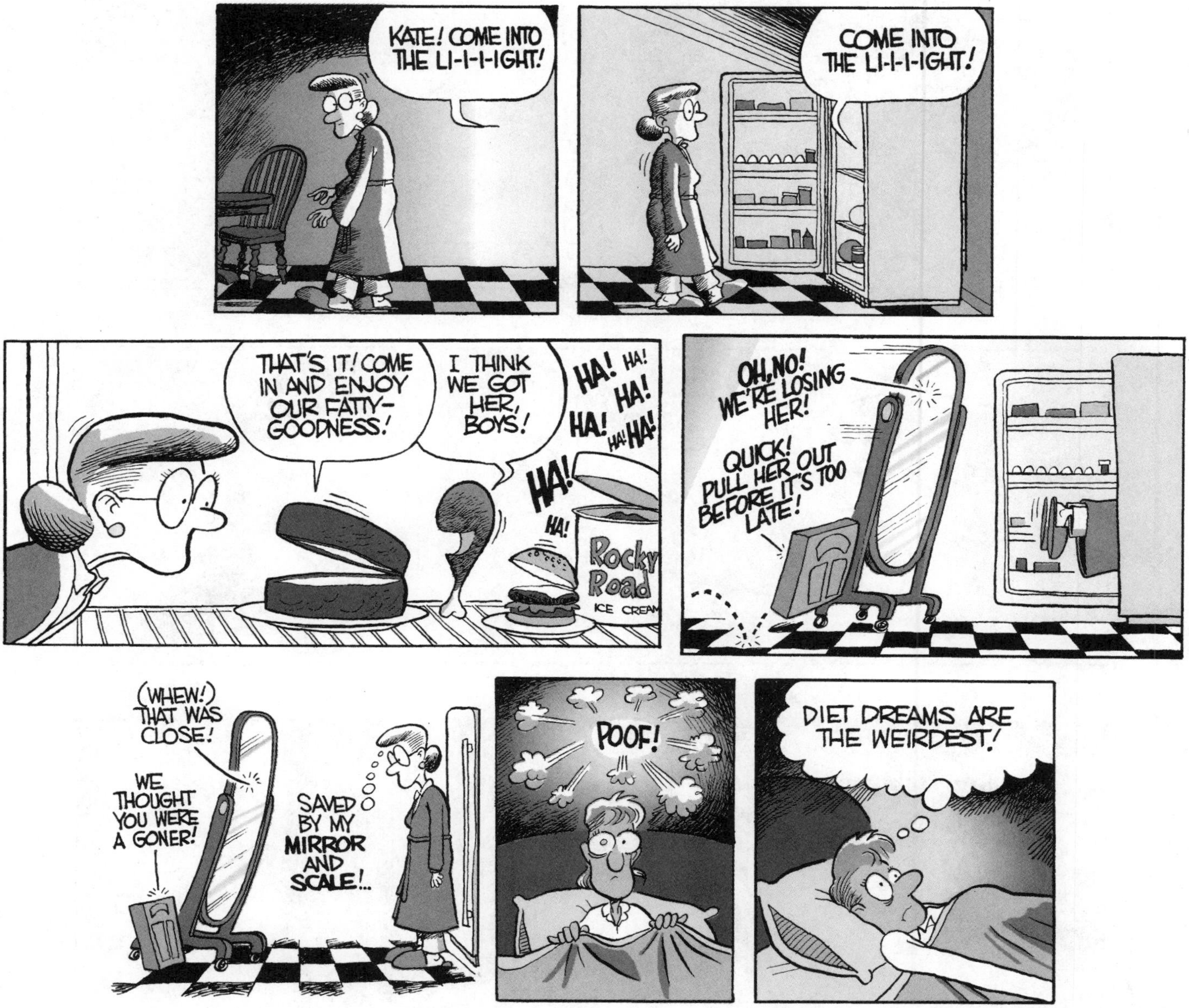
KATE! COME INTO THE LI-I-I-IGHT!
COME INTO THE LI-I-I-IGHT!
THAT'S IT! COME IN AND ENJOY OUR FATTY-GOODNESS!
I THINK WE GOT HER, BOYS!
HA! HA! HA! HA! HA! HA! HA! HA!
Rocky Road ICE CREAM
OH, NO! WE'RE LOSING HER!
QUICK! PULL HER OUT BEFORE IT'S TOO LATE!
(WHEW!) THAT WAS CLOSE!
WE THOUGHT YOU WERE A GONER!
SAVED BY MY MIRROR AND SCALE!..
POOF!
DIET DREAMS ARE THE WEIRDEST!

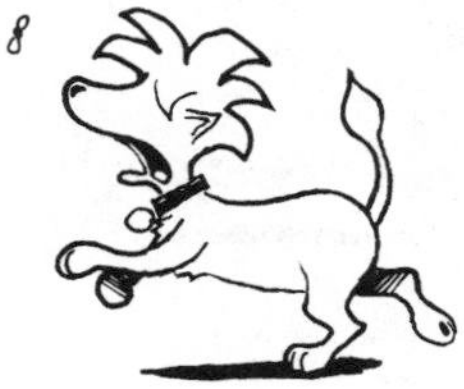

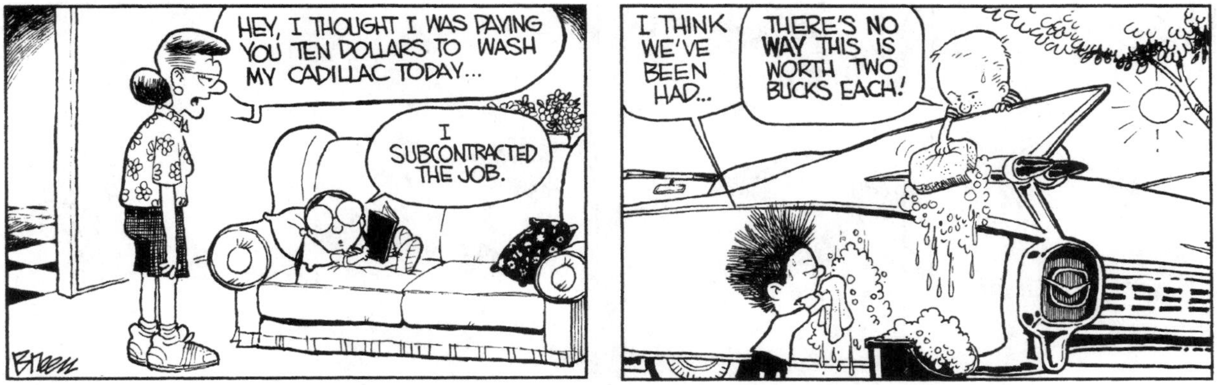
HEY, I THOUGHT I WAS PAYING YOU TEN DOLLARS TO WASH MY CADILLAC TODAY...
I SUBCONTRACTED THE JOB.
I THINK WE'VE BEEN HAD...
THERE'S NO WAY THIS IS WORTH TWO BUCKS EACH!

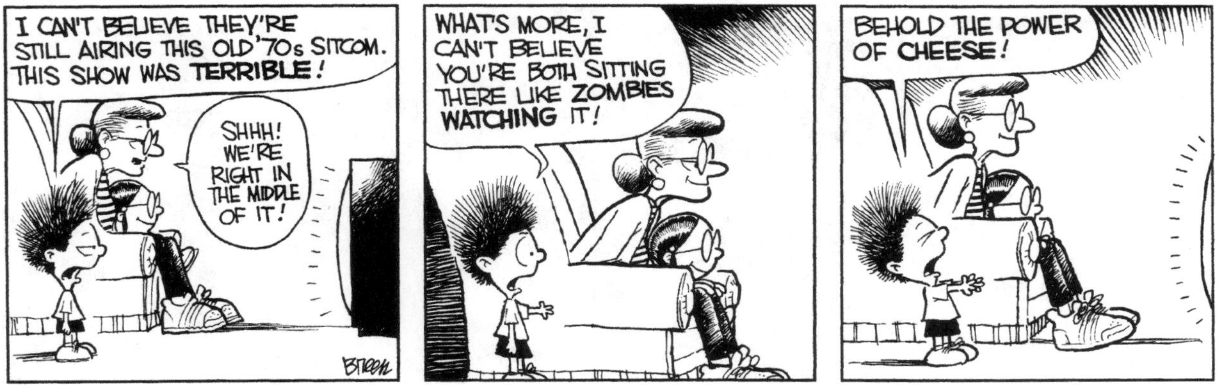
I CAN'T BELIEVE THEY'RE STILL AIRING THIS OLD '70s SITCOM. THIS SHOW WAS TERRIBLE!
SHHH! WE'RE RIGHT IN THE MIDDLE OF IT!
WHAT'S MORE, I CAN'T BELIEVE YOU'RE BOTH SITTING THERE LIKE ZOMBIES WATCHING IT!
BEHOLD THE POWER OF CHEESE!

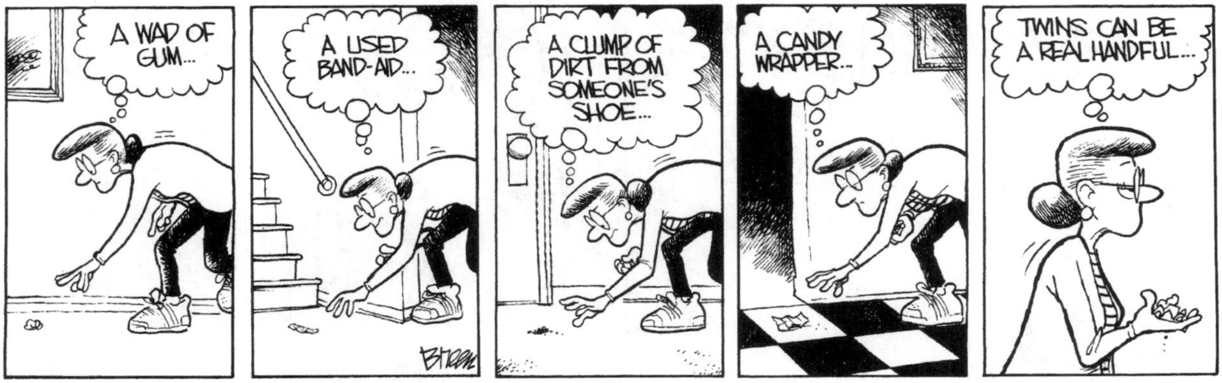
A WAD OF GUM...
A USED BAND-AID...
A CLUMP OF DIRT FROM SOMEONE'S SHOE...
A CANDY WRAPPER...
TWINS CAN BE A REAL HANDFUL...

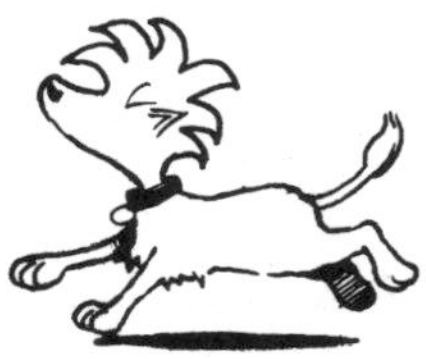

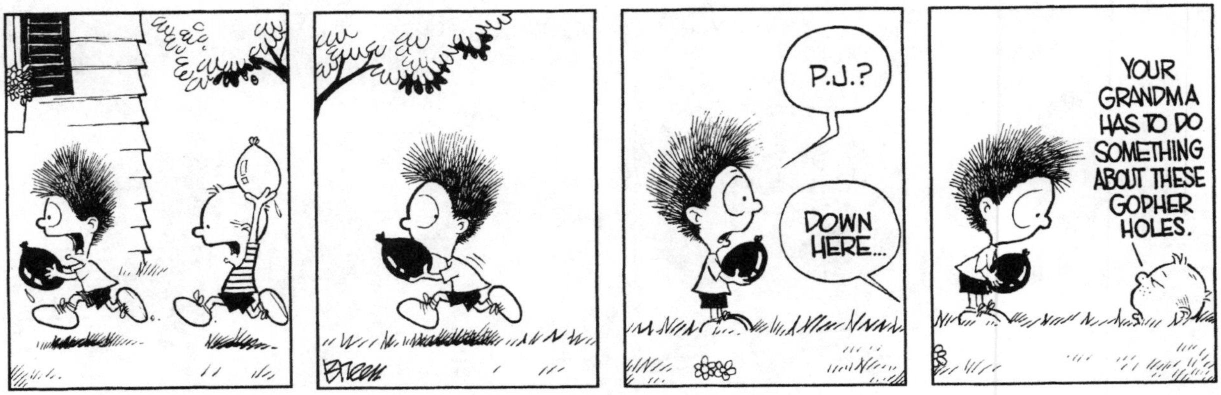
P.J.?
DOWN HERE...
YOUR GRANDMA HAS TO DO SOMETHING ABOUT THESE GOPHER HOLES.

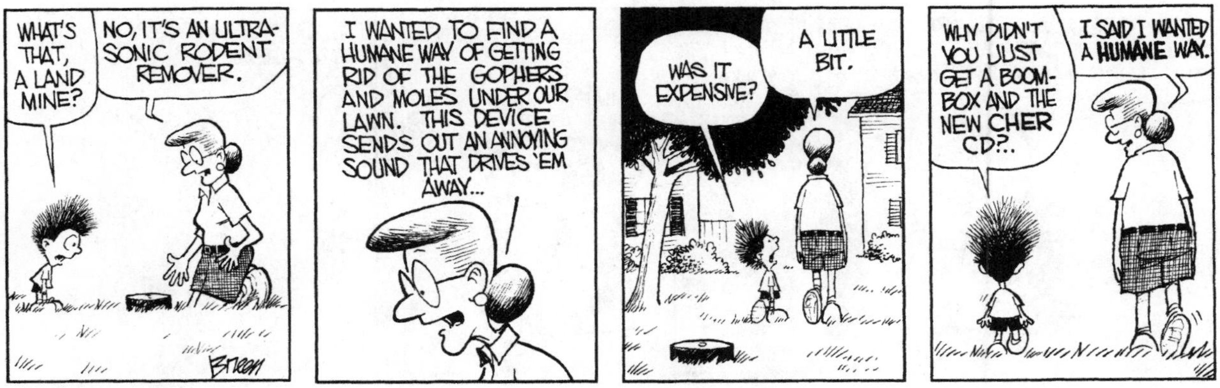
WHAT'S THAT, A LAND MINE?
NO, IT'S AN ULTRA-SONIC RODENT REMOVER.
I WANTED TO FIND A HUMANE WAY OF GETTING RID OF THE GOPHERS AND MOLES UNDER OUR LAWN. THIS DEVICE SENDS OUT AN ANNOYING SOUND THAT DRIVES 'EM AWAY...
WAS IT EXPENSIVE?
A LITTLE BIT.
WHY DIDN'T YOU JUST GET A BOOM-BOX AND THE NEW CHER CD?..
I SAID I WANTED A HUMANE WAY.

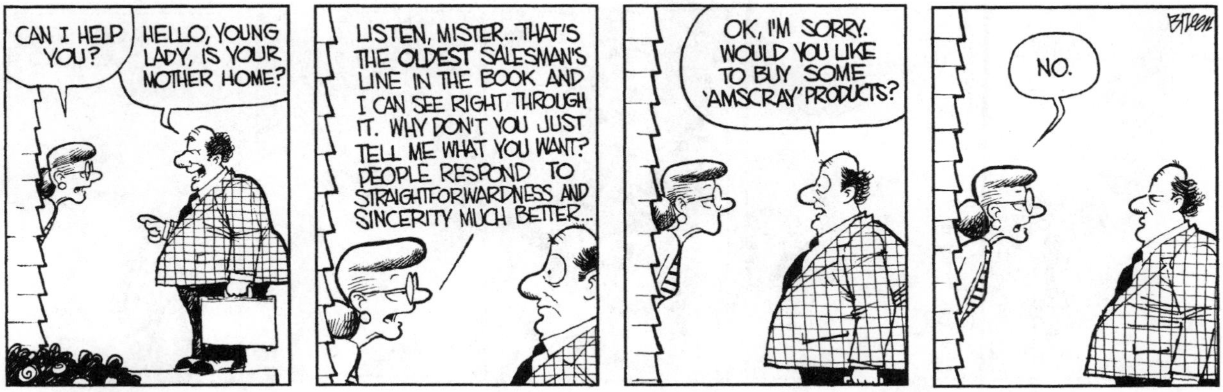
CAN I HELP YOU?
HELLO, YOUNG LADY, IS YOUR MOTHER HOME?
LISTEN, MISTER...THAT'S THE OLDEST SALESMAN'S LINE IN THE BOOK AND I CAN SEE RIGHT THROUGH IT. WHY DON'T YOU JUST TELL ME WHAT YOU WANT? PEOPLE RESPOND TO STRAIGHTFORWARDNESS AND SINCERITY MUCH BETTER...
OK, I'M SORRY. WOULD YOU LIKE TO BUY SOME 'AMSCRAY' PRODUCTS?
NO.

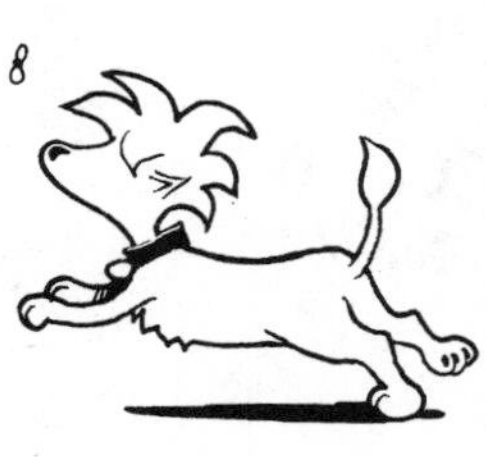

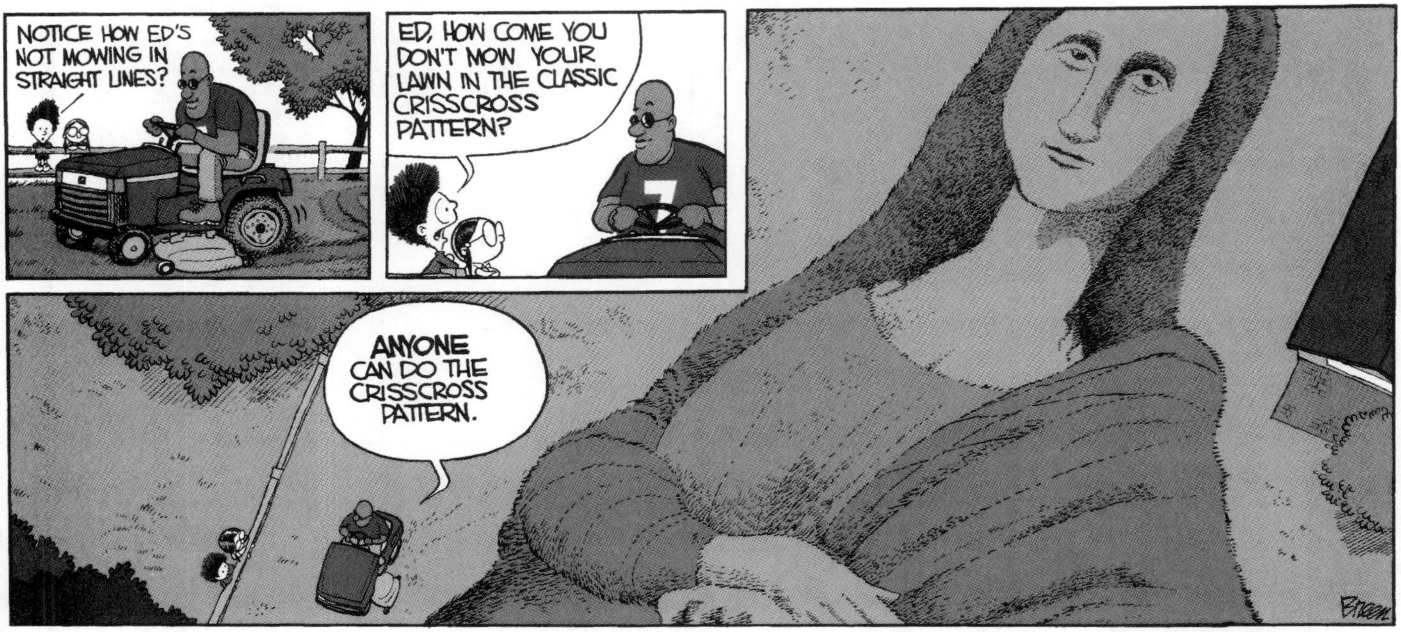
NOTICE HOW ED'S NOT MOWING IN STRAIGHT LINES?
ED, HOW COME YOU DON'T MOW YOUR LAWN IN THE CLASSIC CRISSCROSS PATTERN?
ANYONE CAN DO THE CRISSCROSS PATTERN.
Breen

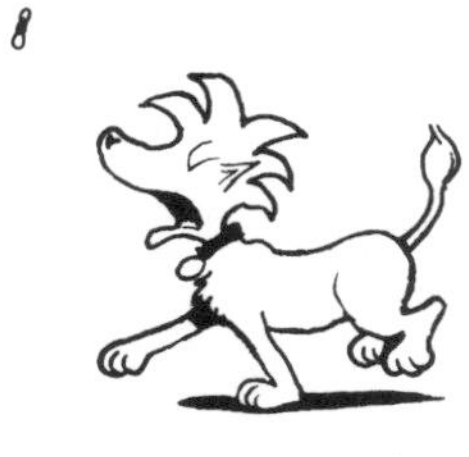

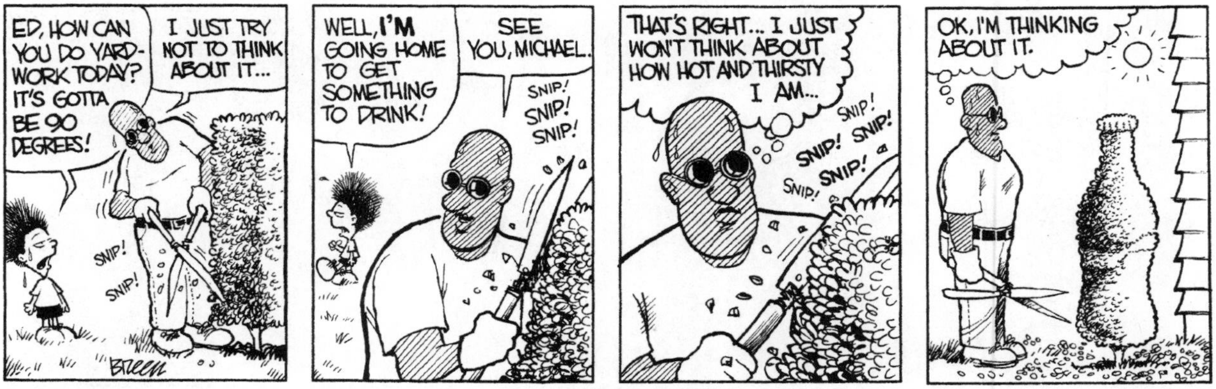
ED, HOW CAN YOU DO YARD-WORK TODAY? IT'S GOTTA BE 90 DEGREES!
I JUST TRY NOT TO THINK ABOUT IT...
SNIP! SNIP!
WELL, I'M GOING HOME TO GET SOMETHING TO DRINK!
SEE YOU, MICHAEL.
SNIP! SNIP! SNIP!
THAT'S RIGHT... I JUST WON'T THINK ABOUT HOW HOT AND THIRSTY I AM...
SNIP! SNIP! SNIP! SNIP! SNIP!
OK, I'M THINKING ABOUT IT.

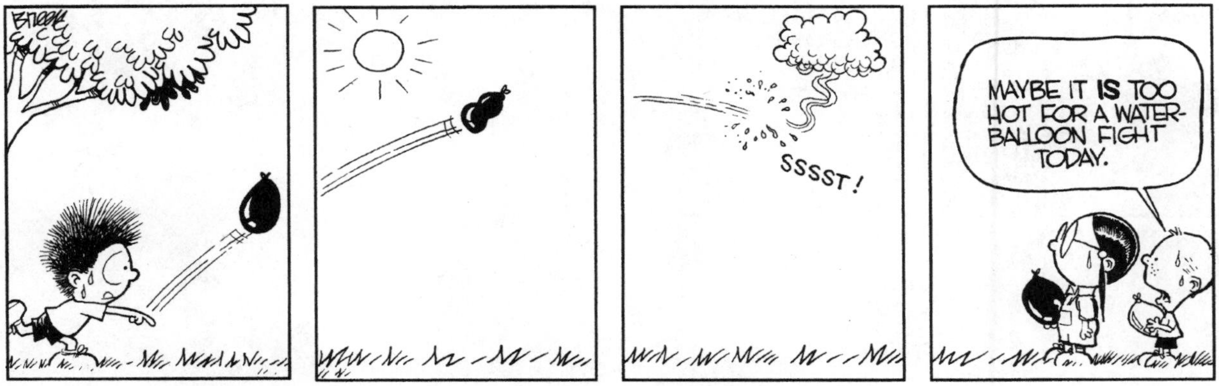
SSSST!
MAYBE IT IS TOO HOT FOR A WATER-BALLOON FIGHT TODAY.

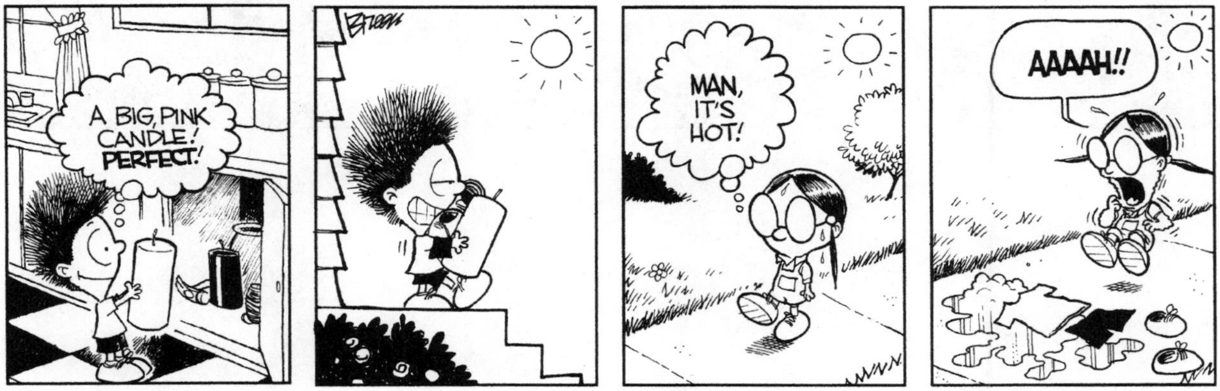
A BIG, PINK CANDLE! PERFECT!
MAN, IT'S HOT!
AAAAH!!

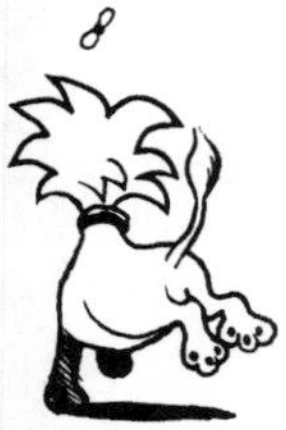

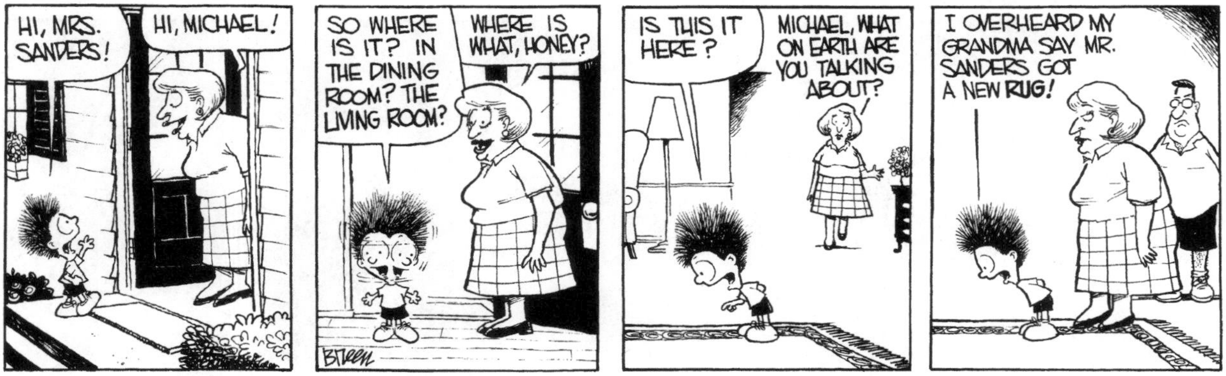
HI, MRS. SANDERS!
HI, MICHAEL!
SO WHERE IS IT? IN THE DINING ROOM? THE LIVING ROOM?
WHERE IS WHAT, HONEY?
IS THIS IT HERE?
MICHAEL, WHAT ON EARTH ARE YOU TALKING ABOUT?
I OVERHEARD MY GRANDMA SAY MR. SANDERS GOT A NEW RUG!

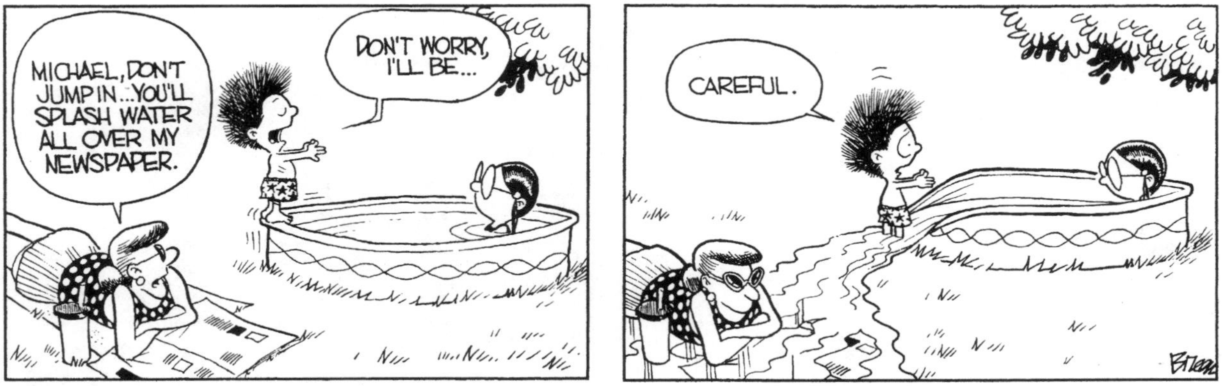
MICHAEL, DON'T JUMP IN...YOU'LL SPLASH WATER ALL OVER MY NEWSPAPER.
DON'T WORRY, I'LL BE...
CAREFUL.

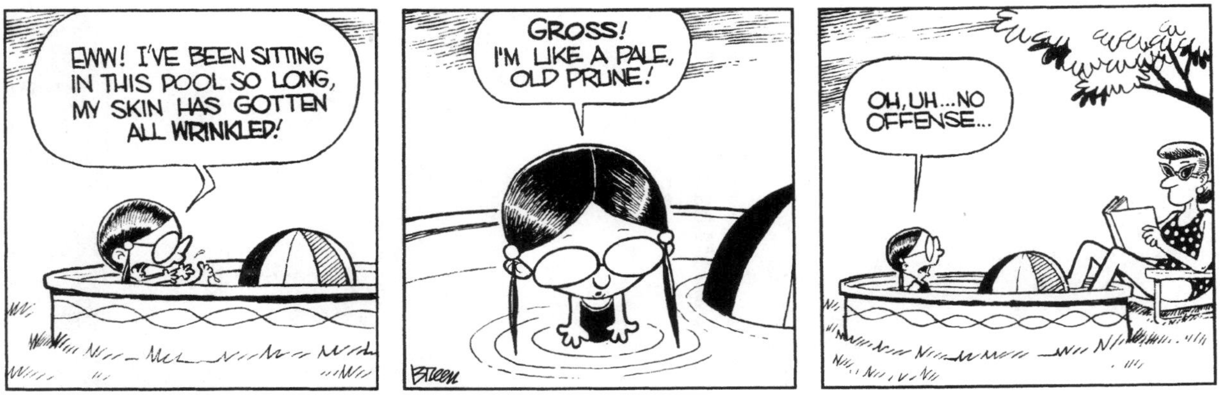
EWW! I'VE BEEN SITTING IN THIS POOL SO LONG, MY SKIN HAS GOTTEN ALL WRINKLED!
GROSS! I'M LIKE A PALE, OLD PRUNE!
OH, UH...NO OFFENSE...

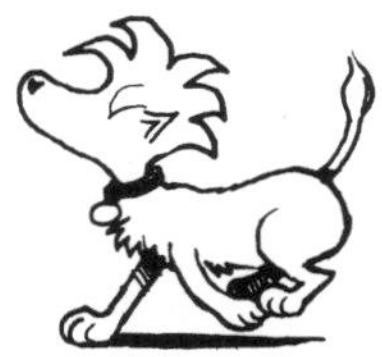

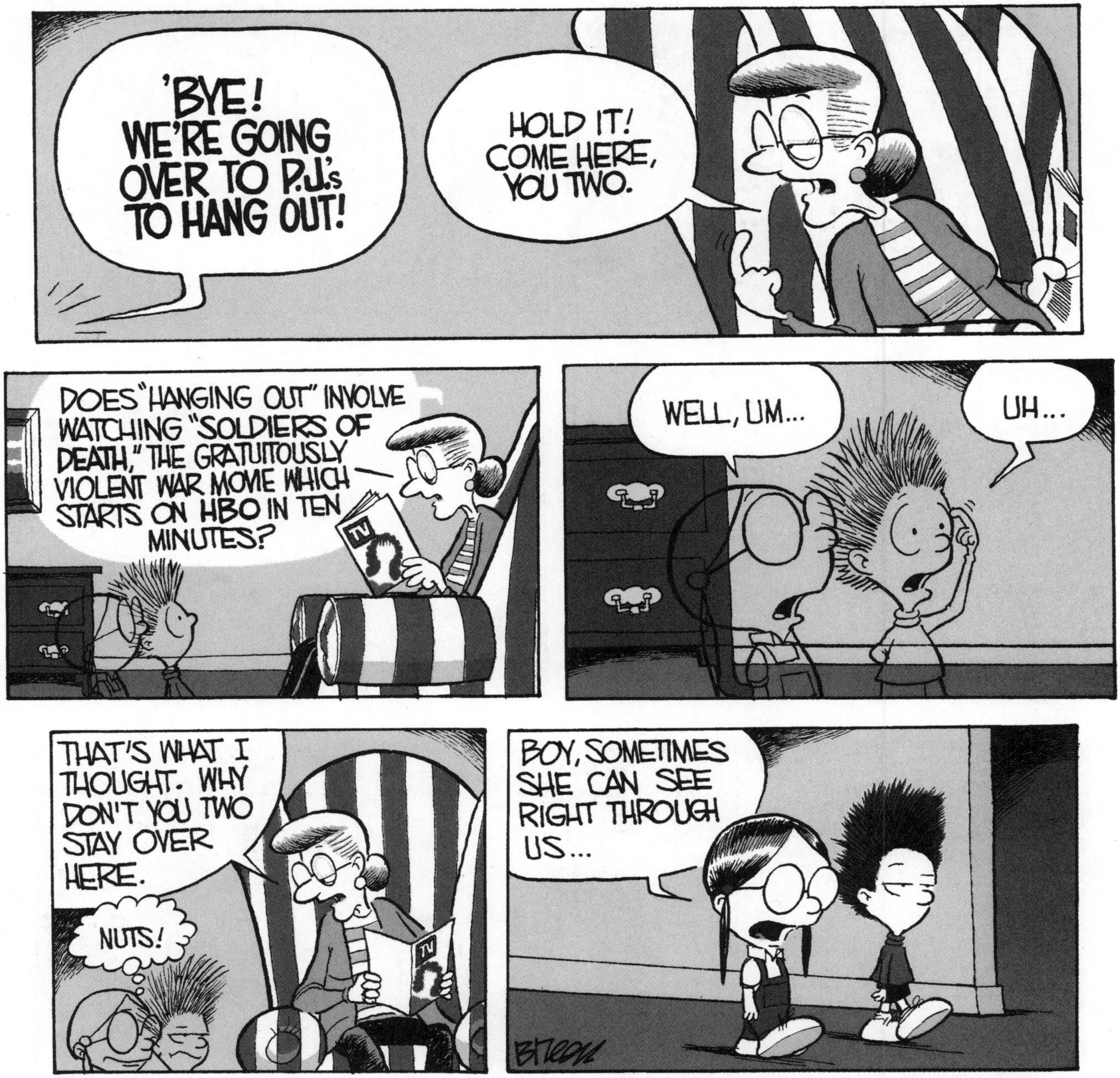
'BYE! WE'RE GOING OVER TO P.J.'s TO HANG OUT!
HOLD IT! COME HERE, YOU TWO.
DOES "HANGING OUT" INVOLVE WATCHING "SOLDIERS OF DEATH," THE GRATUITOUSLY VIOLENT WAR MOVIE WHICH STARTS ON HBO IN TEN MINUTES?
TV
WELL, UM...
UH...
THAT'S WHAT I THOUGHT. WHY DON'T YOU TWO STAY OVER HERE.
NUTS!
TV
BOY, SOMETIMES SHE CAN SEE RIGHT THROUGH US...

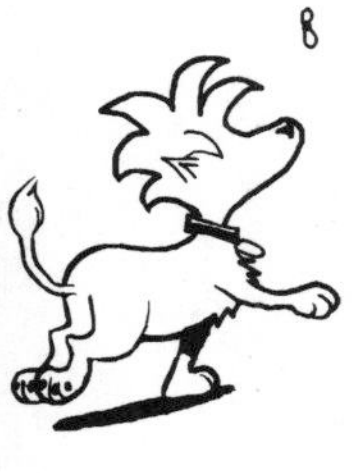

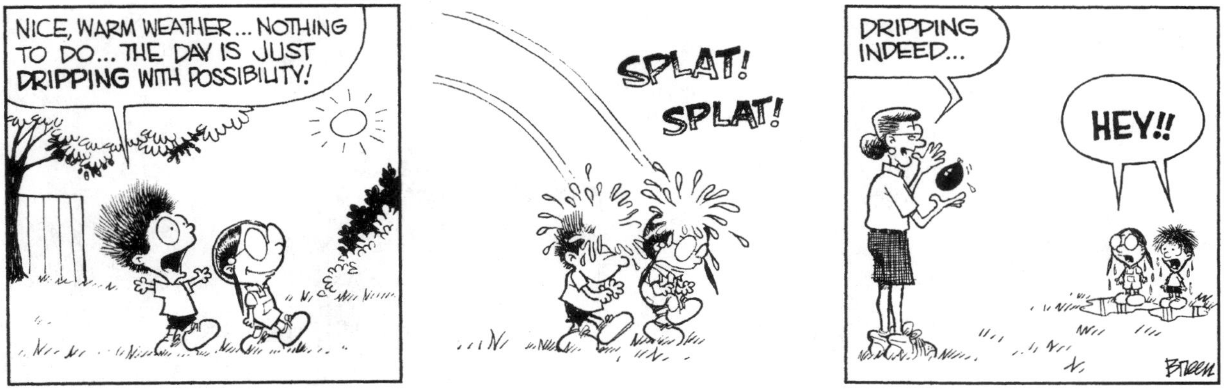
NICE, WARM WEATHER... NOTHING TO DO... THE DAY IS JUST DRIPPING WITH POSSIBILITY!
SPLAT!
SPLAT!
DRIPPING INDEED...
HEY!!

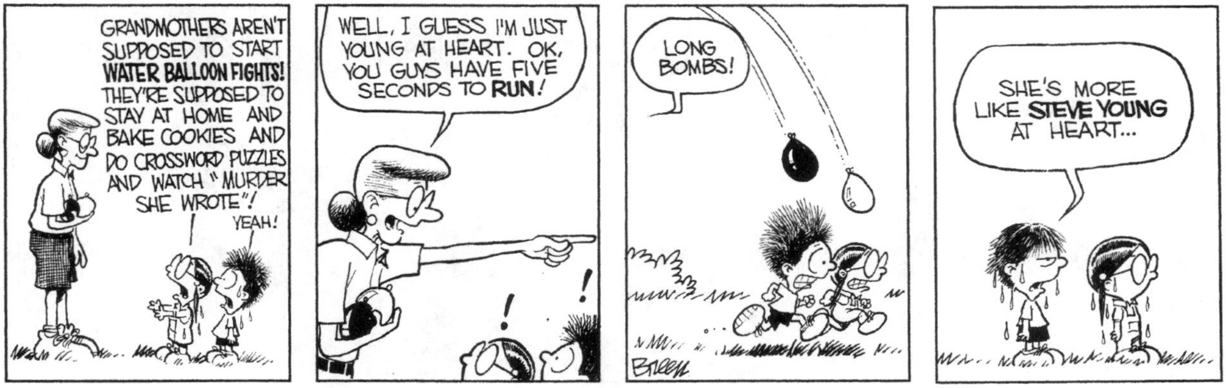
GRANDMOTHERS AREN'T SUPPOSED TO START WATER BALLOON FIGHTS! THEY'RE SUPPOSED TO STAY AT HOME AND BAKE COOKIES AND DO CROSSWORD PUZZLES AND WATCH "MURDER SHE WROTE"!
YEAH!
WELL, I GUESS I'M JUST YOUNG AT HEART. OK, YOU GUYS HAVE FIVE SECONDS TO RUN!
!
!
LONG BOMBS!
SHE'S MORE LIKE STEVE YOUNG AT HEART...

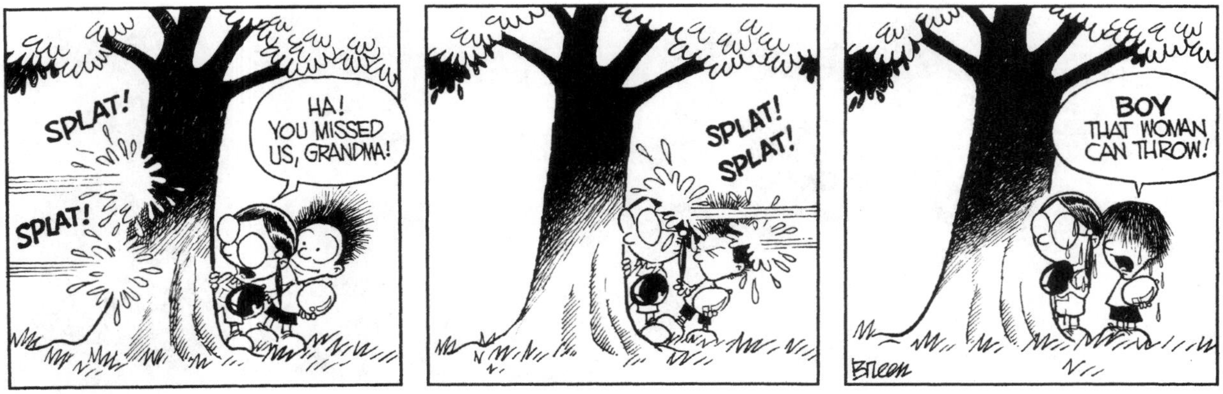
SPLAT!
SPLAT!
HA! YOU MISSED US, GRANDMA!
SPLAT!
SPLAT!
BOY THAT WOMAN CAN THROW!

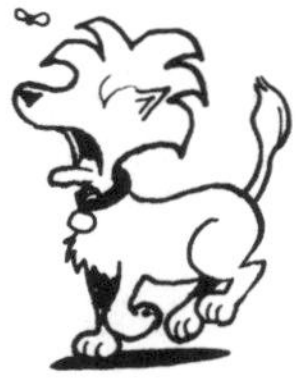

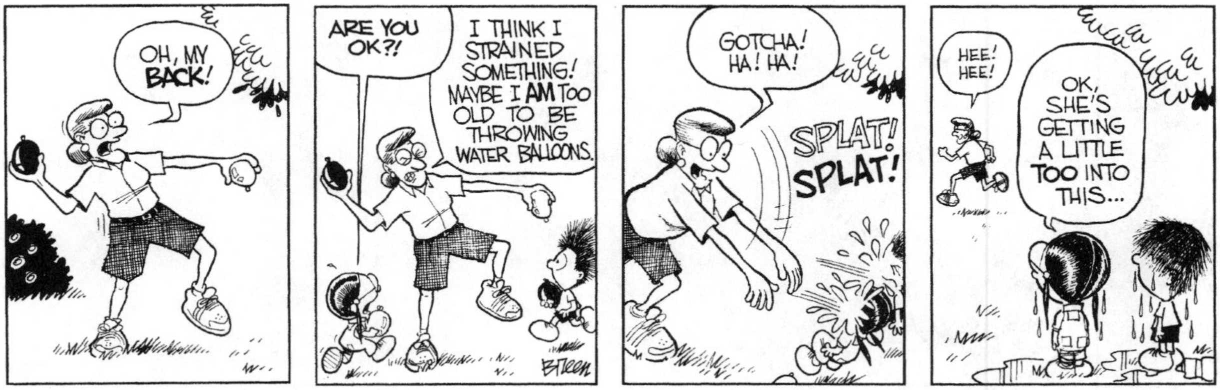
OH, MY BACK!
ARE YOU OK?!
I THINK I STRAINED SOMETHING! MAYBE I AM TOO OLD TO BE THROWING WATER BALLOONS.
GOTCHA! HA! HA!
SPLAT! SPLAT!
HEE! HEE!
OK, SHE'S GETTING A LITTLE TOO INTO THIS...

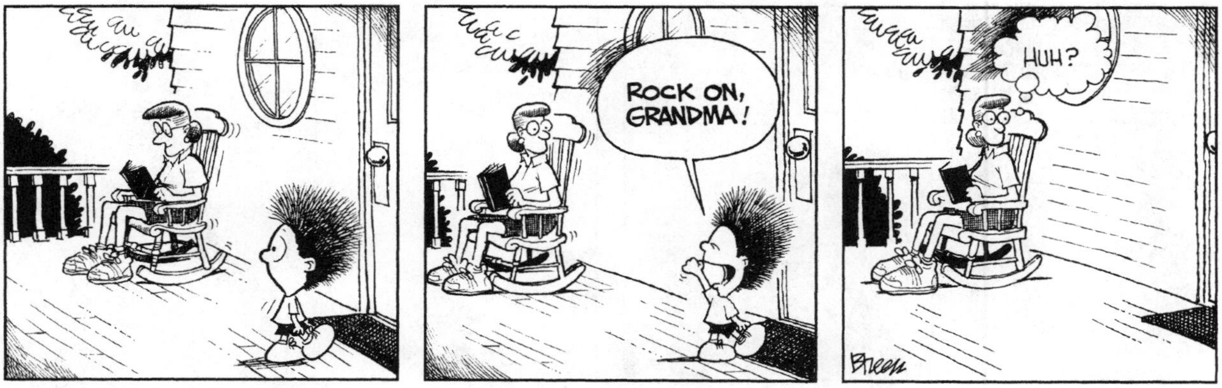
ROCK ON, GRANDMA!
HUH?

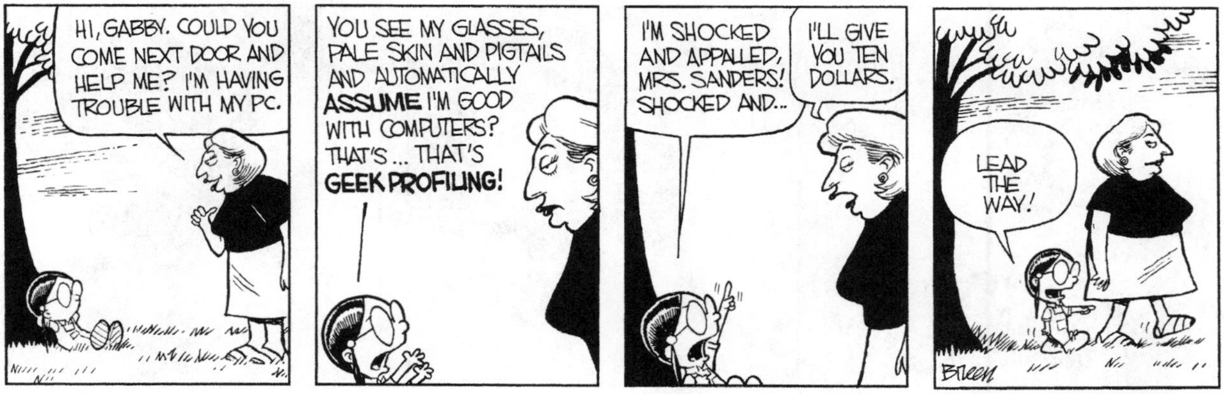
HI, GABBY. COULD YOU COME NEXT DOOR AND HELP ME? I'M HAVING TROUBLE WITH MY PC.
YOU SEE MY GLASSES, PALE SKIN AND PIGTAILS AND AUTOMATICALLY ASSUME I'M GOOD WITH COMPUTERS? THAT'S... THAT'S GEEK PROFILING!
I'M SHOCKED AND APPALLED, MRS. SANDERS! SHOCKED AND...
I'LL GIVE YOU TEN DOLLARS.
LEAD THE WAY!

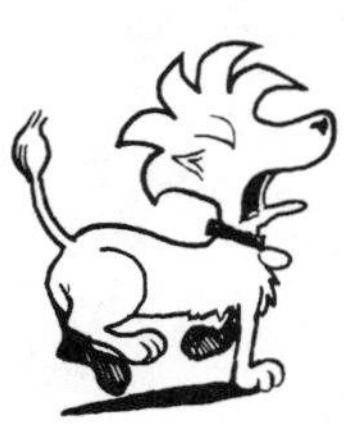

NO WATER FIGHTS IN THE HOUSE, YOU GUYS!
GABBY, YOU'RE TRACKING **MUD** THROUGH THE LIVING ROOM!
MICHAEL, **PLEASE** QUIT PLAYING THAT KAZOO IN MY **EAR**!
@#!*?
BREAK IT UP!
UH-OH... SHE'S TALKING TO HERSELF.
WHAT'S "CALGON"?

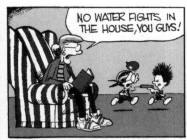

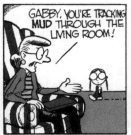

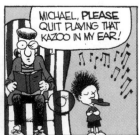

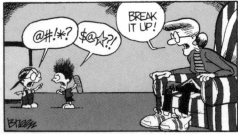

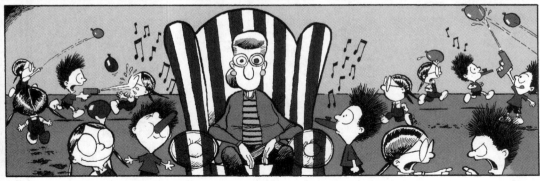

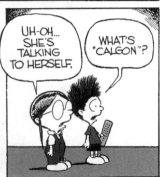

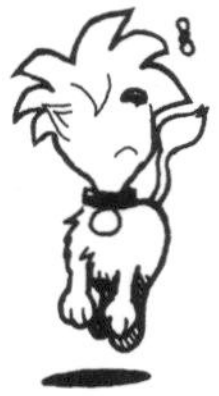

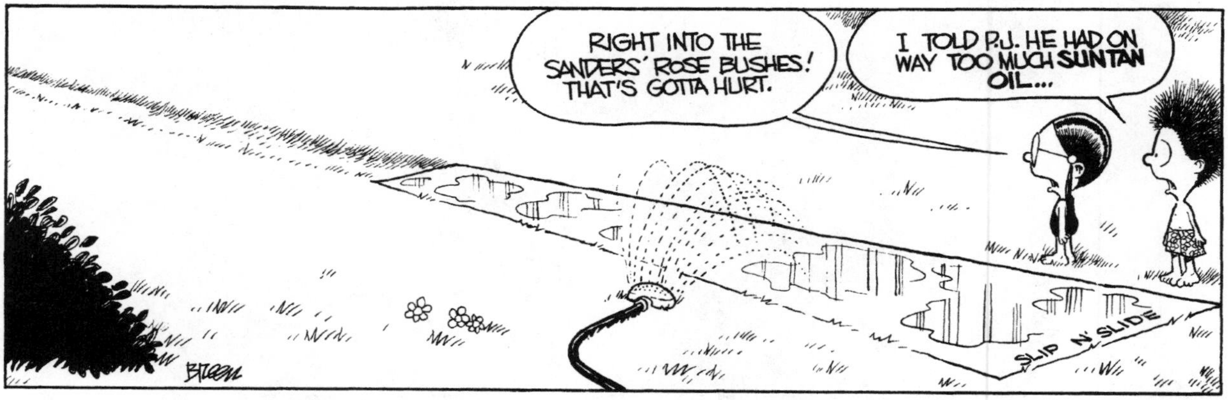
RIGHT INTO THE SANDERS' ROSE BUSHES! THAT'S GOTTA HURT.
I TOLD P.J. HE HAD ON WAY TOO MUCH SUNTAN OIL...
SLIP N' SLIDE

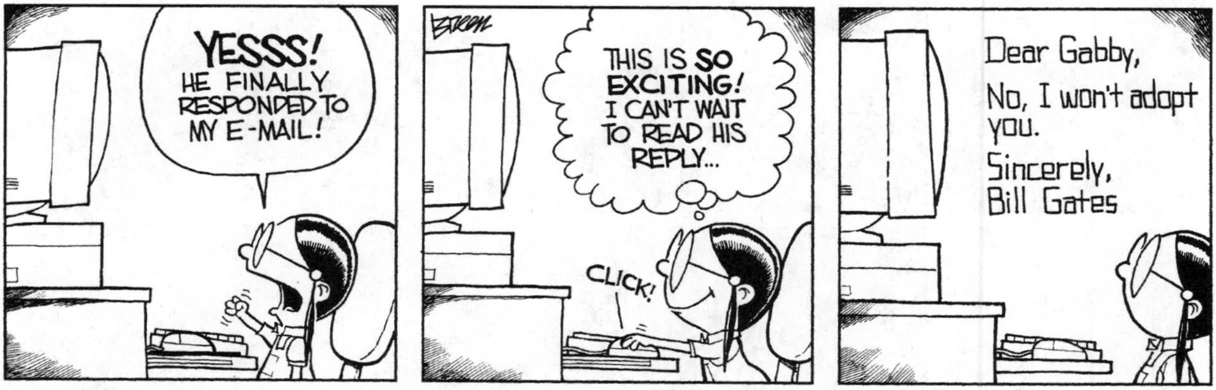
YESSS! HE FINALLY RESPONDED TO MY E-MAIL!
THIS IS SO EXCITING! I CAN'T WAIT TO READ HIS REPLY...
CLICK!
Dear Gabby,
No, I won't adopt you.
Sincerely,
Bill Gates

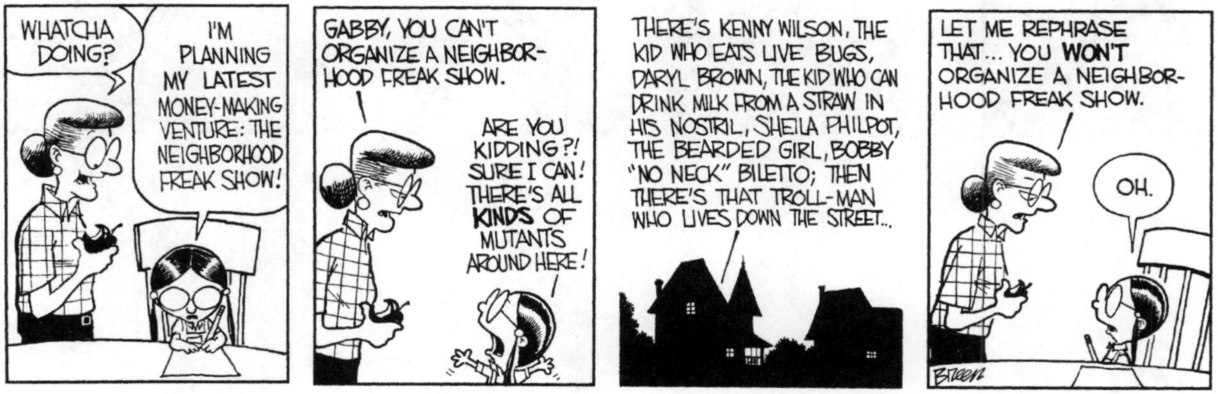
WHATCHA DOING?
I'M PLANNING MY LATEST MONEY-MAKING VENTURE: THE NEIGHBORHOOD FREAK SHOW!
GABBY, YOU CAN'T ORGANIZE A NEIGHBORHOOD FREAK SHOW.
ARE YOU KIDDING?! SURE I CAN! THERE'S ALL KINDS OF MUTANTS AROUND HERE!
THERE'S KENNY WILSON, THE KID WHO EATS LIVE BUGS, DARYL BROWN, THE KID WHO CAN DRINK MILK FROM A STRAW IN HIS NOSTRIL, SHEILA PHILPOT, THE BEARDED GIRL, BOBBY "NO NECK" BILETTO; THEN THERE'S THAT TROLL-MAN WHO LIVES DOWN THE STREET...
LET ME REPHRASE THAT... YOU WON'T ORGANIZE A NEIGHBORHOOD FREAK SHOW.
OH.

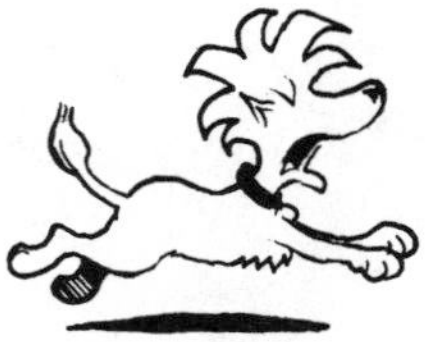

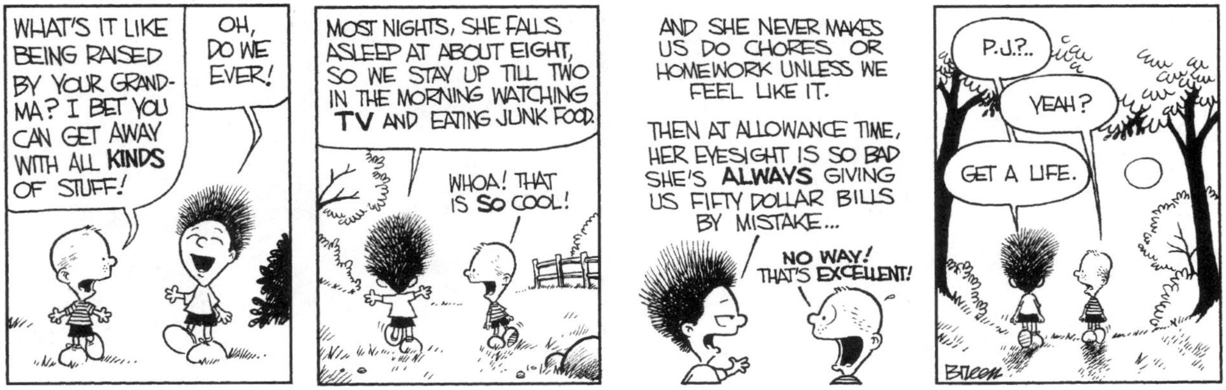
WHAT'S IT LIKE BEING RAISED BY YOUR GRAND-MA? I BET YOU CAN GET AWAY WITH ALL KINDS OF STUFF!
OH, DO WE EVER!
MOST NIGHTS, SHE FALLS ASLEEP AT ABOUT EIGHT, SO WE STAY UP TILL TWO IN THE MORNING WATCHING TV AND EATING JUNK FOOD.
WHOA! THAT IS SO COOL!
AND SHE NEVER MAKES US DO CHORES OR HOMEWORK UNLESS WE FEEL LIKE IT.
THEN AT ALLOWANCE TIME, HER EYESIGHT IS SO BAD SHE'S ALWAYS GIVING US FIFTY DOLLAR BILLS BY MISTAKE...
NO WAY! THAT'S EXCELLENT!
P.J.?..
YEAH?
GET A LIFE.
BTREEN

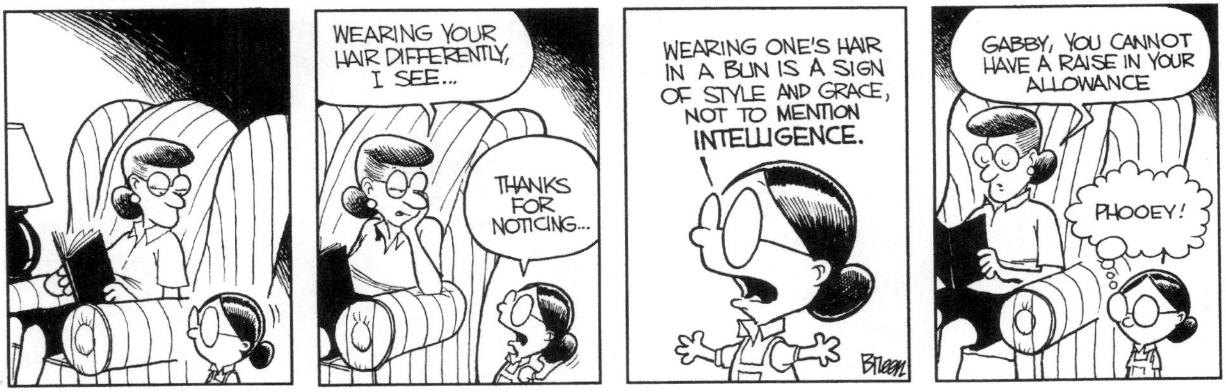
WEARING YOUR HAIR DIFFERENTLY, I SEE...
THANKS FOR NOTICING...
WEARING ONE'S HAIR IN A BUN IS A SIGN OF STYLE AND GRACE, NOT TO MENTION INTELLIGENCE.
BTREEN
GABBY, YOU CANNOT HAVE A RAISE IN YOUR ALLOWANCE
PHOOEY!

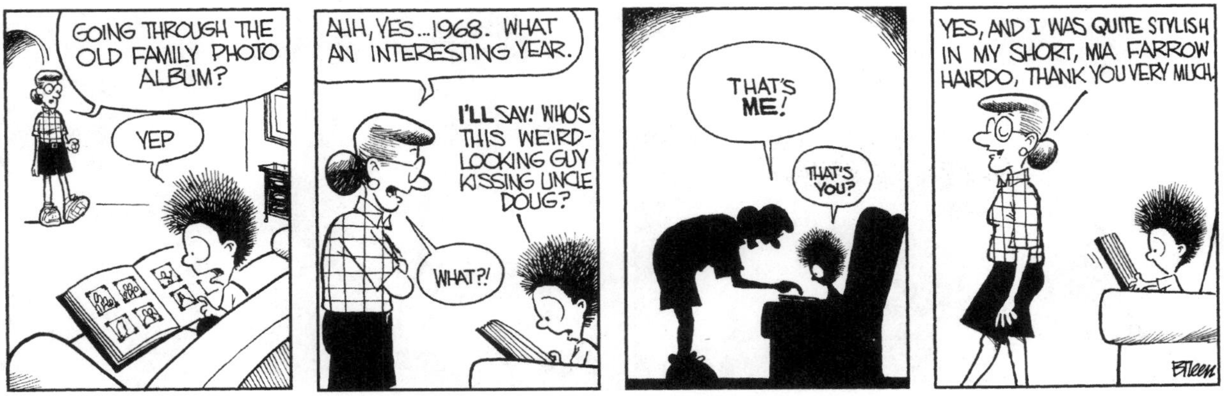
GOING THROUGH THE OLD FAMILY PHOTO ALBUM?
YEP
AHH, YES...1968. WHAT AN INTERESTING YEAR.
I'LL SAY! WHO'S THIS WEIRD-LOOKING GUY KISSING UNCLE DOUG?
WHAT?!
THAT'S ME!
THAT'S YOU?
YES, AND I WAS QUITE STYLISH IN MY SHORT, MIA FARROW HAIRDO, THANK YOU VERY MUCH.
BTREEN

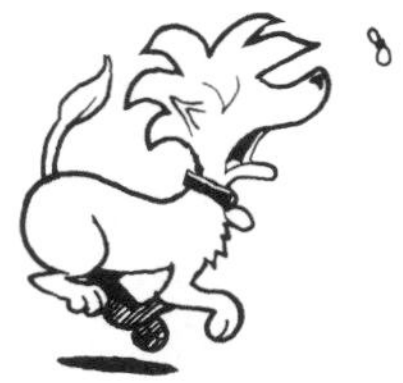

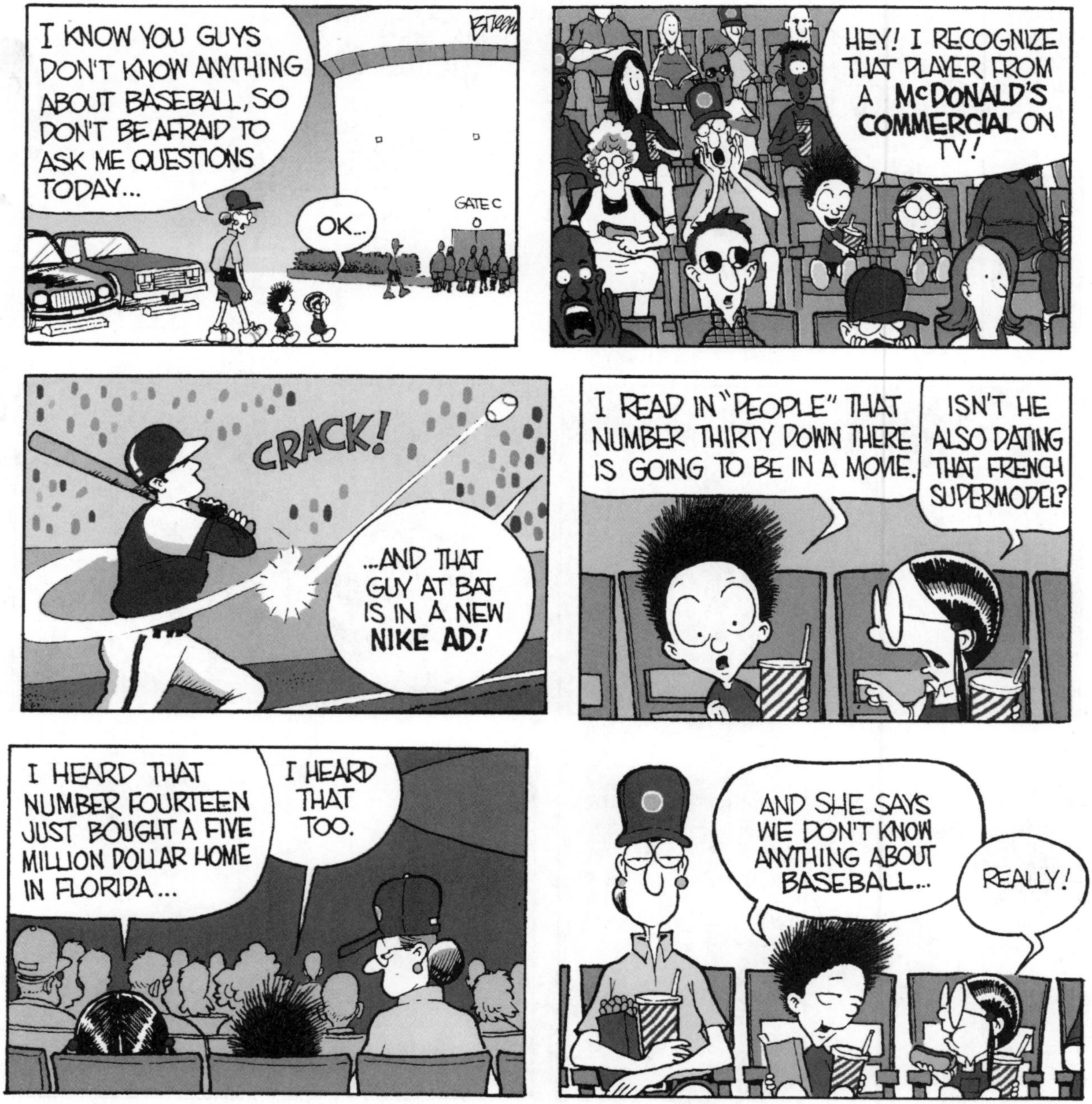
I KNOW YOU GUYS DON'T KNOW ANYTHING ABOUT BASEBALL, SO DON'T BE AFRAID TO ASK ME QUESTIONS TODAY...
OK...
GATE C
HEY! I RECOGNIZE THAT PLAYER FROM A McDONALD'S COMMERCIAL ON TV!
CRACK!
...AND THAT GUY AT BAT IS IN A NEW NIKE AD!
I READ IN "PEOPLE" THAT NUMBER THIRTY DOWN THERE IS GOING TO BE IN A MOVIE.
ISN'T HE ALSO DATING THAT FRENCH SUPERMODEL?
I HEARD THAT NUMBER FOURTEEN JUST BOUGHT A FIVE MILLION DOLLAR HOME IN FLORIDA...
I HEARD THAT TOO.
AND SHE SAYS WE DON'T KNOW ANYTHING ABOUT BASEBALL...
REALLY!

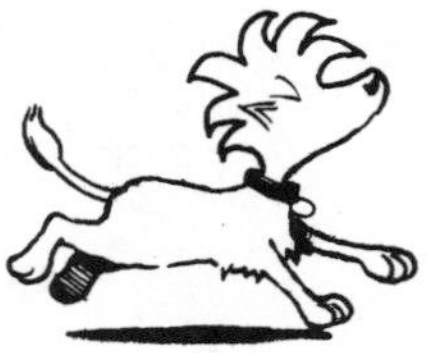

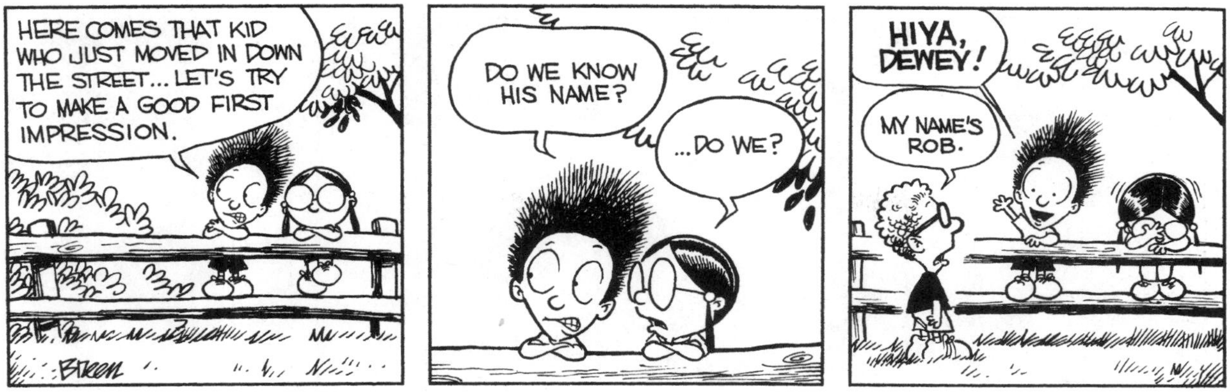
HERE COMES THAT KID WHO JUST MOVED IN DOWN THE STREET... LET'S TRY TO MAKE A GOOD FIRST IMPRESSION.
DO WE KNOW HIS NAME?
...DO WE?
HIYA, DEWEY!
MY NAME'S ROB.

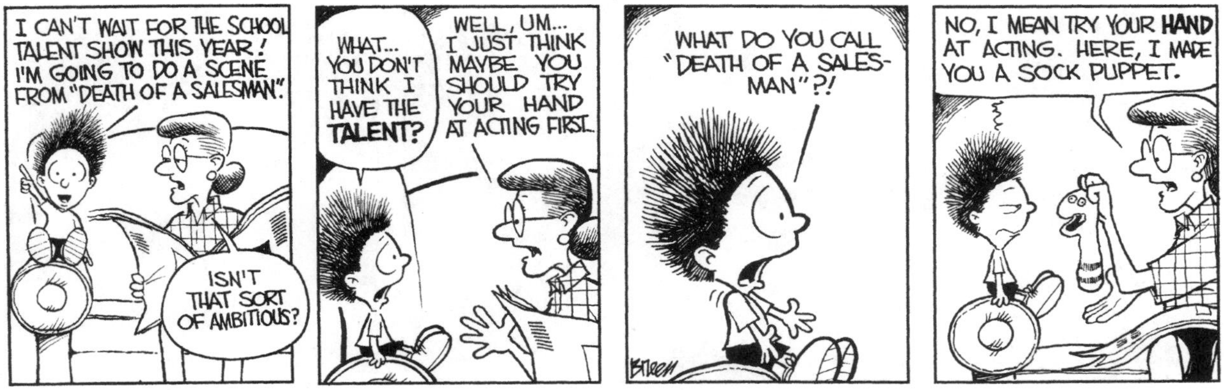
I CAN'T WAIT FOR THE SCHOOL TALENT SHOW THIS YEAR! I'M GOING TO DO A SCENE FROM "DEATH OF A SALESMAN".
ISN'T THAT SORT OF AMBITIOUS?
WHAT... YOU DON'T THINK I HAVE THE TALENT?
WELL, UM... I JUST THINK MAYBE YOU SHOULD TRY YOUR HAND AT ACTING FIRST.
WHAT DO YOU CALL "DEATH OF A SALESMAN"?!
NO, I MEAN TRY YOUR HAND AT ACTING. HERE, I MADE YOU A SOCK PUPPET.

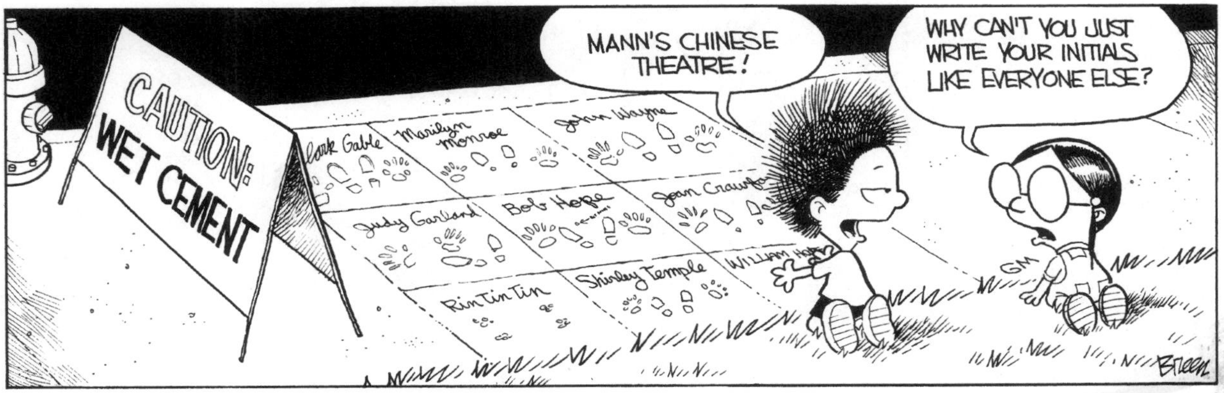
CAUTION: WET CEMENT
Marilyn Monroe
John Wayne
Judy Garland
Bob Hope
Shirley Temple
Rin Tin Tin
MANN'S CHINESE THEATRE!
WHY CAN'T YOU JUST WRITE YOUR INITIALS LIKE EVERYONE ELSE?

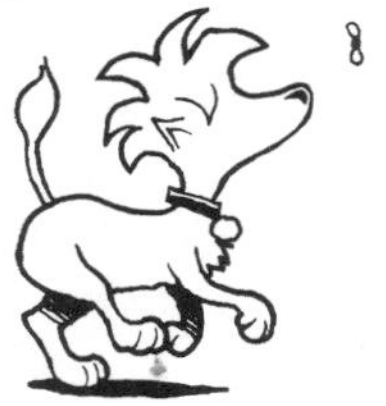

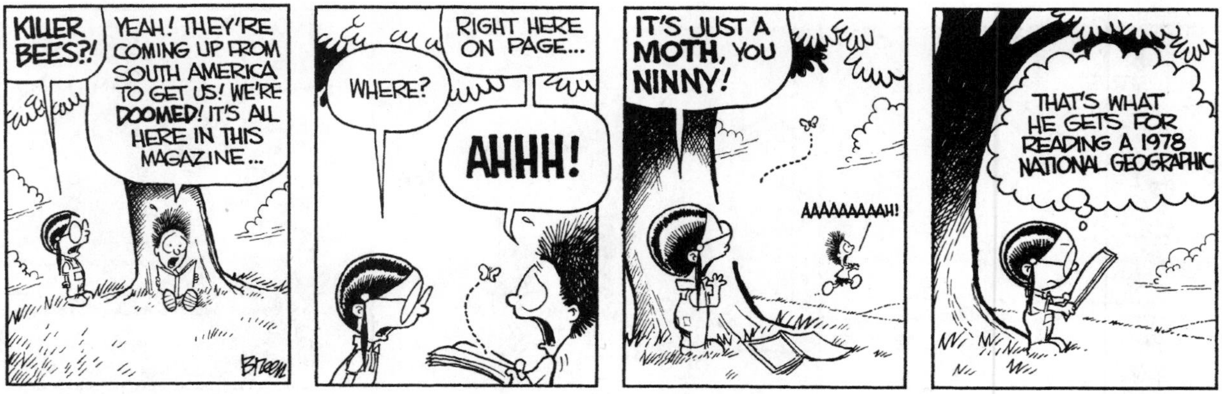
KILLER BEES?!
YEAH! THEY'RE COMING UP FROM SOUTH AMERICA TO GET US! WE'RE DOOMED! IT'S ALL HERE IN THIS MAGAZINE...
WHERE?
RIGHT HERE ON PAGE...
AHHH!
IT'S JUST A MOTH, YOU NINNY!
AAAAAAAAAH!
THAT'S WHAT HE GETS FOR READING A 1978 NATIONAL GEOGRAPHIC

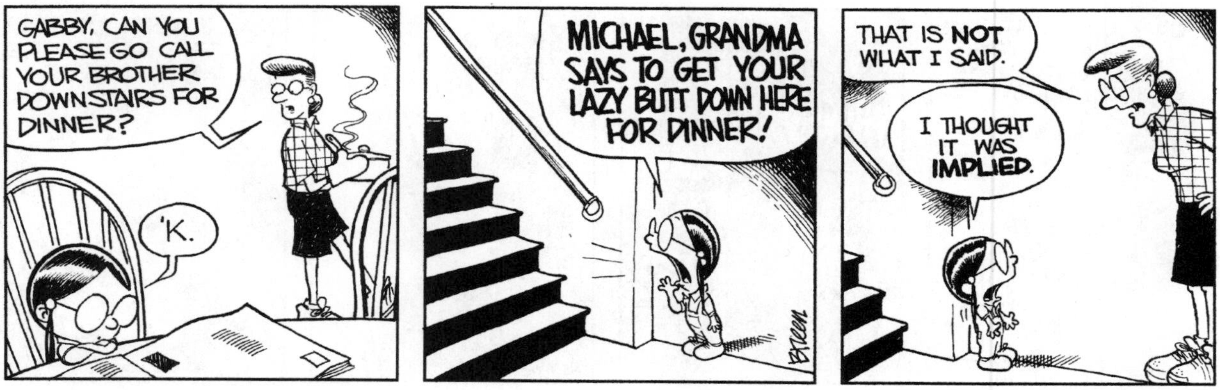
GABBY, CAN YOU PLEASE GO CALL YOUR BROTHER DOWNSTAIRS FOR DINNER?
'K.
MICHAEL, GRANDMA SAYS TO GET YOUR LAZY BUTT DOWN HERE FOR DINNER!
THAT IS NOT WHAT I SAID.
I THOUGHT IT WAS IMPLIED.

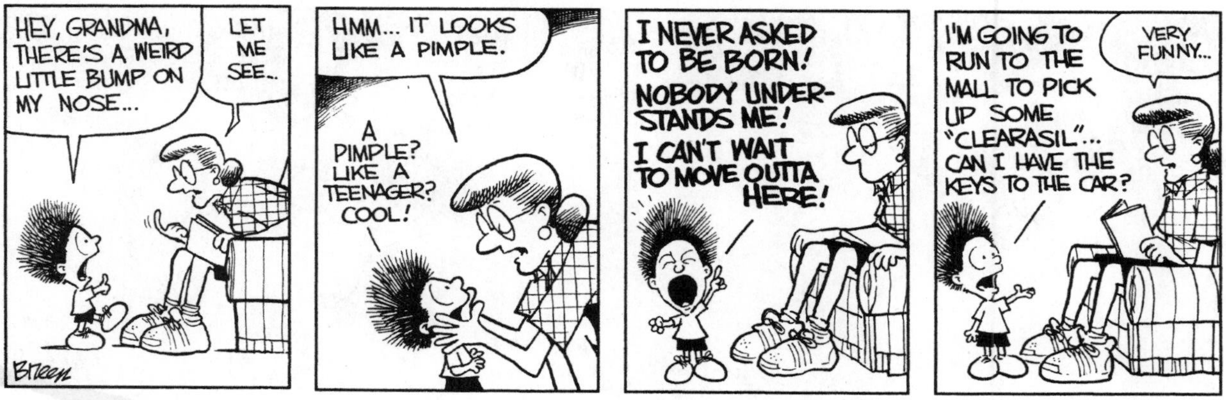
HEY, GRANDMA, THERE'S A WEIRD LITTLE BUMP ON MY NOSE...
LET ME SEE...
HMM... IT LOOKS LIKE A PIMPLE.
A PIMPLE? LIKE A TEENAGER? COOL!
I NEVER ASKED TO BE BORN!
NOBODY UNDER-STANDS ME!
I CAN'T WAIT TO MOVE OUTTA HERE!
I'M GOING TO RUN TO THE MALL TO PICK UP SOME "CLEARASIL"... CAN I HAVE THE KEYS TO THE CAR?
VERY FUNNY...

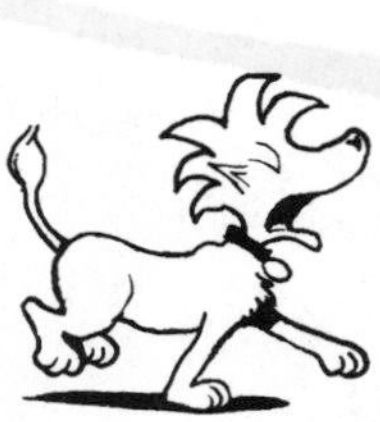

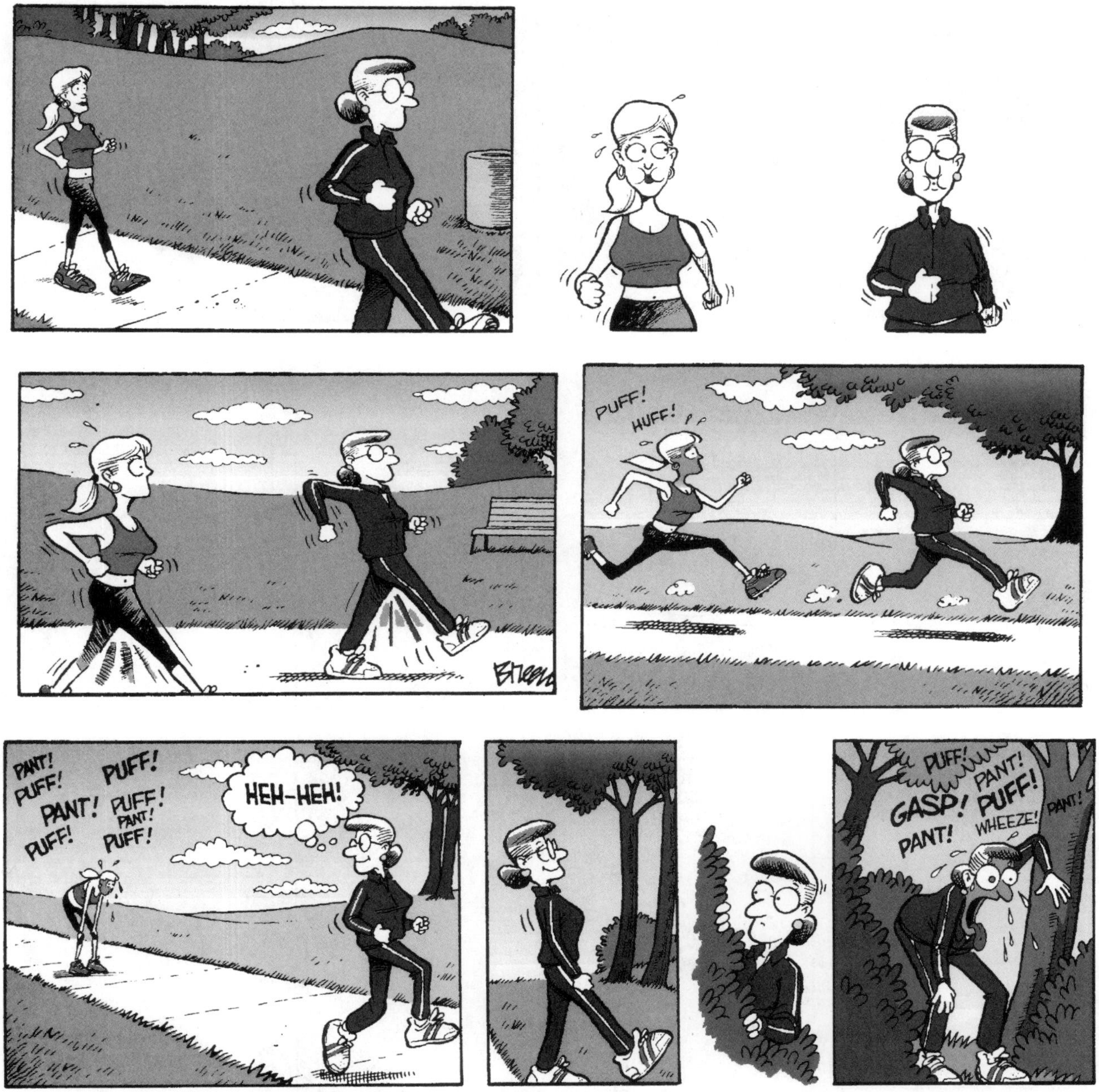
PUFF!
HUFF!
PANT!
PUFF!
PUFF!
PANT!
PUFF!
PANT!
PUFF!
PUFF!
PUFF!
HEH-HEH!
PUFF!
PANT!
PUFF!
GASP!
PANT!
WHEEZE!
PANT!

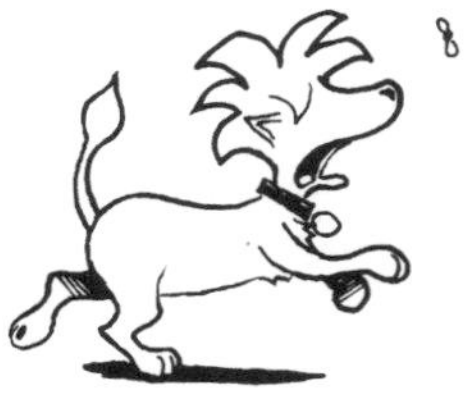

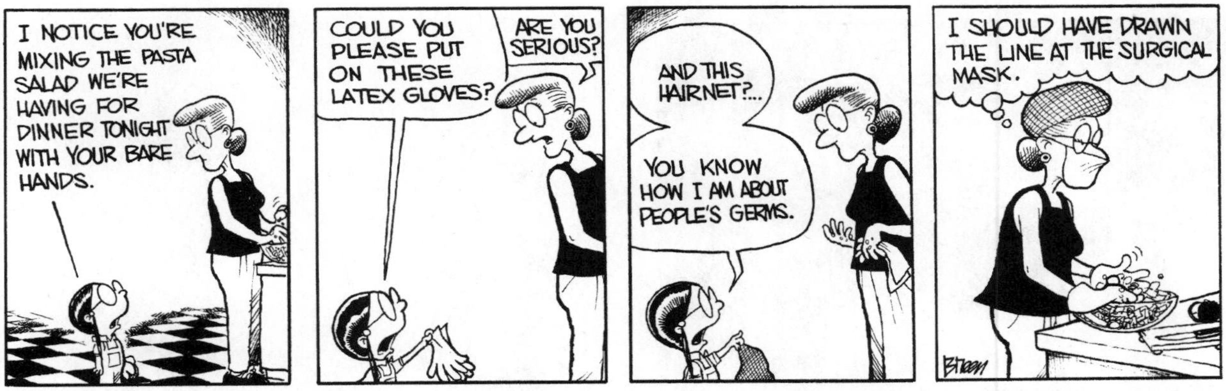
I NOTICE YOU'RE MIXING THE PASTA SALAD WE'RE HAVING FOR DINNER TONIGHT WITH YOUR BARE HANDS.
COULD YOU PLEASE PUT ON THESE LATEX GLOVES?
ARE YOU SERIOUS?
AND THIS HAIRNET?...
YOU KNOW HOW I AM ABOUT PEOPLE'S GERMS.
I SHOULD HAVE DRAWN THE LINE AT THE SURGICAL MASK.

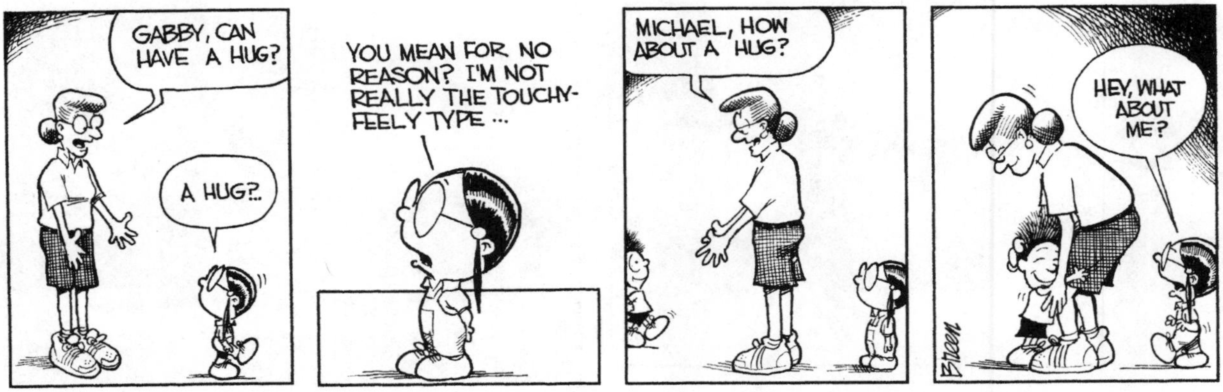
GABBY, CAN HAVE A HUG?
A HUG?..
YOU MEAN FOR NO REASON? I'M NOT REALLY THE TOUCHY-FEELY TYPE ...
MICHAEL, HOW ABOUT A HUG?
HEY, WHAT ABOUT ME?

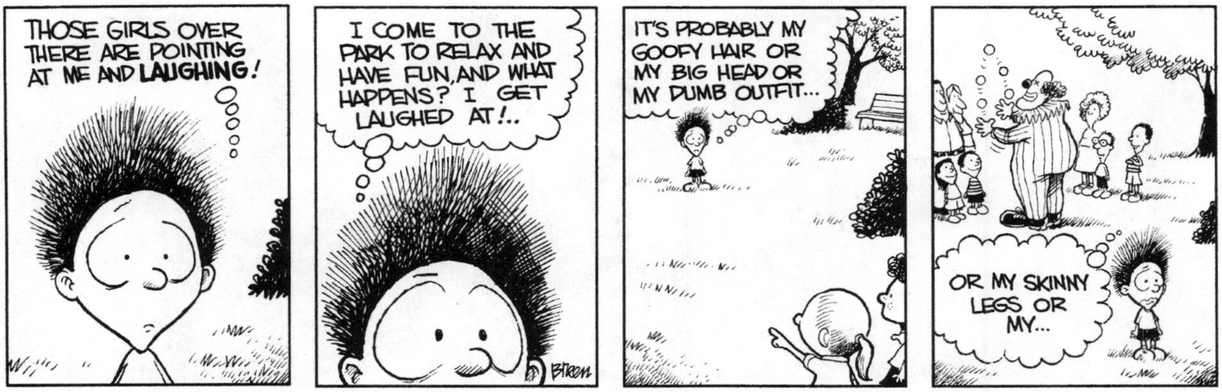
THOSE GIRLS OVER THERE ARE POINTING AT ME AND LAUGHING!
I COME TO THE PARK TO RELAX AND HAVE FUN, AND WHAT HAPPENS? I GET LAUGHED AT!..
IT'S PROBABLY MY GOOFY HAIR OR MY BIG HEAD OR MY DUMB OUTFIT...
OR MY SKINNY LEGS OR MY...

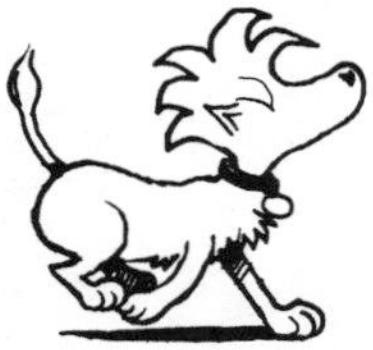

ARE YOU GIRLS TALKING ABOUT ME?
NO.
ARE YOU SURE?
ABSOLUTELY, POSITIVELY SURE.
OK, GOOD. SEE YA!
WE WERE TALKING ABOUT WHO WE THINK ARE THE CUTEST BOYS IN THE NEIGHBORHOOD.

COULD YOU PLEASE TAKE YOUR SHOES OFF BEFORE COMING INTO MY ROOM? THANKS.
MONOPOLY
UM... COULD YOU PLEASE TAKE YOUR SOCKS OFF, TOO?
TELL YOU WHAT... LET'S GO PLAY DOWNSTAIRS.
WHAT?

CLIP!
CLIP!
MICHAEL, COULD YOU PLEASE DO THAT SOMEWHERE ELSE?
CLIP!
CLIP!

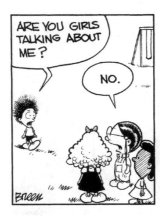

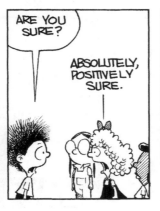

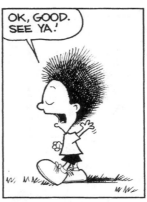

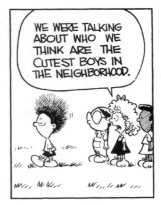

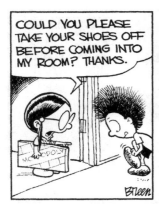

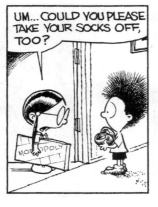

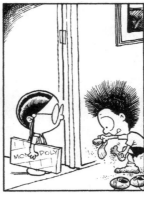

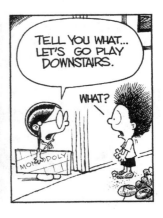

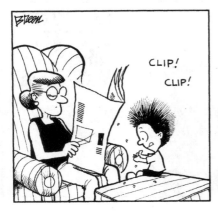

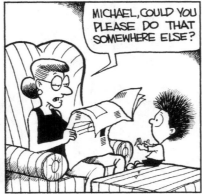

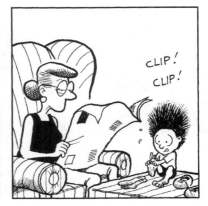

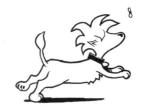

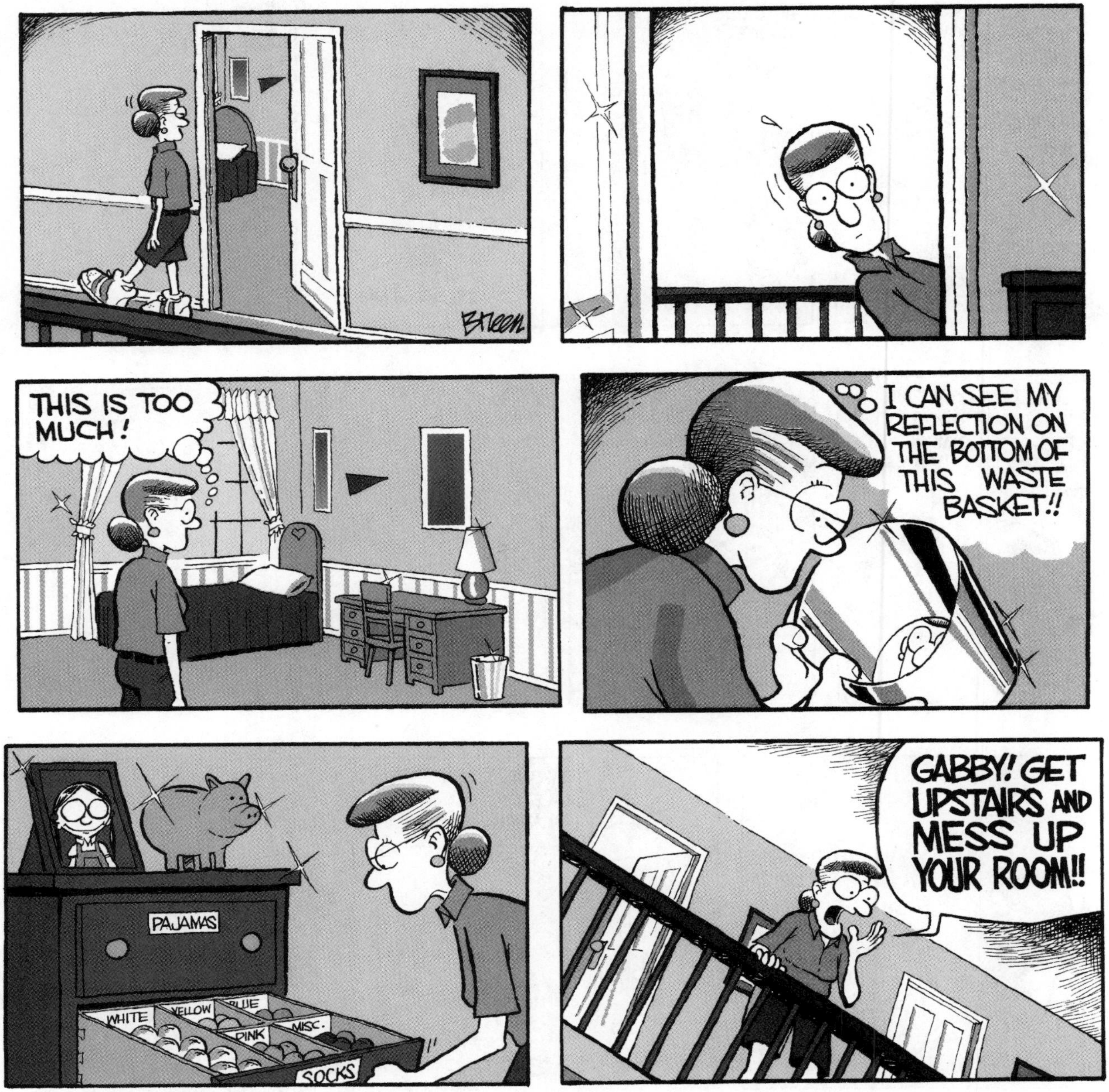
THIS IS TOO MUCH!
I CAN SEE MY REFLECTION ON THE BOTTOM OF THIS WASTE BASKET!!
PAJAMAS
WHITE
YELLOW
BLUE
PINK
MISC.
SOCKS
GABBY! GET UPSTAIRS AND MESS UP YOUR ROOM!!

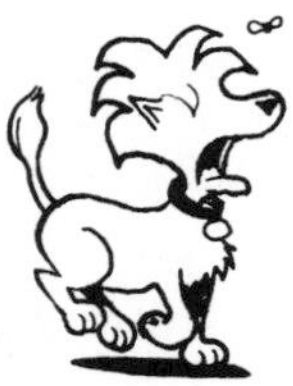

I CAN'T BELIEVE I MADE A **JELLY STAIN** ON THE COUCH! WHAT AM I GONNA DO? YOU GOTTA HELP ME!
HOLD ON— AHA! HERE WE GO...
HINTS FROM HELGA
THIS BOOK SAYS WE HAVE TO DOUSE IT WITH **VINEGAR**. JUST A SEC, I'LL GET SOME FROM THE KITCHEN
OK, HURRY!
THIS OUGHTA DO THE TRICK.
GUNKA! GUNKA! GUNKA!
WAIT A MINUTE...
GUNKA! GUNKA! GUNKA!
OOPS.
JELLY STAIN, NOT JELLYFISH STING!!

WELL, I HID THAT JELLY STAIN I MADE ON THE COUCH.
WITH A PURPLE MAGIC MARKER? YOU DIDN'T.
YOU DID.
I THINK IT'S PRETTY CONVINCING... IF YOU SQUINT YOUR EYES AND STAND BACK HERE.

WHY CAN'T I HAVE A RAISE IN MY ALLOWANCE? I CAN HARDLY BUY ANYTHING WITH THREE DOLLARS A WEEK.
YOU CAN BUY EVEN LESS WITH **NOTHING** A WEEK...
MANAGEMENT WANTS TO PLAY HARDBALL, HUH?.. I'M AFRAID THAT LEAVES ME WITH NO OTHER CHOICE.
ON STRIKE

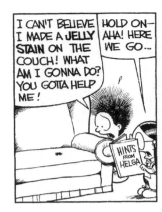

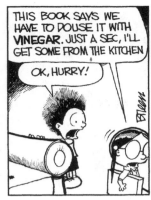

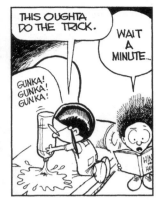

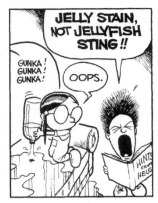

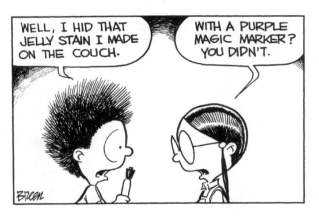

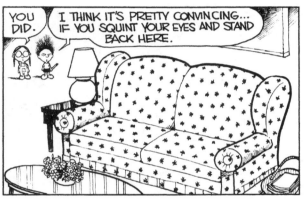

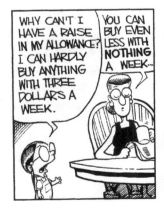

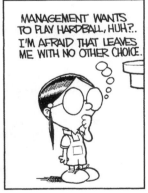

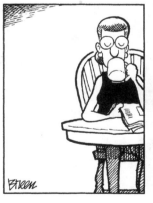

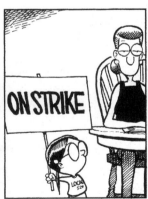

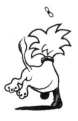

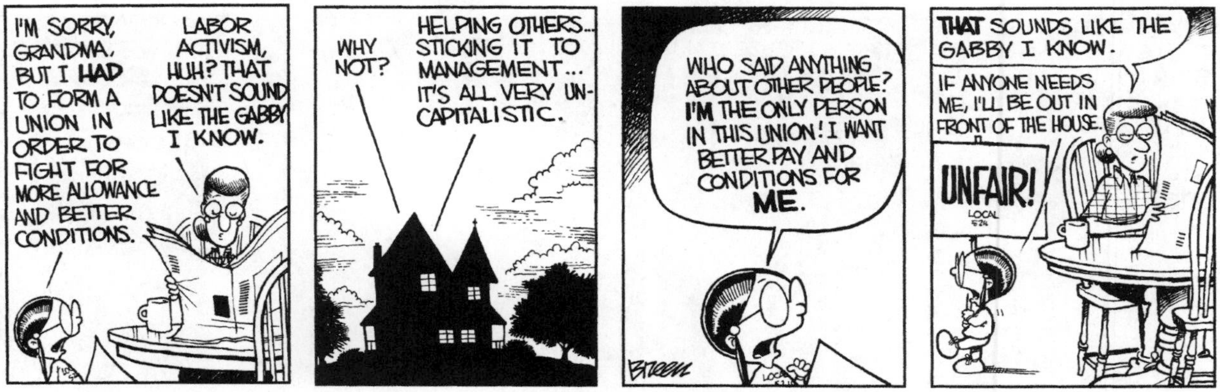
I'M SORRY, GRANDMA, BUT I HAD TO FORM A UNION IN ORDER TO FIGHT FOR MORE ALLOWANCE AND BETTER CONDITIONS.
LABOR ACTIVISM, HUH? THAT DOESN'T SOUND LIKE THE GABBY I KNOW.
WHY NOT?
HELPING OTHERS... STICKING IT TO MANAGEMENT... IT'S ALL VERY UN-CAPITALISTIC.
WHO SAID ANYTHING ABOUT OTHER PEOPLE? I'M THE ONLY PERSON IN THIS UNION! I WANT BETTER PAY AND CONDITIONS FOR ME.
THAT SOUNDS LIKE THE GABBY I KNOW.
IF ANYONE NEEDS ME, I'LL BE OUT IN FRONT OF THE HOUSE.
UNFAIR!

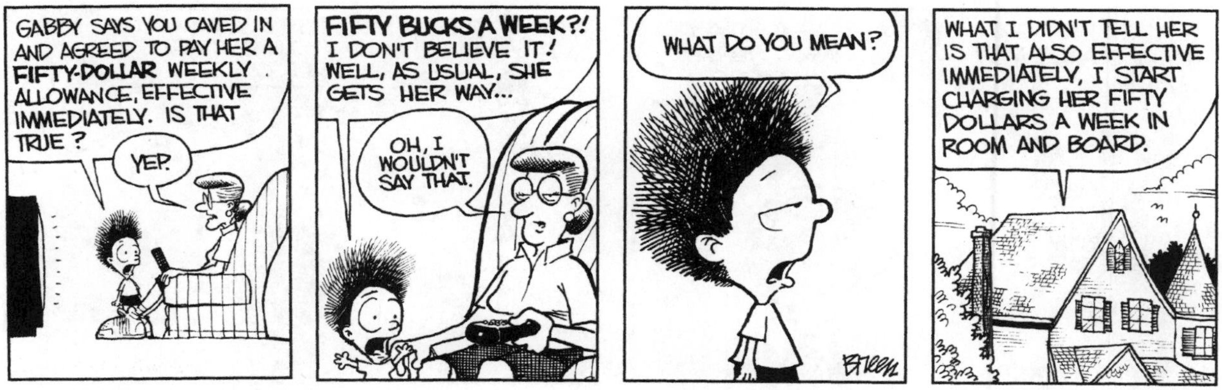
GABBY SAYS YOU CAVED IN AND AGREED TO PAY HER A FIFTY-DOLLAR WEEKLY ALLOWANCE, EFFECTIVE IMMEDIATELY. IS THAT TRUE?
YEP.
FIFTY BUCKS A WEEK?! I DON'T BELIEVE IT! WELL, AS USUAL, SHE GETS HER WAY...
OH, I WOULDN'T SAY THAT.
WHAT DO YOU MEAN?
WHAT I DIDN'T TELL HER IS THAT ALSO EFFECTIVE IMMEDIATELY, I START CHARGING HER FIFTY DOLLARS A WEEK IN ROOM AND BOARD.

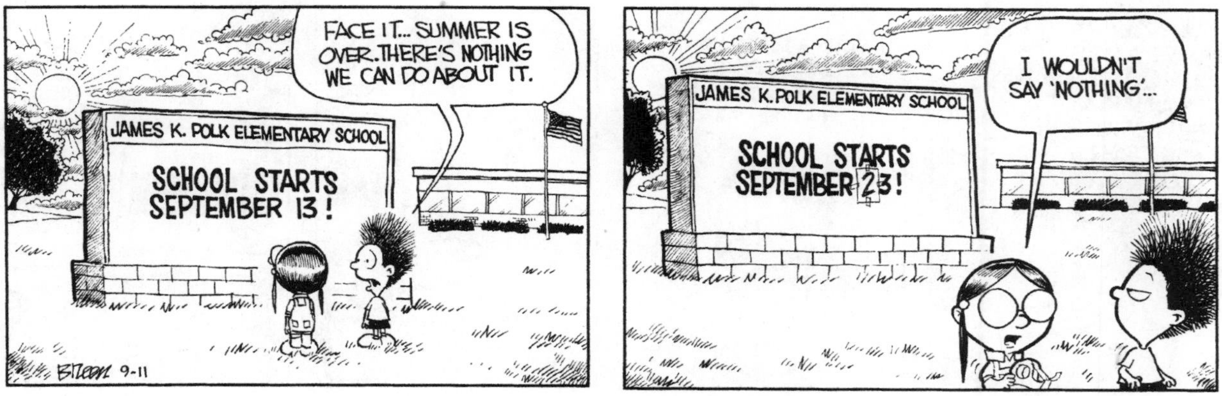
FACE IT... SUMMER IS OVER. THERE'S NOTHING WE CAN DO ABOUT IT.
JAMES K. POLK ELEMENTARY SCHOOL
SCHOOL STARTS SEPTEMBER 13!
9-11
I WOULDN'T SAY 'NOTHING'...
JAMES K. POLK ELEMENTARY SCHOOL
SCHOOL STARTS SEPTEMBER 23!

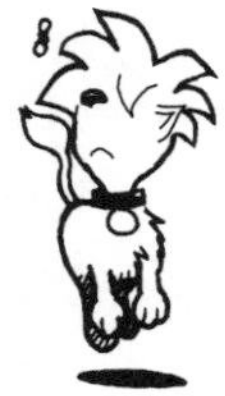

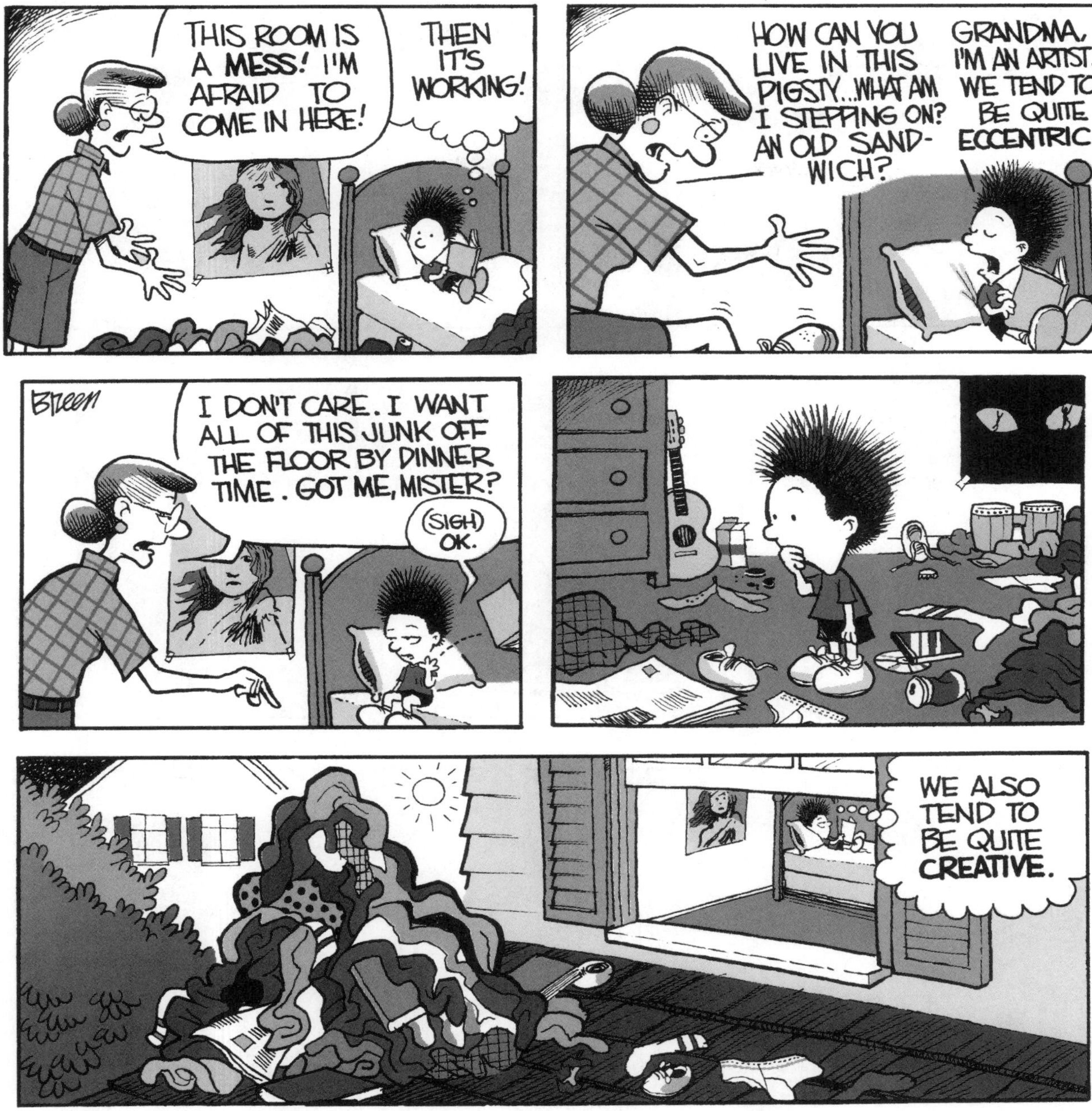
THIS ROOM IS A MESS! I'M AFRAID TO COME IN HERE!
THEN IT'S WORKING!
HOW CAN YOU LIVE IN THIS PIGSTY...WHAT AM I STEPPING ON? AN OLD SAND-WICH?
GRANDMA, I'M AN ARTIST. WE TEND TO BE QUITE ECCENTRIC.
BREEN
I DON'T CARE. I WANT ALL OF THIS JUNK OFF THE FLOOR BY DINNER TIME. GOT ME, MISTER?
(SIGH) OK.
WE ALSO TEND TO BE QUITE CREATIVE.

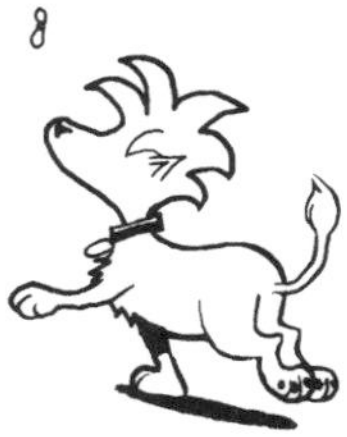
8

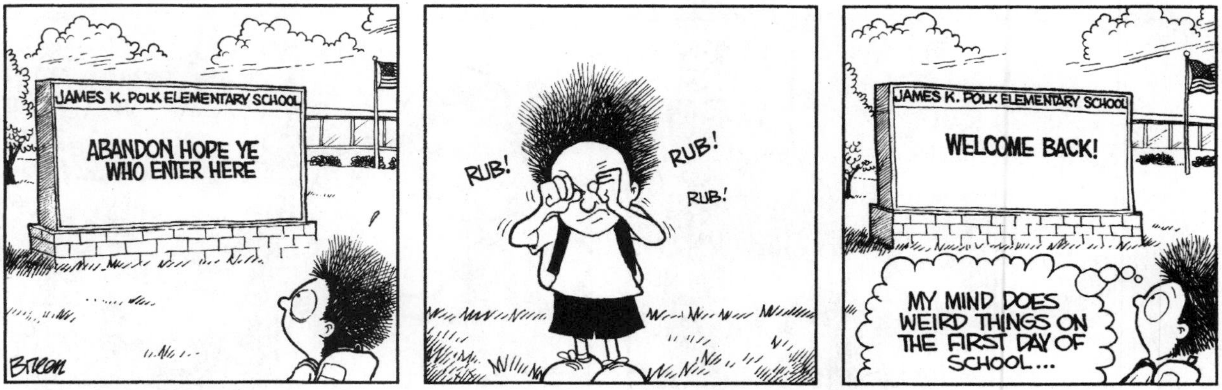
JAMES K. POLK ELEMENTARY SCHOOL
ABANDON HOPE YE WHO ENTER HERE
RUB!
RUB!
RUB!
JAMES K. POLK ELEMENTARY SCHOOL
WELCOME BACK!
MY MIND DOES WEIRD THINGS ON THE FIRST DAY OF SCHOOL...

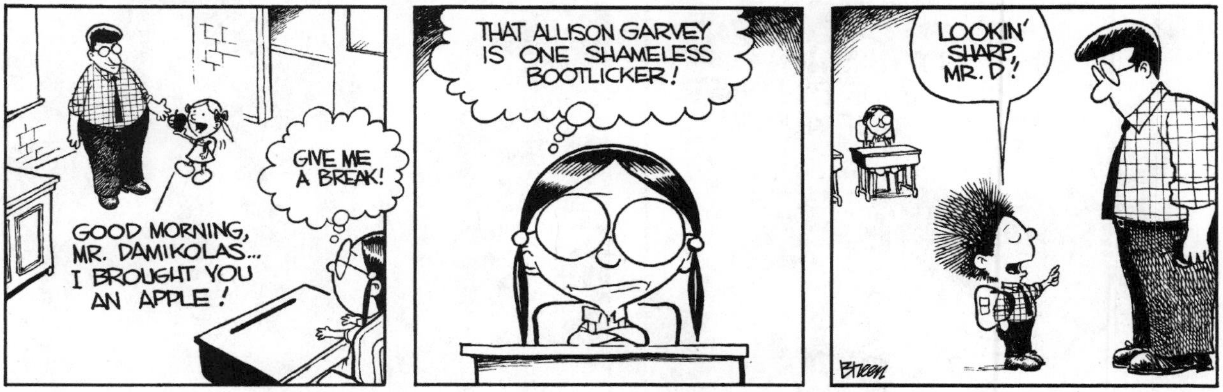
GOOD MORNING, MR. DAMIKOLAS... I BROUGHT YOU AN APPLE!
GIVE ME A BREAK!
THAT ALLISON GARVEY IS ONE SHAMELESS BOOTLICKER!
LOOKIN' SHARP, MR. D!

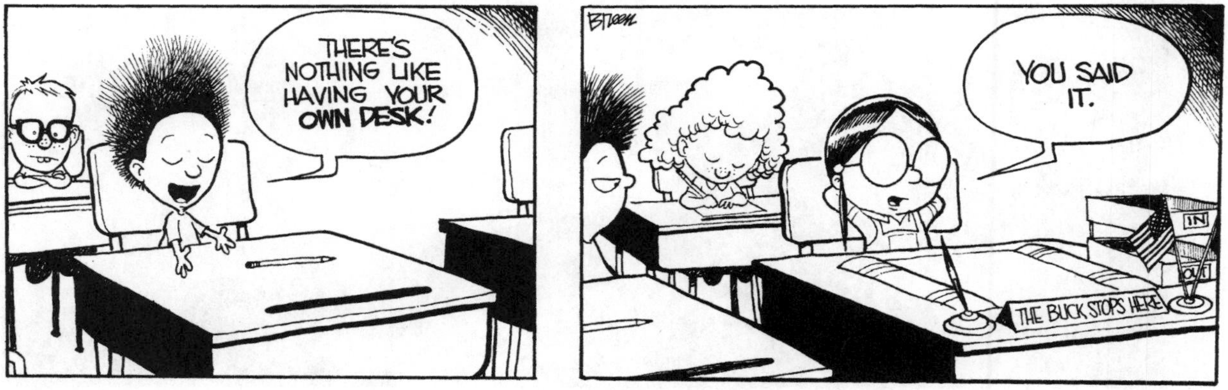
THERE'S NOTHING LIKE HAVING YOUR **OWN DESK**!
YOU SAID IT.
IN
OUT
THE BUCK STOPS HERE

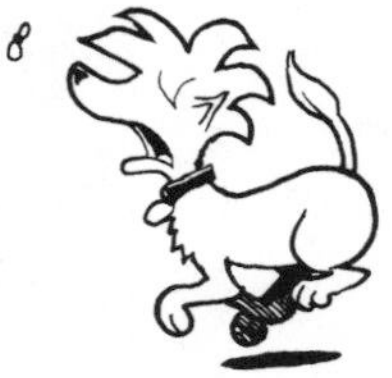

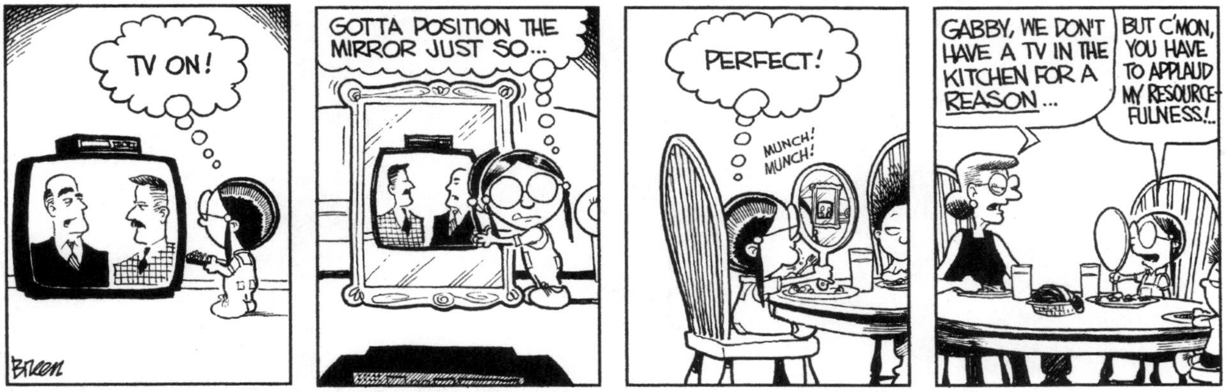
TV ON!
GOTTA POSITION THE MIRROR JUST SO...
PERFECT!
MUNCH! MUNCH!
GABBY, WE DON'T HAVE A TV IN THE KITCHEN FOR A REASON...
BUT C'MON, YOU HAVE TO APPLAUD MY RESOURCE-FULNESS!..

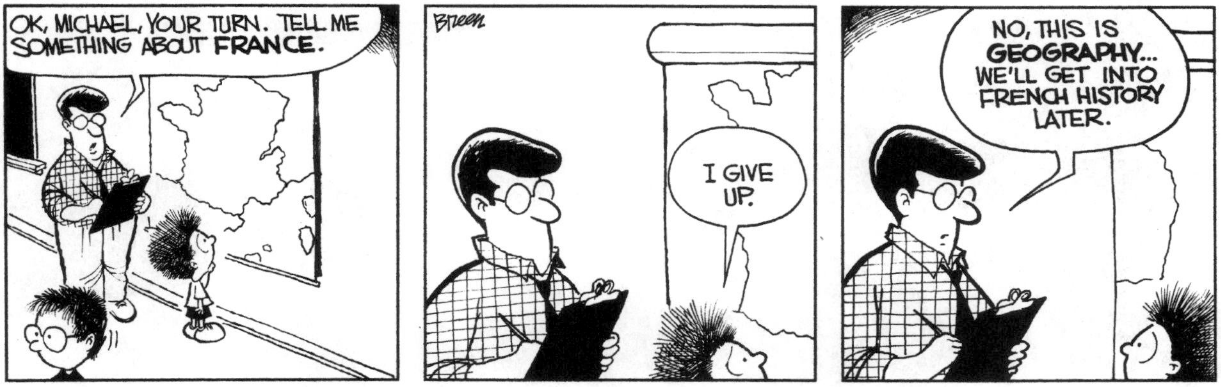
OK, MICHAEL, YOUR TURN. TELL ME SOMETHING ABOUT FRANCE.
I GIVE UP.
NO, THIS IS GEOGRAPHY... WE'LL GET INTO FRENCH HISTORY LATER.

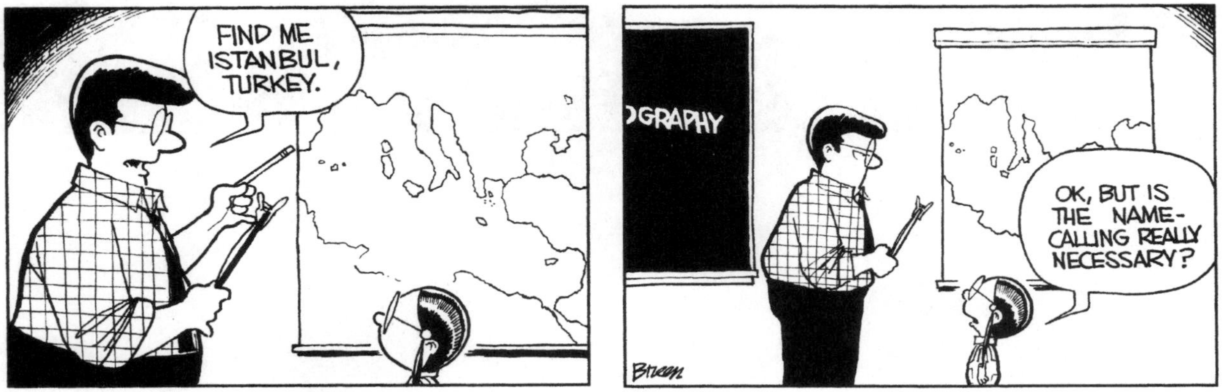
FIND ME ISTANBUL, TURKEY.
OGRAPHY
OK, BUT IS THE NAME-CALLING REALLY NECESSARY?

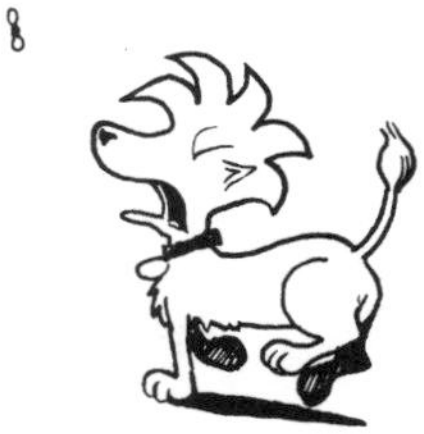

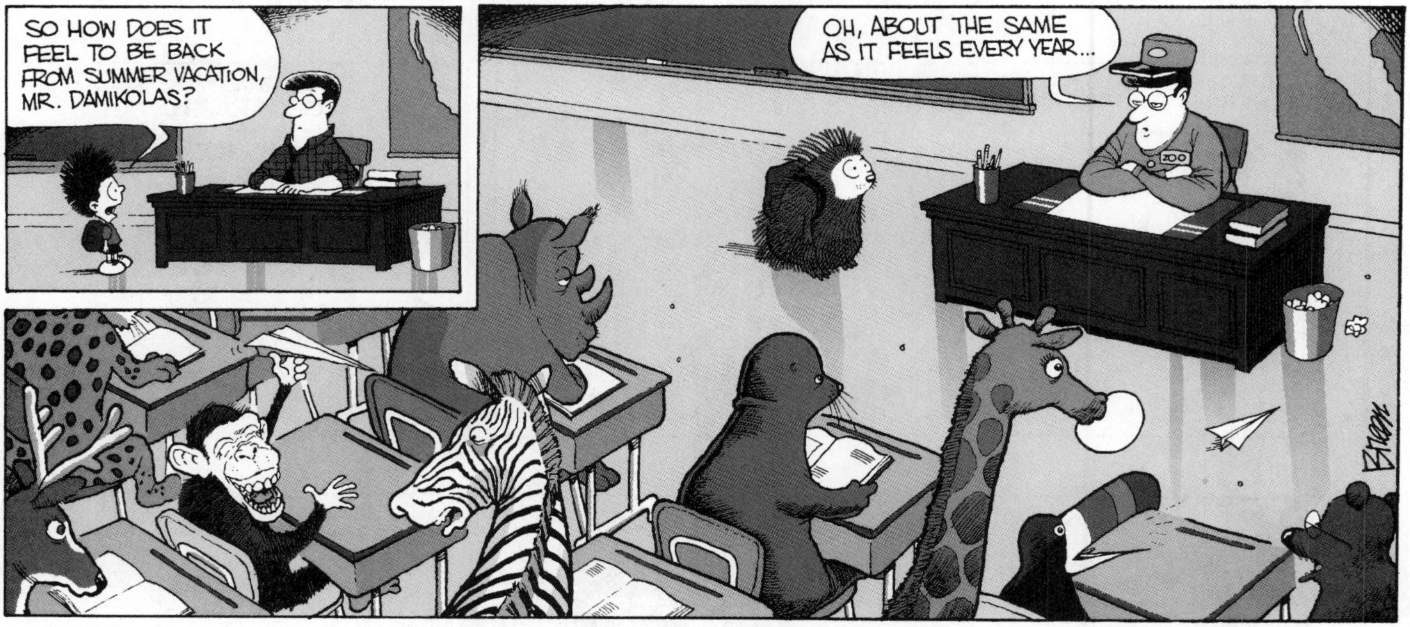
SO HOW DOES IT FEEL TO BE BACK FROM SUMMER VACATION, MR. DAMIKOLAS?
OH, ABOUT THE SAME AS IT FEELS EVERY YEAR...
ZOO

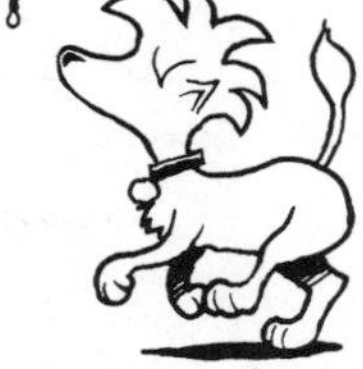

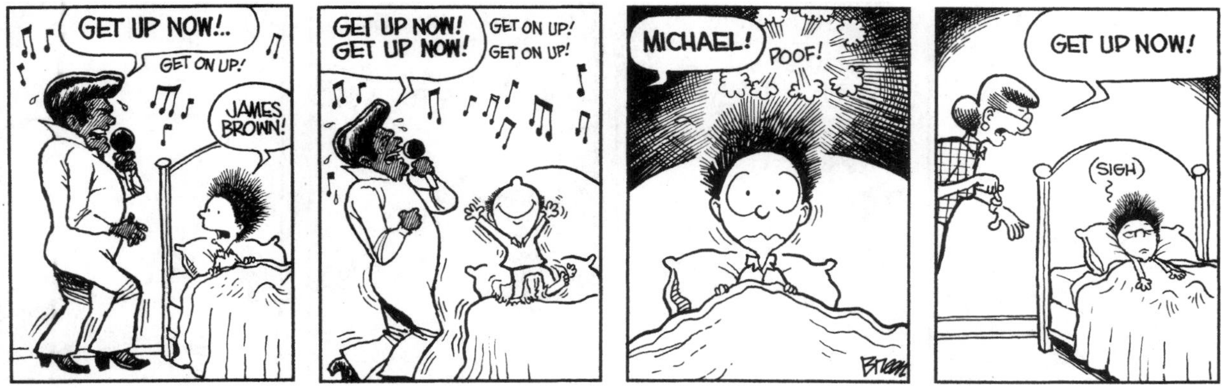
GET UP NOW!..
GET ON UP!
JAMES BROWN!
GET UP NOW!
GET UP NOW!
GET ON UP!
GET ON UP!
MICHAEL!
POOF!
GET UP NOW!
(SIGH)

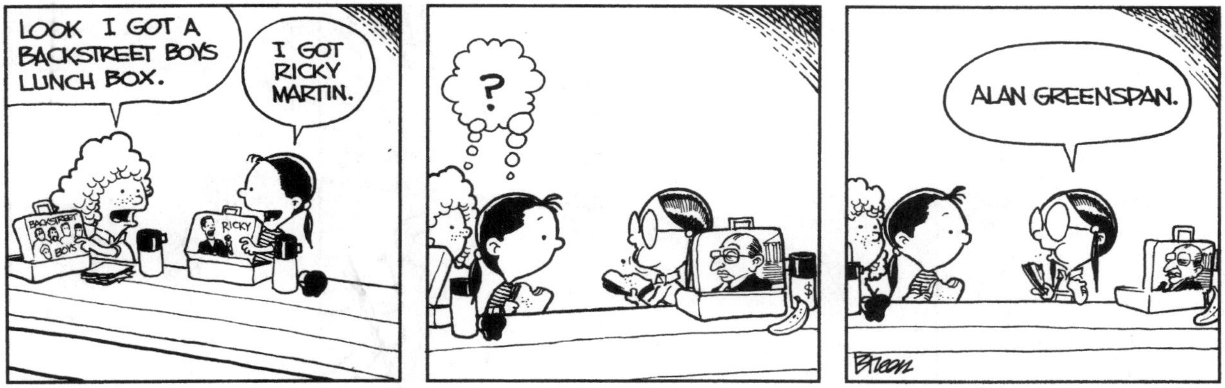
LOOK I GOT A BACKSTREET BOYS LUNCH BOX.
I GOT RICKY MARTIN.
?
ALAN GREENSPAN.

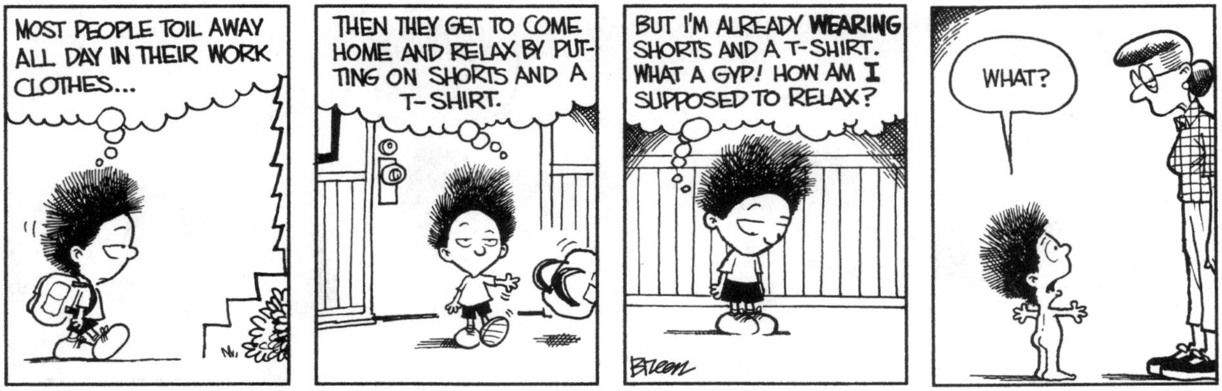
MOST PEOPLE TOIL AWAY ALL DAY IN THEIR WORK CLOTHES...
THEN THEY GET TO COME HOME AND RELAX BY PUTTING ON SHORTS AND A T-SHIRT.
BUT I'M ALREADY WEARING SHORTS AND A T-SHIRT. WHAT A GYP! HOW AM I SUPPOSED TO RELAX?
WHAT?

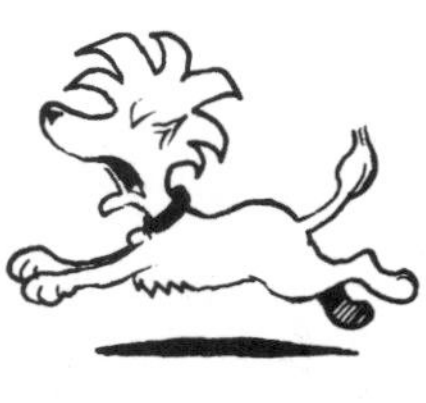

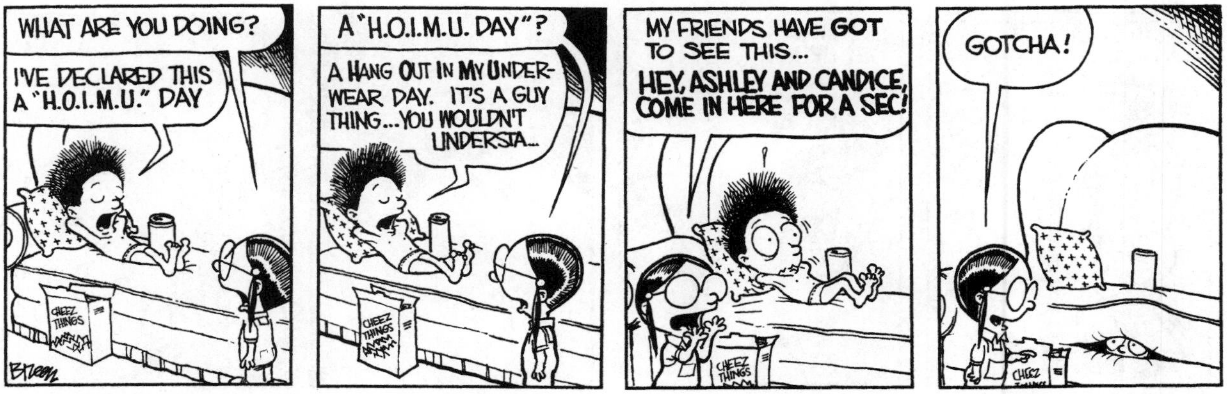
WHAT ARE YOU DOING?
I'VE DECLARED THIS A "H.O.I.M.U." DAY
A "H.O.I.M.U. DAY"?
A HANG OUT IN MY UNDERWEAR DAY. IT'S A GUY THING...YOU WOULDN'T UNDERSTA...
MY FRIENDS HAVE GOT TO SEE THIS...
HEY, ASHLEY AND CANDICE, COME IN HERE FOR A SEC!
!
GOTCHA!
CHEEZ THINGS

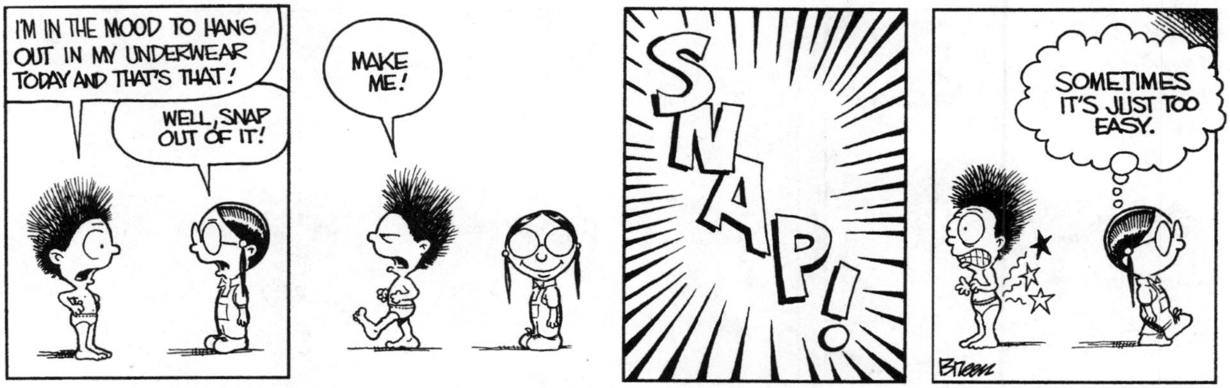
I'M IN THE MOOD TO HANG OUT IN MY UNDERWEAR TODAY AND THAT'S THAT!
WELL, SNAP OUT OF IT!
MAKE ME!
SNAP!
SOMETIMES IT'S JUST TOO EASY.

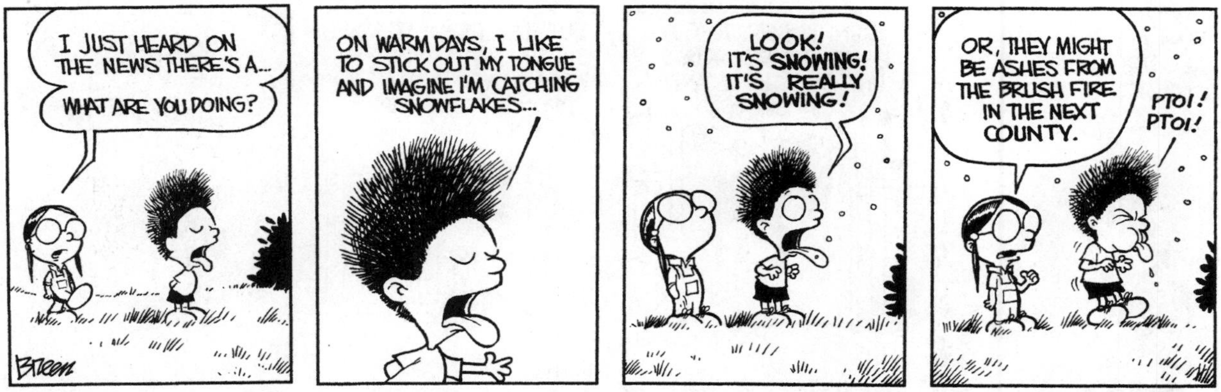
I JUST HEARD ON THE NEWS THERE'S A...
WHAT ARE YOU DOING?
ON WARM DAYS, I LIKE TO STICK OUT MY TONGUE AND IMAGINE I'M CATCHING SNOWFLAKES...
LOOK! IT'S SNOWING! IT'S REALLY SNOWING!
OR, THEY MIGHT BE ASHES FROM THE BRUSH FIRE IN THE NEXT COUNTY.
PTOI! PTOI!

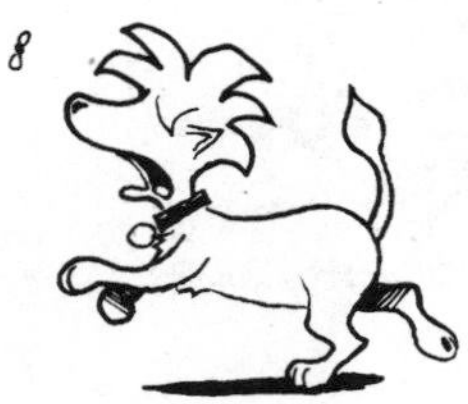

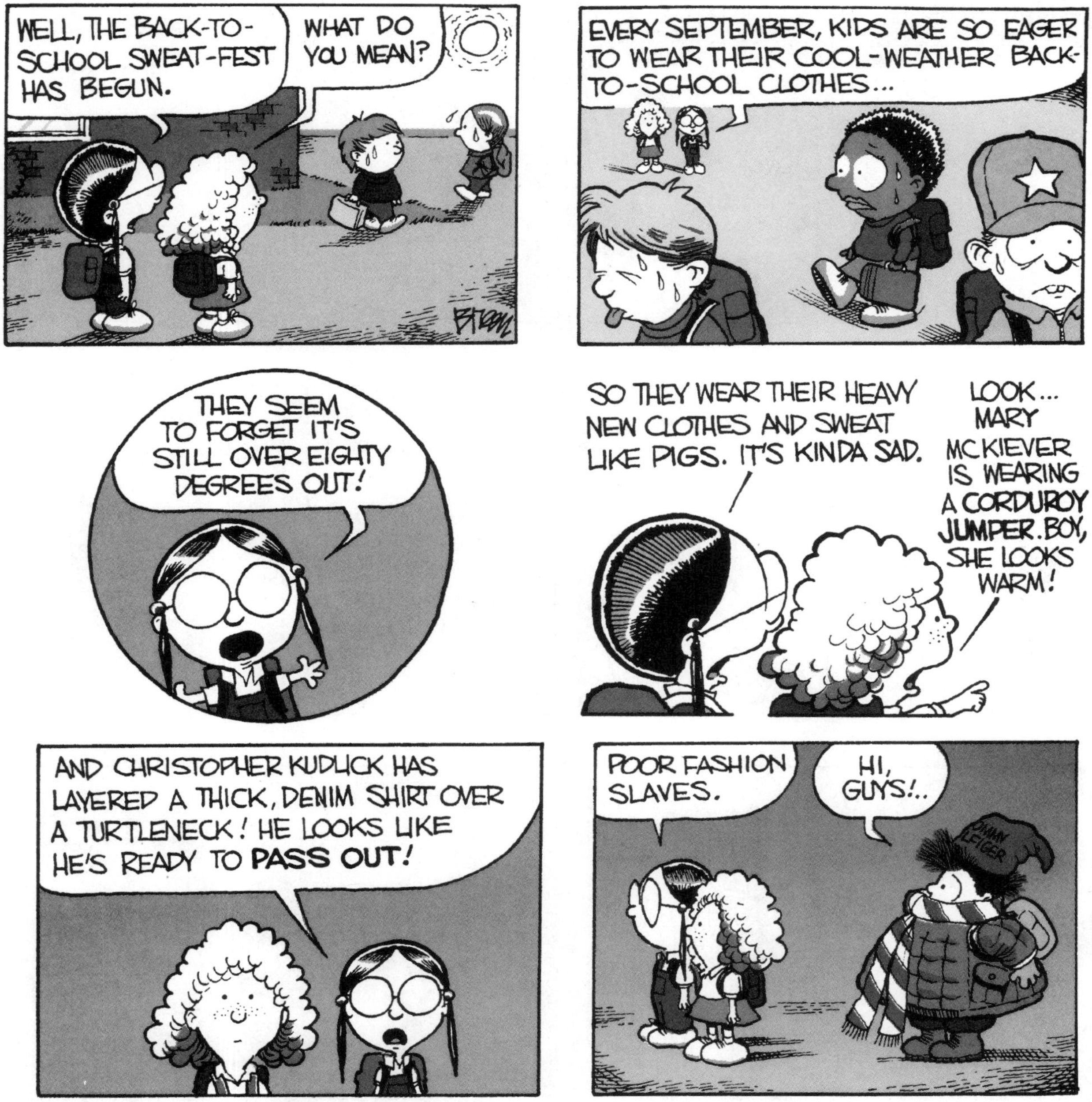
WELL, THE BACK-TO-SCHOOL SWEAT-FEST HAS BEGUN.
WHAT DO YOU MEAN?
EVERY SEPTEMBER, KIDS ARE SO EAGER TO WEAR THEIR COOL-WEATHER BACK-TO-SCHOOL CLOTHES...
THEY SEEM TO FORGET IT'S STILL OVER EIGHTY DEGREES OUT!
SO THEY WEAR THEIR HEAVY NEW CLOTHES AND SWEAT LIKE PIGS. IT'S KINDA SAD.
LOOK... MARY MCKIEVER IS WEARING A CORDUROY JUMPER. BOY, SHE LOOKS WARM!
AND CHRISTOPHER KUDLICK HAS LAYERED A THICK, DENIM SHIRT OVER A TURTLENECK! HE LOOKS LIKE HE'S READY TO PASS OUT!
POOR FASHION SLAVES.
HI, GUYS!..

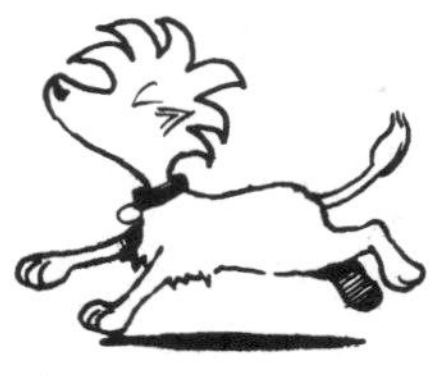

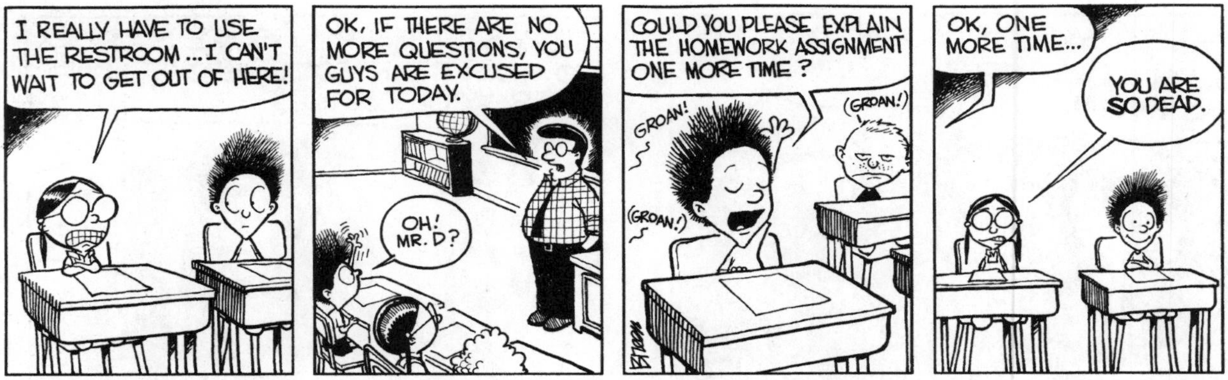

I REALLY HAVE TO USE THE RESTROOM ...I CAN'T WAIT TO GET OUT OF HERE!
OK, IF THERE ARE NO MORE QUESTIONS, YOU GUYS ARE EXCUSED FOR TODAY.
OH! MR. D?
COULD YOU PLEASE EXPLAIN THE HOMEWORK ASSIGNMENT ONE MORE TIME ?
GROAN!
(GROAN!)
(GROAN!)
OK, ONE MORE TIME...
YOU ARE SO DEAD.

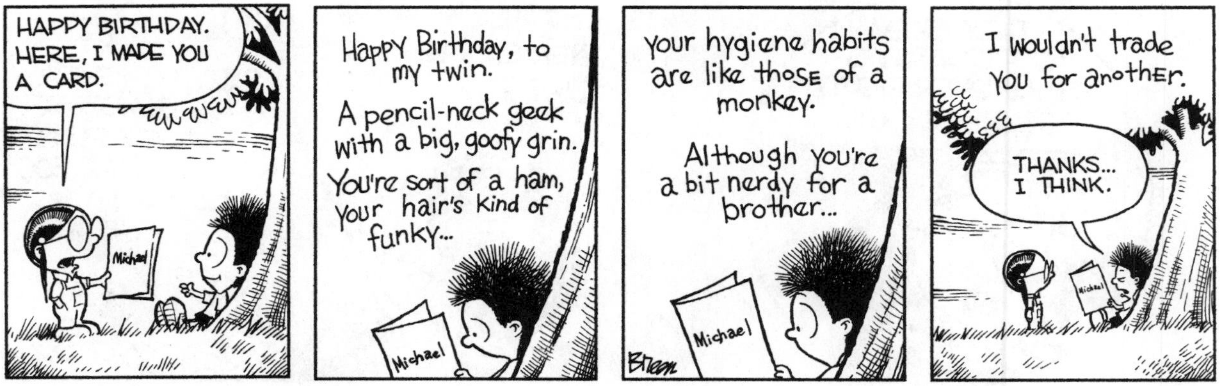

HAPPY BIRTHDAY. HERE, I MADE YOU A CARD.
Michael
Happy Birthday, to my twin.
A pencil-neck geek with a big, goofy grin.
You're sort of a ham, your hair's kind of funky...
Michael
Your hygiene habits are like those of a monkey.
Although you're a bit nerdy for a brother...
Michael
I wouldn't trade you for another.
THANKS... I THINK.
Michael

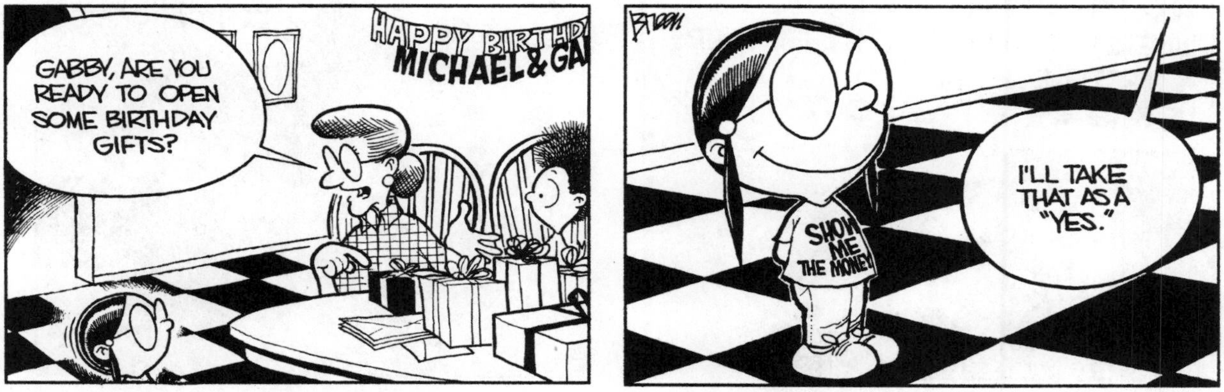

HAPPY BIRTHD
MICHAEL&GA
GABBY, ARE YOU READY TO OPEN SOME BIRTHDAY GIFTS?
SHOW ME THE MONEY
I'LL TAKE THAT AS A "YES."

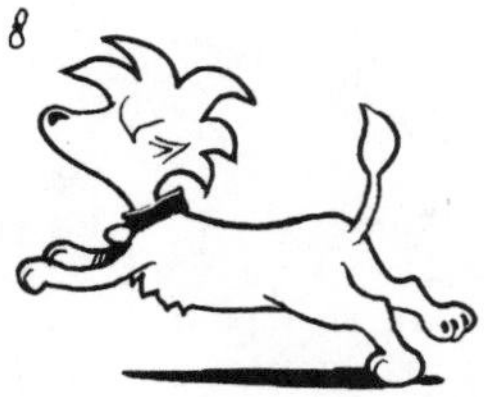

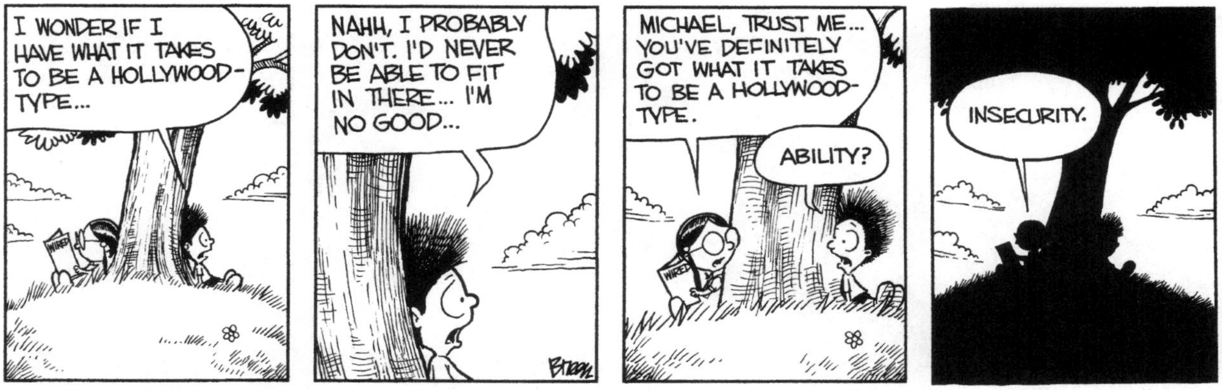
I WONDER IF I HAVE WHAT IT TAKES TO BE A HOLLYWOOD-TYPE...
NAHH, I PROBABLY DON'T. I'D NEVER BE ABLE TO FIT IN THERE... I'M NO GOOD...
MICHAEL, TRUST ME... YOU'VE DEFINITELY GOT WHAT IT TAKES TO BE A HOLLYWOOD-TYPE.
ABILITY?
INSECURITY.

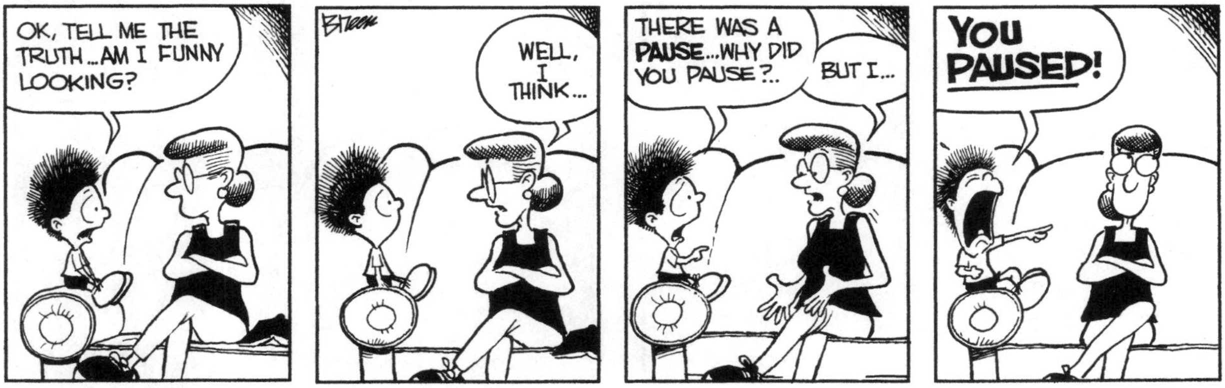
OK, TELL ME THE TRUTH...AM I FUNNY LOOKING?
WELL, I THINK...
THERE WAS A **PAUSE**...WHY DID YOU PAUSE?..
BUT I...
YOU PAUSED!

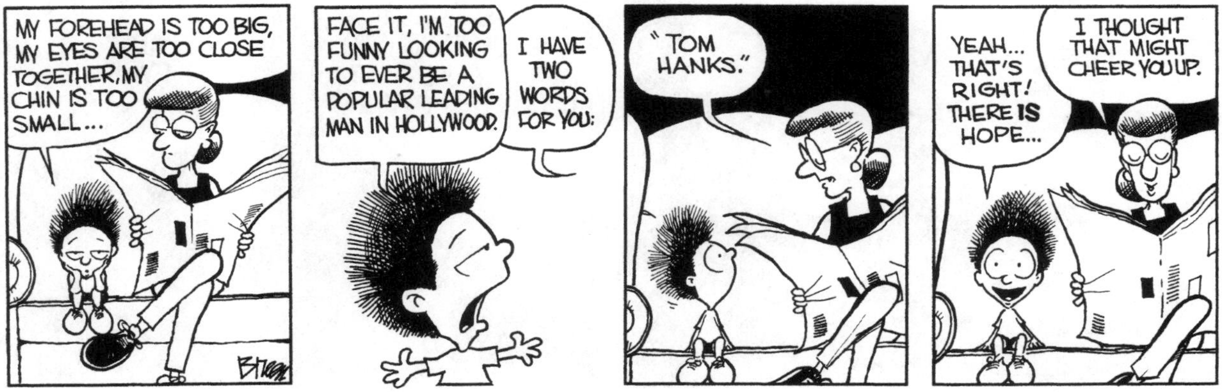
MY FOREHEAD IS TOO BIG, MY EYES ARE TOO CLOSE TOGETHER, MY CHIN IS TOO SMALL...
FACE IT, I'M TOO FUNNY LOOKING TO EVER BE A POPULAR LEADING MAN IN HOLLYWOOD.
I HAVE TWO WORDS FOR YOU:
"TOM HANKS."
YEAH... THAT'S RIGHT! THERE **IS** HOPE...
I THOUGHT THAT MIGHT CHEER YOU UP.

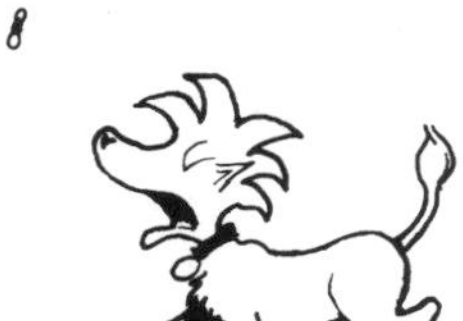

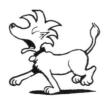

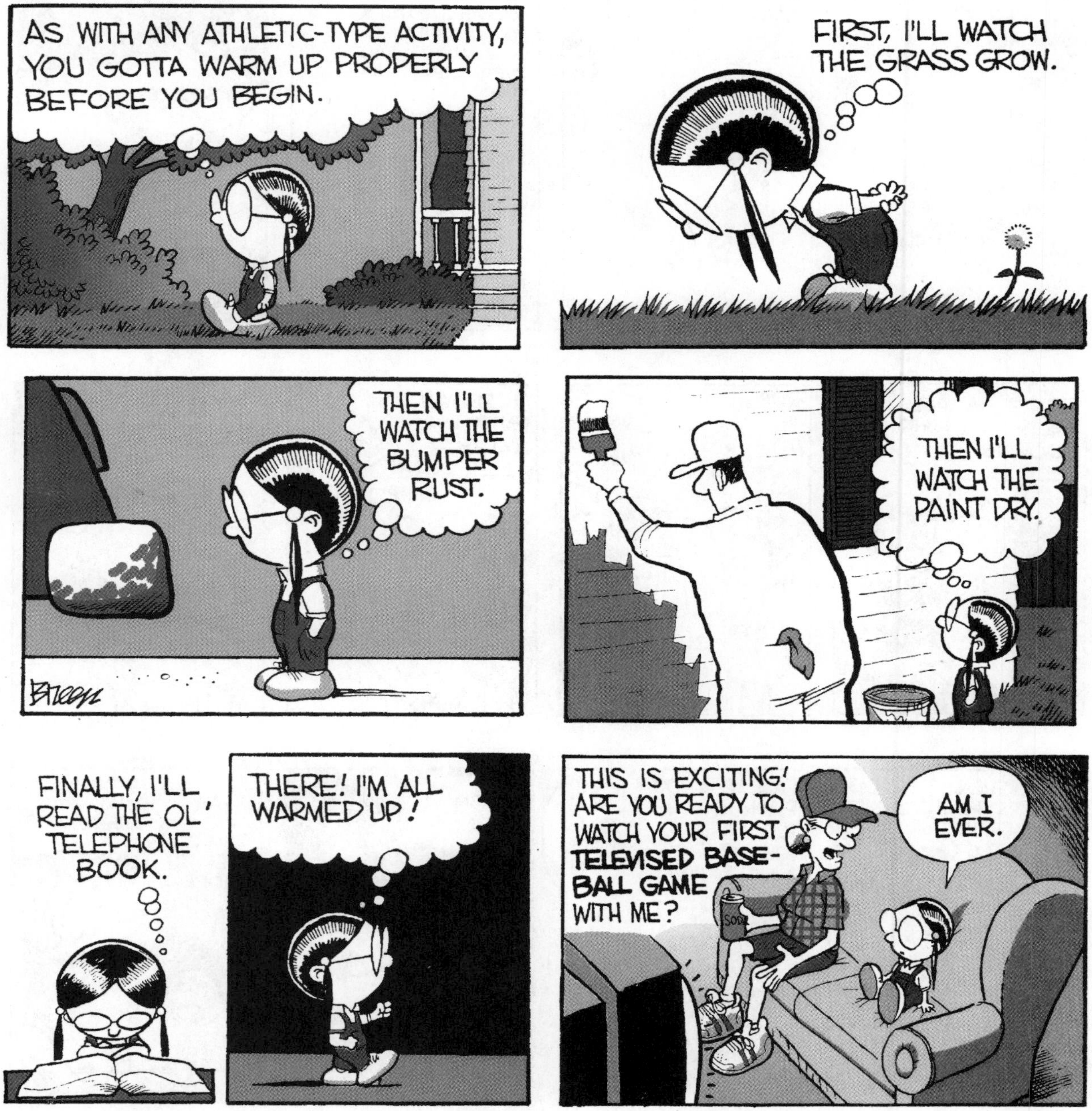
AS WITH ANY ATHLETIC-TYPE ACTIVITY, YOU GOTTA WARM UP PROPERLY BEFORE YOU BEGIN.
FIRST, I'LL WATCH THE GRASS GROW.
THEN I'LL WATCH THE BUMPER RUST.
THEN I'LL WATCH THE PAINT DRY.
FINALLY, I'LL READ THE OL' TELEPHONE BOOK.
THERE! I'M ALL WARMED UP!
THIS IS EXCITING! ARE YOU READY TO WATCH YOUR FIRST **TELEVISED BASE-BALL GAME** WITH ME?
AM I EVER.
SODA

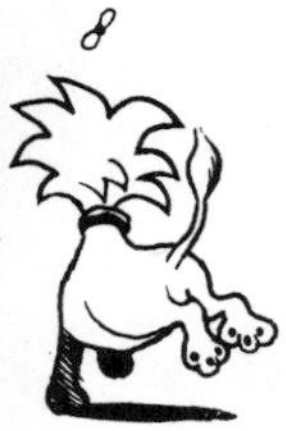

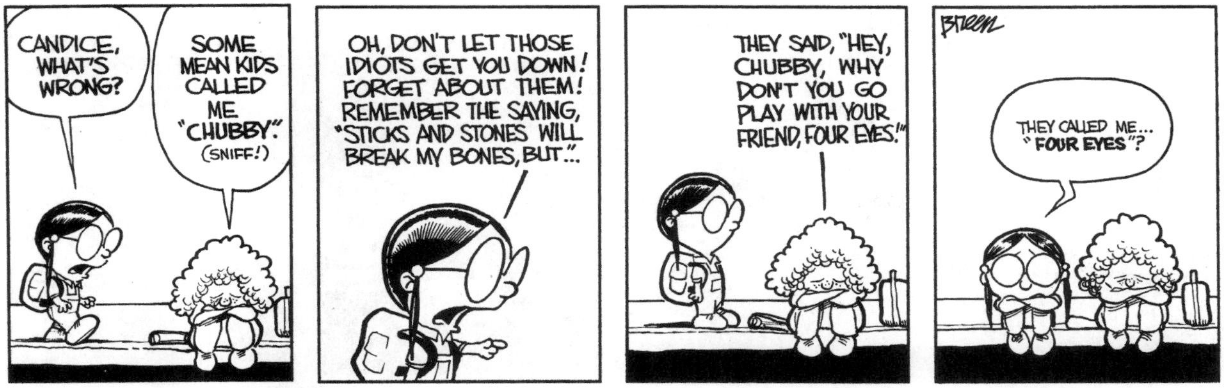
CANDICE, WHAT'S WRONG?
SOME MEAN KIDS CALLED ME "CHUBBY." (SNIFF!)
OH, DON'T LET THOSE IDIOTS GET YOU DOWN! FORGET ABOUT THEM! REMEMBER THE SAYING, "STICKS AND STONES WILL BREAK MY BONES, BUT..."
THEY SAID, "HEY, CHUBBY, WHY DON'T YOU GO PLAY WITH YOUR FRIEND, FOUR EYES!"
THEY CALLED ME... "FOUR EYES"?

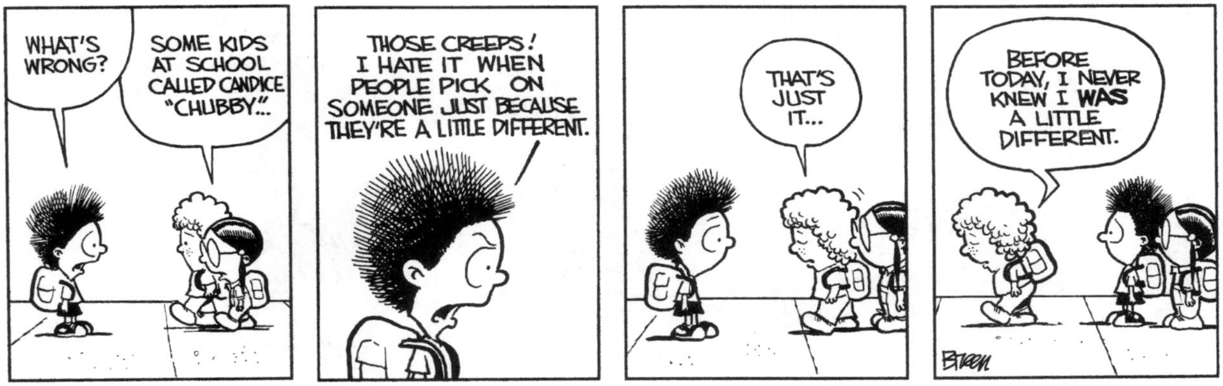
WHAT'S WRONG?
SOME KIDS AT SCHOOL CALLED CANDICE "CHUBBY."
THOSE CREEPS! I HATE IT WHEN PEOPLE PICK ON SOMEONE JUST BECAUSE THEY'RE A LITTLE DIFFERENT.
THAT'S JUST IT...
BEFORE TODAY, I NEVER KNEW I WAS A LITTLE DIFFERENT.

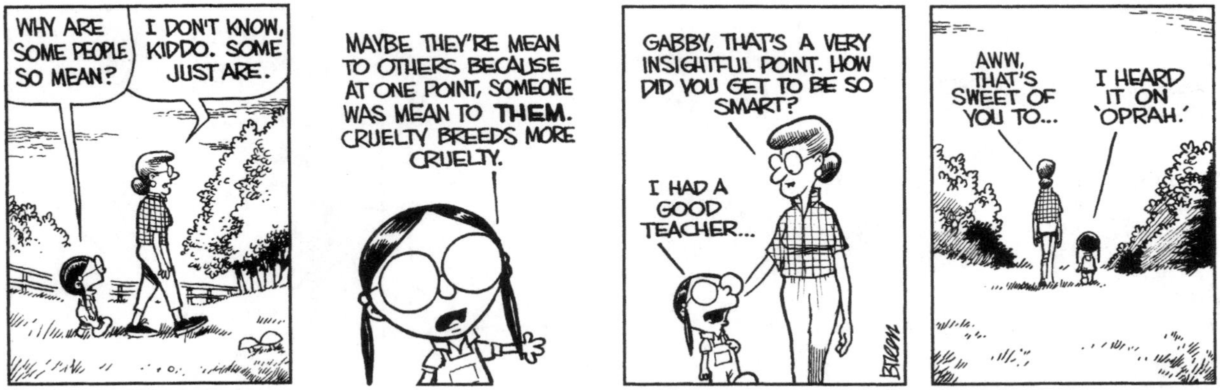
WHY ARE SOME PEOPLE SO MEAN?
I DON'T KNOW, KIDDO. SOME JUST ARE.
MAYBE THEY'RE MEAN TO OTHERS BECAUSE AT ONE POINT, SOMEONE WAS MEAN TO THEM. CRUELTY BREEDS MORE CRUELTY.
GABBY, THAT'S A VERY INSIGHTFUL POINT. HOW DID YOU GET TO BE SO SMART?
I HAD A GOOD TEACHER...
AWW, THAT'S SWEET OF YOU TO...
I HEARD IT ON 'OPRAH.'

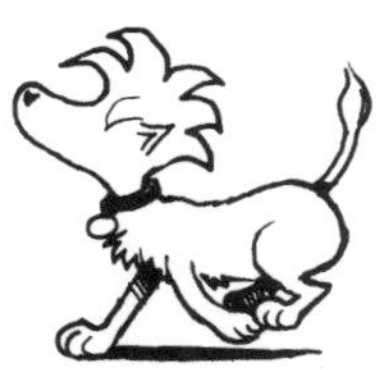

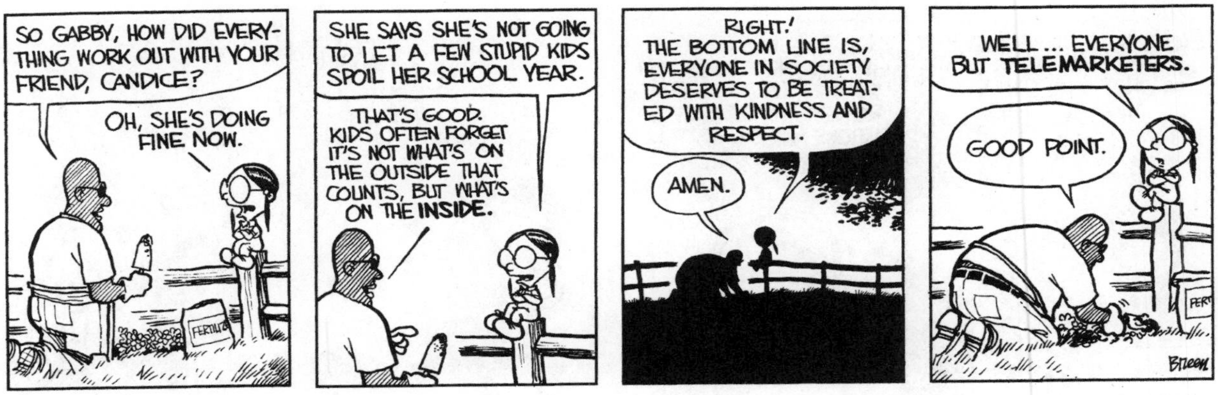
SO GABBY, HOW DID EVERYTHING WORK OUT WITH YOUR FRIEND, CANDICE?
OH, SHE'S DOING FINE NOW.
SHE SAYS SHE'S NOT GOING TO LET A FEW STUPID KIDS SPOIL HER SCHOOL YEAR.
THAT'S GOOD. KIDS OFTEN FORGET IT'S NOT WHAT'S ON THE OUTSIDE THAT COUNTS, BUT WHAT'S ON THE **INSIDE**.
RIGHT! THE BOTTOM LINE IS, EVERYONE IN SOCIETY DESERVES TO BE TREATED WITH KINDNESS AND RESPECT.
AMEN.
WELL ... EVERYONE BUT **TELEMARKETERS**.
GOOD POINT.
FERTILIZ
BREEN

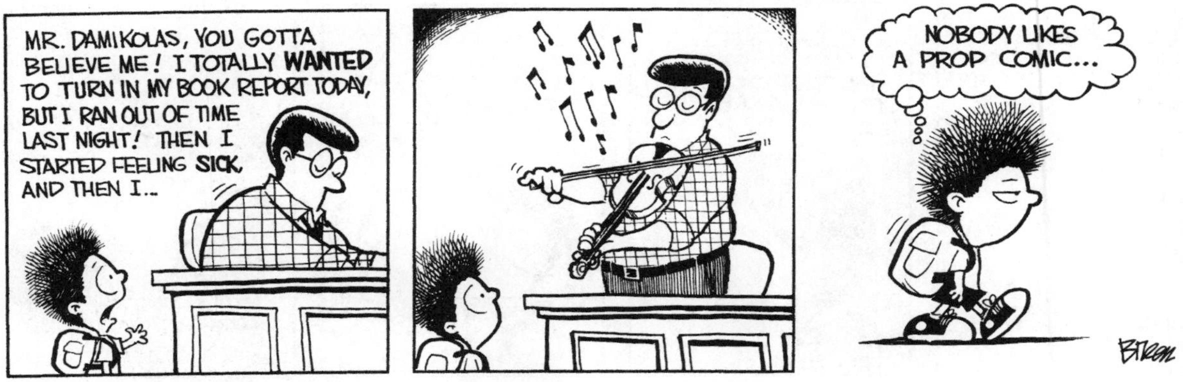
MR. DAMIKOLAS, YOU GOTTA BELIEVE ME! I TOTALLY **WANTED** TO TURN IN MY BOOK REPORT TODAY, BUT I RAN OUT OF TIME LAST NIGHT! THEN I STARTED FEELING **SICK**, AND THEN I...
NOBODY LIKES A PROP COMIC...
BREEN

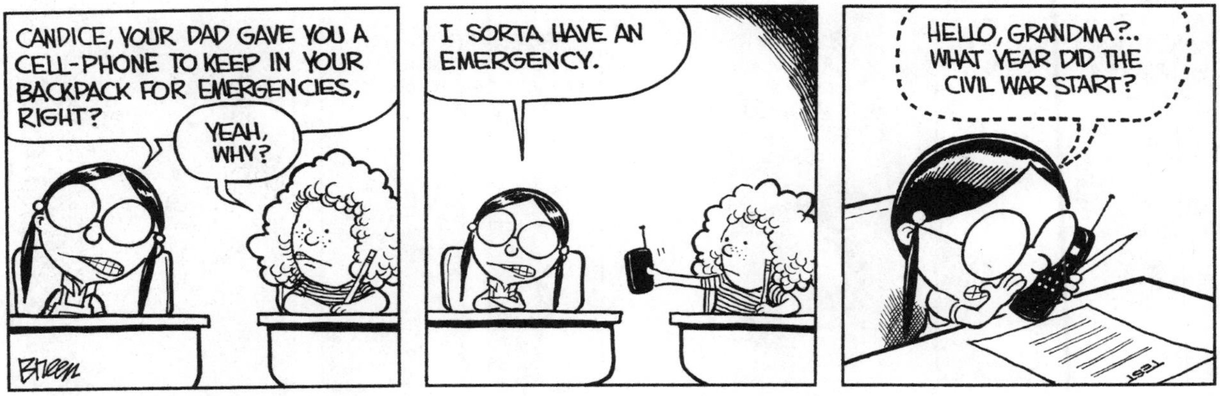
CANDICE, YOUR DAD GAVE YOU A CELL-PHONE TO KEEP IN YOUR BACKPACK FOR EMERGENCIES, RIGHT?
YEAH, WHY?
I SORTA HAVE AN EMERGENCY.
HELLO, GRANDMA?.. WHAT YEAR DID THE CIVIL WAR START?
TEST
BREEN

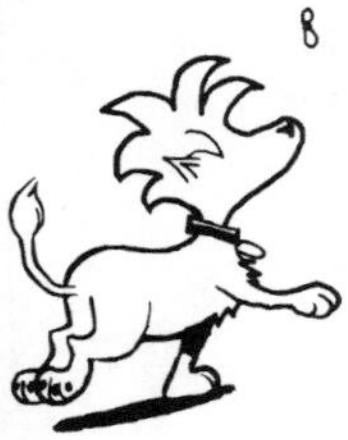

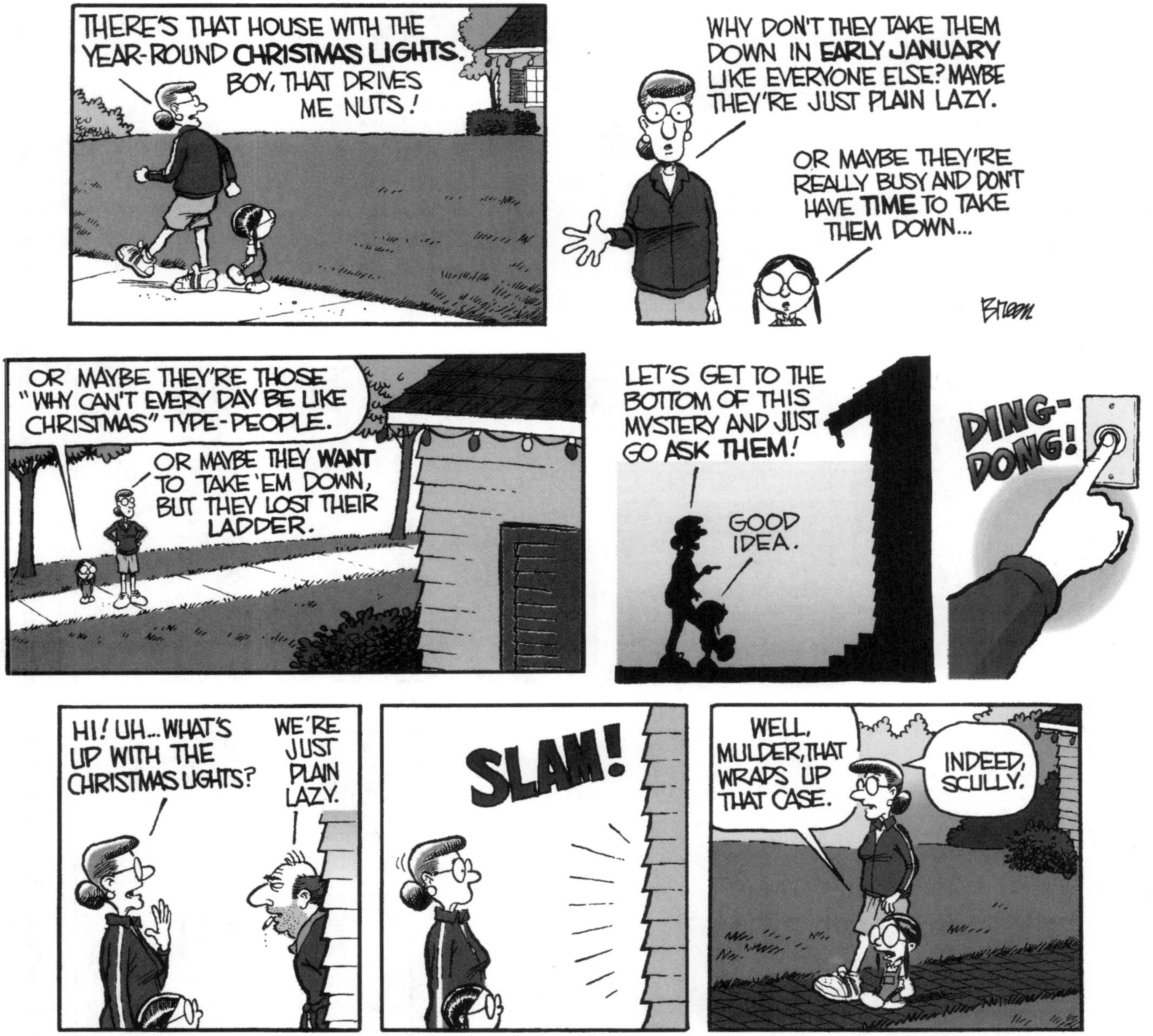
THERE'S THAT HOUSE WITH THE YEAR-ROUND CHRISTMAS LIGHTS.
BOY, THAT DRIVES ME NUTS!
WHY DON'T THEY TAKE THEM DOWN IN EARLY JANUARY LIKE EVERYONE ELSE? MAYBE THEY'RE JUST PLAIN LAZY.
OR MAYBE THEY'RE REALLY BUSY AND DON'T HAVE TIME TO TAKE THEM DOWN...
OR MAYBE THEY'RE THOSE "WHY CAN'T EVERY DAY BE LIKE CHRISTMAS" TYPE-PEOPLE.
OR MAYBE THEY WANT TO TAKE 'EM DOWN, BUT THEY LOST THEIR LADDER.
LET'S GET TO THE BOTTOM OF THIS MYSTERY AND JUST GO ASK THEM!
GOOD IDEA.
DING-DONG!
HI! UH...WHAT'S UP WITH THE CHRISTMAS LIGHTS?
WE'RE JUST PLAIN LAZY.
SLAM!
WELL, MULDER, THAT WRAPS UP THAT CASE.
INDEED, SCULLY.

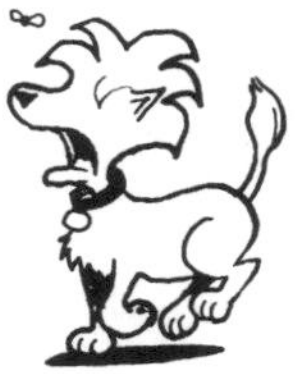

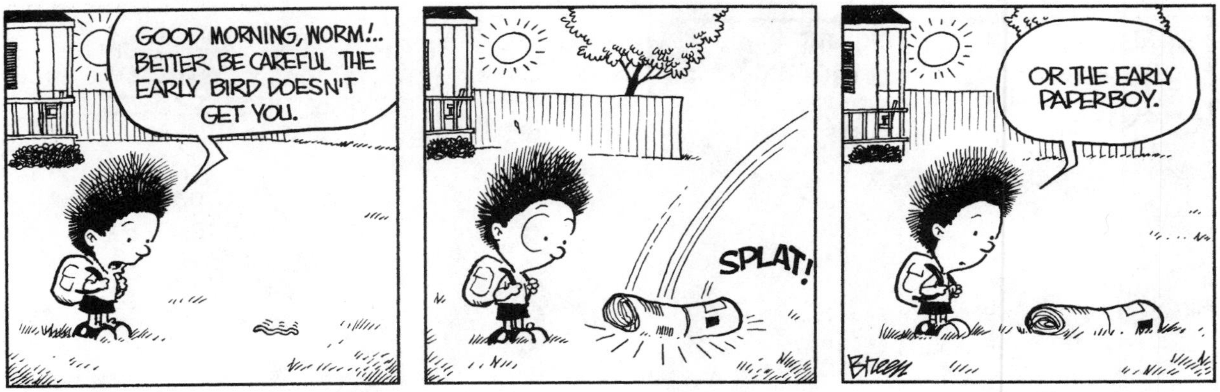
GOOD MORNING, WORM!.. BETTER BE CAREFUL THE EARLY BIRD DOESN'T GET YOU.
SPLAT!
OR THE EARLY PAPERBOY.

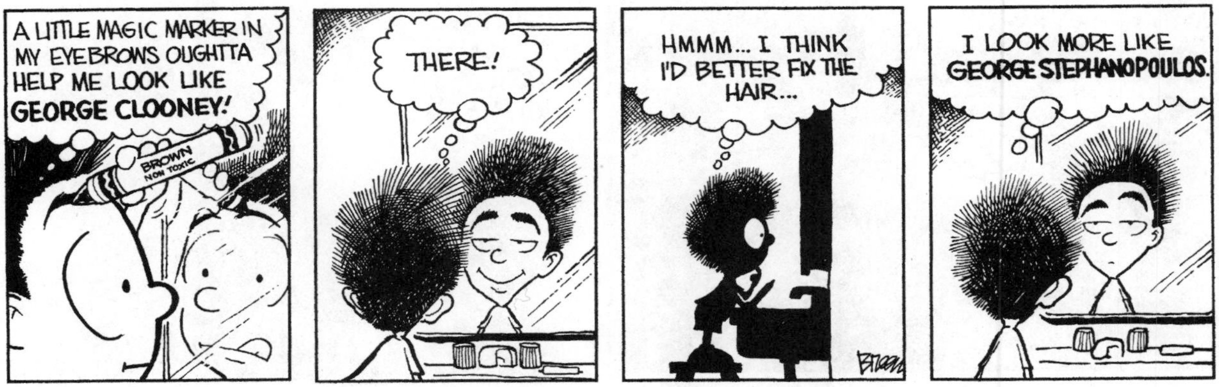
A LITTLE MAGIC MARKER IN MY EYEBROWS OUGHTTA HELP ME LOOK LIKE GEORGE CLOONEY!
BROWN NON TOXIC
THERE!
HMMM... I THINK I'D BETTER FIX THE HAIR...
I LOOK MORE LIKE GEORGE STEPHANOPOULOS.

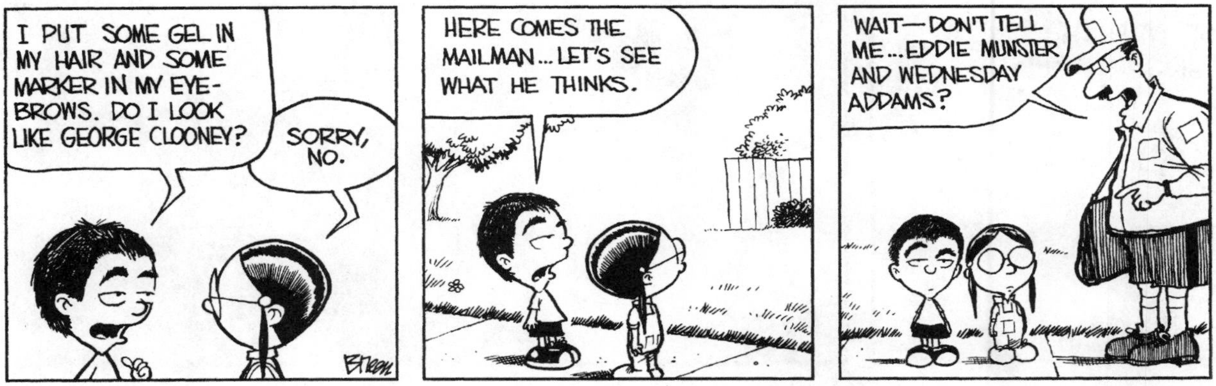
I PUT SOME GEL IN MY HAIR AND SOME MARKER IN MY EYE-BROWS. DO I LOOK LIKE GEORGE CLOONEY?
SORRY, NO.
HERE COMES THE MAILMAN... LET'S SEE WHAT HE THINKS.
WAIT—DON'T TELL ME...EDDIE MUNSTER AND WEDNESDAY ADDAMS?

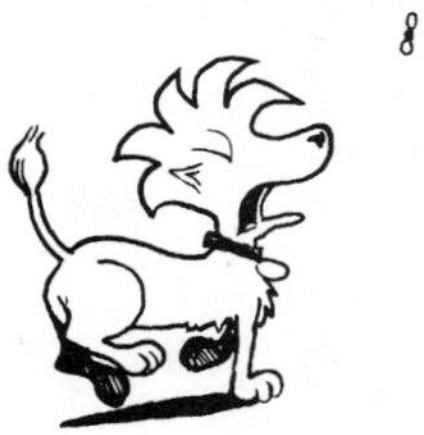

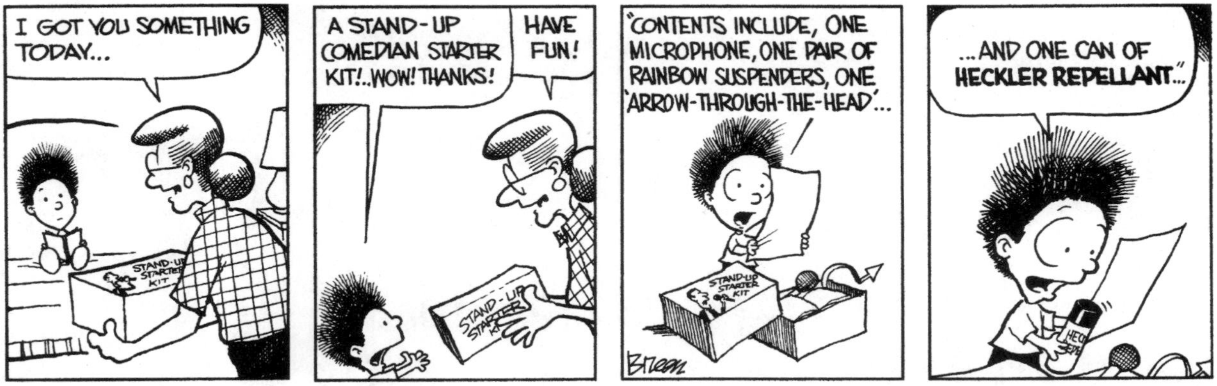
I GOT YOU SOMETHING TODAY...
STAND-UP STARTER KIT
A STAND-UP COMEDIAN STARTER KIT!..WOW! THANKS!
HAVE FUN!
STAND-UP STARTER KIT
"CONTENTS INCLUDE, ONE MICROPHONE, ONE PAIR OF RAINBOW SUSPENDERS, ONE 'ARROW-THROUGH-THE-HEAD'...
STAND-UP STARTER KIT
...AND ONE CAN OF HECKLER REPELLANT."

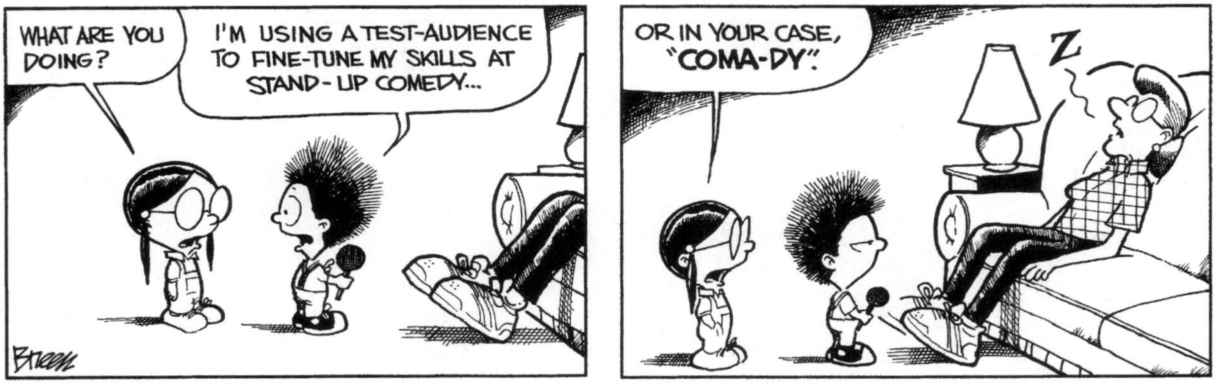
WHAT ARE YOU DOING?
I'M USING A TEST-AUDIENCE TO FINE-TUNE MY SKILLS AT STAND-UP COMEDY...
OR IN YOUR CASE, "COMA-DY."
Z

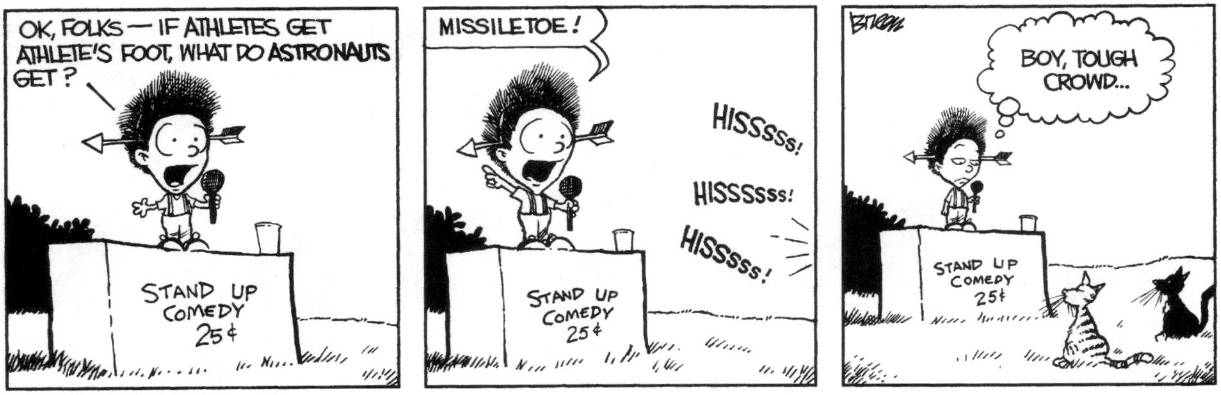
OK, FOLKS — IF ATHLETES GET ATHLETE'S FOOT, WHAT DO ASTRONAUTS GET?
STAND UP COMEDY 25¢
MISSILETOE!
HISSSSS!
HISSSSSS!
HISSSSSS!
STAND UP COMEDY 25¢
BOY, TOUGH CROWD...
STAND UP COMEDY 25¢

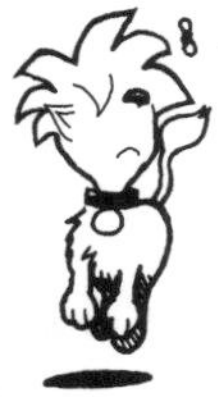

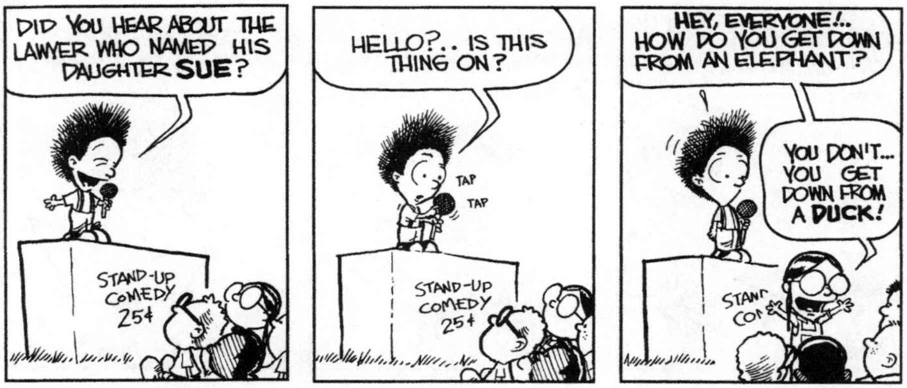
DID YOU HEAR ABOUT THE LAWYER WHO NAMED HIS DAUGHTER SUE?
STAND-UP COMEDY 25¢
HELLO?.. IS THIS THING ON?
TAP
TAP
STAND-UP COMEDY 25¢
HEY, EVERYONE!.. HOW DO YOU GET DOWN FROM AN ELEPHANT?
YOU DON'T... YOU GET DOWN FROM A DUCK!
I WONDER IF THIS EVER HAPPENS TO JERRY SEINFELD.
HA! HA! HA! HA! HA! HA! HA! HA! HA! HA! HA! HA! HA!
BREEN

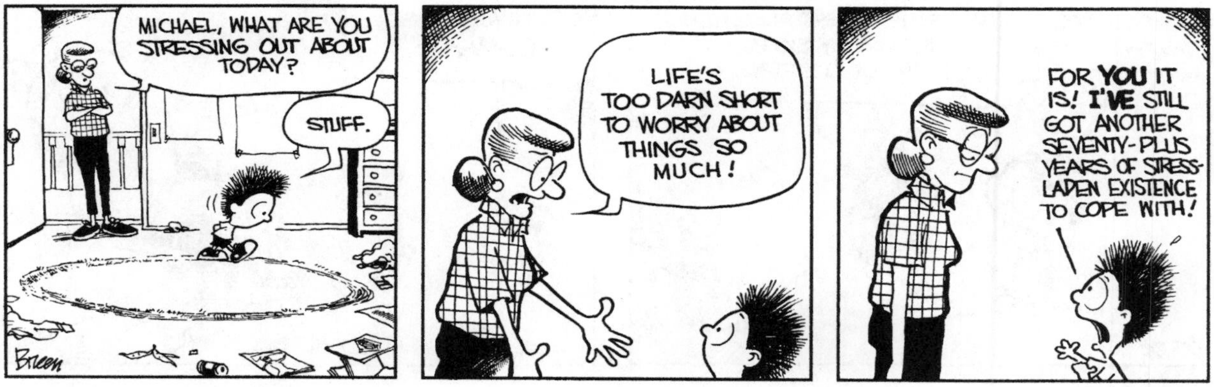
MICHAEL, WHAT ARE YOU STRESSING OUT ABOUT TODAY?
STUFF.
BREEN
LIFE'S TOO DARN SHORT TO WORRY ABOUT THINGS SO MUCH!
FOR YOU IT IS! I'VE STILL GOT ANOTHER SEVENTY-PLUS YEARS OF STRESS-LADEN EXISTENCE TO COPE WITH!

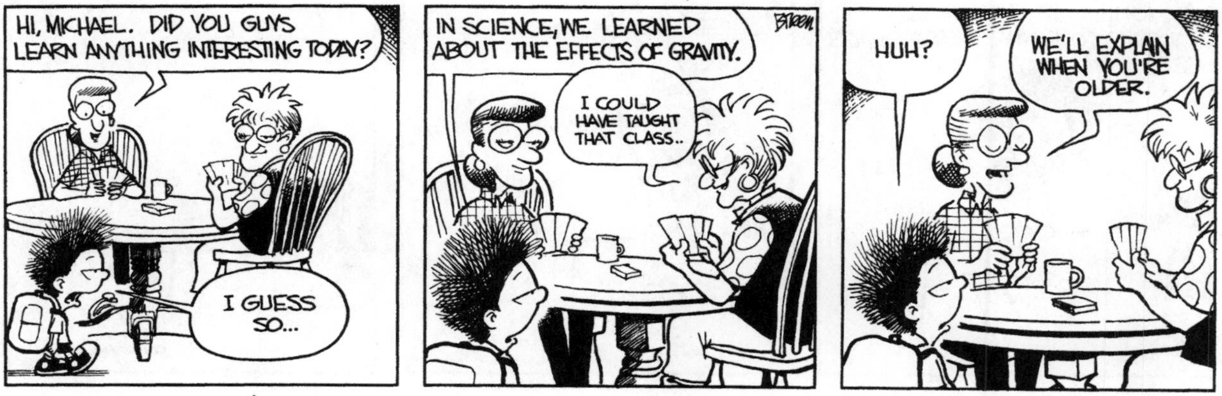
HI, MICHAEL. DID YOU GUYS LEARN ANYTHING INTERESTING TODAY?
I GUESS SO...
IN SCIENCE, WE LEARNED ABOUT THE EFFECTS OF GRAVITY.
BREEN
I COULD HAVE TAUGHT THAT CLASS..
HUH?
WE'LL EXPLAIN WHEN YOU'RE OLDER.

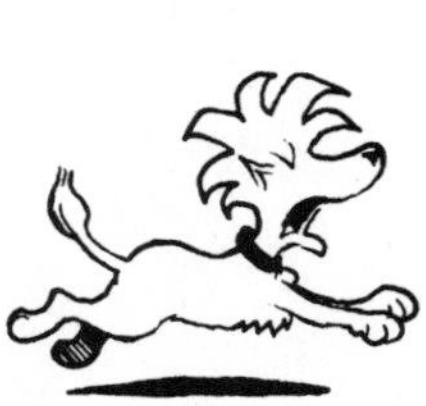

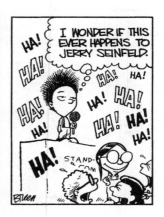

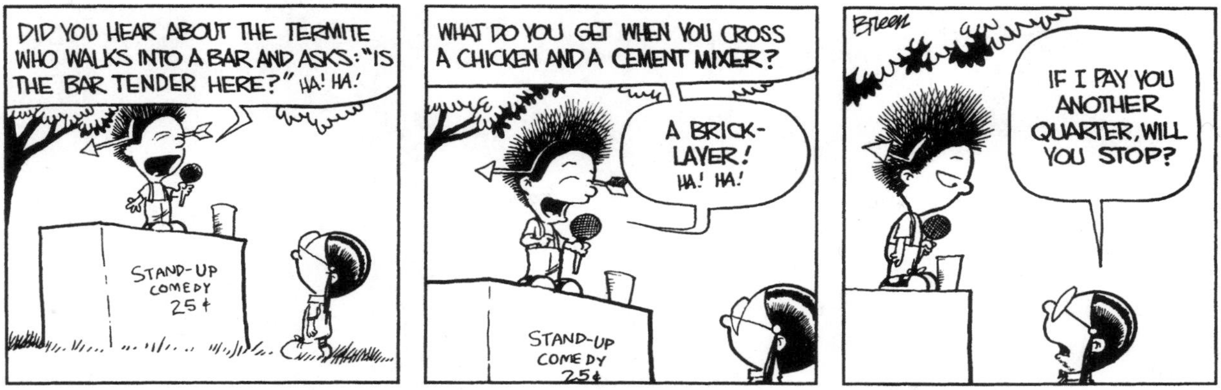
DID YOU HEAR ABOUT THE TERMITE WHO WALKS INTO A BAR AND ASKS: "IS THE BAR TENDER HERE?" HA! HA!
STAND-UP COMEDY 25¢
WHAT DO YOU GET WHEN YOU CROSS A CHICKEN AND A CEMENT MIXER?
A BRICK-LAYER! HA! HA!
STAND-UP COMEDY 25¢
IF I PAY YOU ANOTHER QUARTER, WILL YOU STOP?

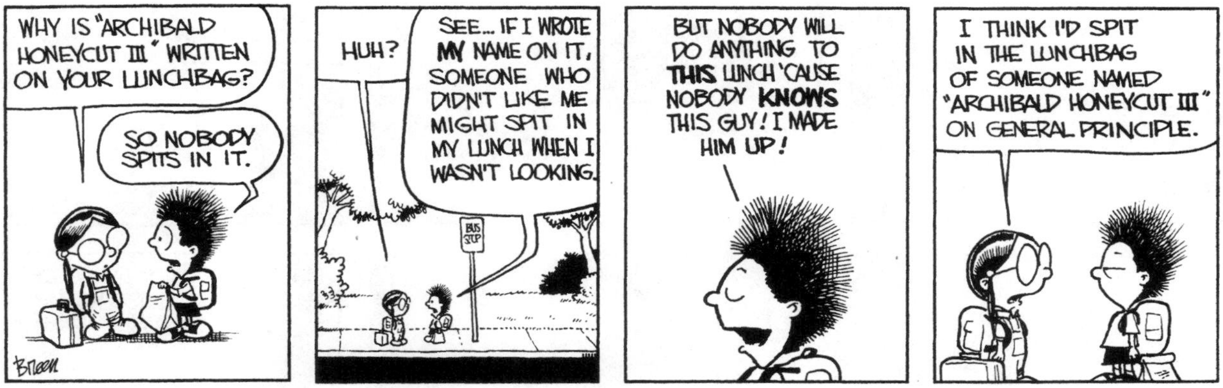
WHY IS "ARCHIBALD HONEYCUT III" WRITTEN ON YOUR LUNCHBAG?
SO NOBODY SPITS IN IT.
HUH?
SEE... IF I WROTE MY NAME ON IT, SOMEONE WHO DIDN'T LIKE ME MIGHT SPIT IN MY LUNCH WHEN I WASN'T LOOKING.
BUS STOP
BUT NOBODY WILL DO ANYTHING TO THIS LUNCH 'CAUSE NOBODY KNOWS THIS GUY! I MADE HIM UP!
I THINK I'D SPIT IN THE LUNCHBAG OF SOMEONE NAMED "ARCHIBALD HONEYCUT III" ON GENERAL PRINCIPLE.

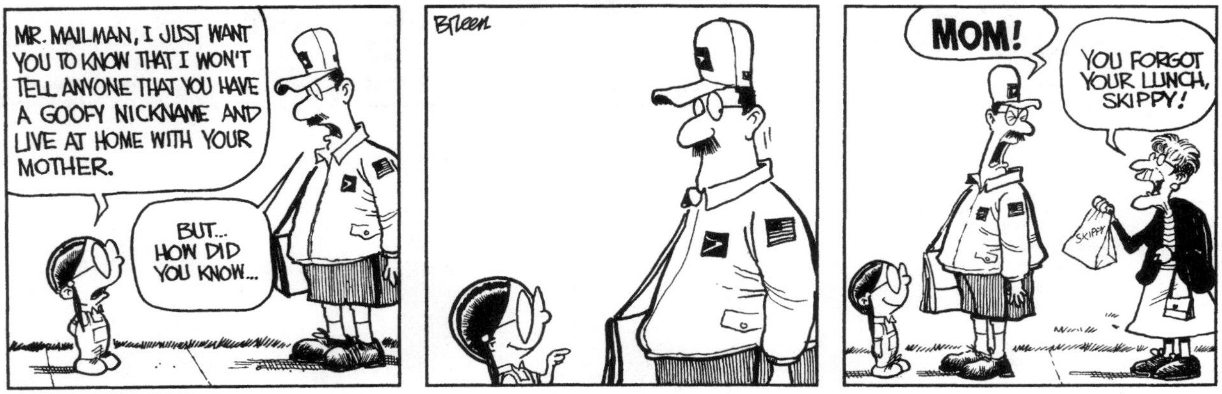
MR. MAILMAN, I JUST WANT YOU TO KNOW THAT I WON'T TELL ANYONE THAT YOU HAVE A GOOFY NICKNAME AND LIVE AT HOME WITH YOUR MOTHER.
BUT... HOW DID YOU KNOW...
MOM!
YOU FORGOT YOUR LUNCH, SKIPPY!
SKIPPY

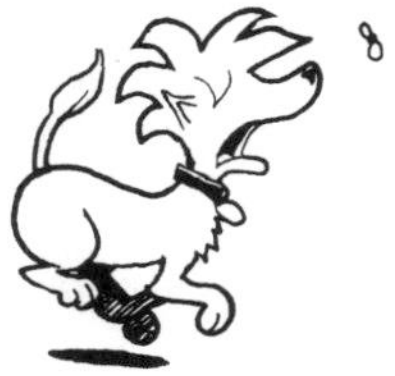

MICHAEL, RUN INSIDE AND RETURN THE VIDEO...
THE MATRIX
OK.
WARNING: STIFF PENALTY IF VIDEO IS NOT REWOUND!
UH-OH.
VIDEO RETURN
KING KONG
EXCUSE ME, WHAT EXACTLY IS THE STIFF PENALTY IF A VIDEO ISN'T REWOUND?
UPON YOUR NEXT VISIT, WE MAKE YOU WATCH TWENTY MINUTES OF AN `ERNEST' MOVIE.
NEW RELEASES:
PENALTY BOX
I'LL BE BACK.
ON YOUR SECOND OFFENSE, WE MAKE IT AN ADAM SANDLER FILM.
KING KONG

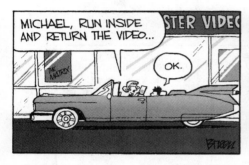

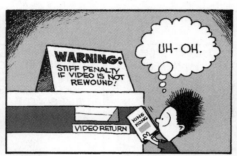

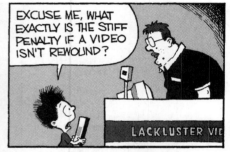

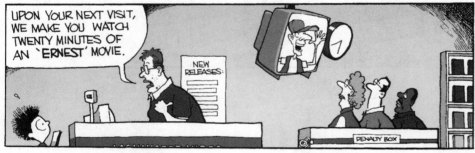

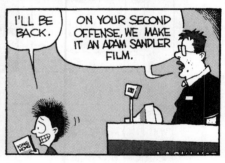

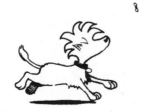

WHY ARE WE PARKING HERE?
I HAVE TO RUN INTO THE AUTO PARTS STORE ACROSS THE STREET...
I NEED TO GET SOME OIL FOR THAT SQUEAKY PASSENGER DOOR.
THIS DOOR SQUEAKS? I GUESS I'VE NEVER NOTICED...
SQUEEK
HEY... WHAT DO YOU KNOW... IT **DOES** SQUEAK. WE SHOULD FIX THIS.
MICHAEL, BE CAREFUL OF THE ON-COMING...
SNAP!
VOILÁ!.. YOU FIXED IT.

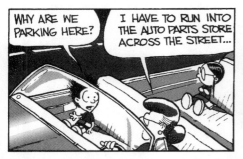

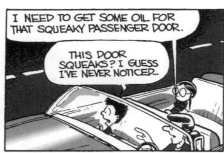

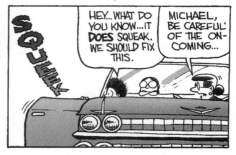

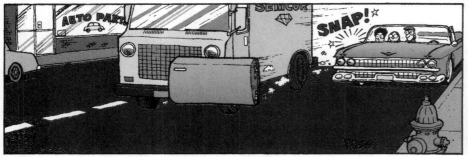

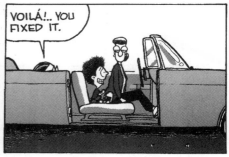

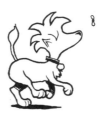

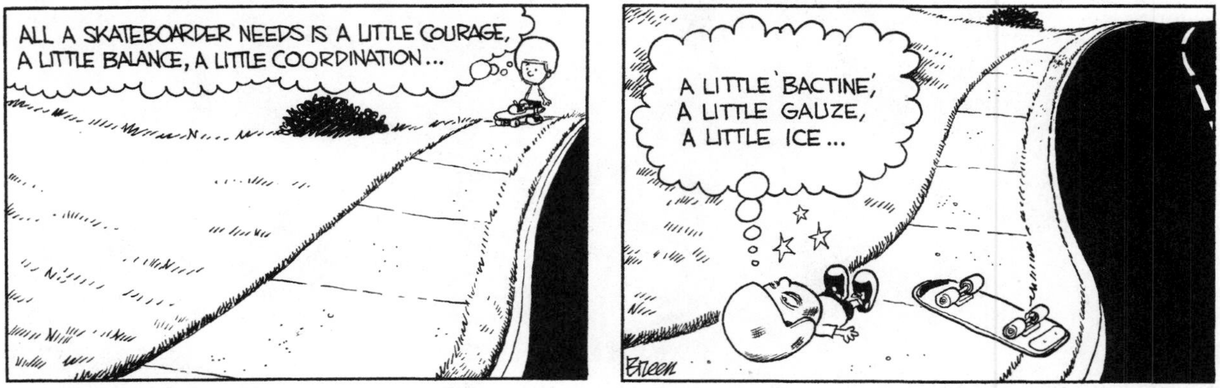
ALL A SKATEBOARDER NEEDS IS A LITTLE COURAGE, A LITTLE BALANCE, A LITTLE COORDINATION...
A LITTLE 'BACTINE,' A LITTLE GAUZE, A LITTLE ICE...
BREEN

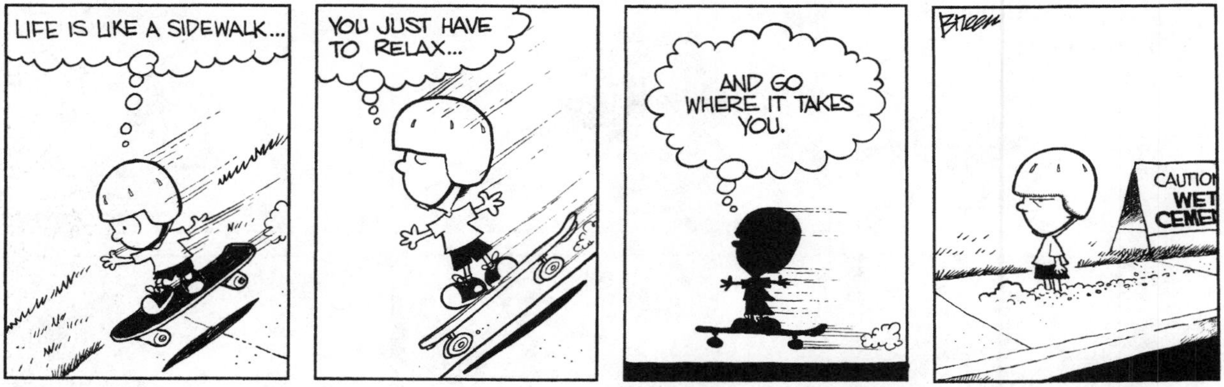
LIFE IS LIKE A SIDEWALK...
YOU JUST HAVE TO RELAX...
AND GO WHERE IT TAKES YOU.
BREEN
CAUTIO
WET
CEME

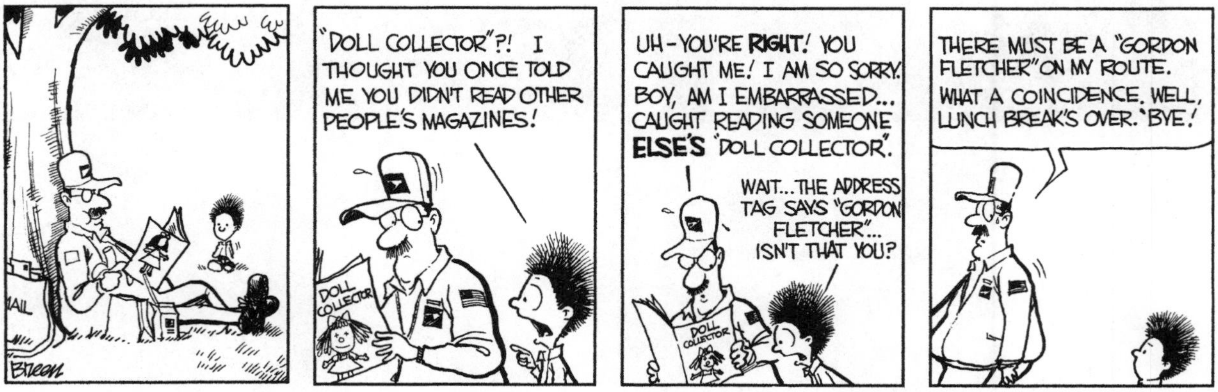
BREEN
"DOLL COLLECTOR"?! I THOUGHT YOU ONCE TOLD ME YOU DIDN'T READ OTHER PEOPLE'S MAGAZINES!
DOLL COLLECTOR
UH-YOU'RE **RIGHT**! YOU CAUGHT ME! I AM SO SORRY. BOY, AM I EMBARRASSED... CAUGHT READING SOMEONE **ELSE'S** "DOLL COLLECTOR".
WAIT... THE ADDRESS TAG SAYS "GORDON FLETCHER"... ISN'T THAT YOU?
DOLL COLLECTOR
THERE MUST BE A "GORDON FLETCHER" ON MY ROUTE. WHAT A COINCIDENCE. WELL, LUNCH BREAK'S OVER. 'BYE!

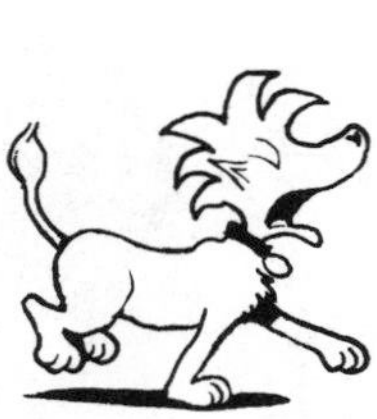

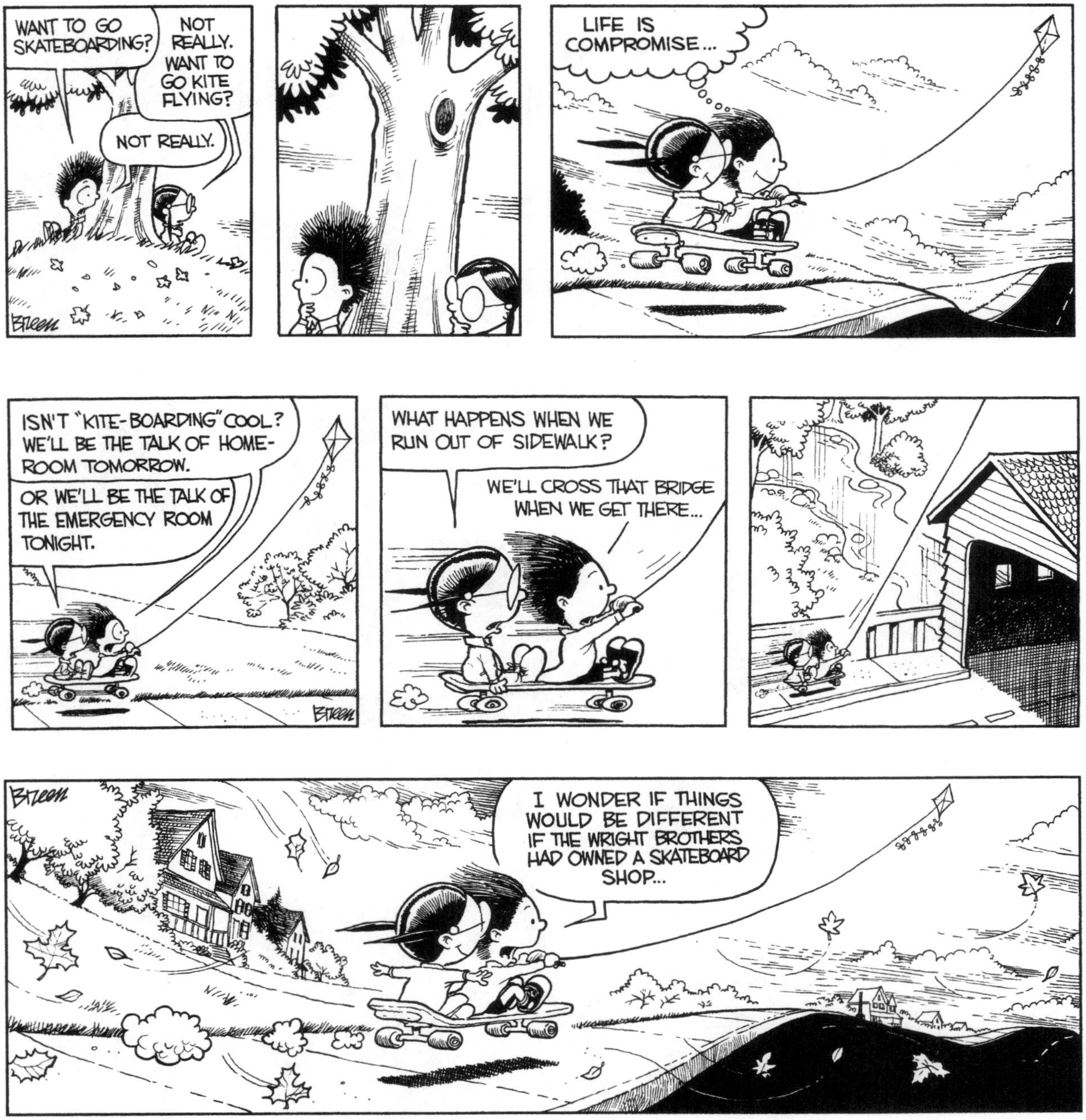
WANT TO GO SKATEBOARDING?
NOT REALLY. WANT TO GO KITE FLYING?
NOT REALLY.
LIFE IS COMPROMISE...
ISN'T "KITE-BOARDING" COOL? WE'LL BE THE TALK OF HOME-ROOM TOMORROW.
OR WE'LL BE THE TALK OF THE EMERGENCY ROOM TONIGHT.
WHAT HAPPENS WHEN WE RUN OUT OF SIDEWALK?
WE'LL CROSS THAT BRIDGE WHEN WE GET THERE...
I WONDER IF THINGS WOULD BE DIFFERENT IF THE WRIGHT BROTHERS HAD OWNED A SKATEBOARD SHOP...

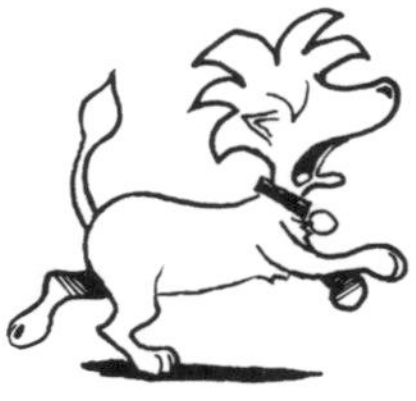

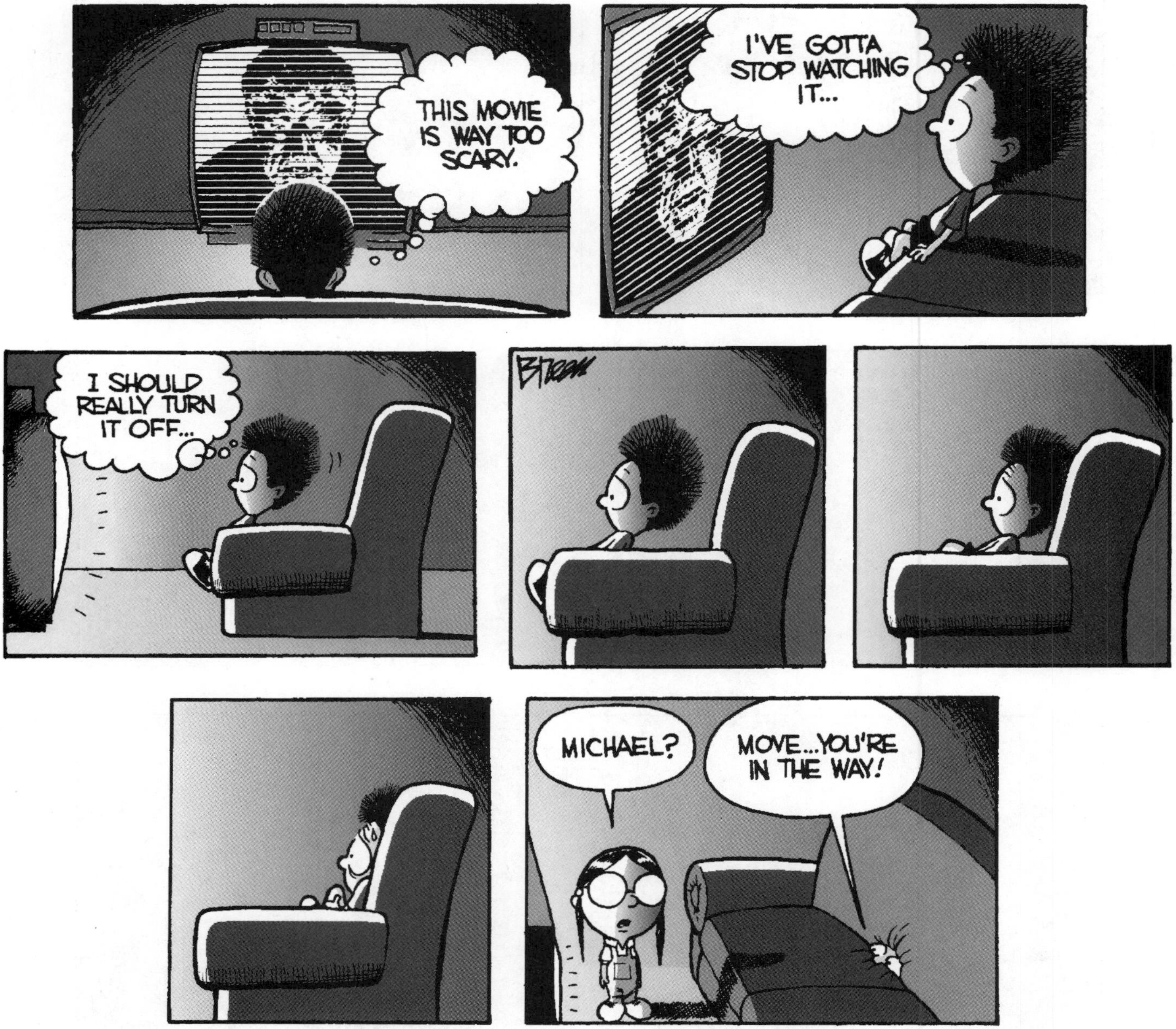
THIS MOVIE IS WAY TOO SCARY.
I'VE GOTTA STOP WATCHING IT...
I SHOULD REALLY TURN IT OFF...
MICHAEL?
MOVE...YOU'RE IN THE WAY!

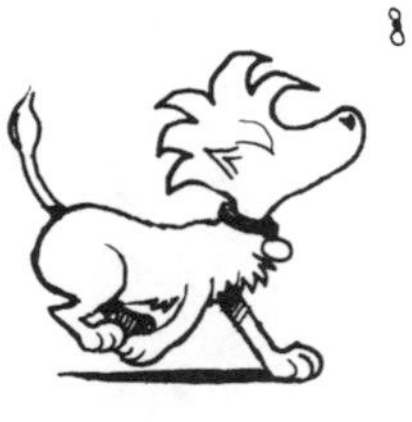

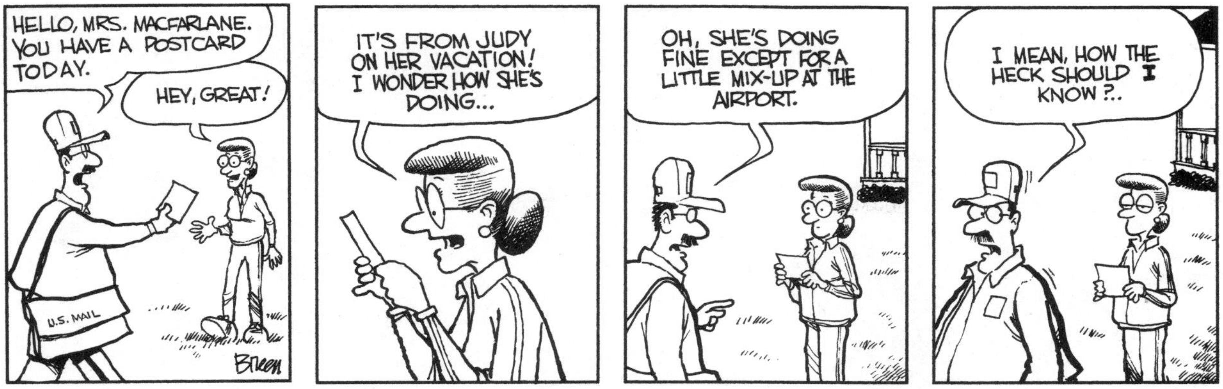
HELLO, MRS. MACFARLANE. YOU HAVE A POSTCARD TODAY.
HEY, GREAT!
U.S. MAIL
IT'S FROM JUDY ON HER VACATION! I WONDER HOW SHE'S DOING...
OH, SHE'S DOING FINE EXCEPT FOR A LITTLE MIX-UP AT THE AIRPORT.
I MEAN, HOW THE HECK SHOULD I KNOW?..

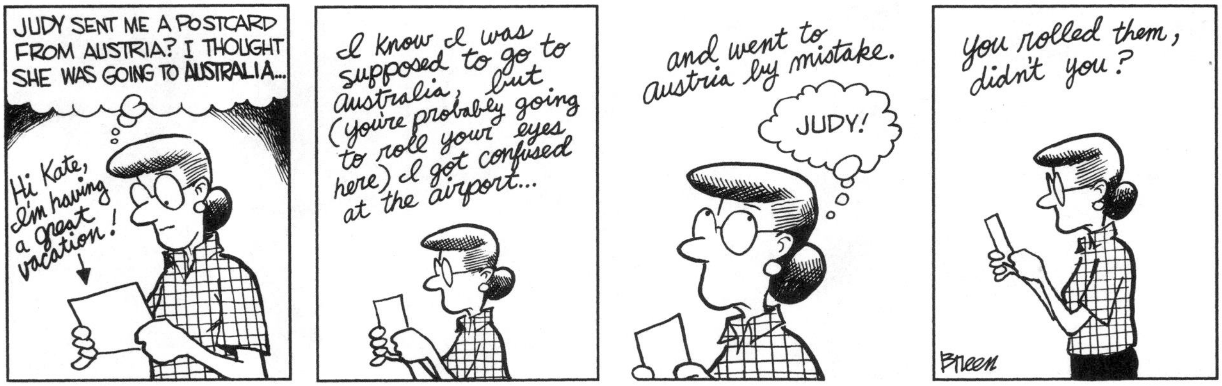
JUDY SENT ME A POSTCARD FROM AUSTRIA? I THOUGHT SHE WAS GOING TO AUSTRALIA...
Hi Kate, I'm having a great vacation!
I know I was supposed to go to Australia, but (you're probably going to roll your eyes here) I got confused at the airport...
and went to Austria by mistake.
JUDY!
You rolled them, didn't you?

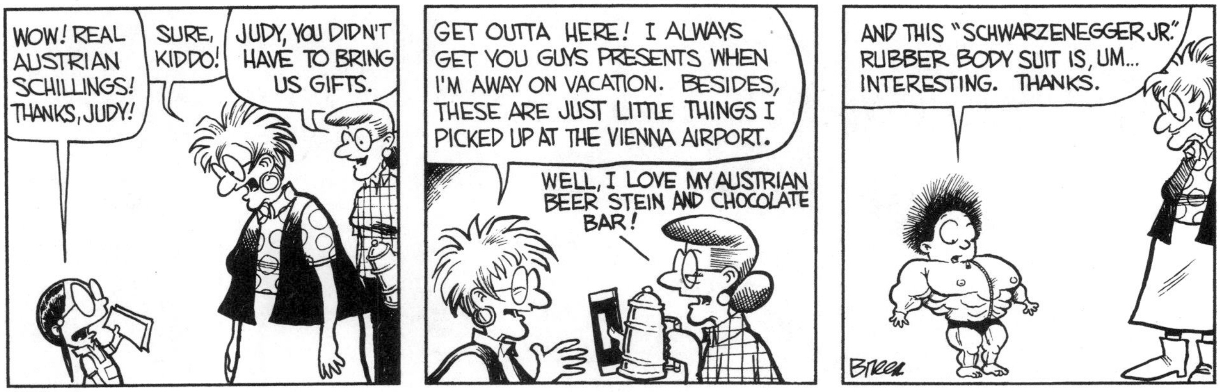
WOW! REAL AUSTRIAN SCHILLINGS! THANKS, JUDY!
SURE, KIDDO!
JUDY, YOU DIDN'T HAVE TO BRING US GIFTS.
GET OUTTA HERE! I ALWAYS GET YOU GUYS PRESENTS WHEN I'M AWAY ON VACATION. BESIDES, THESE ARE JUST LITTLE THINGS I PICKED UP AT THE VIENNA AIRPORT.
WELL, I LOVE MY AUSTRIAN BEER STEIN AND CHOCOLATE BAR!
AND THIS "SCHWARZENEGGER JR." RUBBER BODY SUIT IS, UM... INTERESTING. THANKS.

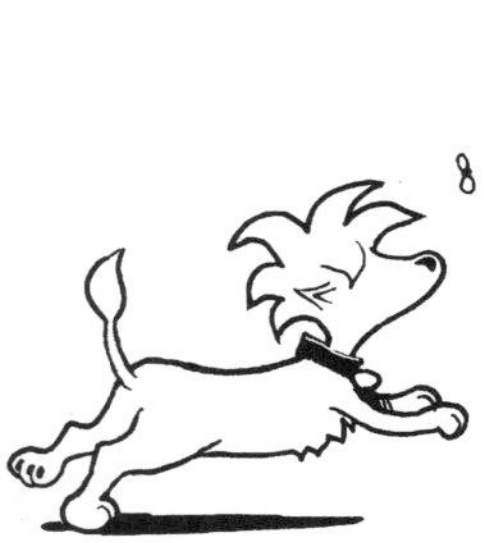

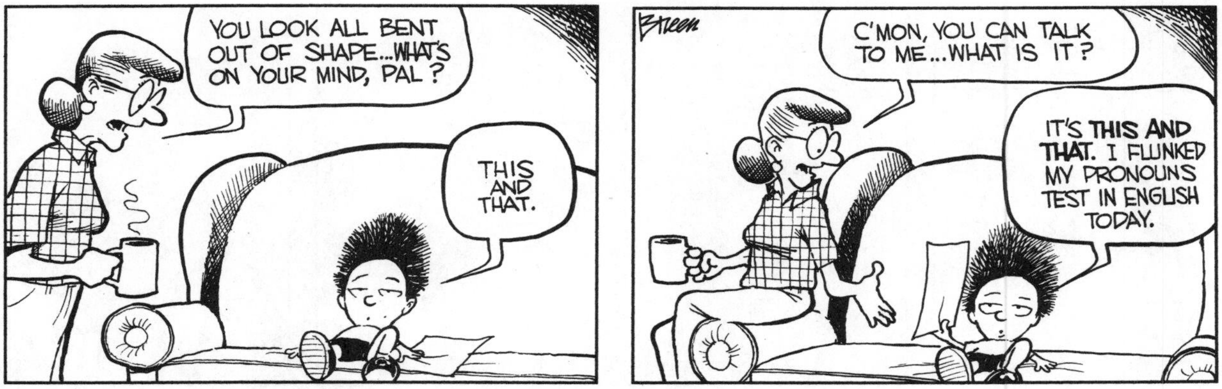
YOU LOOK ALL BENT OUT OF SHAPE...WHAT'S ON YOUR MIND, PAL?
THIS AND THAT.
C'MON, YOU CAN TALK TO ME...WHAT IS IT?
IT'S **THIS AND THAT.** I FLUNKED MY PRONOUNS TEST IN ENGLISH TODAY.

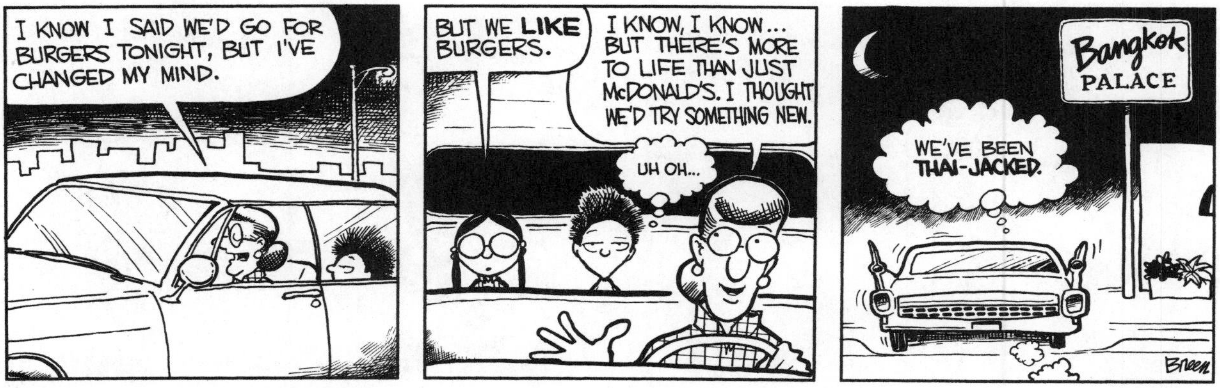
I KNOW I SAID WE'D GO FOR BURGERS TONIGHT, BUT I'VE CHANGED MY MIND.
BUT WE **LIKE** BURGERS.
I KNOW, I KNOW... BUT THERE'S MORE TO LIFE THAN JUST McDONALD'S. I THOUGHT WE'D TRY SOMETHING NEW.
UH OH...
Bangkok PALACE
WE'VE BEEN **THAI-JACKED.**

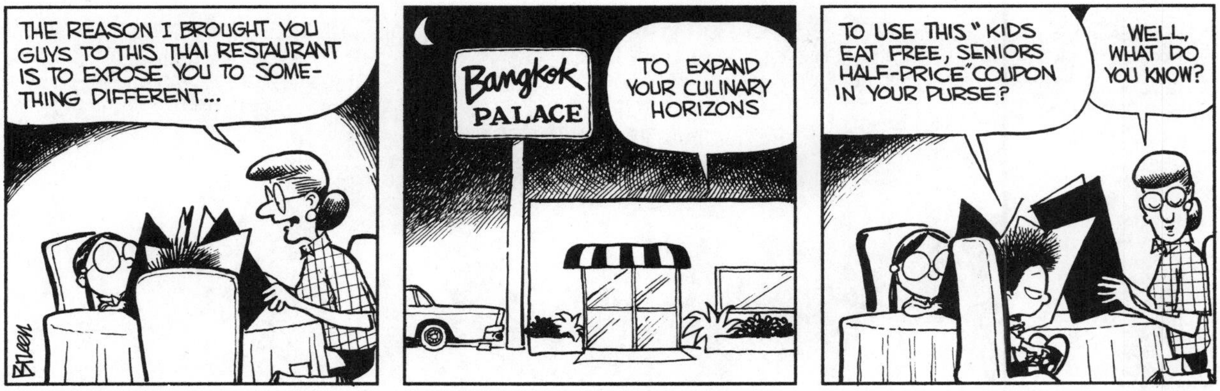
THE REASON I BROUGHT YOU GUYS TO THIS THAI RESTAURANT IS TO EXPOSE YOU TO SOME-THING DIFFERENT...
Bangkok PALACE
TO EXPAND YOUR CULINARY HORIZONS
TO USE THIS "KIDS EAT FREE, SENIORS HALF-PRICE" COUPON IN YOUR PURSE?
WELL, WHAT DO YOU KNOW?

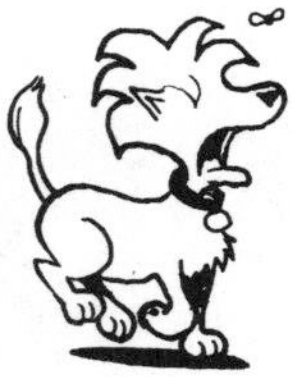

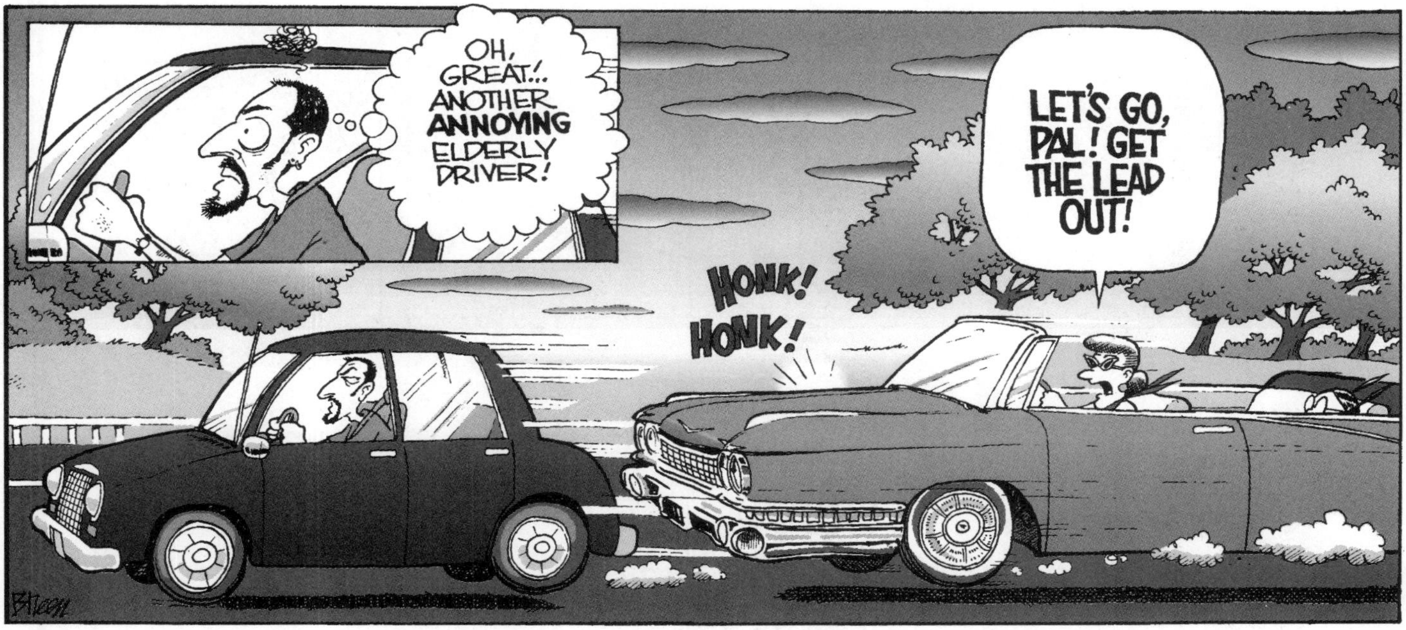
OH, GREAT!.. ANOTHER **ANNOYING** ELDERLY DRIVER!
HONK! HONK!
LET'S GO, PAL! GET THE LEAD OUT!

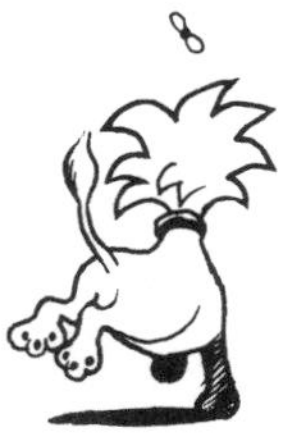

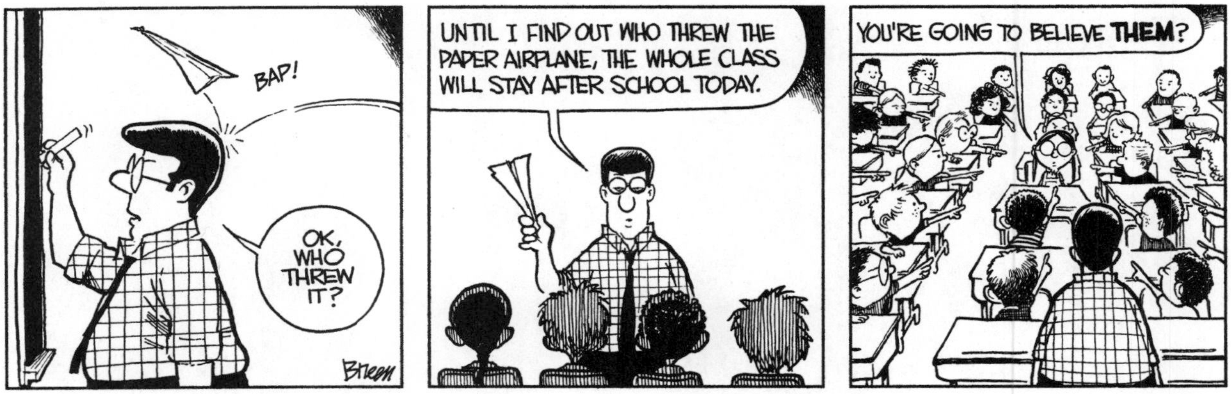
BAP!
OK, WHO THREW IT?
UNTIL I FIND OUT WHO THREW THE PAPER AIRPLANE, THE WHOLE CLASS WILL STAY AFTER SCHOOL TODAY.
YOU'RE GOING TO BELIEVE **THEM**?

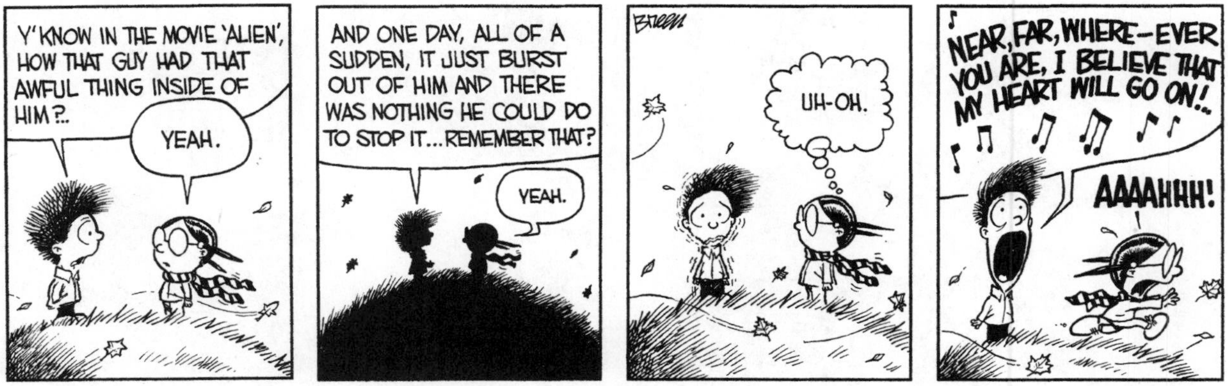
Y'KNOW IN THE MOVIE 'ALIEN', HOW THAT GUY HAD THAT AWFUL THING INSIDE OF HIM?..
YEAH.
AND ONE DAY, ALL OF A SUDDEN, IT JUST BURST OUT OF HIM AND THERE WAS NOTHING HE COULD DO TO STOP IT... REMEMBER THAT?
YEAH.
UH-OH.
NEAR, FAR, WHERE-EVER YOU ARE, I BELIEVE THAT MY HEART WILL GO ON!..
AAAAHHH!

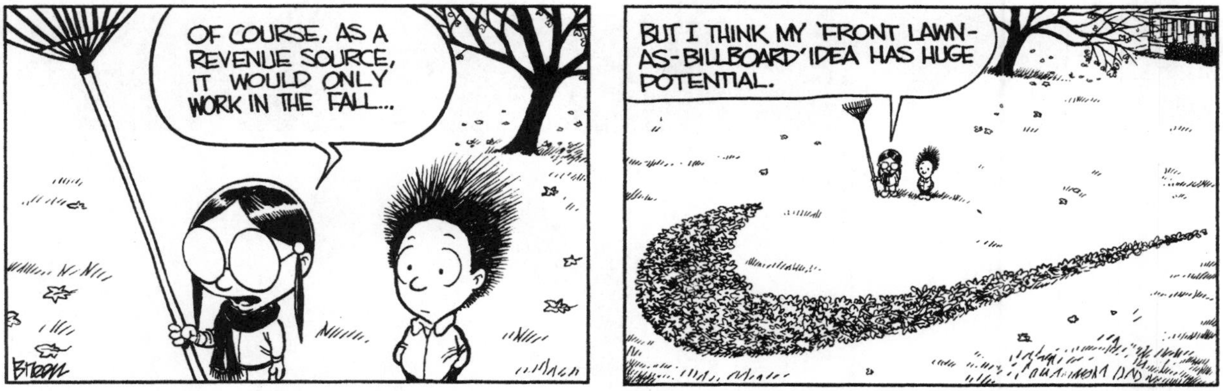
OF COURSE, AS A REVENUE SOURCE, IT WOULD ONLY WORK IN THE FALL...
BUT I THINK MY 'FRONT LAWN-AS-BILLBOARD' IDEA HAS HUGE POTENTIAL.

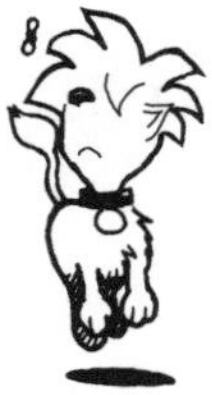

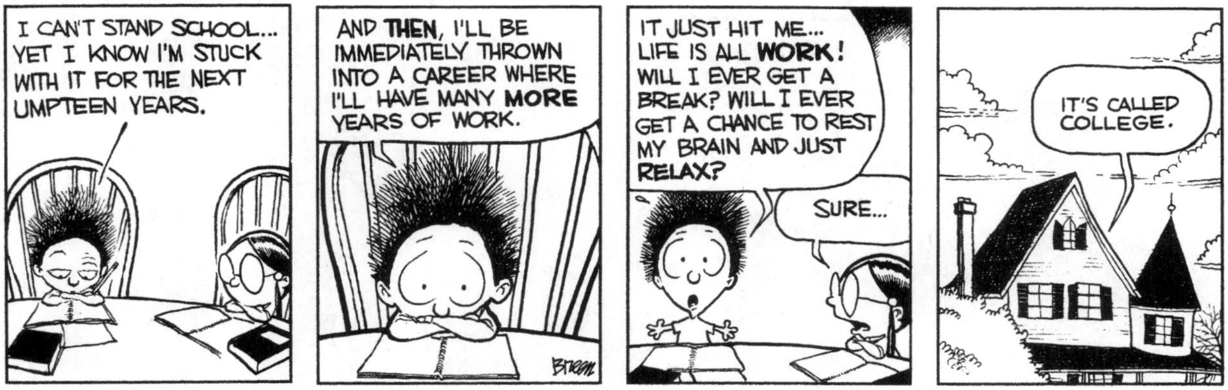
I CAN'T STAND SCHOOL... YET I KNOW I'M STUCK WITH IT FOR THE NEXT UMPTEEN YEARS.
AND **THEN**, I'LL BE IMMEDIATELY THROWN INTO A CAREER WHERE I'LL HAVE MANY **MORE** YEARS OF WORK.
IT JUST HIT ME... LIFE IS ALL **WORK**! WILL I EVER GET A BREAK? WILL I EVER GET A CHANCE TO REST MY BRAIN AND JUST **RELAX**?
SURE...
IT'S CALLED COLLEGE.

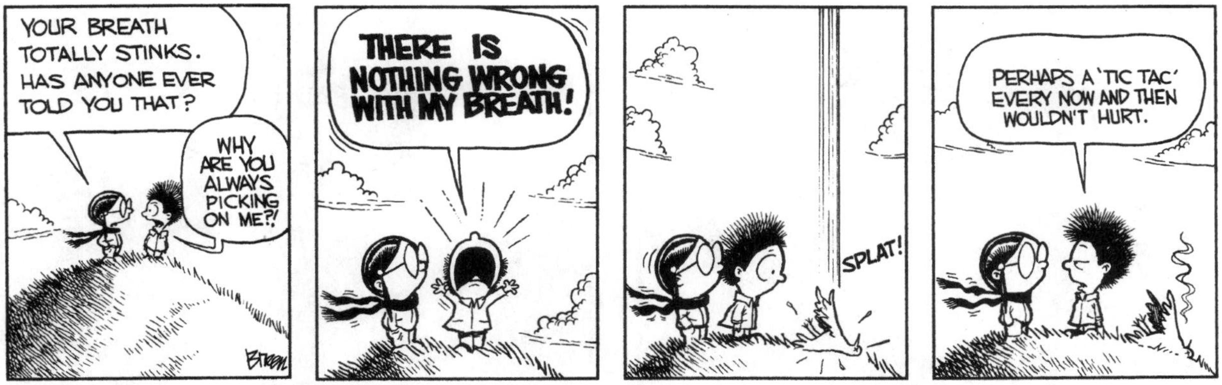
YOUR BREATH TOTALLY STINKS. HAS ANYONE EVER TOLD YOU THAT?
WHY ARE YOU ALWAYS PICKING ON ME?!
THERE IS NOTHING WRONG WITH MY BREATH!
SPLAT!
PERHAPS A 'TIC TAC' EVERY NOW AND THEN WOULDN'T HURT.

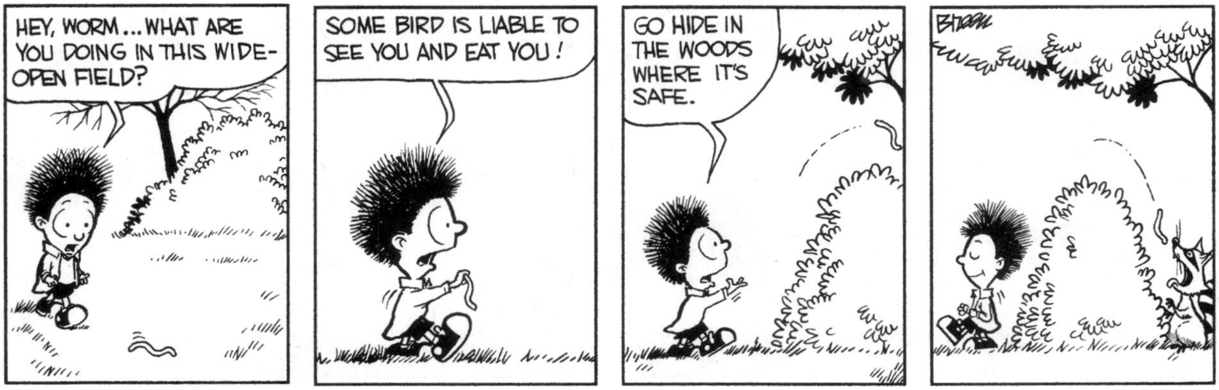
HEY, WORM... WHAT ARE YOU DOING IN THIS WIDE-OPEN FIELD?
SOME BIRD IS LIABLE TO SEE YOU AND EAT YOU!
GO HIDE IN THE WOODS WHERE IT'S SAFE.

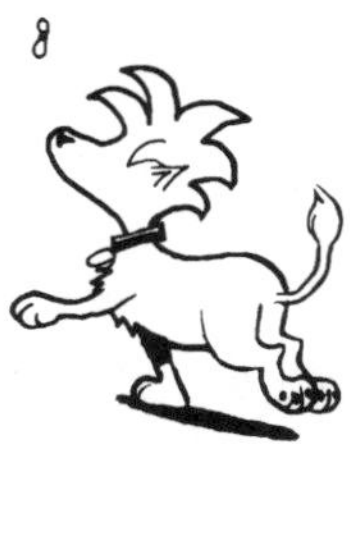

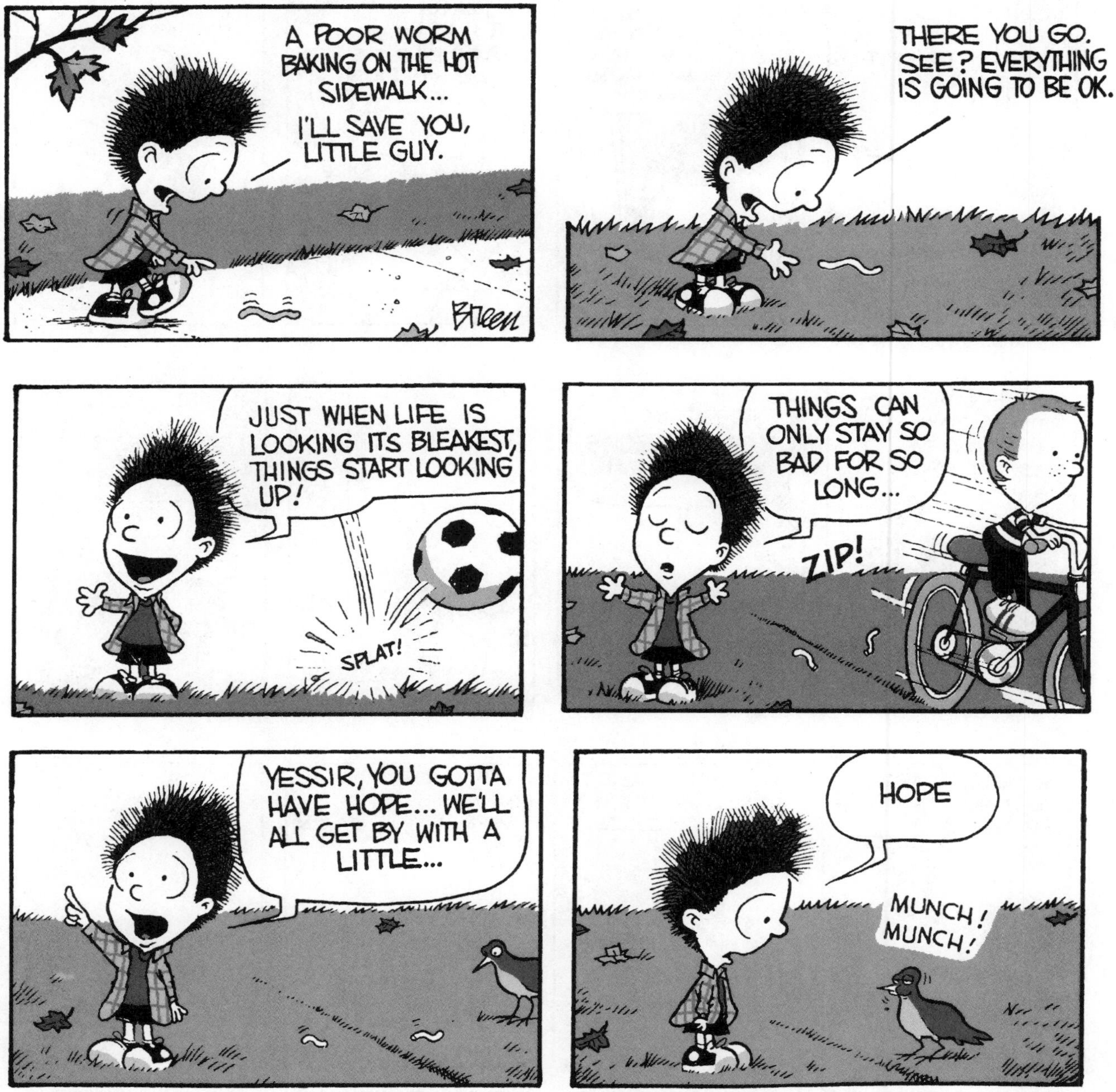
A POOR WORM BAKING ON THE HOT SIDEWALK...
I'LL SAVE YOU, LITTLE GUY.
THERE YOU GO. SEE? EVERYTHING IS GOING TO BE OK.
JUST WHEN LIFE IS LOOKING ITS BLEAKEST, THINGS START LOOKING UP!
SPLAT!
THINGS CAN ONLY STAY SO BAD FOR SO LONG...
ZIP!
YESSIR, YOU GOTTA HAVE HOPE... WE'LL ALL GET BY WITH A LITTLE...
HOPE
MUNCH! MUNCH!

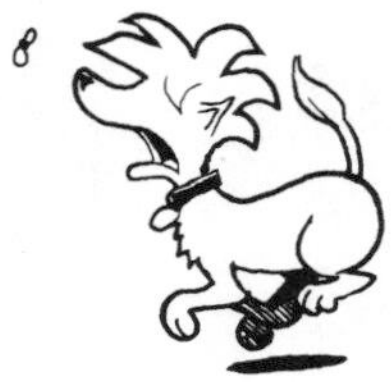

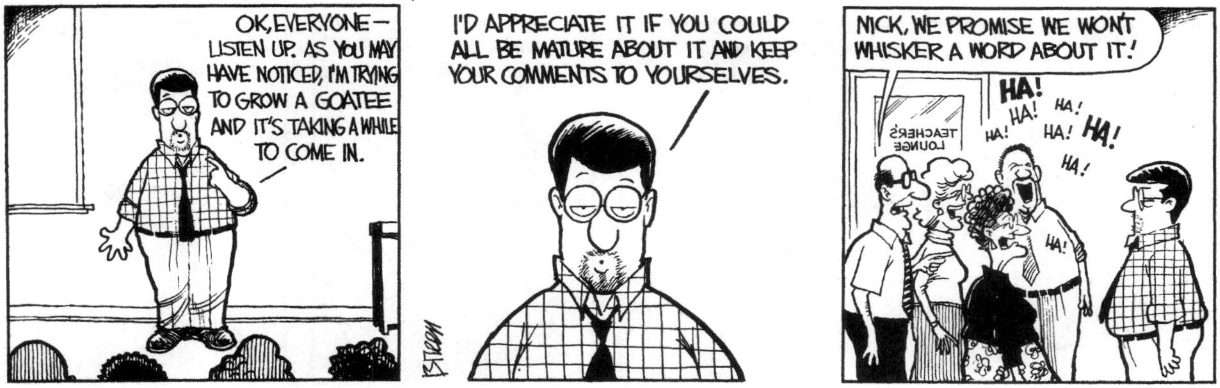
OK, EVERYONE— LISTEN UP. AS YOU MAY HAVE NOTICED, I'M TRYING TO GROW A GOATEE AND IT'S TAKING A WHILE TO COME IN.
I'D APPRECIATE IT IF YOU COULD ALL BE MATURE ABOUT IT AND KEEP YOUR COMMENTS TO YOURSELVES.
NICK, WE PROMISE WE WON'T WHISKER A WORD ABOUT IT!
HA! HA! HA! HA! HA! HA! HA! HA!

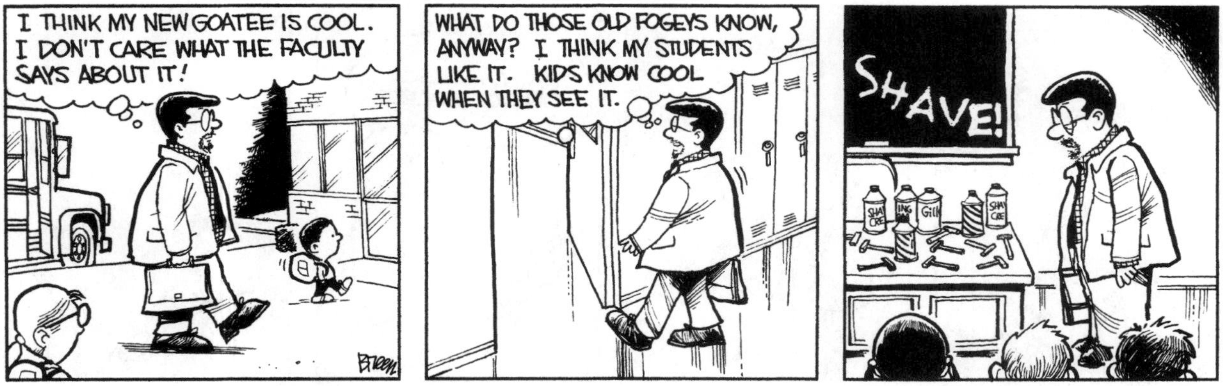
I THINK MY NEW GOATEE IS COOL. I DON'T CARE WHAT THE FACULTY SAYS ABOUT IT!
WHAT DO THOSE OLD FOGEYS KNOW, ANYWAY? I THINK MY STUDENTS LIKE IT. KIDS KNOW COOL WHEN THEY SEE IT.
SHAVE!

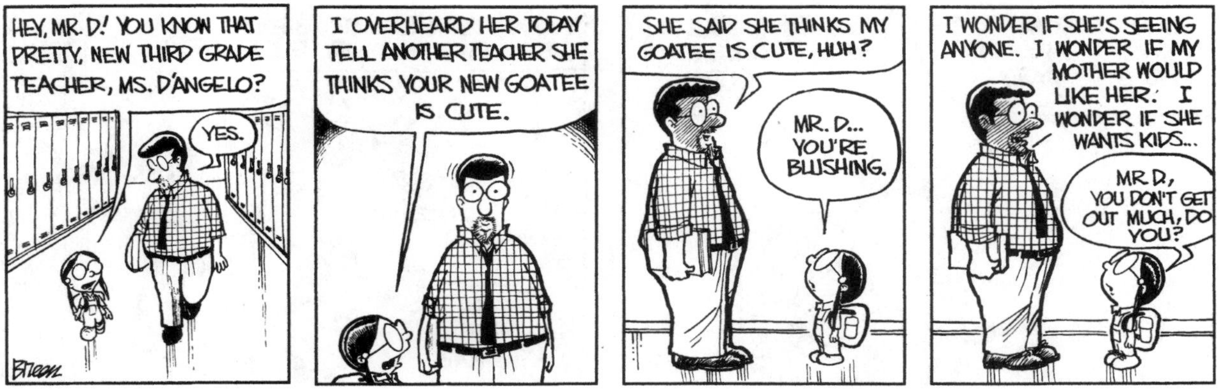
HEY, MR. D! YOU KNOW THAT PRETTY, NEW THIRD GRADE TEACHER, MS. D'ANGELO?
YES.
I OVERHEARD HER TODAY TELL ANOTHER TEACHER SHE THINKS YOUR NEW GOATEE IS CUTE.
SHE SAID SHE THINKS MY GOATEE IS CUTE, HUH?
MR. D... YOU'RE BLUSHING.
I WONDER IF SHE'S SEEING ANYONE. I WONDER IF MY MOTHER WOULD LIKE HER. I WONDER IF SHE WANTS KIDS...
MR. D, YOU DON'T GET OUT MUCH, DO YOU?

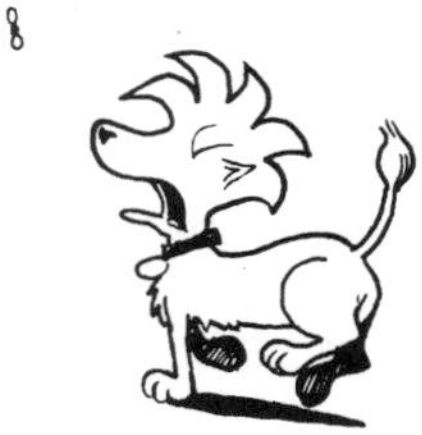

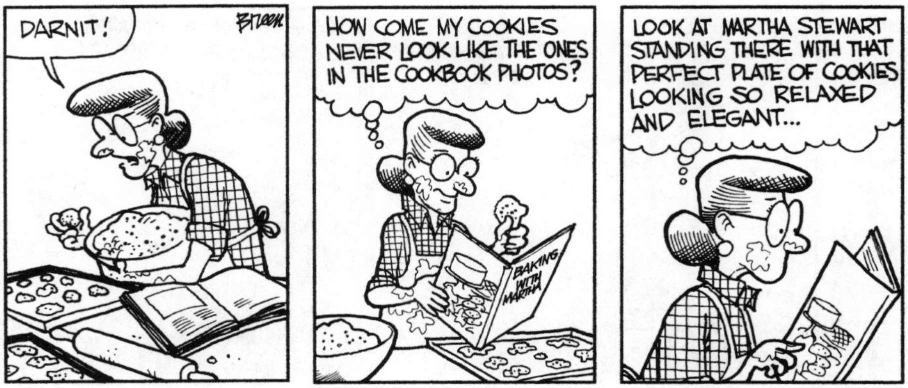
DARNIT!
HOW COME MY COOKIES NEVER LOOK LIKE THE ONES IN THE COOKBOOK PHOTOS?
BAKING WITH MARTHA
LOOK AT MARTHA STEWART STANDING THERE WITH THAT PERFECT PLATE OF COOKIES LOOKING SO RELAXED AND ELEGANT...
I COULD JUST SLAP HER.

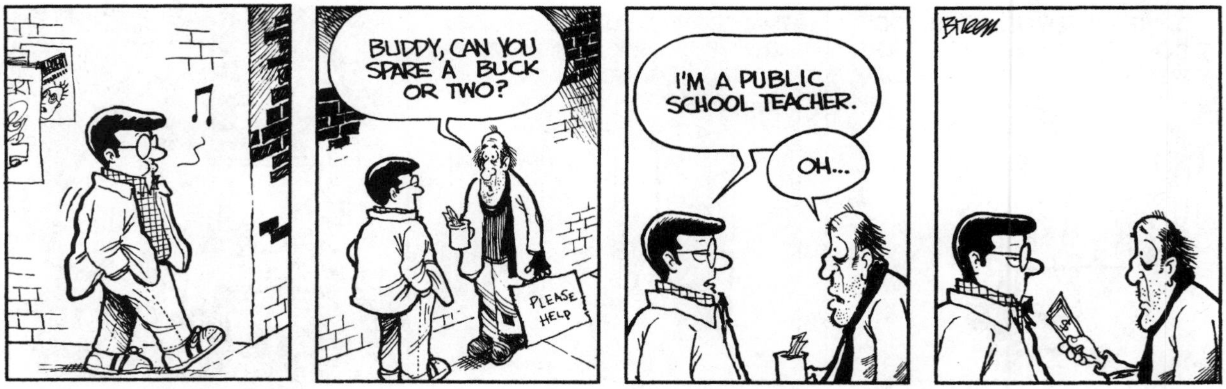
BUDDY, CAN YOU SPARE A BUCK OR TWO?
PLEASE HELP
I'M A PUBLIC SCHOOL TEACHER.
OH...

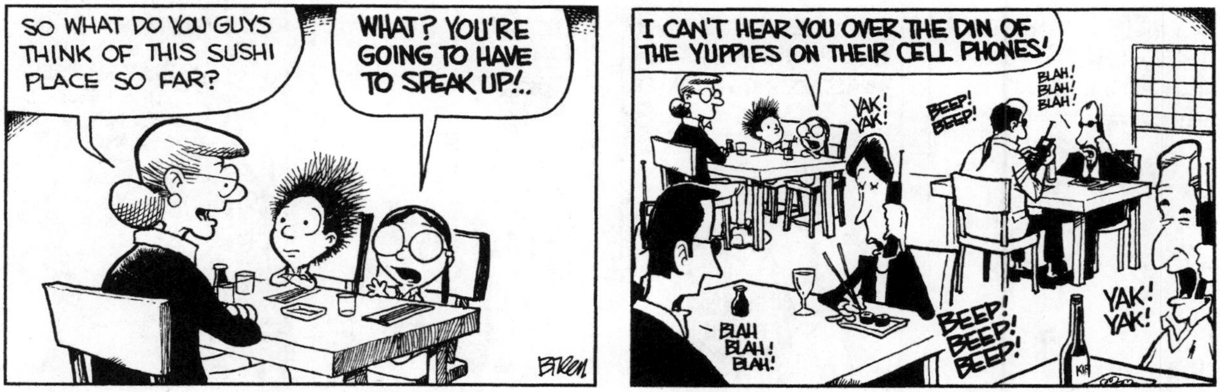
SO WHAT DO YOU GUYS THINK OF THIS SUSHI PLACE SO FAR?
WHAT? YOU'RE GOING TO HAVE TO SPEAK UP!..
I CAN'T HEAR YOU OVER THE DIN OF THE YUPPIES ON THEIR CELL PHONES!
YAK! YAK!
BEEP! BEEP!
BLAH! BLAH! BLAH!
BLAH BLAH! BLAH!
BEEP! BEEP! BEEP!
YAK! YAK!

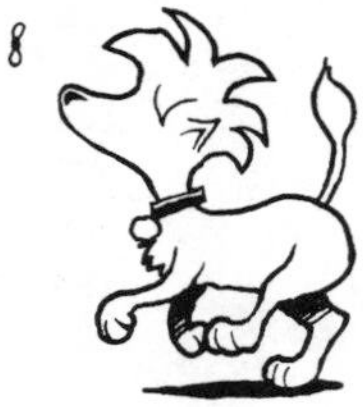

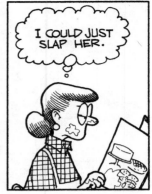

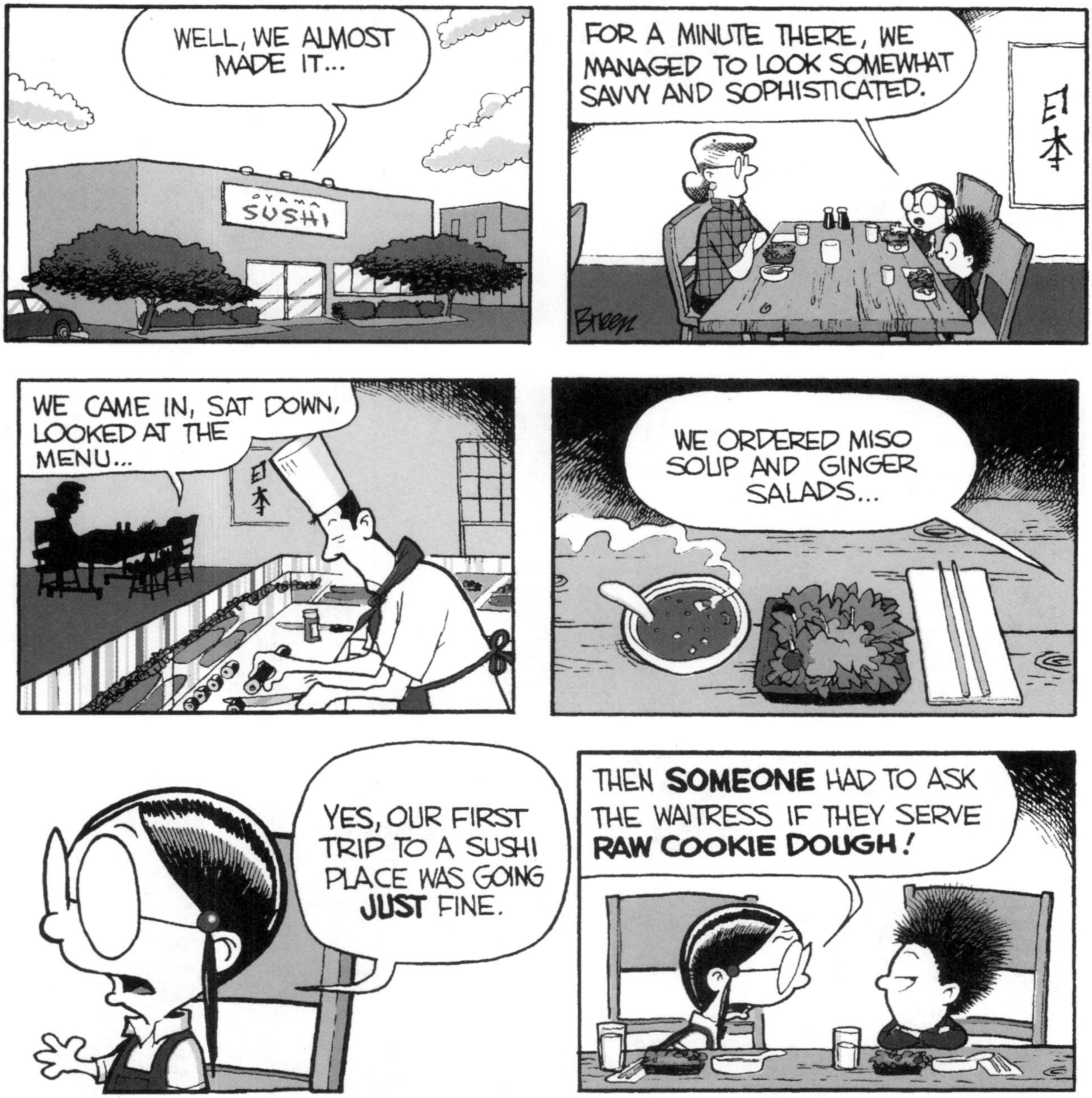
WELL, WE ALMOST MADE IT...
OYAMA SUSHI
FOR A MINUTE THERE, WE MANAGED TO LOOK SOMEWHAT SAVVY AND SOPHISTICATED.
日本
WE CAME IN, SAT DOWN, LOOKED AT THE MENU...
WE ORDERED MISO SOUP AND GINGER SALADS...
YES, OUR FIRST TRIP TO A SUSHI PLACE WAS GOING JUST FINE.
THEN SOMEONE HAD TO ASK THE WAITRESS IF THEY SERVE RAW COOKIE DOUGH!

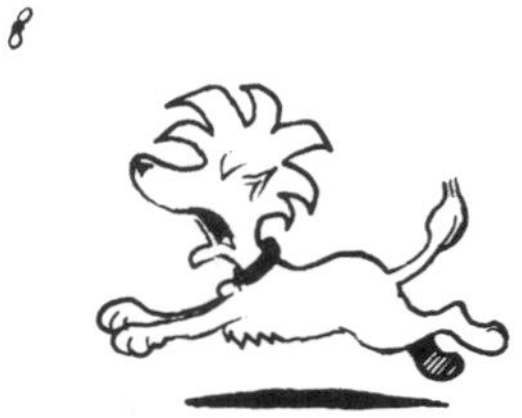

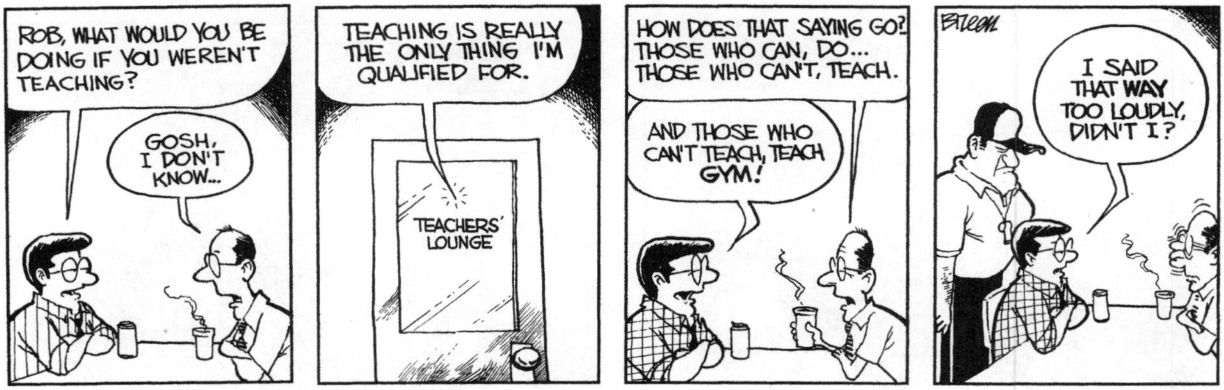
ROB, WHAT WOULD YOU BE DOING IF YOU WEREN'T TEACHING?
GOSH, I DON'T KNOW...
TEACHING IS REALLY THE ONLY THING I'M QUALIFIED FOR.
TEACHERS' LOUNGE
HOW DOES THAT SAYING GO? THOSE WHO CAN, DO... THOSE WHO CAN'T, TEACH.
AND THOSE WHO CAN'T TEACH, TEACH GYM!
I SAID THAT WAY TOO LOUDLY, DIDN'T I?

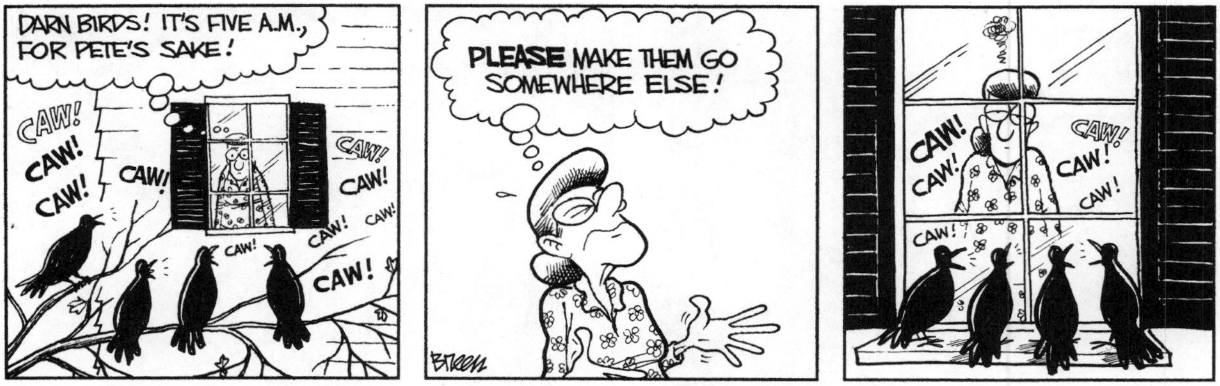
DARN BIRDS! IT'S FIVE A.M., FOR PETE'S SAKE!
CAW! CAW! CAW! CAW! CAW! CAW! CAW! CAW! CAW! CAW!
PLEASE MAKE THEM GO SOMEWHERE ELSE!
CAW! CAW! CAW! CAW! CAW! CAW!

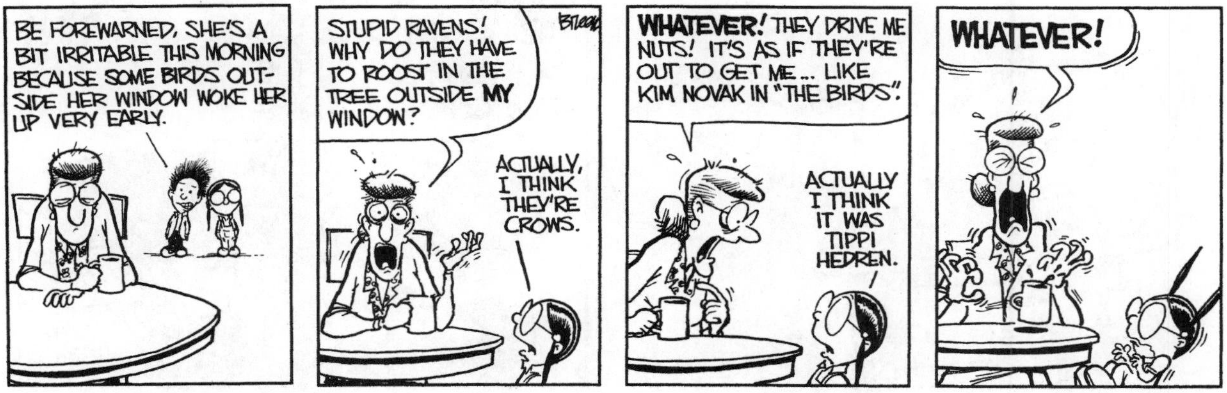
BE FOREWARNED, SHE'S A BIT IRRITABLE THIS MORNING BECAUSE SOME BIRDS OUTSIDE HER WINDOW WOKE HER UP VERY EARLY.
STUPID RAVENS! WHY DO THEY HAVE TO ROOST IN THE TREE OUTSIDE MY WINDOW?
ACTUALLY, I THINK THEY'RE CROWS.
WHATEVER! THEY DRIVE ME NUTS! IT'S AS IF THEY'RE OUT TO GET ME... LIKE KIM NOVAK IN "THE BIRDS".
ACTUALLY I THINK IT WAS TIPPI HEDREN.
WHATEVER!

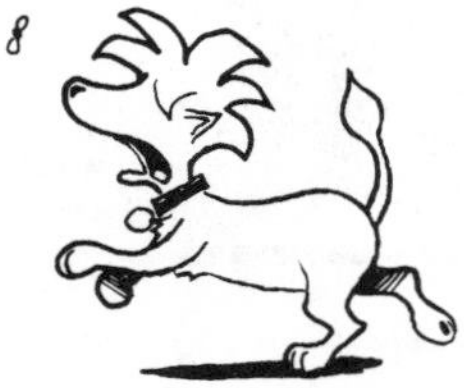

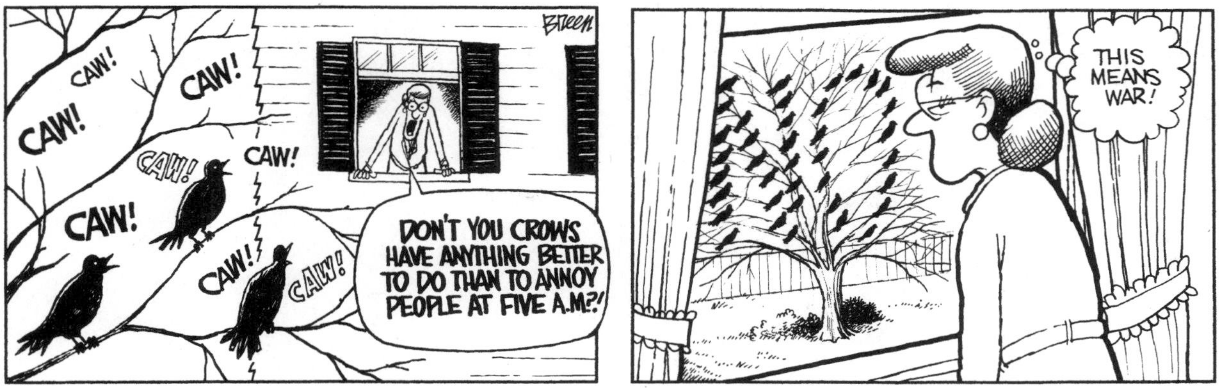
CAW!
CAW!
CAW!
CAW!
CAW!
CAW!
CAW!
CAW!
DON'T YOU CROWS HAVE ANYTHING BETTER TO DO THAN TO ANNOY PEOPLE AT FIVE A.M?!
THIS MEANS WAR!

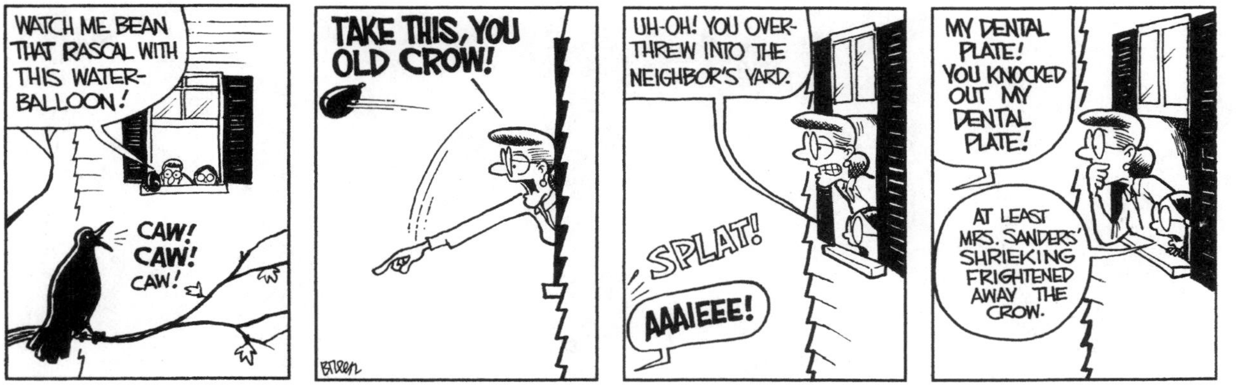
WATCH ME BEAN THAT RASCAL WITH THIS WATER-BALLOON!
CAW! CAW! CAW!
TAKE THIS, YOU OLD CROW!
UH-OH! YOU OVER-THREW INTO THE NEIGHBOR'S YARD.
SPLAT!
AAAIEEE!
MY DENTAL PLATE! YOU KNOCKED OUT MY DENTAL PLATE!
AT LEAST MRS. SANDERS' SHRIEKING FRIGHTENED AWAY THE CROW.

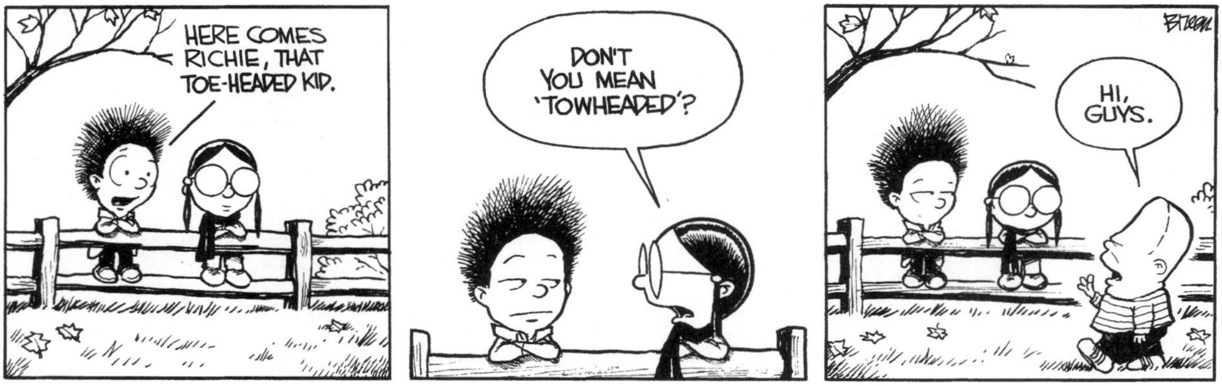
HERE COMES RICHIE, THAT TOE-HEADED KID.
DON'T YOU MEAN 'TOWHEADED'?
HI, GUYS.

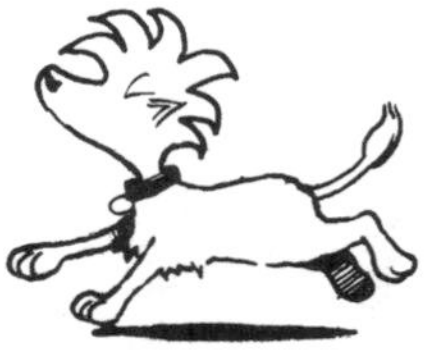

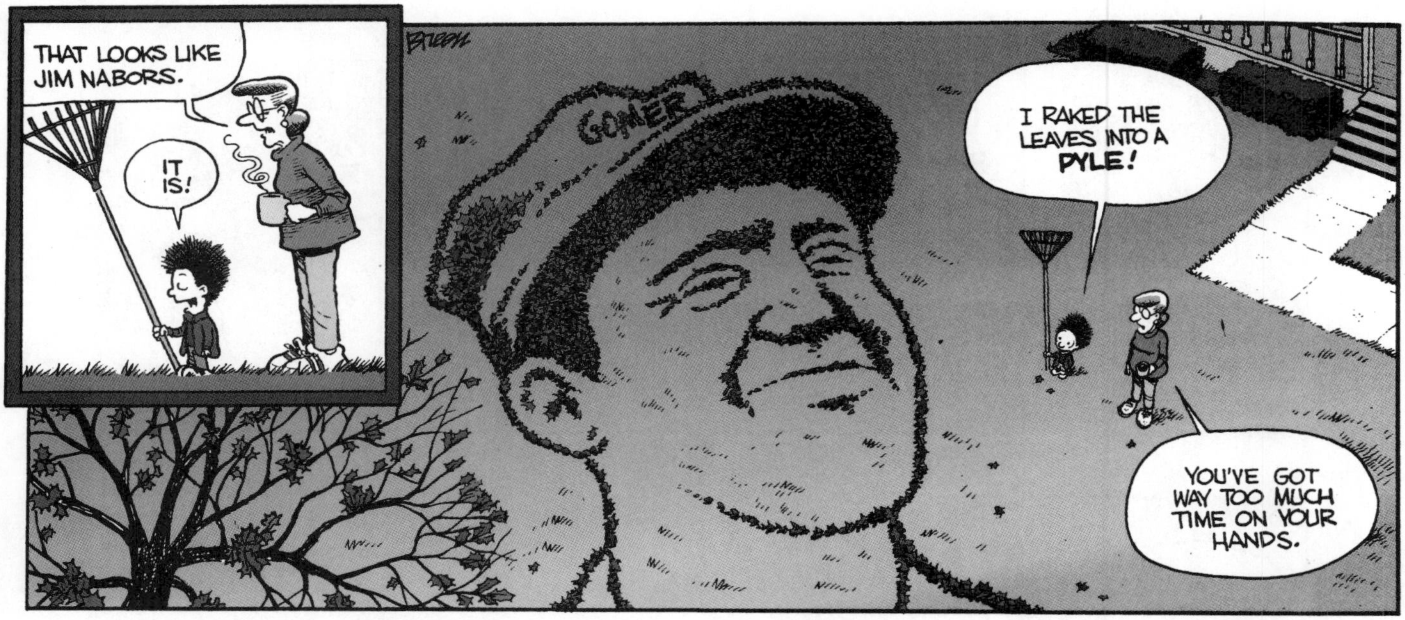
THAT LOOKS LIKE JIM NABORS.
IT IS!
GOMER
I RAKED THE LEAVES INTO A PYLE!
YOU'VE GOT WAY TOO MUCH TIME ON YOUR HANDS.

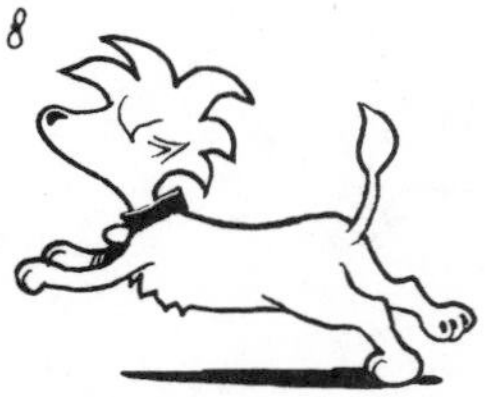

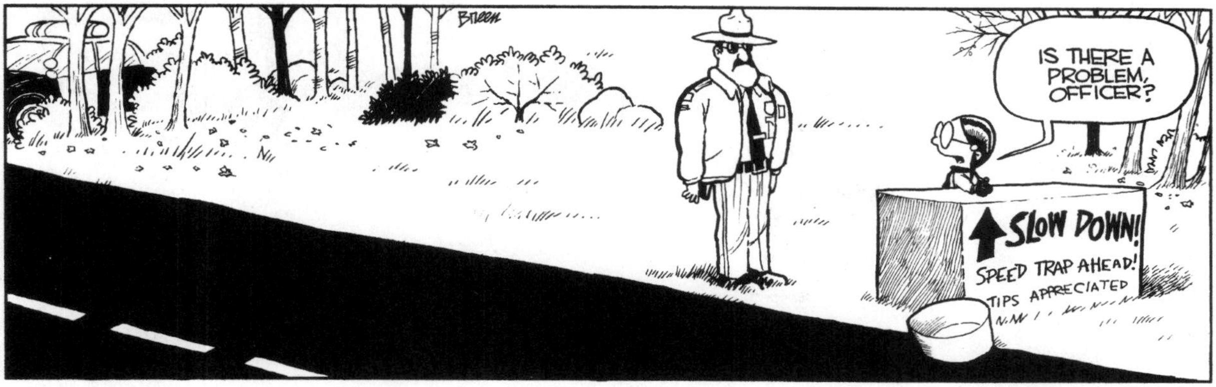

IS THERE A PROBLEM, OFFICER?
SLOW DOWN!
SPEED TRAP AHEAD!
TIPS APPRECIATED

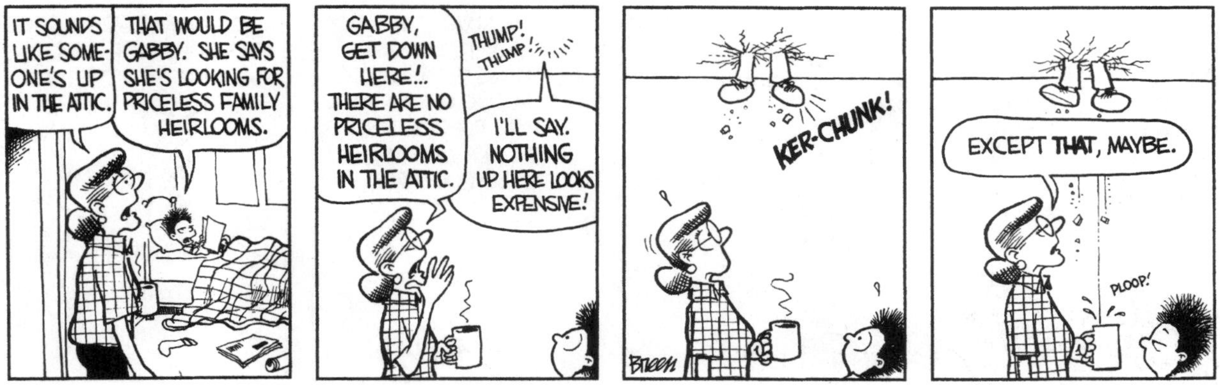

IT SOUNDS LIKE SOME-ONE'S UP IN THE ATTIC.
THAT WOULD BE GABBY. SHE SAYS SHE'S LOOKING FOR PRICELESS FAMILY HEIRLOOMS.
GABBY, GET DOWN HERE!.. THERE ARE NO PRICELESS HEIRLOOMS IN THE ATTIC.
THUMP! THUMP!
I'LL SAY. NOTHING UP HERE LOOKS EXPENSIVE!
KER-CHUNK!
EXCEPT THAT, MAYBE.
PLOOP!

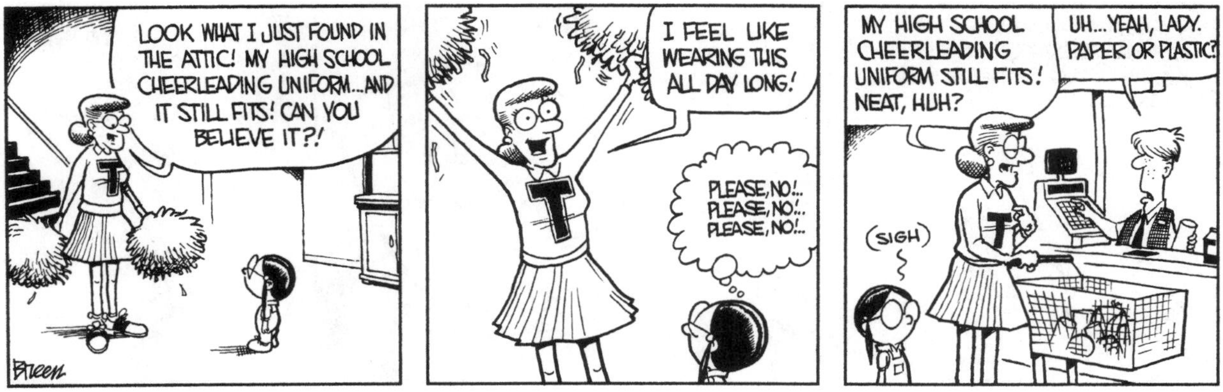

LOOK WHAT I JUST FOUND IN THE ATTIC! MY HIGH SCHOOL CHEERLEADING UNIFORM...AND IT STILL FITS! CAN YOU BELIEVE IT?!
I FEEL LIKE WEARING THIS ALL DAY LONG!
PLEASE, NO!.. PLEASE, NO!.. PLEASE, NO!..
MY HIGH SCHOOL CHEERLEADING UNIFORM STILL FITS! NEAT, HUH?
UH...YEAH, LADY. PAPER OR PLASTIC?
(SIGH)

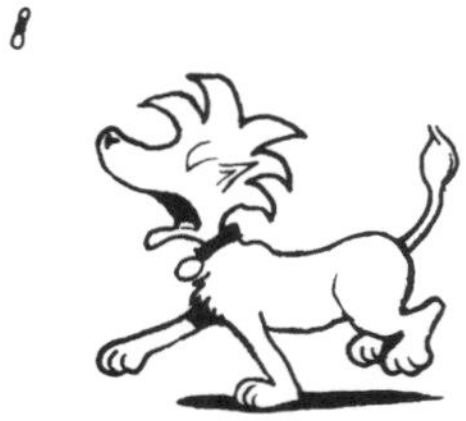

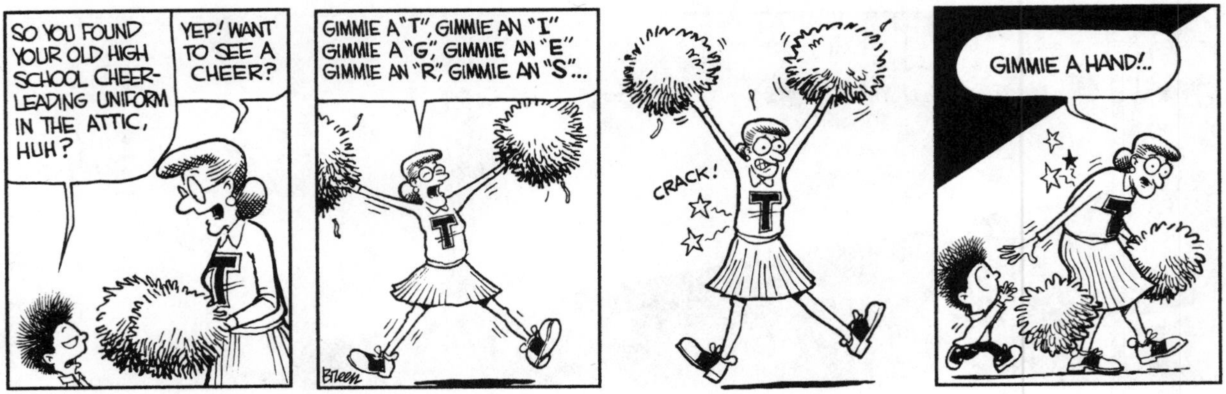
SO YOU FOUND YOUR OLD HIGH SCHOOL CHEER-LEADING UNIFORM IN THE ATTIC, HUH?
YEP! WANT TO SEE A CHEER?
GIMMIE A "T", GIMMIE AN "I" GIMMIE A "G", GIMMIE AN "E" GIMMIE AN "R", GIMMIE AN "S"...
CRACK!
GIMMIE A HAND!..

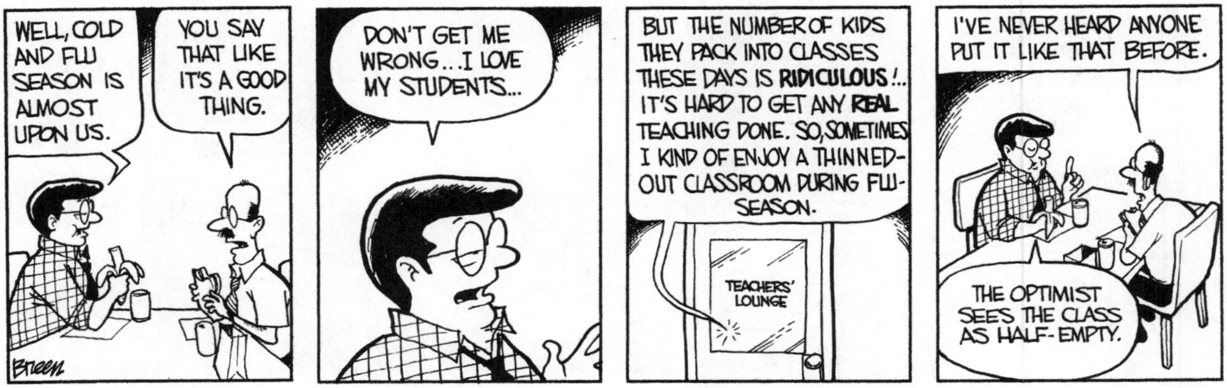
WELL, COLD AND FLU SEASON IS ALMOST UPON US.
YOU SAY THAT LIKE IT'S A GOOD THING.
DON'T GET ME WRONG... I LOVE MY STUDENTS...
BUT THE NUMBER OF KIDS THEY PACK INTO CLASSES THESE DAYS IS RIDICULOUS!... IT'S HARD TO GET ANY REAL TEACHING DONE. SO, SOMETIMES I KIND OF ENJOY A THINNED-OUT CLASSROOM DURING FLU-SEASON.
TEACHERS' LOUNGE
I'VE NEVER HEARD ANYONE PUT IT LIKE THAT BEFORE.
THE OPTIMIST SEES THE CLASS AS HALF-EMPTY.

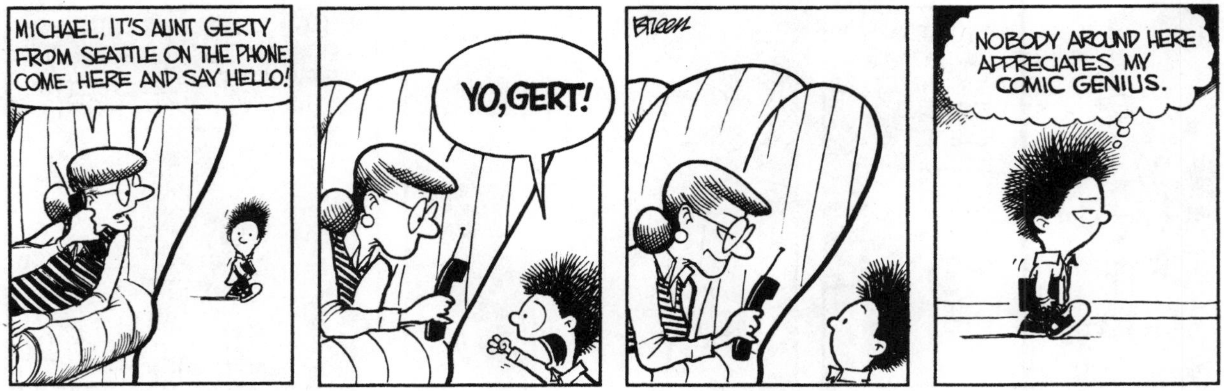
MICHAEL, IT'S AUNT GERTY FROM SEATTLE ON THE PHONE. COME HERE AND SAY HELLO!
YO, GERT!
NOBODY AROUND HERE APPRECIATES MY COMIC GENIUS.

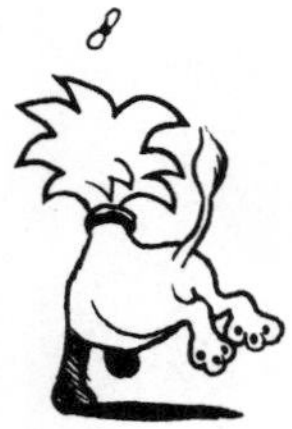

GROSS! YOU NEED TO WASH THE DIRT FROM BEHIND YOUR EARS!
NOTHING GOOD HAS EVER RESULTED FROM POOR HYGIENE!
WOULD YOU JUST LET ME BE?
WHEN WAS THE LAST TIME YOU TOOK A BATH, ANY-WAY?
FRIDAY...
OF LAST WEEK.
!
NO, SIR... NOTHING GOOD WHATSOEVER.

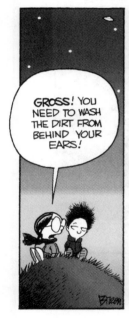

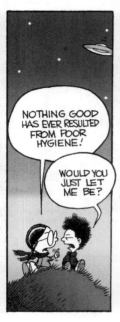

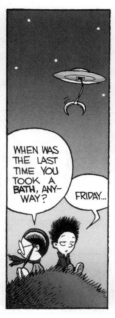

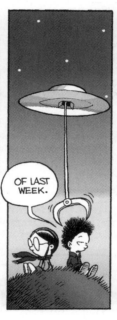

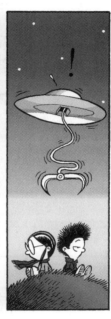

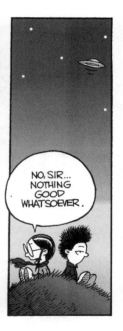

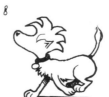

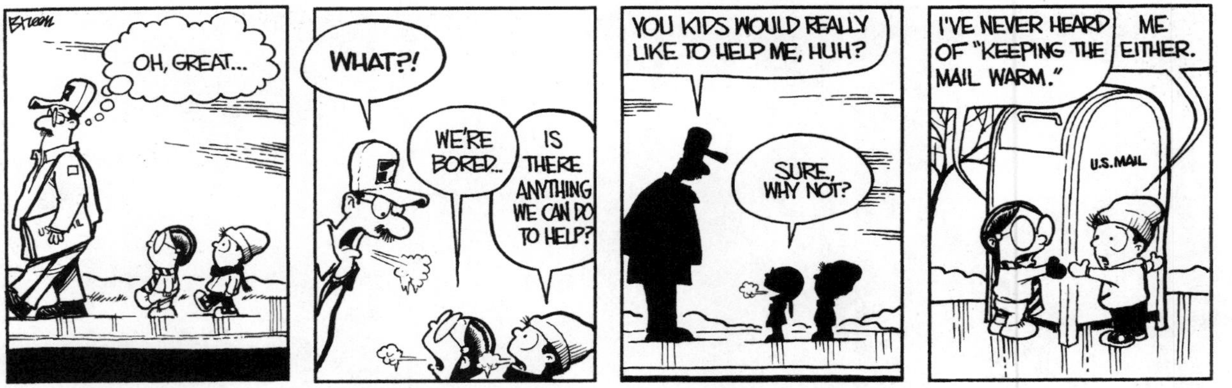
OH, GREAT...
WHAT?!
WE'RE BORED...
IS THERE ANYTHING WE CAN DO TO HELP?
YOU KIDS WOULD REALLY LIKE TO HELP ME, HUH?
SURE, WHY NOT?
U.S. MAIL
I'VE NEVER HEARD OF "KEEPING THE MAIL WARM."
ME EITHER.

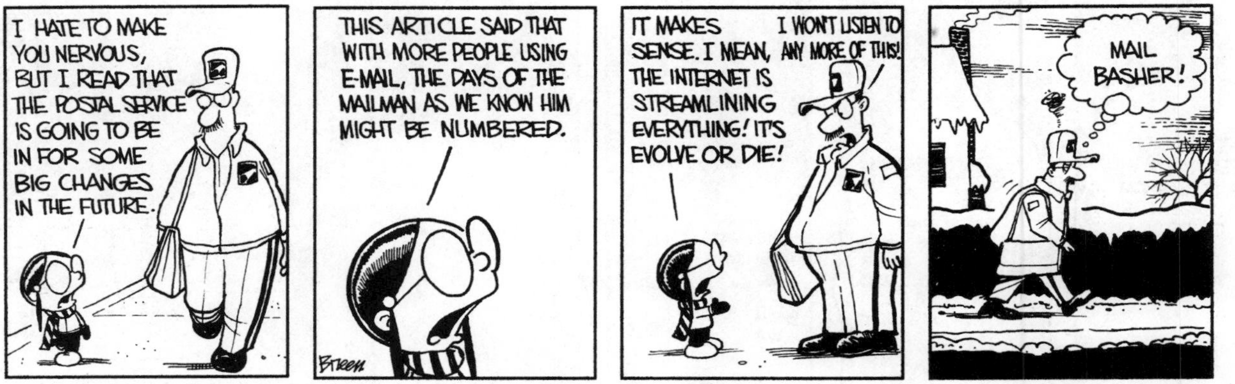
I HATE TO MAKE YOU NERVOUS, BUT I READ THAT THE POSTAL SERVICE IS GOING TO BE IN FOR SOME BIG CHANGES IN THE FUTURE.
THIS ARTICLE SAID THAT WITH MORE PEOPLE USING E-MAIL, THE DAYS OF THE MAILMAN AS WE KNOW HIM MIGHT BE NUMBERED.
IT MAKES SENSE. I MEAN, THE INTERNET IS STREAMLINING EVERYTHING! IT'S EVOLVE OR DIE!
I WON'T LISTEN TO ANY MORE OF THIS!
MAIL BASHER!

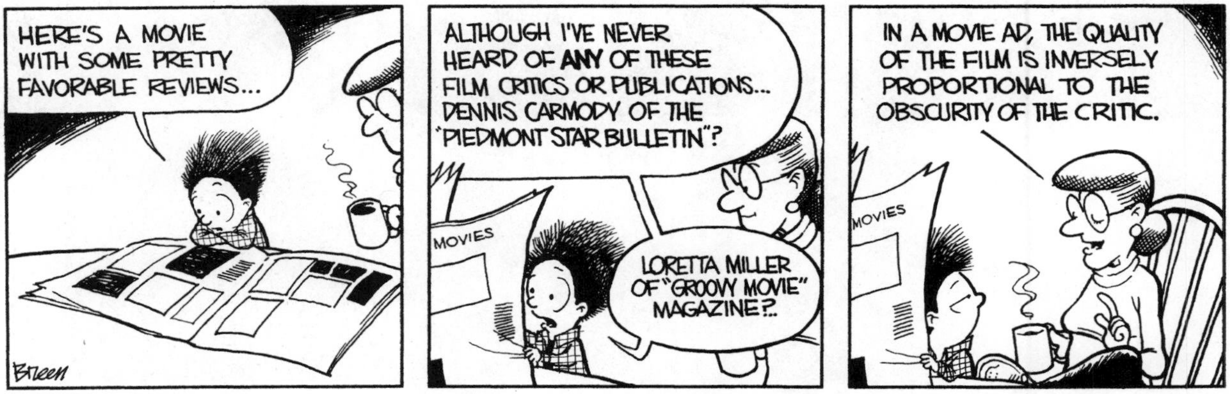
HERE'S A MOVIE WITH SOME PRETTY FAVORABLE REVIEWS...
ALTHOUGH I'VE NEVER HEARD OF ANY OF THESE FILM CRITICS OR PUBLICATIONS... DENNIS CARMODY OF THE "PIEDMONT STAR BULLETIN"?
MOVIES
LORETTA MILLER OF "GROOVY MOVIE" MAGAZINE?..
IN A MOVIE AD, THE QUALITY OF THE FILM IS INVERSELY PROPORTIONAL TO THE OBSCURITY OF THE CRITIC.
MOVIES

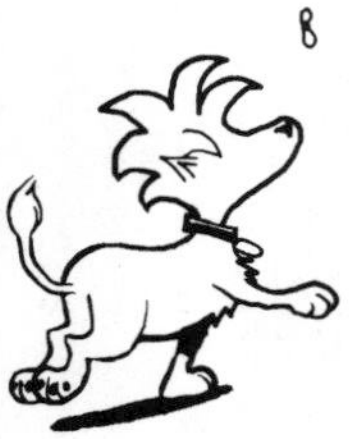

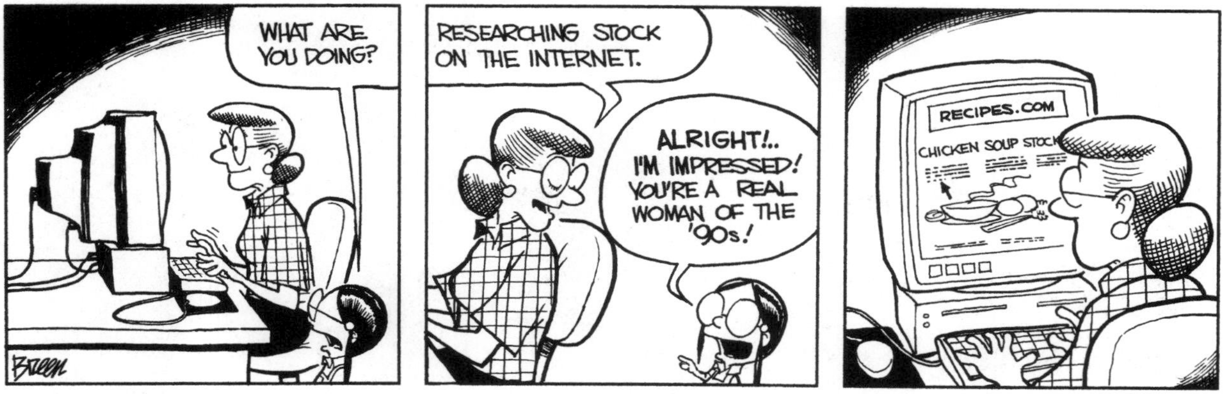
WHAT ARE YOU DOING?
RESEARCHING STOCK ON THE INTERNET.
ALRIGHT!.. I'M IMPRESSED! YOU'RE A REAL WOMAN OF THE '90s!
RECIPES.COM
CHICKEN SOUP STOCK

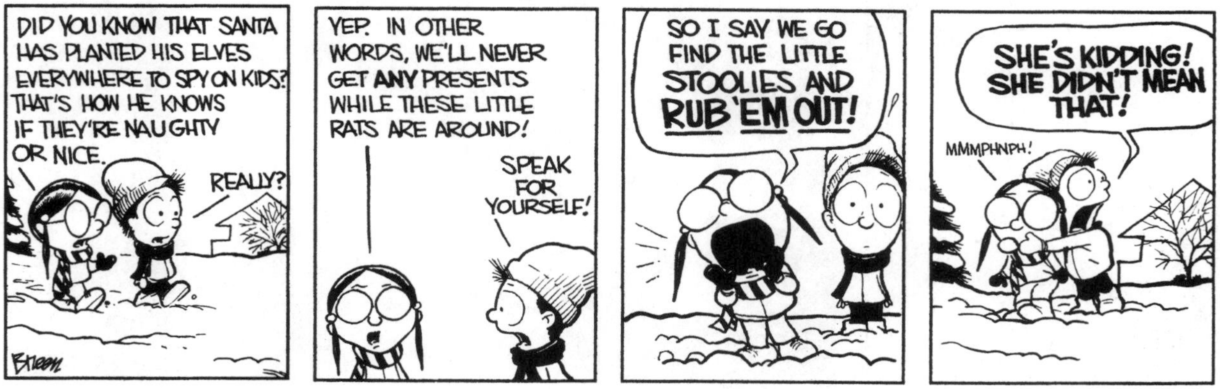
DID YOU KNOW THAT SANTA HAS PLANTED HIS ELVES EVERYWHERE TO SPY ON KIDS? THAT'S HOW HE KNOWS IF THEY'RE NAUGHTY OR NICE.
REALLY?
YEP. IN OTHER WORDS, WE'LL NEVER GET ANY PRESENTS WHILE THESE LITTLE RATS ARE AROUND!
SPEAK FOR YOURSELF!
SO I SAY WE GO FIND THE LITTLE STOOLIES AND RUB 'EM OUT!
MMMPHNPH!
SHE'S KIDDING! SHE DIDN'T MEAN THAT!

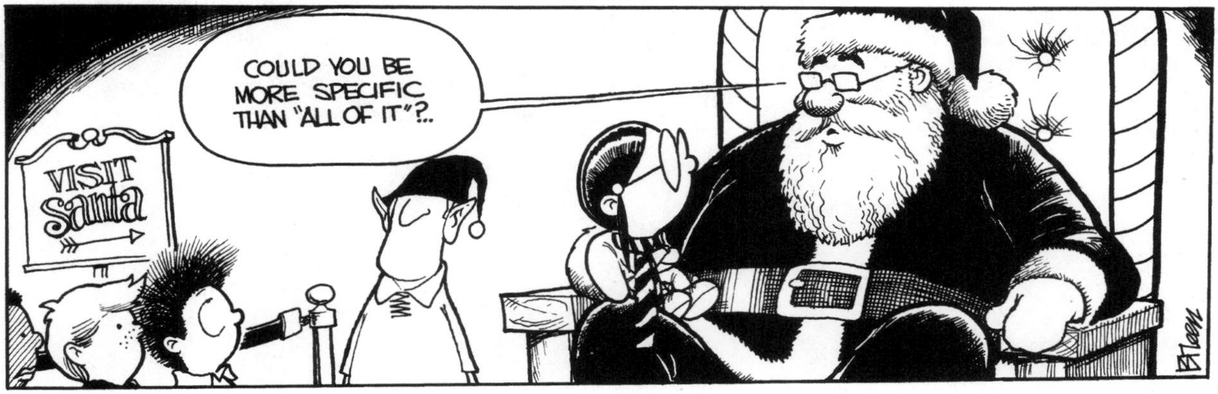
COULD YOU BE MORE SPECIFIC THAN "ALL OF IT"?..
VISIT Santa

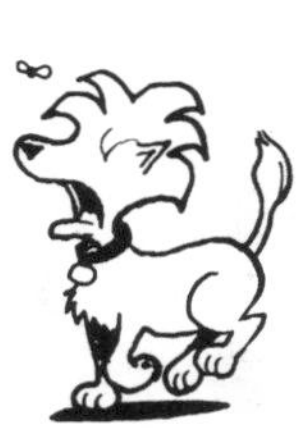

THIS 'MILLENNIUM BUG' COMPUTER GLITCH HAS SOME PEOPLE PRETTY SCARED...
Y2K
IT SAYS HERE THEY'RE STOCK-PILING MONTHS WORTH OF FOOD AND PROVISIONS IN CASE THE WHOLE SYSTEM BREAKS DOWN.
I THINK THAT'S KINDA NUTTY...
Y2K
BUT TO EACH HIS OWN.
Y2K

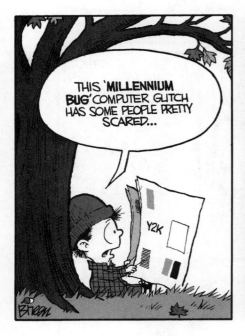

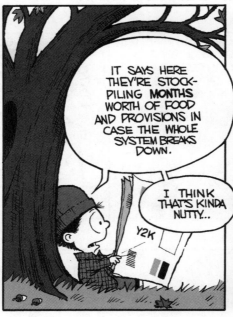

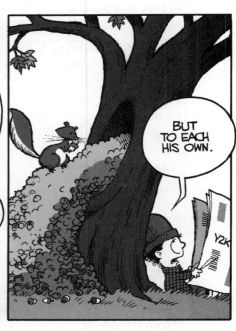

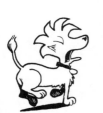

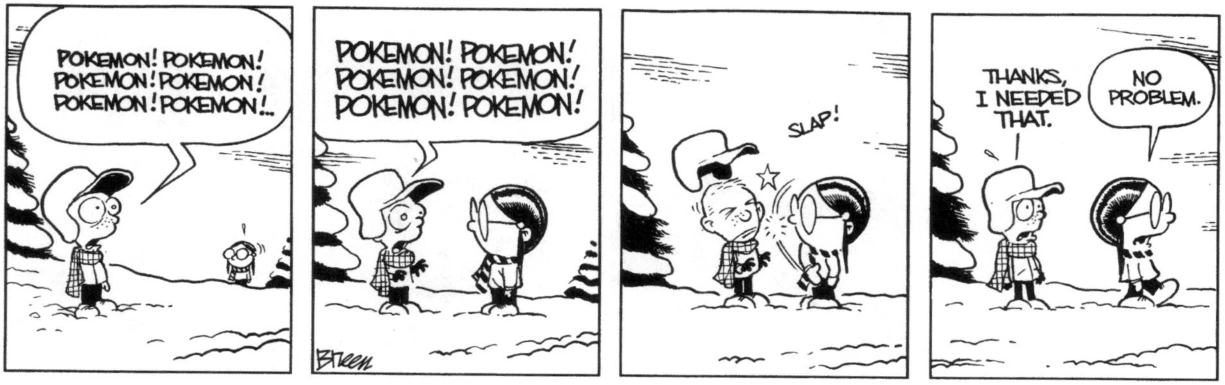
POKEMON! POKEMON! POKEMON! POKEMON! POKEMON! POKEMON!..
POKEMON! POKEMON! POKEMON! POKEMON! POKEMON! POKEMON!
SLAP!
THANKS, I NEEDED THAT.
NO PROBLEM.

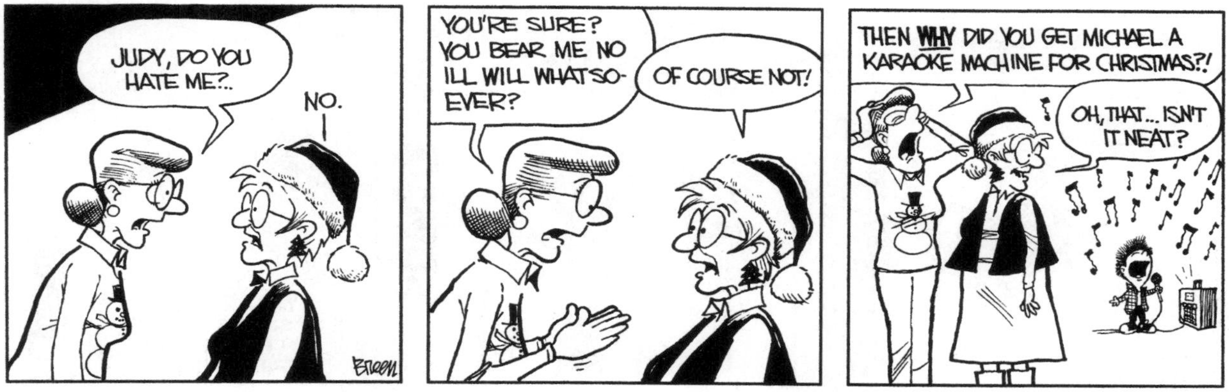
JUDY, DO YOU HATE ME?..
NO.
YOU'RE SURE? YOU BEAR ME NO ILL WILL WHATSO-EVER?
OF COURSE NOT!
THEN WHY DID YOU GET MICHAEL A KARAOKE MACHINE FOR CHRISTMAS?!
OH, THAT... ISN'T IT NEAT?

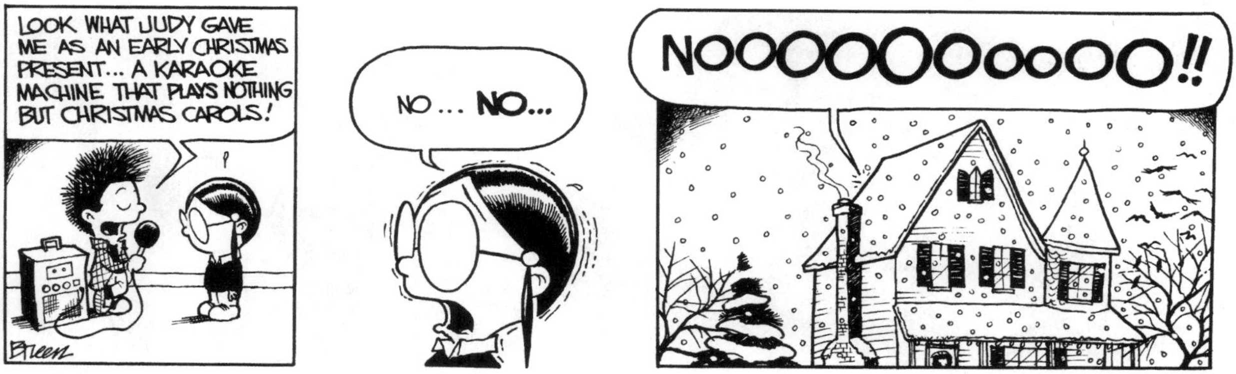
LOOK WHAT JUDY GAVE ME AS AN EARLY CHRISTMAS PRESENT... A KARAOKE MACHINE THAT PLAYS NOTHING BUT CHRISTMAS CAROLS!
NO ... NO...
NOOOOOOOoooOO!!

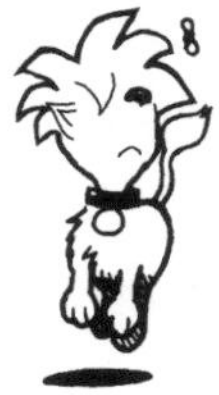

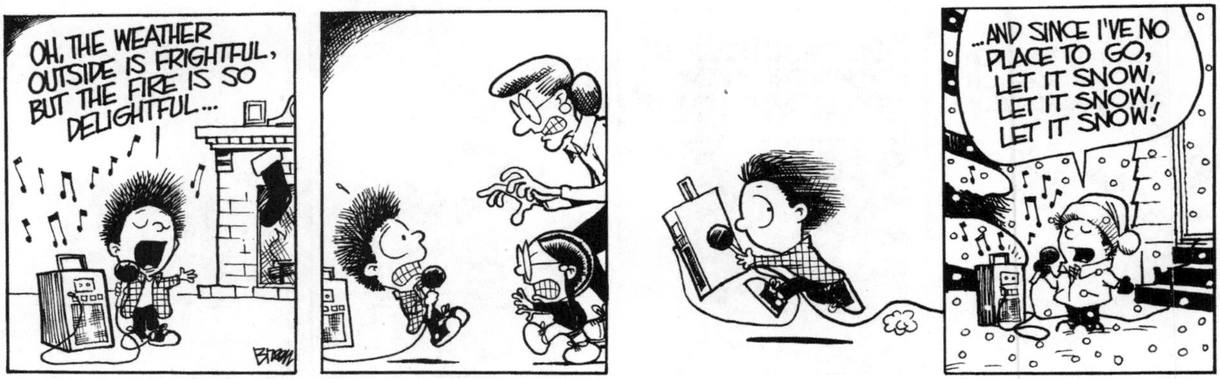
OH, THE WEATHER OUTSIDE IS FRIGHTFUL, BUT THE FIRE IS SO DELIGHTFUL...
...AND SINCE I'VE NO PLACE TO GO, LET IT SNOW, LET IT SNOW, LET IT SNOW!

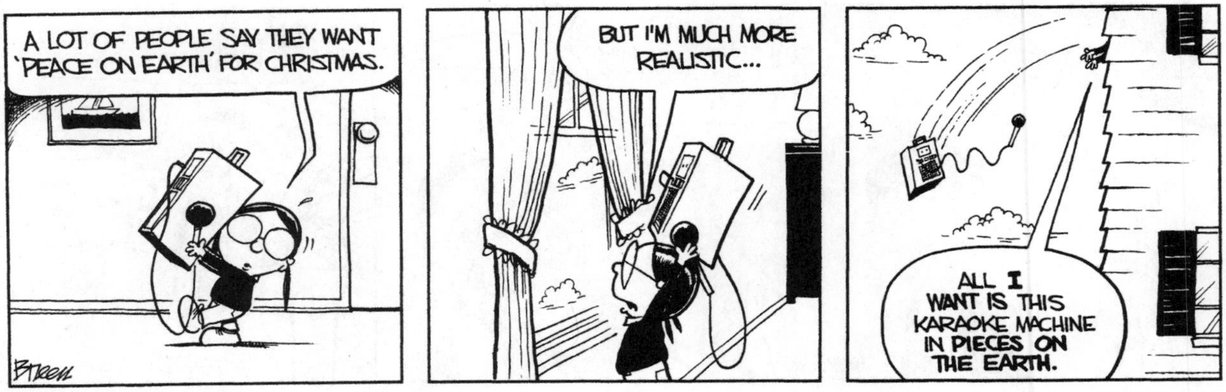
A LOT OF PEOPLE SAY THEY WANT 'PEACE ON EARTH' FOR CHRISTMAS.
BUT I'M MUCH MORE REALISTIC...
ALL I WANT IS THIS KARAOKE MACHINE IN PIECES ON THE EARTH.

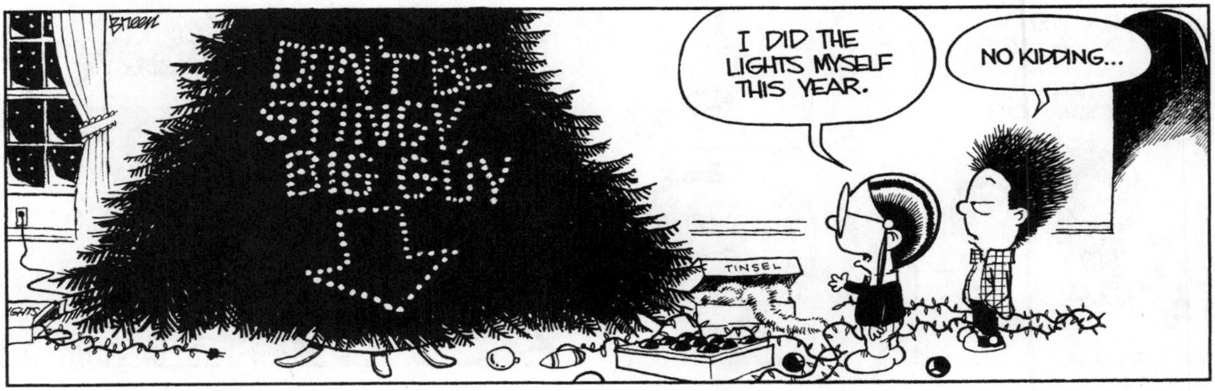
DON'T BE STINGY BIG GUY
TINSEL
I DID THE LIGHTS MYSELF THIS YEAR.
NO KIDDING...

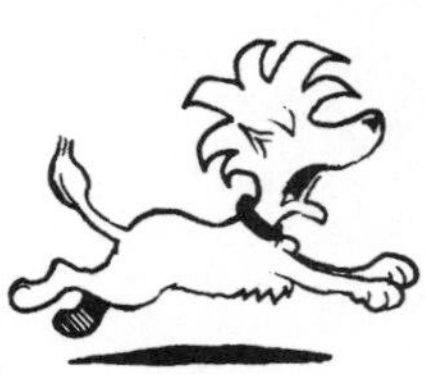

WE GO THROUGH THIS EVERY YEAR WHEN IT GETS COLD OUTSIDE...
I JUST DON'T GET IT!..
IS IT THE PEOPLE?
IS IT THE COST?
WHAT'S WRONG WITH JOINING A **GYM**?!
THIRTY- SIX, THIRTY-SEVEN... QUIET, I'LL LOSE COUNT!.. THIRTY-EIGHT...

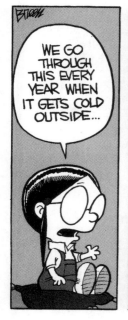

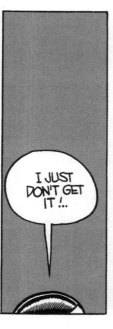

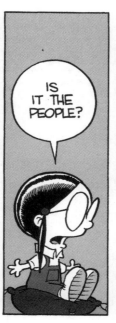

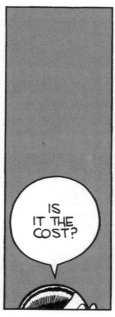

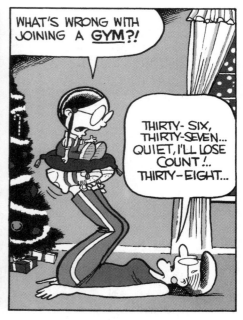

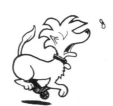

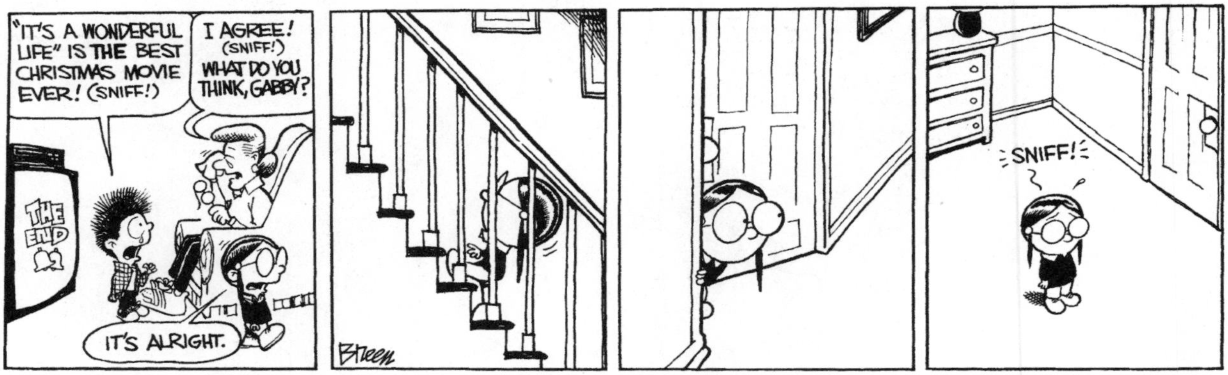
"IT'S A WONDERFUL LIFE" IS THE BEST CHRISTMAS MOVIE EVER! (SNIFF!)
I AGREE! (SNIFF!) WHAT DO YOU THINK, GABBY?
THE END
IT'S ALRIGHT.
SNIFF!
BREEN

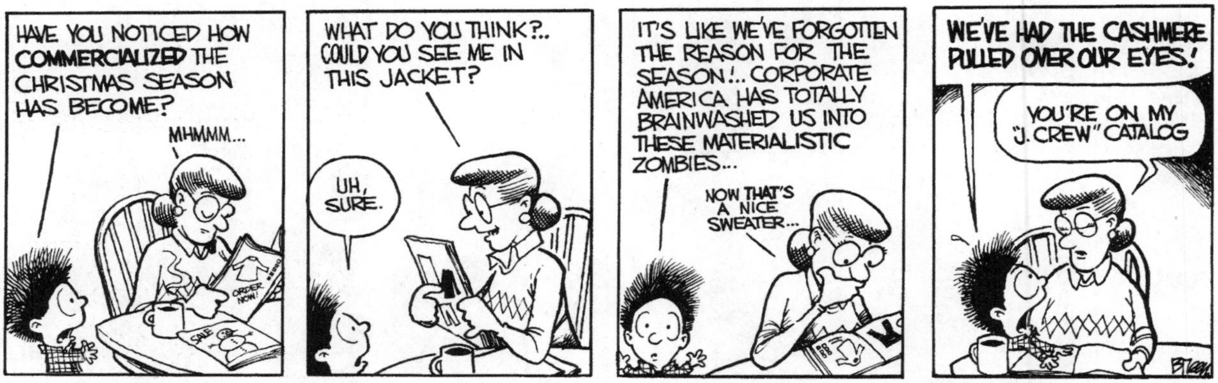
HAVE YOU NOTICED HOW COMMERCIALIZED THE CHRISTMAS SEASON HAS BECOME?
MHMMM...
ORDER NOW!
SALE
WHAT DO YOU THINK?.. COULD YOU SEE ME IN THIS JACKET?
UH, SURE.
IT'S LIKE WE'VE FORGOTTEN THE REASON FOR THE SEASON!.. CORPORATE AMERICA HAS TOTALLY BRAINWASHED US INTO THESE MATERIALISTIC ZOMBIES...
NOW THAT'S A NICE SWEATER...
WE'VE HAD THE CASHMERE PULLED OVER OUR EYES!
YOU'RE ON MY "J. CREW" CATALOG
BREEN

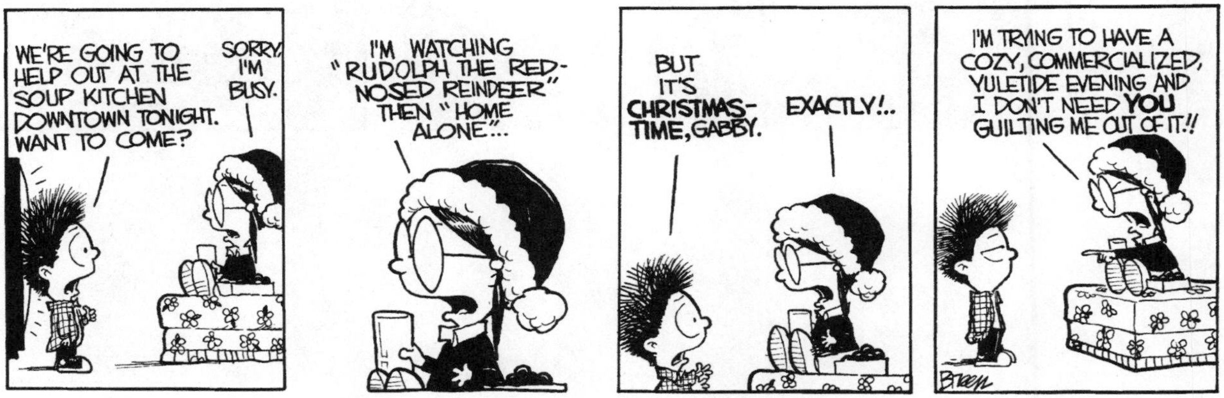
WE'RE GOING TO HELP OUT AT THE SOUP KITCHEN DOWNTOWN TONIGHT. WANT TO COME?
SORRY. I'M BUSY.
I'M WATCHING "RUDOLPH THE RED-NOSED REINDEER" THEN "HOME ALONE".
BUT IT'S CHRISTMAS-TIME, GABBY.
EXACTLY!..
I'M TRYING TO HAVE A COZY, COMMERCIALIZED, YULETIDE EVENING AND I DON'T NEED YOU GUILTING ME OUT OF IT!!
BREEN

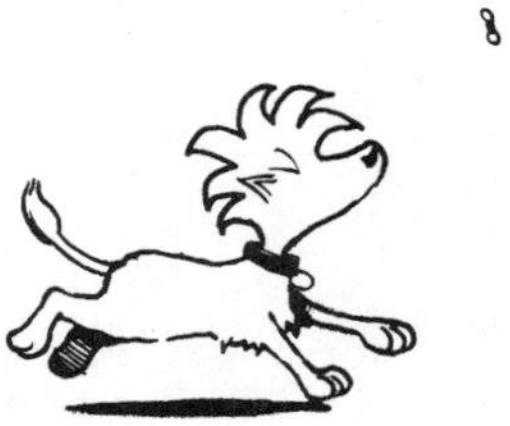

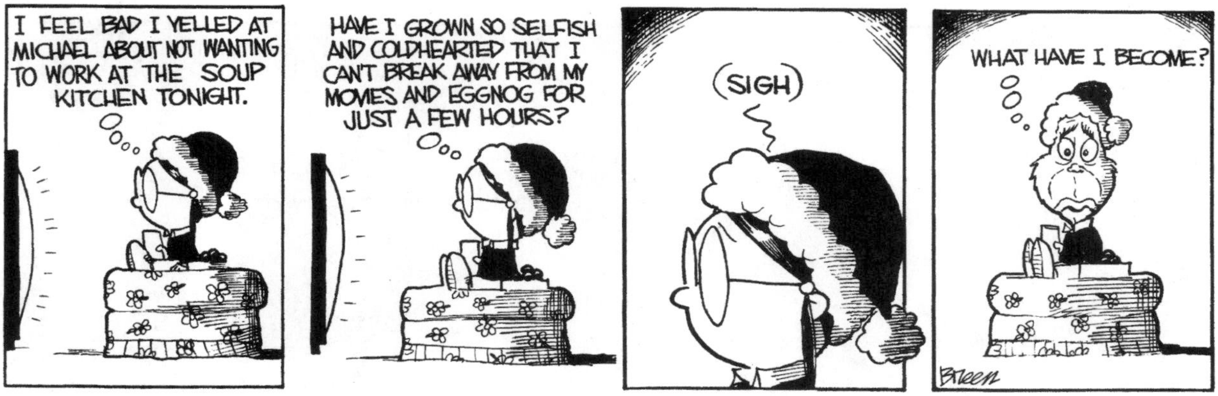
I FEEL BAD I YELLED AT MICHAEL ABOUT NOT WANTING TO WORK AT THE SOUP KITCHEN TONIGHT.
HAVE I GROWN SO SELFISH AND COLDHEARTED THAT I CAN'T BREAK AWAY FROM MY MOVIES AND EGGNOG FOR JUST A FEW HOURS?
(SIGH)
WHAT HAVE I BECOME?
BREEN

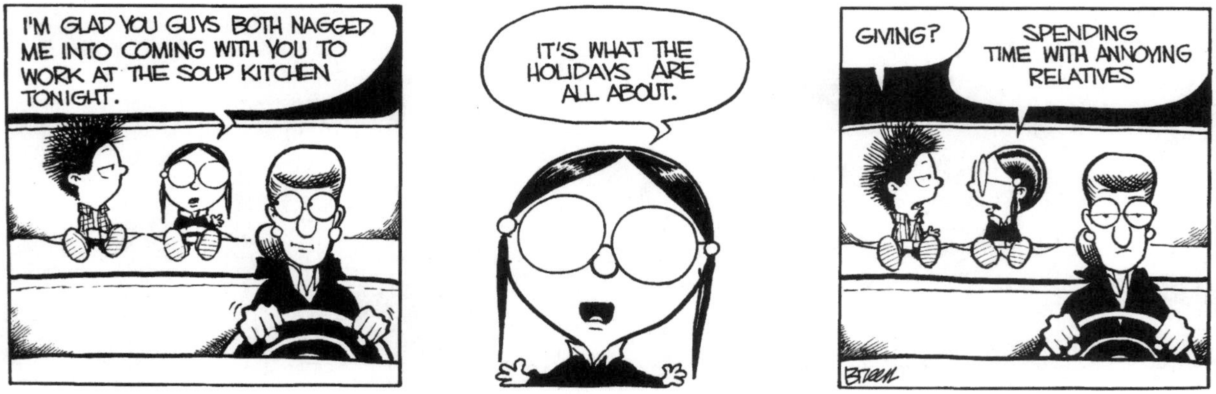
I'M GLAD YOU GUYS BOTH NAGGED ME INTO COMING WITH YOU TO WORK AT THE SOUP KITCHEN TONIGHT.
IT'S WHAT THE HOLIDAYS ARE ALL ABOUT.
GIVING?
SPENDING TIME WITH ANNOYING RELATIVES
BREEN

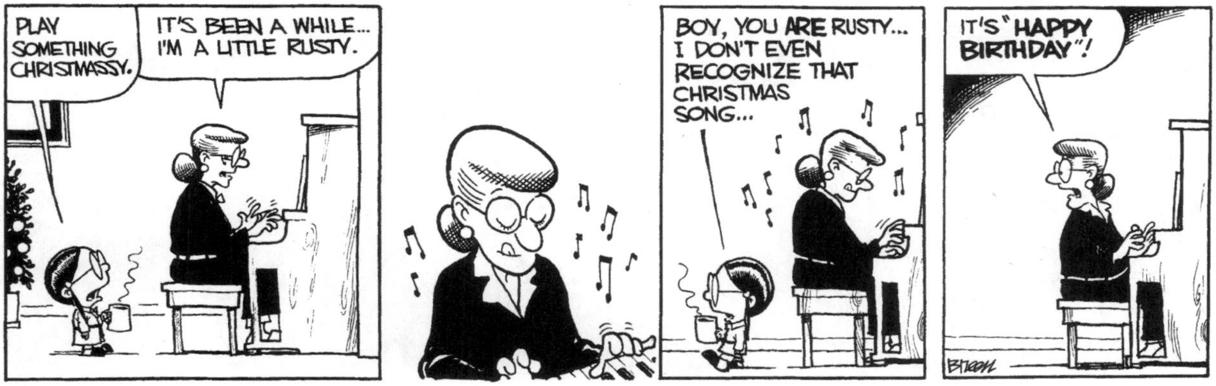
PLAY SOMETHING CHRISTMASSY.
IT'S BEEN A WHILE... I'M A LITTLE RUSTY.
BOY, YOU ARE RUSTY... I DON'T EVEN RECOGNIZE THAT CHRISTMAS SONG...
IT'S "HAPPY BIRTHDAY"!
BREEN

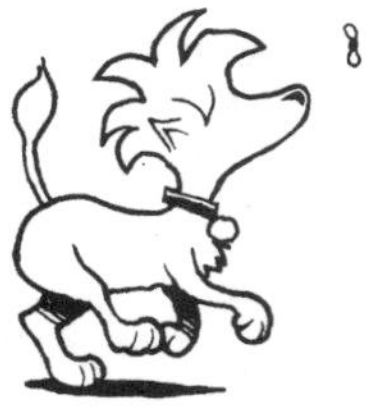

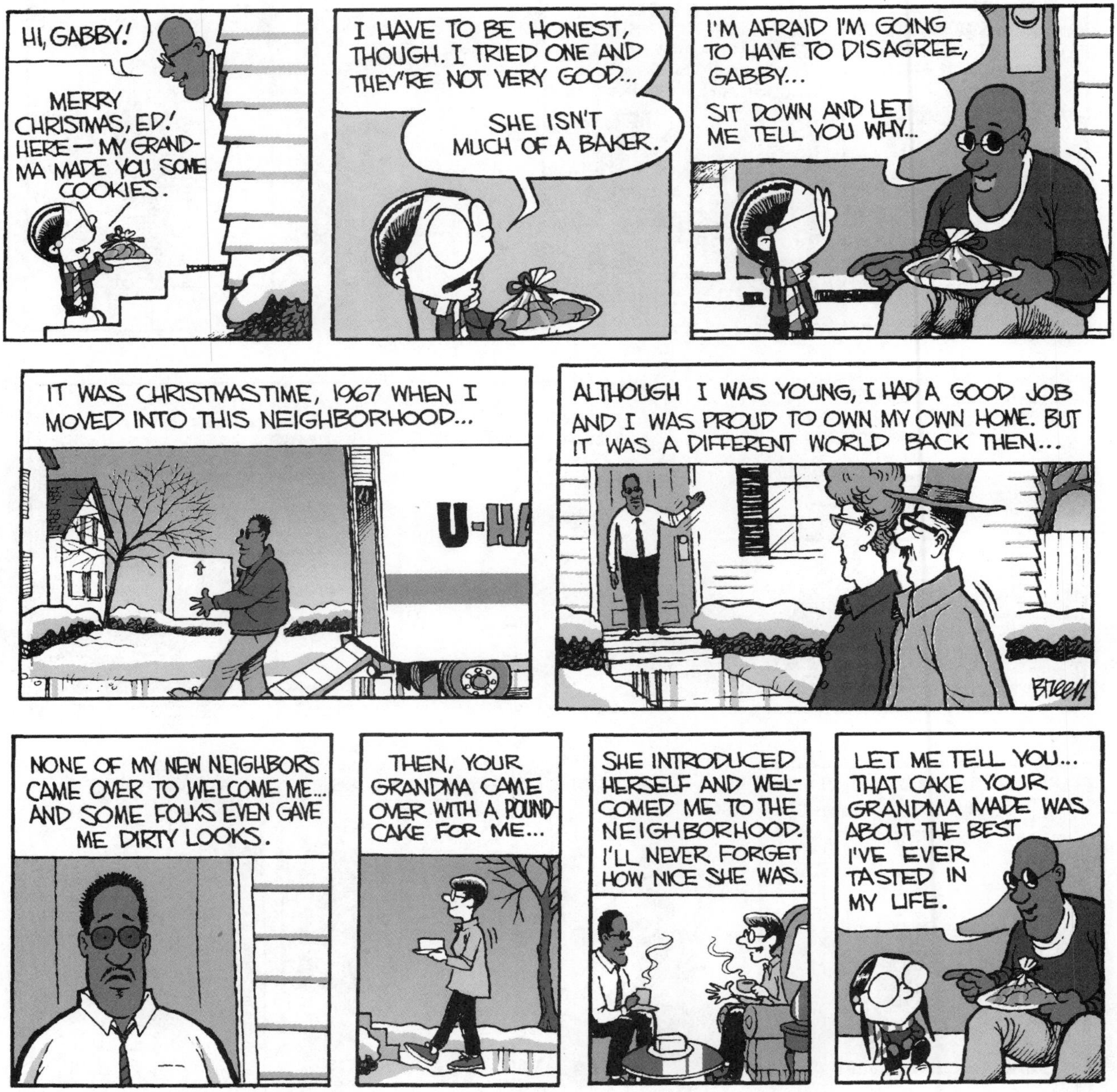
HI, GABBY!
MERRY CHRISTMAS, ED! HERE — MY GRANDMA MADE YOU SOME COOKIES.
I HAVE TO BE HONEST, THOUGH. I TRIED ONE AND THEY'RE NOT VERY GOOD...
SHE ISN'T MUCH OF A BAKER.
I'M AFRAID I'M GOING TO HAVE TO DISAGREE, GABBY...
SIT DOWN AND LET ME TELL YOU WHY...
IT WAS CHRISTMASTIME, 1967 WHEN I MOVED INTO THIS NEIGHBORHOOD...
U-HA
ALTHOUGH I WAS YOUNG, I HAD A GOOD JOB AND I WAS PROUD TO OWN MY OWN HOME. BUT IT WAS A DIFFERENT WORLD BACK THEN...
BREEN
NONE OF MY NEW NEIGHBORS CAME OVER TO WELCOME ME... AND SOME FOLKS EVEN GAVE ME DIRTY LOOKS.
THEN, YOUR GRANDMA CAME OVER WITH A POUND-CAKE FOR ME...
SHE INTRODUCED HERSELF AND WELCOMED ME TO THE NEIGHBORHOOD. I'LL NEVER FORGET HOW NICE SHE WAS.
LET ME TELL YOU... THAT CAKE YOUR GRANDMA MADE WAS ABOUT THE BEST I'VE EVER TASTED IN MY LIFE.

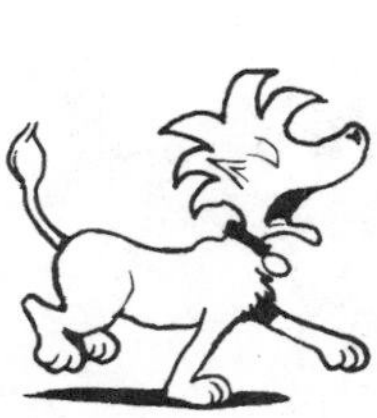

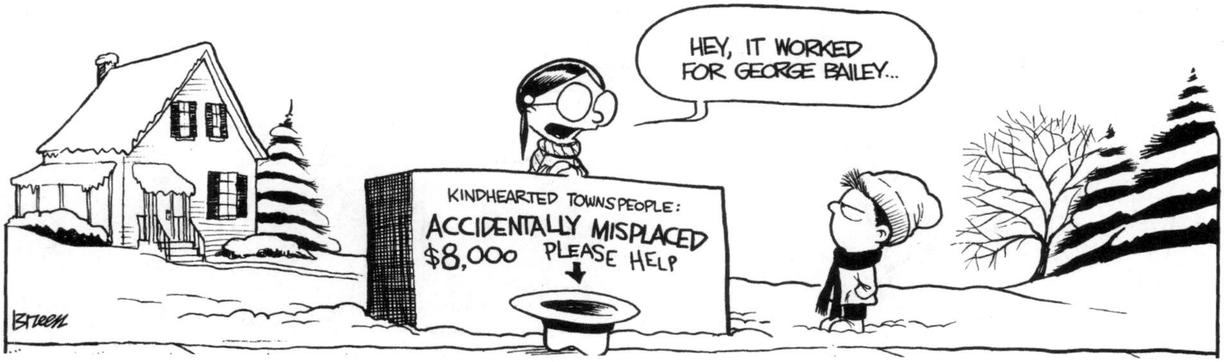
HEY, IT WORKED FOR GEORGE BAILEY...
KINDHEARTED TOWNSPEOPLE:
ACCIDENTALLY MISPLACED $8,000 PLEASE HELP

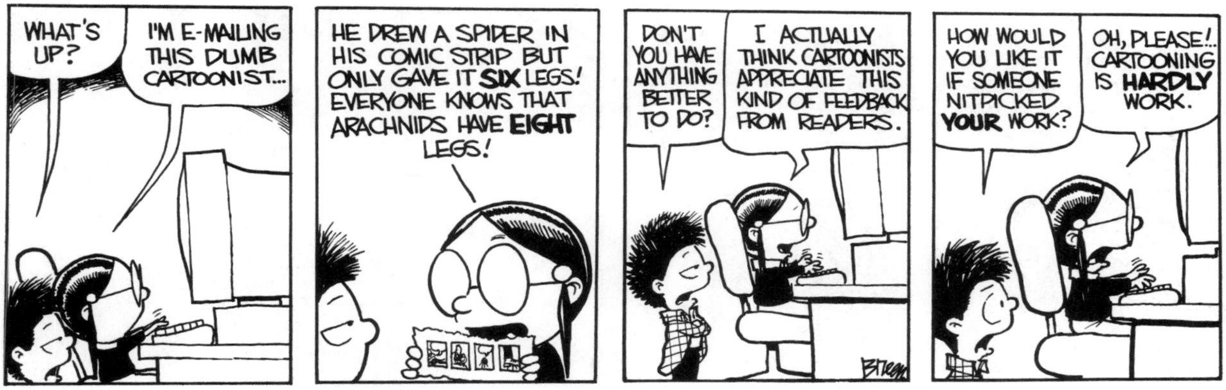
WHAT'S UP?
I'M E-MAILING THIS DUMB CARTOONIST...
HE DREW A SPIDER IN HIS COMIC STRIP BUT ONLY GAVE IT SIX LEGS! EVERYONE KNOWS THAT ARACHNIDS HAVE EIGHT LEGS!
DON'T YOU HAVE ANYTHING BETTER TO DO?
I ACTUALLY THINK CARTOONISTS APPRECIATE THIS KIND OF FEEDBACK FROM READERS.
HOW WOULD YOU LIKE IT IF SOMEONE NITPICKED YOUR WORK?
OH, PLEASE!.. CARTOONING IS HARDLY WORK.

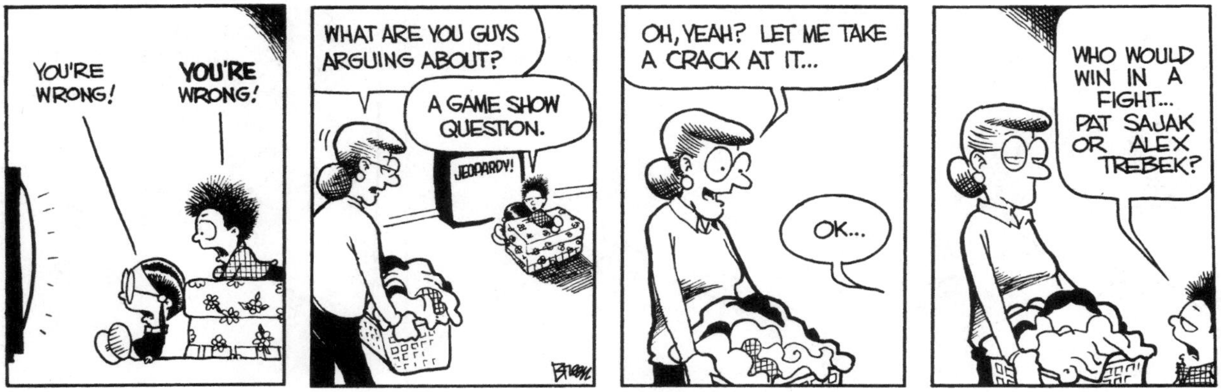
YOU'RE WRONG!
YOU'RE WRONG!
WHAT ARE YOU GUYS ARGUING ABOUT?
A GAME SHOW QUESTION.
JEOPARDY!
OH, YEAH? LET ME TAKE A CRACK AT IT...
OK...
WHO WOULD WIN IN A FIGHT... PAT SAJAK OR ALEX TREBEK?

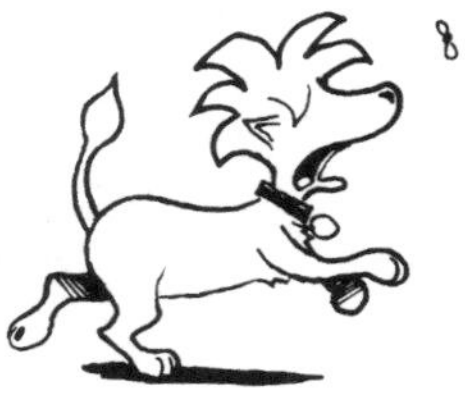

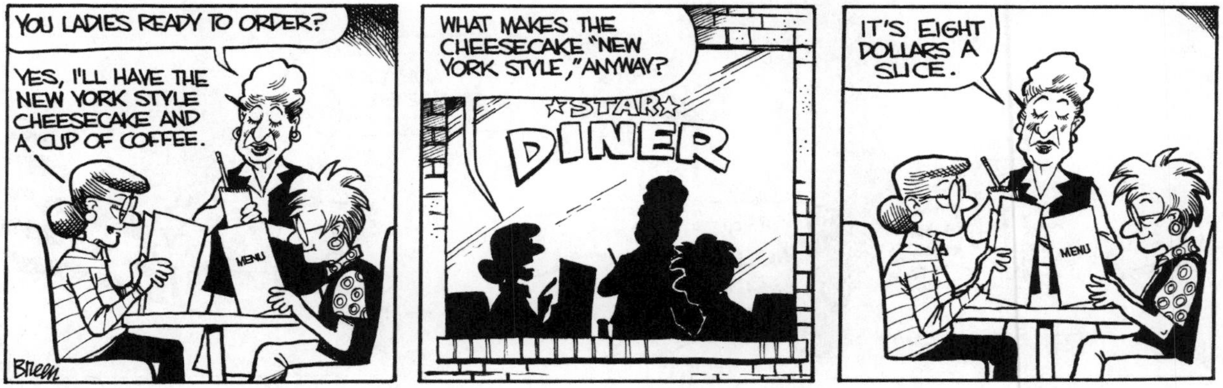
YOU LADIES READY TO ORDER?
YES, I'LL HAVE THE NEW YORK STYLE CHEESECAKE AND A CUP OF COFFEE.
MENU
WHAT MAKES THE CHEESECAKE "NEW YORK STYLE," ANYWAY?
STAR
DINER
IT'S EIGHT DOLLARS A SLICE.
MENU

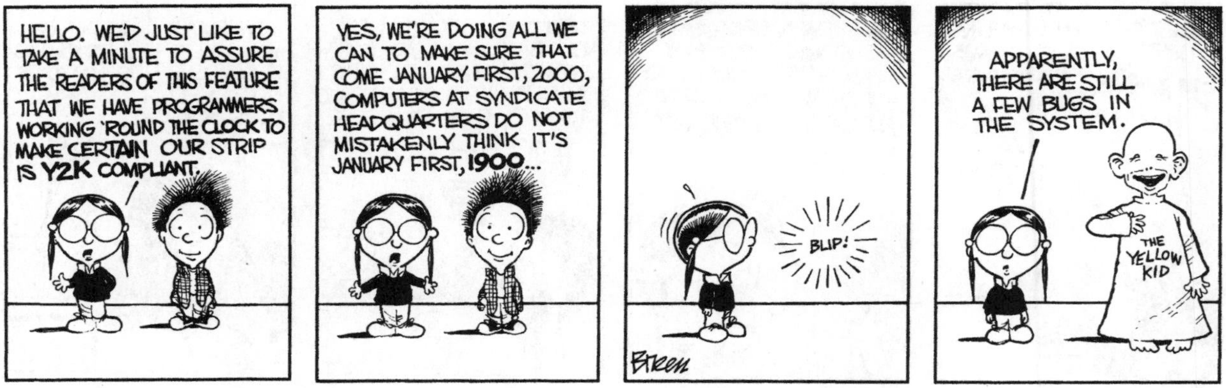
HELLO. WE'D JUST LIKE TO TAKE A MINUTE TO ASSURE THE READERS OF THIS FEATURE THAT WE HAVE PROGRAMMERS WORKING 'ROUND THE CLOCK TO MAKE CERTAIN OUR STRIP IS Y2K COMPLIANT.
YES, WE'RE DOING ALL WE CAN TO MAKE SURE THAT COME JANUARY FIRST, 2000, COMPUTERS AT SYNDICATE HEADQUARTERS DO NOT MISTAKENLY THINK IT'S JANUARY FIRST, 1900...
BLIP!
APPARENTLY, THERE ARE STILL A FEW BUGS IN THE SYSTEM.
THE YELLOW KID

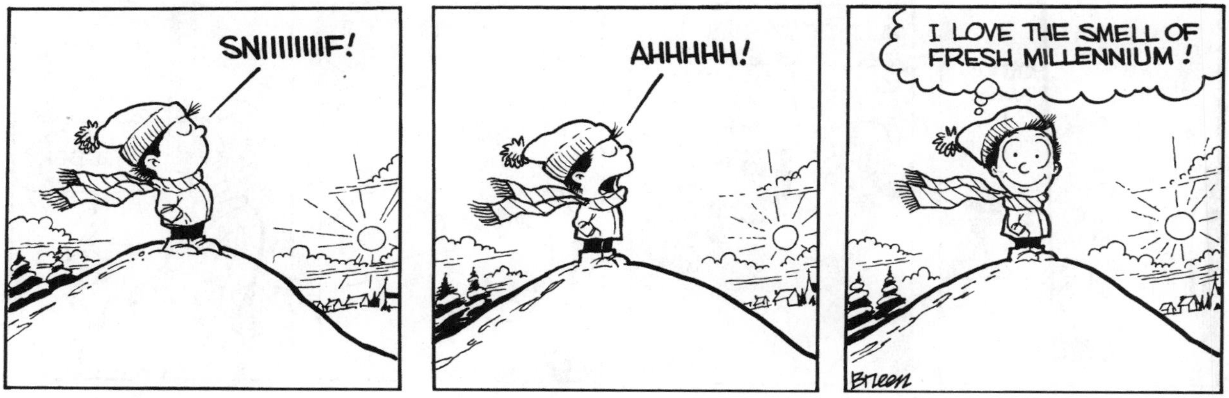
SNIIIIIIIF!
AHHHHH!
I LOVE THE SMELL OF FRESH MILLENNIUM!

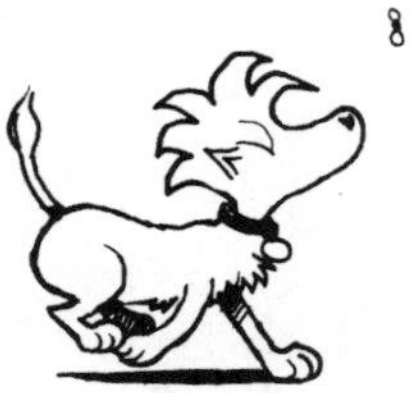

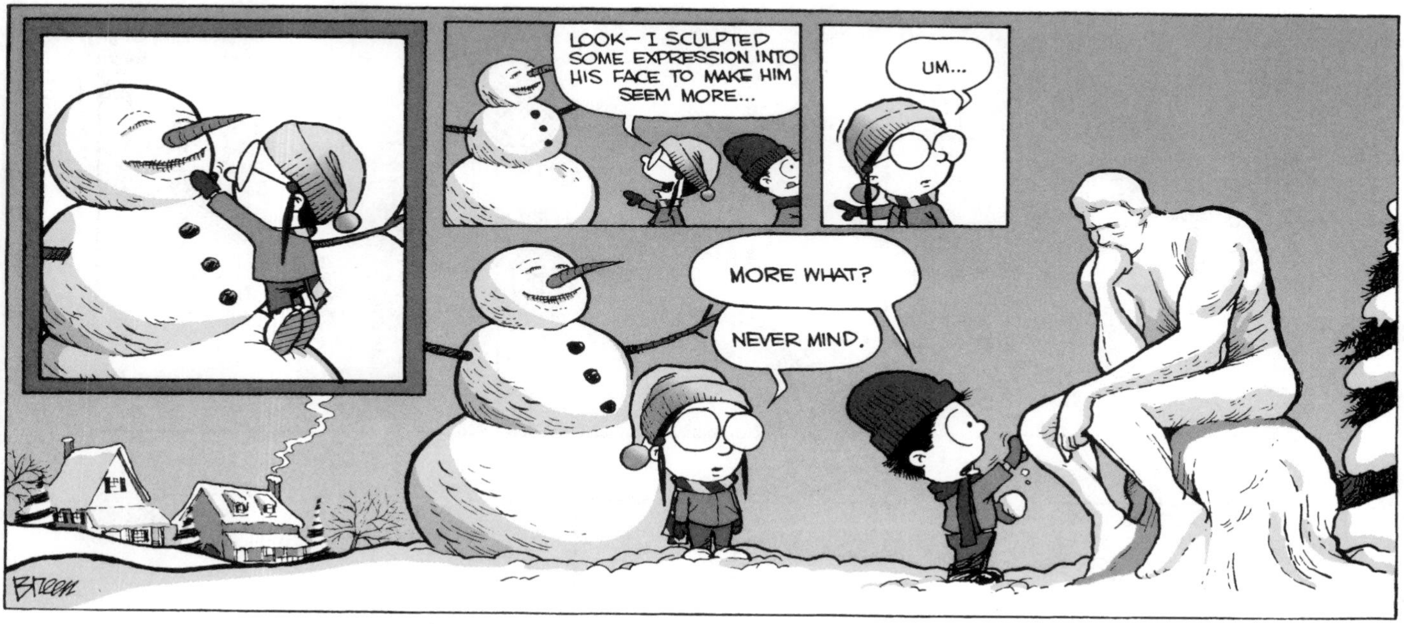
LOOK— I SCULPTED SOME EXPRESSION INTO HIS FACE TO MAKE HIM SEEM MORE...
UM...
MORE WHAT?
NEVER MIND.
BREEN

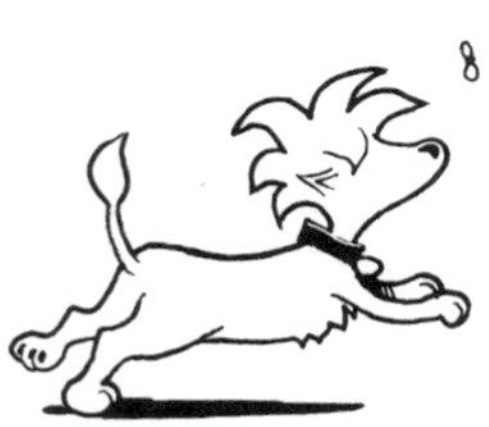

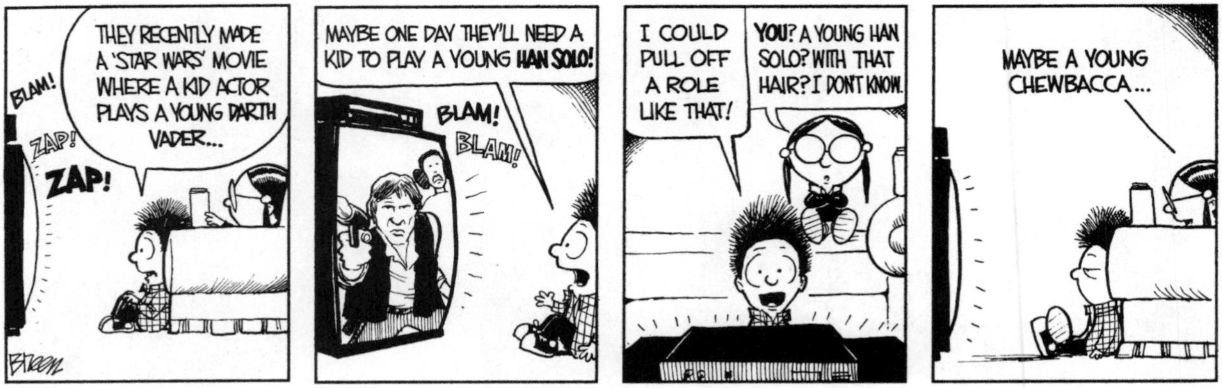
THEY RECENTLY MADE A 'STAR WARS' MOVIE WHERE A KID ACTOR PLAYS A YOUNG DARTH VADER...
BLAM!
ZAP!
ZAP!
MAYBE ONE DAY THEY'LL NEED A KID TO PLAY A YOUNG HAN SOLO!
BLAM!
BLAM!
I COULD PULL OFF A ROLE LIKE THAT!
YOU? A YOUNG HAN SOLO? WITH THAT HAIR? I DON'T KNOW.
MAYBE A YOUNG CHEWBACCA...

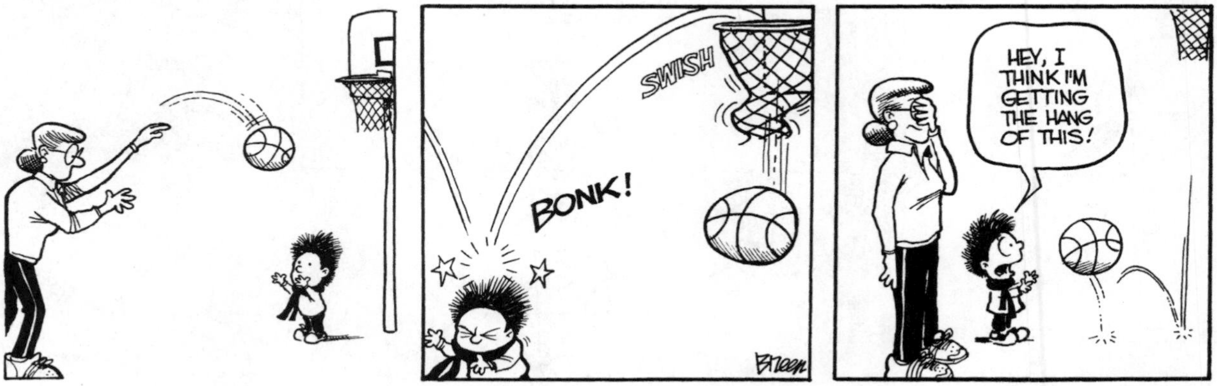
SWISH
BONK!
HEY, I THINK I'M GETTING THE HANG OF THIS!

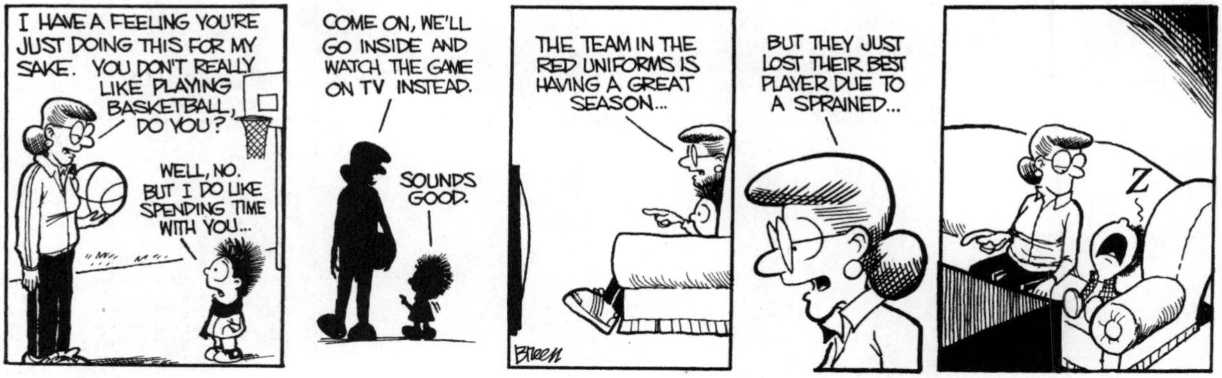
I HAVE A FEELING YOU'RE JUST DOING THIS FOR MY SAKE. YOU DON'T REALLY LIKE PLAYING BASKETBALL, DO YOU?
WELL, NO. BUT I DO LIKE SPENDING TIME WITH YOU...
COME ON, WE'LL GO INSIDE AND WATCH THE GAME ON TV INSTEAD.
SOUNDS GOOD.
THE TEAM IN THE RED UNIFORMS IS HAVING A GREAT SEASON...
BUT THEY JUST LOST THEIR BEST PLAYER DUE TO A SPRAINED...
Z

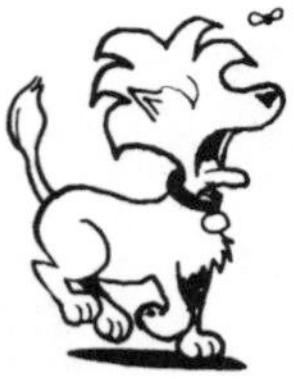

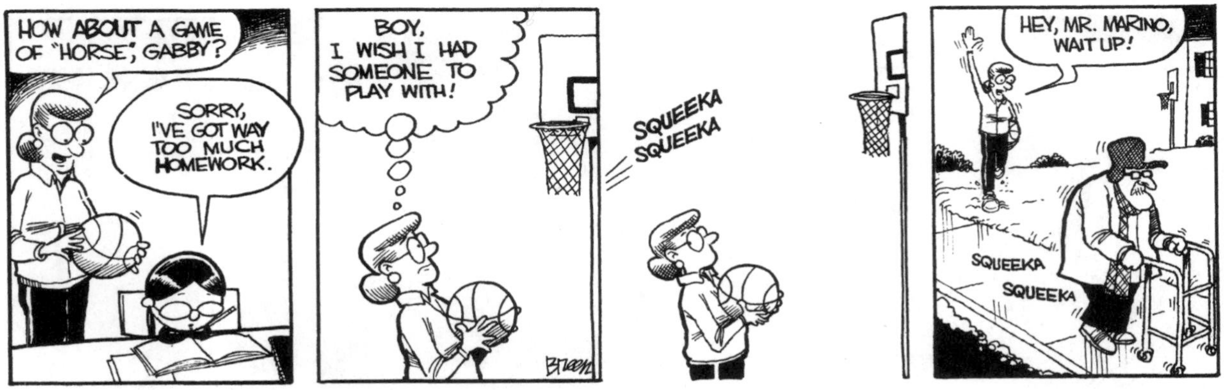
HOW ABOUT A GAME OF "HORSE," GABBY?
SORRY, I'VE GOT WAY TOO MUCH HOMEWORK.
BOY, I WISH I HAD SOMEONE TO PLAY WITH!
SQUEEKA SQUEEKA
HEY, MR. MARINO, WAIT UP!
SQUEEKA
SQUEEKA

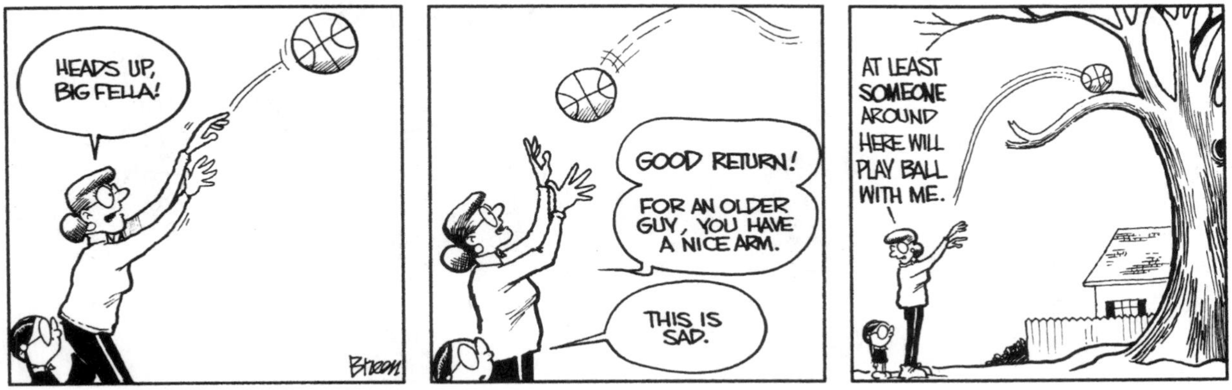
HEADS UP, BIG FELLA!
GOOD RETURN!
FOR AN OLDER GUY, YOU HAVE A NICE ARM.
THIS IS SAD.
AT LEAST SOMEONE AROUND HERE WILL PLAY BALL WITH ME.

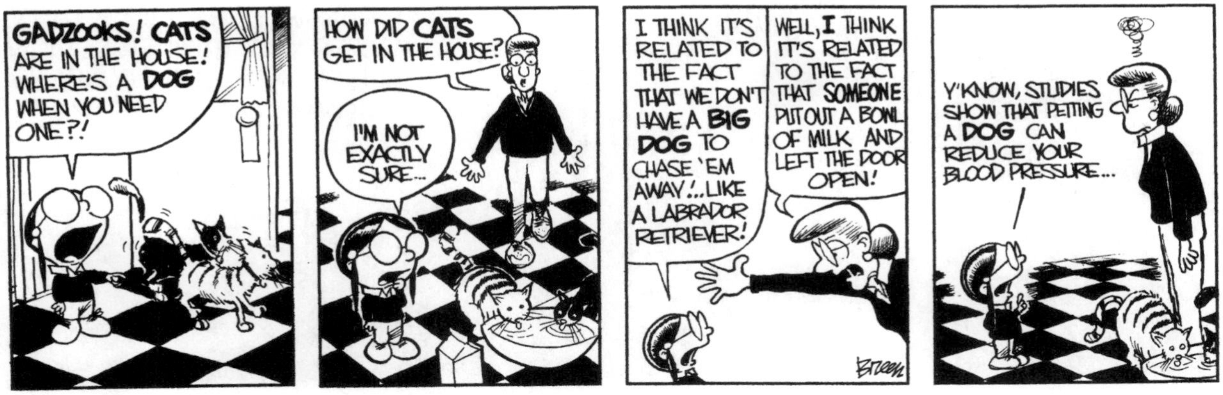
GADZOOKS! CATS ARE IN THE HOUSE! WHERE'S A DOG WHEN YOU NEED ONE?!
HOW DID CATS GET IN THE HOUSE?
I'M NOT EXACTLY SURE...
I THINK IT'S RELATED TO THE FACT THAT WE DON'T HAVE A BIG DOG TO CHASE 'EM AWAY!..LIKE A LABRADOR RETRIEVER!
WELL, I THINK IT'S RELATED TO THE FACT THAT SOMEONE PUT OUT A BOWL OF MILK AND LEFT THE DOOR OPEN!
Y'KNOW, STUDIES SHOW THAT PETTING A DOG CAN REDUCE YOUR BLOOD PRESSURE...

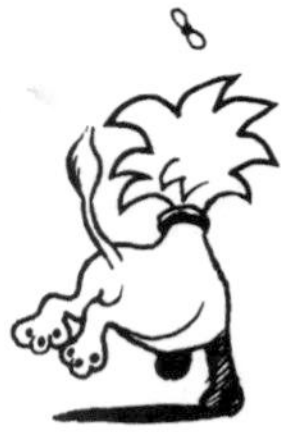

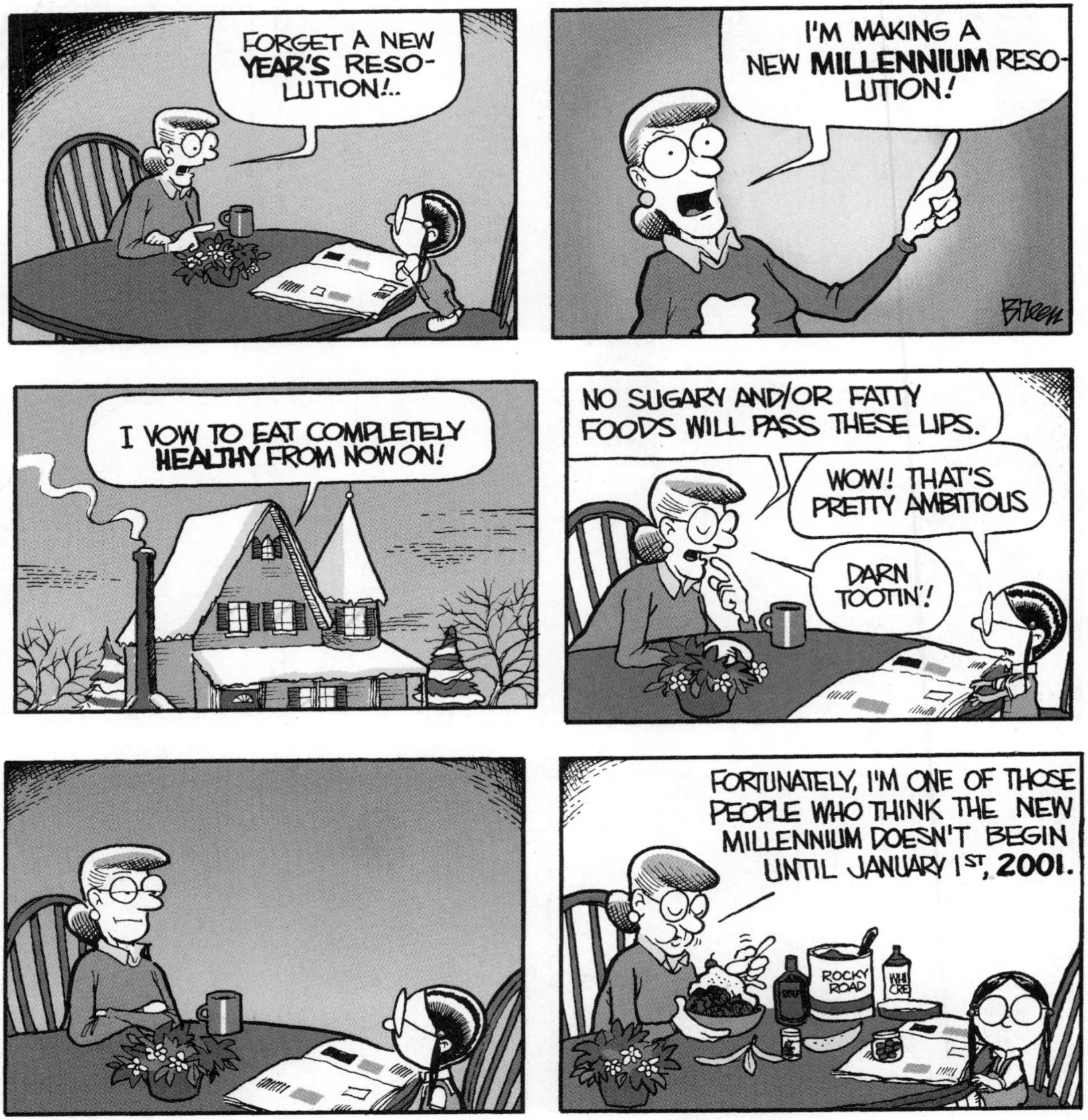
FORGET A NEW YEAR'S RESO-LUTION!..
I'M MAKING A NEW MILLENNIUM RESO-LUTION!
I VOW TO EAT COMPLETELY HEALTHY FROM NOW ON!
NO SUGARY AND/OR FATTY FOODS WILL PASS THESE LIPS.
WOW! THAT'S PRETTY AMBITIOUS
DARN TOOTIN'!
FORTUNATELY, I'M ONE OF THOSE PEOPLE WHO THINK THE NEW MILLENNIUM DOESN'T BEGIN UNTIL JANUARY 1ST, 2001.
ROCKY ROAD

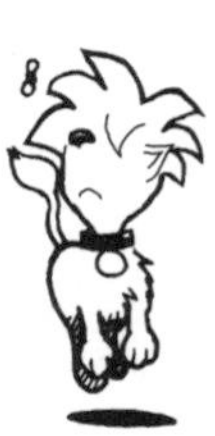

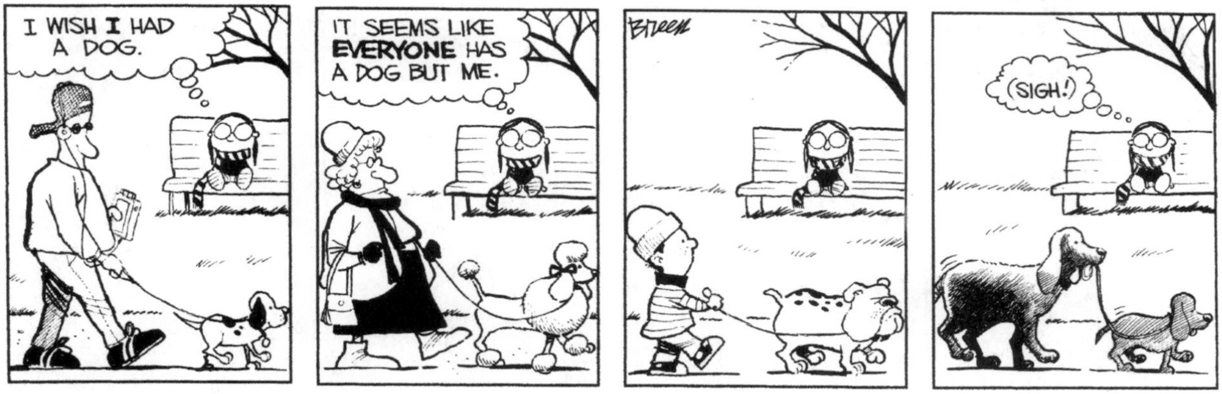
I WISH **I** HAD A DOG.
IT SEEMS LIKE **EVERYONE** HAS A DOG BUT ME.
(SIGH!)

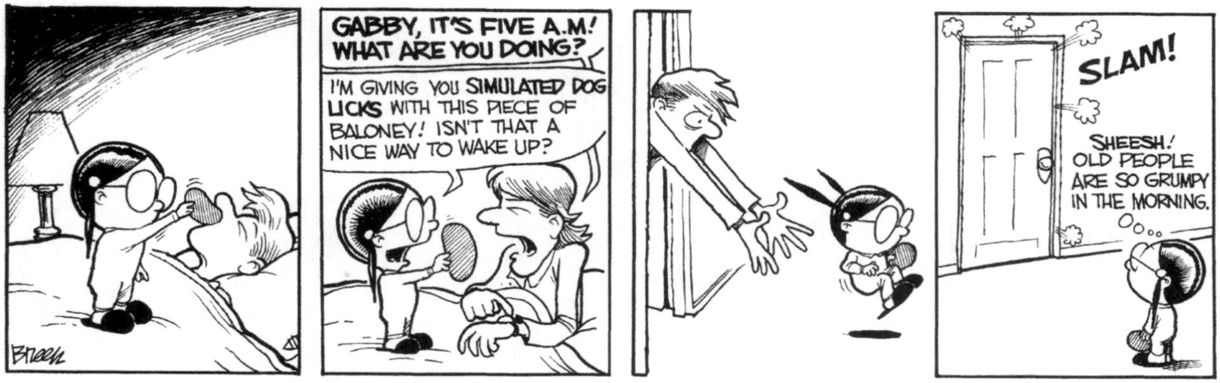
GABBY, IT'S FIVE A.M! WHAT ARE YOU DOING?
I'M GIVING YOU **SIMULATED DOG LICKS** WITH THIS PIECE OF BALONEY! ISN'T THAT A NICE WAY TO WAKE UP?
SLAM!
SHEESH! OLD PEOPLE ARE SO GRUMPY IN THE MORNING.

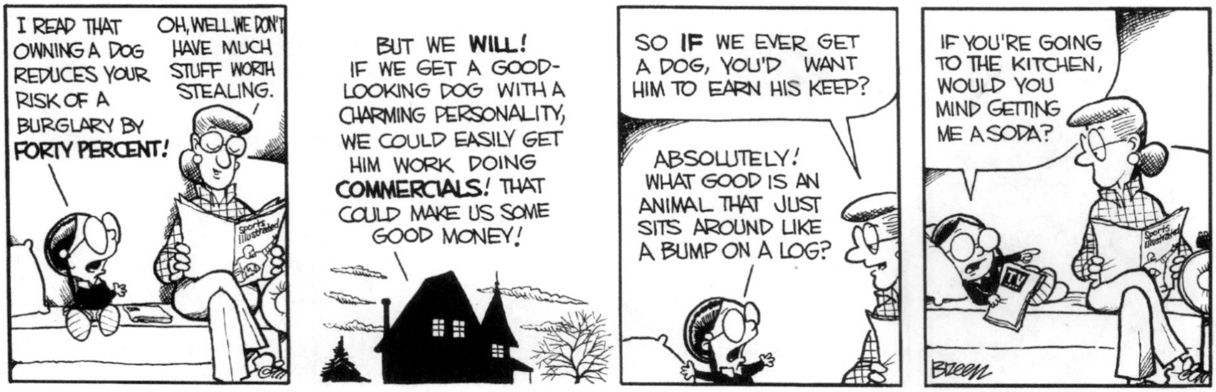
I READ THAT OWNING A DOG REDUCES YOUR RISK OF A BURGLARY BY **FORTY PERCENT**!
OH, WELL. WE DON'T HAVE MUCH STUFF WORTH STEALING.
BUT WE **WILL**! IF WE GET A GOOD-LOOKING DOG WITH A CHARMING PERSONALITY, WE COULD EASILY GET HIM WORK DOING **COMMERCIALS**! THAT COULD MAKE US SOME GOOD MONEY!
SO **IF** WE EVER GET A DOG, YOU'D WANT HIM TO EARN HIS KEEP?
ABSOLUTELY! WHAT GOOD IS AN ANIMAL THAT JUST SITS AROUND LIKE A BUMP ON A LOG?
IF YOU'RE GOING TO THE KITCHEN, WOULD YOU MIND GETTING ME A SODA?

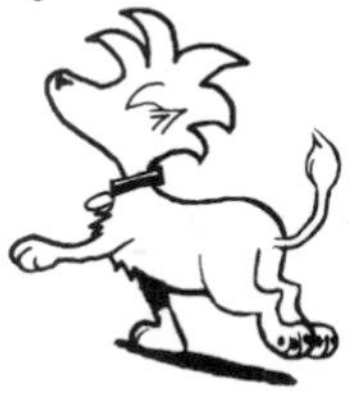

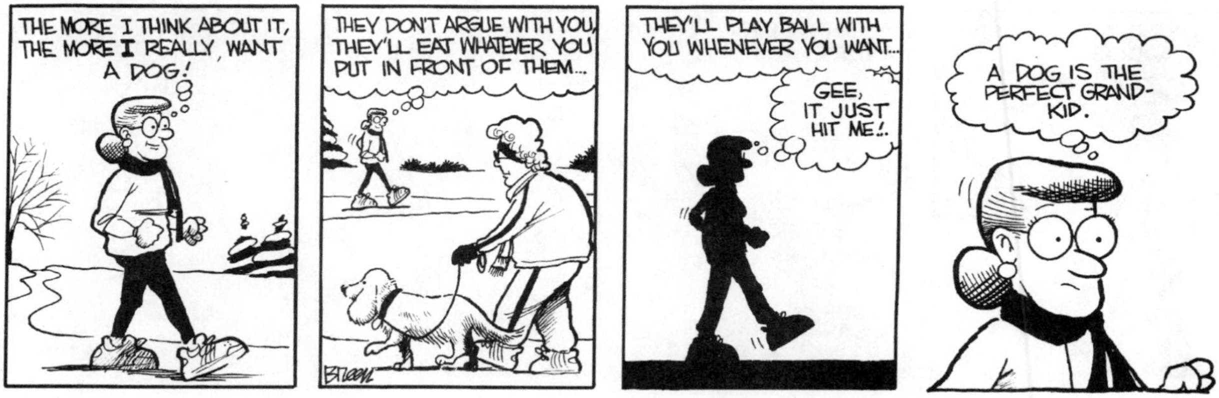
THE MORE I THINK ABOUT IT, THE MORE I REALLY, WANT A DOG!
THEY DON'T ARGUE WITH YOU, THEY'LL EAT WHATEVER YOU PUT IN FRONT OF THEM...
THEY'LL PLAY BALL WITH YOU WHENEVER YOU WANT...
GEE, IT JUST HIT ME!.
A DOG IS THE PERFECT GRAND-KID.

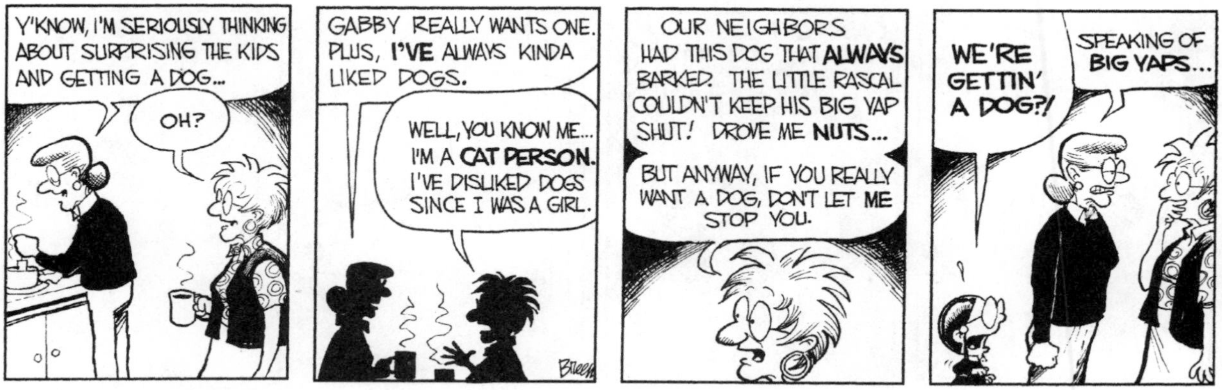
Y'KNOW, I'M SERIOUSLY THINKING ABOUT SURPRISING THE KIDS AND GETTING A DOG...
OH?
GABBY REALLY WANTS ONE. PLUS, I'VE ALWAYS KINDA LIKED DOGS.
WELL, YOU KNOW ME... I'M A CAT PERSON. I'VE DISLIKED DOGS SINCE I WAS A GIRL.
OUR NEIGHBORS HAD THIS DOG THAT ALWAYS BARKED. THE LITTLE RASCAL COULDN'T KEEP HIS BIG YAP SHUT! DROVE ME NUTS...
BUT ANYWAY, IF YOU REALLY WANT A DOG, DON'T LET ME STOP YOU.
WE'RE GETTIN' A DOG?!
SPEAKING OF BIG YAPS...

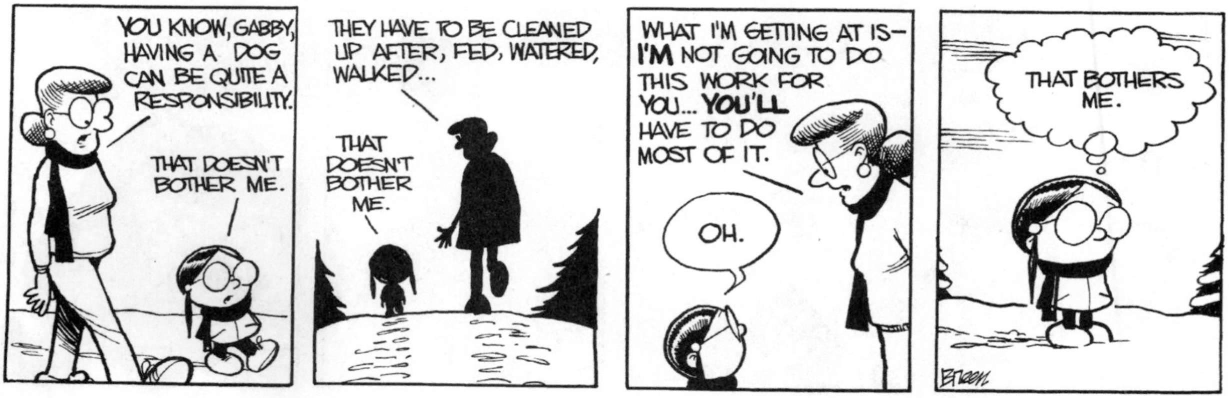
YOU KNOW, GABBY, HAVING A DOG CAN BE QUITE A RESPONSIBILITY.
THAT DOESN'T BOTHER ME.
THEY HAVE TO BE CLEANED UP AFTER, FED, WATERED, WALKED...
THAT DOESN'T BOTHER ME.
WHAT I'M GETTING AT IS— I'M NOT GOING TO DO THIS WORK FOR YOU... YOU'LL HAVE TO DO MOST OF IT.
OH.
THAT BOTHERS ME.

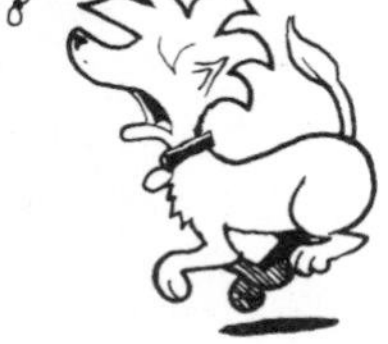